T0344305

Limitations and Future Applications of Quantum Cryptography

Neeraj Kumar
Babasaheb Bhimrao Ambedkar University, Lucknow, India

Alka Agrawal
Babasaheb Bhimrao Ambedkar University, Lucknow, India

Brijesh K. Chaurasia
Indian Institute of Information Technology, India

Raees Ahmad Khan
Indian Institute of Information Technology, India

A volume in the Advances in Information Security,
Privacy, and Ethics (AISPE) Book Series

Published in the United States of America by
IGI Global
Information Science Reference (an imprint of IGI Global)
701 E. Chocolate Avenue
Hershey PA, USA 17033
Tel: 717-533-8845
Fax: 717-533-8661
E-mail: cust@igi-global.com
Web site: http://www.igi-global.com

Copyright © 2021 by IGI Global. All rights reserved. No part of this publication may be reproduced, stored or distributed in
any form or by any means, electronic or mechanical, including photocopying, without written permission from the publisher.
Product or company names used in this set are for identification purposes only. Inclusion of the names of the products or
companies does not indicate a claim of ownership by IGI Global of the trademark or registered trademark.

Library of Congress Cataloging-in-Publication Data

Names: Kumar, Neeraj, 1981- editor. | Agrawal, Alka, 1977- editor. |
    Chaurasia, Brijesh Kumar, 1975- editor. | Khan, R. A. (Raees Ahmad),
    editor.
Title: Limitations and future applications of quantum cryptography / Neeraj
    Kumar, Alka Agrawal, Brijesh Kumar Chaurasia, and Raees Ahmad Khan,
    editor.
Description: Hershey, PA : Information Science Reference, [2021] | Includes
    bibliographical references and index. | Summary: "This book is for
    security experts as well as for IoT developers to help them understand
    the concepts related to quantum cryptography and classical cryptography
    and providing a direction to security professionals and IoT solution
    developers toward using approaches of Quantum Cryptography as available
    computational power increases"-- Provided by publisher.
Identifiers: LCCN 2020026779 (print) | LCCN 2020026780 (ebook) | ISBN
    9781799866770 (hardcover) | ISBN 9781799866787 (paperback) | ISBN
    9781799866794 (ebook)
Subjects: LCSH: Quantum computing. | Cryptography. | Data encryption
    (Computer science) | Internet of things.
Classification: LCC QA76.889 .L569 2021 (print) | LCC QA76.889 (ebook) |
    DDC 004.67/8--dc23
LC record available at https://lccn.loc.gov/2020026779
LC ebook record available at https://lccn.loc.gov/2020026780

This book is published in the IGI Global book series Advances in Information Security, Privacy, and Ethics (AISPE) (ISSN:
1948-9730; eISSN: 1948-9749)

British Cataloguing in Publication Data
A Cataloguing in Publication record for this book is available from the British Library.

All work contributed to this book is new, previously-unpublished material. The views expressed in this book are those of the
authors, but not necessarily of the publisher.

For electronic access to this publication, please contact: eresources@igi-global.com.

Advances in Information Security, Privacy, and Ethics (AISPE) Book Series

Manish Gupta
State University of New York, USA

ISSN:1948-9730
EISSN:1948-9749

MISSION

As digital technologies become more pervasive in everyday life and the Internet is utilized in ever increasing ways by both private and public entities, concern over digital threats becomes more prevalent.

The **Advances in Information Security, Privacy, & Ethics (AISPE) Book Series** provides cutting-edge research on the protection and misuse of information and technology across various industries and settings. Comprised of scholarly research on topics such as identity management, cryptography, system security, authentication, and data protection, this book series is ideal for reference by IT professionals, academicians, and upper-level students.

COVERAGE

- Tracking Cookies
- Network Security Services
- Telecommunications Regulations
- Computer ethics
- Electronic Mail Security
- Privacy Issues of Social Networking
- Cookies
- Security Classifications
- Internet Governance
- Access Control

IGI Global is currently accepting manuscripts for publication within this series. To submit a proposal for a volume in this series, please contact our Acquisition Editors at Acquisitions@igi-global.com or visit: http://www.igi-global.com/publish/.

The Advances in Information Security, Privacy, and Ethics (AISPE) Book Series (ISSN 1948-9730) is published by IGI Global, 701 E. Chocolate Avenue, Hershey, PA 17033-1240, USA, www.igi-global.com. This series is composed of titles available for purchase individually; each title is edited to be contextually exclusive from any other title within the series. For pricing and ordering information please visit http://www.igi-global.com/book-series/advances-information-security-privacy-ethics/37157. Postmaster: Send all address changes to above address. © © 2021 IGI Global. All rights, including translation in other languages reserved by the publisher. No part of this series may be reproduced or used in any form or by any means – graphics, electronic, or mechanical, including photocopying, recording, taping, or information and retrieval systems – without written permission from the publisher, except for non commercial, educational use, including classroom teaching purposes. The views expressed in this series are those of the authors, but not necessarily of IGI Global.

Titles in this Series

For a list of additional titles in this series, please visit: www.igi-global.com/book-series

Advancements in Security and Privacy Initiatives for Multimedia Images
Ashwani Kumar (Vardhaman College of Engineering, India) and Seelam Sai Satyanarayana Reddy (Vardhaman College of Engineering, India)
Information Science Reference • © 2021 • 278pp • H/C (ISBN: 9781799827955) • US $215.00

Blockchain Applications in IoT Security
Harshita Patel (Vellore Institute of Technology, India) and Ghanshyam Singh Thakur (Maulana Azad National Institute of Technology, India)
Information Science Reference • © 2021 • 275pp • H/C (ISBN: 9781799824145) • US $215.00

Real-Time and Retrospective Analyses of Cyber Security
David Anthony Bird (British Computer Society, UK)
Information Science Reference • © 2021 • 267pp • H/C (ISBN: 9781799839798) • US $195.00

Transdisciplinary Perspectives on Risk Management and Cyber Intelligence
Luisa Dall'Acqua (University of Bologna, Italy & LS TCO, Italy) and Irene Maria Gironacci (Swinburne University of Technology, Australia)
Information Science Reference • © 2021 • 273pp • H/C (ISBN: 9781799843399) • US $195.00

Handbook of Research on Cyber Crime and Information Privacy
Maria Manuela Cruz-Cunha (Polytechnic Institute of Cávado and Ave, Portugal) and Nuno Ricardo Mateus-Coelho (Polytechnic Institute of Management and Technology, Portugal)
Information Science Reference • © 2021 • 753pp • H/C (ISBN: 9781799857280) • US $425.00

Large-Scale Data Streaming, Processing, and Blockchain Security
Hemraj Saini (Jaypee University of Information Technology, India) Geetanjali Rathee (Jaypee University of Information Technology, India) and Dinesh Kumar Saini (Sohar University, Oman)
Information Science Reference • © 2021 • 285pp • H/C (ISBN: 9781799834441) • US $225.00

Privacy Concerns Surrounding Personal Information Sharing on Health and Fitness Mobile Apps
Devjani Sen (Algonquin College, Canada) and Rukhsana Ahmed (University at Albany, SUNY, USA)
Information Science Reference • © 2021 • 335pp • H/C (ISBN: 9781799834878) • US $215.00

701 East Chocolate Avenue, Hershey, PA 17033, USA
Tel: 717-533-8845 x100 • Fax: 717-533-8661
E-Mail: cust@igi-global.com • www.igi-global.com

Table of Contents

Detailed Table of Contents

Chapter 1

    Satish Rupraoji Billewar, Vivekanand Institute of Management Studies and Research,
        Mumbai University, India
    Gaurav Vishnu Londhe, NMIMS Mumbai, India
    Sunil Bahiru Ghane, Sardar Patel Institute of Technology, Mumbai, India

History repeats itself. Quantum cryptography has started a revolution of quantum computing and has repeated the days of Einstein's research paper on "Theory of Relativity," which changed the world's perceptions of physics completely written based on Newton's laws. Quantum cryptography is going to change the definition of computers right from scratch. The last century was witness of a space race between US and USSR. This century would be witness of quantum computing race between US and China. It has changed the dimensions of operating systems, software, hardware, databases, and applications. Quantum computers are in a phase to replace the conventional computers and they are reaching to the level called quantum supremacy. The chapter covers the details of the basic principles and work methodology of quantum cryptography, the contribution of various pioneers, advantages over classical cryptography, its applications, future scope, and limitations simultaneously. The chapter covers the contribution of leading countries and organizations in quantum revolution.

Chapter 2

    Kamaljit I. Lakhtaria, Gujarat University, India
    Vrunda Gadesha, Gujarat University, India

When we aim to demonstrate that a programmable quantum device can solve complex problems which cannot be addressed by classic computers, this fundamental goal is known as quantum supremacy. This concept has changed every fundamental rule of computation. In this chapter, the detailed concept of quantum computing and quantum supremacy is explained along with various open source tools and real-time applications of this technology. The major base concepts, quantum computing, the difference between classical and quantum computer on physical level, programing quantum device, and the experiment-quantum supremacy are explained conceptually. This chapter also includes an introduction of the tools Cirq and OpenFermion plus the applications like quantum simulation, error mitigation technique, quantum machine learning, and quantum optimization, which are explained with illustrations.

    S. Venkata Lakshmi, Sri Krishna College of Engineering and Technology, India
    Sujatha Krishnamoorthy, Wenzhou-Kean University, China
    Mudassir Khan, King Khalid University, Saudi Arabia
    Neeraj Kumar, Babasaheb Bhimrao Ambedkar University, Lucknow, India
    Varsha Sahni, CT India, India

Cryptography is used for the secure communication in which two parties are involved. The most popular cryptographic issue is the transmission of confidential messages. The privacy is maintained using the cryptographic protocol. The security of quantum cryptography relies more on physics including quantum mechanics and statistics rather than on solving mathematical problems. A well-known application of quantum cryptography is quantum key distribution (QKD) that is used to establish communication by generating cryptographic keys. Moreover, it is based on the Heisenberg uncertainty principle that ensures the security and prevents from eavesdropping. Basically, quantum cryptography with faint laser pulses, polarization coding, phase coding, and frequency coding have been discussed.

    Nilay R. Mistry, Gujarat Forensic Sciences University, India
    Ankit Y. Dholakiya, Gujarat Forensic Sciences University, India
    Jay P. Prajapati, Gujarat Forensic Sciences University, India

Quantum internet is an innovative approach to secure communication. Quantum internet is the next revolution in technology that enables the devices to perform operations that are beyond the classical internet. Quantum internet with quantum cryptography is one of the best solutions for secure data communication. Quantum internet uses the fundamental laws of quantum physics, which make it secure against sophisticated network attacks. In this research, the authors described quantum cryptography, which enhances the secure transmission over quantum internet using cryptographic protocols. These protocols use random bits transformations, which prevent attackers to make out the patterns of random bits transformations. Also, they introduced the conceptual OSI model for quantum internet, which makes it easy to understand the working of the quantum internet at different layers. Quantum internet can be implemented in intelligence network, satellite communication, critical infrastructure, etc. This can mark a significant change in secure communication.

    Renata Wong, Nanjing University, China
    Amandeep Singh Bhatia, Chitkara University Institute of Engineering and Technology,
       Chitkara University, Patiala, India

In the last two decades, the interest in quantum computation has increased significantly among research communities. Quantum computing is the field that investigates the computational power and other properties of computers on the basis of the underlying quantum-mechanical principles. The main purpose is to find quantum algorithms that are significantly faster than any existing classical algorithms solving the same problem. While the quantum computers currently freely available to wider public count no more than two dozens of qubits, and most recently developed quantum devices offer some 50-60 qubits, quantum computer hardware is expected to grow in terms of qubit counts, fault tolerance, and resistance to decoherence. The main objective of this chapter is to present an introduction to the core quantum computing algorithms developed thus far for the field of cryptography.

Chapter 6

Aarti Dadheech, Institute of Technology, Nirma University, India

Quantum cryptography is a branch of cryptography that is a mixture of quantum mechanics and classical cryptography. The study of quantum cryptography is to design cryptographic algorithms and protocols that are against quantum computing attacks. In this chapter, the authors focus on analyzing characteristics of the quantum-proof cryptosystem and its applications in the future internet. Lattice-based cryptography provides a much stronger belief of security, in that the average-case of certain problems is equivalent to the worst-case of those problems. With the increase in cryptanalytic attacks conventional cryptographic schemes will soon become obsolete. As the reality of quantum computing approaches, these cryptosystems will need to be replaced with efficient quantum-resistant cryptosystems. We need an alternate security mechanism which is as hard as the existing number theoretic approaches. In this chapter, the authors discuss the security dimension of lattice-based cryptography whose strength lies in the hardness of lattice problems and also study its application areas.

Chapter 7

Anand Sharma, Mody University of Science and Technology, Lakshmangarh, India
Alekha Parimal Bhatt, Capgemini IT India Pvt. Ltd., India

IoT-based healthcare is especially susceptible as many IoT devices are developed without keeping in mind the security issue. In addition, such smart devices may be connected to global networks to access anytime, anywhere. There are some security challenges like mobility, computational limitation, scalability, communication media, dynamic topology, and above all the data confidentiality in storage or in transmission. There are some security protocols and methodology which is used in IoT-based healthcare systems like steganography, AES cryptosystems, and RSA cryptographic techniques. Therefore, it is necessary to use quantum cryptography system to make sure the security, privacy, and integrity of the patient's data received and transmitted from IoT-based healthcare systems. Quantum cryptography is a very fascinating domain in cyber security that utilizes quantum mechanics to extend a cryptosystem that is supposed to be the unbreakable secure system.

Chapter 8

Binod Kumar, JSPM's Rajarshi Shahu College of Engineering, India
Sheetal B. Prasad, SRM Institute of Science and Technology, India
Parashu Ram Pal, ABES Engineering College, India
Pankaj Pathak, Symbiosis Institute of Digital and Telecom Management, Symbiosis International University, India

Quantum computation has the ability to revolutionize the treatment of patients. Quantum computing can help to detect diseases by identifying and forecasting malfunctions. But there's a threat associated here (i.e., healthcare data among the most popular cybercriminal targets, IoT devices notoriously lacking in effective safeguards, and quantum computers on the brink of an encryption/decryption breakthrough). Health agencies need a security prognosis and treatment plan as soon as possible. Healthcare companies recently worry more about the quantum security threats. The biggest threat of healthcare data breaches has come in the form of identity theft. There should be a strong mechanism to combat the security gaps in existing healthcare industry. If the healthcare data are available on the network, an attacker may try to modify, intercept, or even view this data stream. With the use of quantum security, the quantum state of these photons changes alert the security pros that someone is trying to breach the link.

Chapter 9

Sandeep Kumar Sharma, Department of Computer Science and IT, Khwaja Moinuddin Chishti Language University, India
Mazhar Khaliq, Department of Computer Science and IT, Khwaja Moinuddin Chishti Language University, India

Quantum computing has immense computational advantages. It escorts today's world of computing towards qubits universe of computing by the logical superposition technique. Various new technologies will come to reality with replacement of existing problem-solving methodology. The development of quantum computing imposes significant impact on cyber security and digital forensics technologies. Cybercrimes may be dramatically increased and malicious code will get ability to harm speedily. The quantum computing in software forensics methodology needs to develop in order to counter the challenges such as traceability of malicious code automation, sources of malicious code generation, intellectual property right theft issues, source code validation, plagiarism, breach of copyright issues, and an acquisition of digital evidence with quality and quantity with the wings of quantum forensics. This chapter aims to concentrate on the key issues of quantum computing approach in the field of software forensics with ontological aspects.

Chapter 10

Bably Dolly, Babasaheb Bhimrao Ambedkar University, Lucknow, India
Deepa Raj, Babasaheb Bhimrao Ambedkar University, Lucknow, India

Image processing via the quantum platform is an emerging area for researchers. Researchers are more interested to move on towards quantum image processing instead of classical image processing. This chapter starts with the review of different quantum image computing-based research papers with a brief idea of the ethics which inspire quantum computing in the background and focus on the current scenario of recent trends of quantum image representation, pitfalls, and summarization of the pros and cons of it, with the limitations of the technologies used and focus on the recent work to be going on and application of it in a different field. In the next, it will focus on the different methods used by the researcher in the previous papers. The next section discussed the different methods based on quantum image representation used. Some different techniques of image storage, retrieval, and representation in a quantum system are discussed. Also, this chapter briefs the pros and cons of using different techniques in quantum systems in comparison to classical systems.

Chapter 11

Sabyasachi Pramanik, Haldia Institute of Technology, India
Ramkrishna Ghosh, Haldia Institute of Technology, India
Digvijay Pandey, Department of Technical Education, India & Institution of Engineering
and Technology, India
Mangesh M. Ghonge, Sandip Institute of Technology and Research Centre, India

The immense measure of classified information has been moved on the internet. Information security turns out to be progressively significant for some applications, for instance, private transmission, video observation, military, and clinical applications. Lately, there has been a great deal of enthusiasm for steganography and steganalysis. Steganography is the specialty of covering up and transmitting information through clearly harmless transporters with an end goal to disguise the presence of information. The advanced picture information, for example, BMP, JPEG, and GIF, are generally utilized as a transporter for steganography. Here the mystery message is implanted into a picture (or any media) called spread picture and afterward sent to the beneficiary who extricates the mystery message from the spread message. This picture ought not to be discernible from the spread picture, with the goal that the aggressor can't find any implanted message. The authors have proposed three approaches of steganography that can easily support message privacy.

Chapter 12

Amandeep Singh Bhatia, Chitkara University Institute of Engineering and Technology,
Chitkara University, Patiala, India
Renata Wong, Nanjing University, China

Quantum computing is a new exciting field which can be exploited to great speed and innovation in machine learning and artificial intelligence. Quantum machine learning at crossroads explores the interaction between quantum computing and machine learning, supplementing each other to create models and also to accelerate existing machine learning models predicting better and accurate classifications. The main purpose is to explore methods, concepts, theories, and algorithms that focus and utilize quantum computing features such as superposition and entanglement to enhance the abilities of machine learning computations enormously faster. It is a natural goal to study the present and future quantum technologies with machine learning that can enhance the existing classical algorithms. The objective of this chapter is to facilitate the reader to grasp the key components involved in the field to be able to understand the essentialities of the subject and thus can compare computations of quantum computing with its counterpart classical machine learning algorithms.

Chapter 13

Bhanu Chander, Pondicherry University, India

The basic idea of artificial intelligence and machine learning is that machines have the talent to learn from data, previous experience, and perform the work in future consequences. In the era of the digitalized world which holds big data has long-established machine learning methods consistently with requisite high-quality computational resources in numerous useful and realistic tasks. At the same time, quantum machine learning methods work exponentially faster than their counterparts by making use of quantum mechanics. Through taking advantage of quantum effects such as interference or entanglement, quantum computers can proficiently explain selected issues that are supposed to be tough for traditional machines. Quantum computing is unexpectedly related to that of kernel methods in machine learning. Hence, this chapter provides quantum computation, advance of QML techniques, QML kernel space and optimization, and future work of QML.

Preface

INTRODUCTION

"If you want to make a simulation of nature, you'd better make it quantum mechanical, and by golly it's a wonderful problem, because it doesn't look so easy" By Richard Phillips Feynman

Research communities are interested evocatively research in quantum computation. Quantum computing is a beautiful combination of quantum physics, computer science, and information theory. Quantum algorithms are significantly faster than any existing classical algorithms solving the problem. The purpose of Quantum Computing is to explore the computational power and other properties of computers on the root of the core quantum-mechanical principles.

"A quantum computer is a device for computation that makes direct use of quantum mechanical phenomena, such as superposition and entanglement, to perform operations on data. The basic principle behind quantum computation is that quantum properties can be used to represent data and perform operations on these data". The concept of quantum computing is based on two fundamental principles of quantum mechanics: superposition and entanglement. Quantum mechanics has played an ever-increasing role in the development of new and more efficient computing devices. Quantum mechanics inspires the working of classical computers and communication devices, from the transistor through the laser to the latest hardware advances that increase the speed and power and decrease the size of computer and communications components. The fundamental unit of information in the world of quantum computing is known as a qubit.

Each qubit is capable of being in more than one state at any given point in time and hence can take superposition of both 0 and 1. The imagination for qubit as an electron located in a magnetic field, where its state can be either lined-up with the field (i.e., spin-up or 0) or not lined-up with the field (i.e., spin-down or 1). Unlike classical computers, smallest particle's behavior is responsible for energy and time-efficient operations. Quantum computing employs the ability of sub-atomic particles for multi-state presence at specific time. The electron's state is changed using an energy pulse.

Instead of using bits, qubits are used in quantum computing, which is a key indicator in the high level of safety and security this type of cryptography ensures. If interfered with or eavesdropped in, qubits will delete or refuse to send, which keeps the information safe. This is vital in the current era where sensitive and important personal information can be digitally shared online. Quantum cryptography is an important branch of cryptography, which is the combination of quantum mechanics and classical cryptography. In computer networks, a large amount of data is transferred worldwide daily, including anything from military plans to a country's sensitive information, and data breaches can be disastrous. This is where quantum cryptography comes into play. (Shor, 1994). By not being dependent on computational power, it can easily replace classical cryptography. Cryptography is the key technologies to ensure the security of the information system. The security of communication can be guaranteed by Heisenberg's uncertainty principle and quantum no-cloning theory (Peres, 2006).

In 1993, the scheme that teleports an unknown quantum state was proposed, According to the concept of quantum teleportation the classic information is obtained by the sender measuring the quantum state of the original, which will be told by the sender in the way of classical communication. Quantum information is the rest of the information that the sender does not extract in the measurement, and it is passed to the recipient by measurement. (Bennett, et.-el., 1993).

Quantum information processing includes quantum computing, quantum cryptography, quantum communications, and quantum games, explores the implications of using quantum mechanics instead of classical mechanics for information and its processing. It is not only computation is done from classical to quantum but Quantum computing has changed the conception of computation. This book is concerned with theory foundation conventional computing and cryptography are replaced with a quantum application and quantum cryptography in the current era of technological development.

To design cryptographic algorithms and protocols are the main goal of the research in quantum cryptography for quantum computing attacks. Exploring quantum cryptographic algorithms and protocols will be a crucial part of cyberspace security issues.

The ongoing efforts to build quantum computers and applications of quantum cryptography a dynamic area which is still so emergent. Last decades researcher have combine Influential revolutionary theories, information theory and quantum mechanics .The innovative view is quantum information theory as connection with physics novel algorithms, applications and protocols. Information theory includes the foundations of both computer science and communications, abstracted away the physical world so effectively that it became possible to talk about the major issues within computer science and communications, such as the efficiency of an algorithm or the robustness of a communication protocol.

The early 1980s saw the beginning of quantum computing with physicist Paul Benioff's proposal of a quantum mechanical model of the Turing machine. According to David Deutsch, an Oxford University theoretical physicist who is considered the father of quantum computing, suggested the idea of the quantum mechanical Turing machine. Few quantum phenomena related to entangle particles could not simulated by The Turing machine that led to the hypothesis that possibly, Quantum processes could be used to accelerate general computation. To generate the model of information theory foremost computation have to re-establish and mapping classical to quantum model. Quantum entanglement is the most common explanation given for relation of quantum information processing works and multipartite entanglement to take a deep view for quantum computing. Quantum computing respects the Church -Turing Thesis, according to which any computational problem that can be solved by a classical computer is also solved by quantum computer. But the focal intense regards complexity of problem solved by quantum computer over classical computer (Tseng et al., 2007). Many existing public key cryptography (RSA ELGamal, elliptic curve cryptography (ECC) and etc.) will be no longer safe in the quantum computation due to the appearances of the quantum computer (ElGamal, 1985; Rivest et al., 1978).Under quantum computer, discrete logarithm problem or the integer factorization problem will no longer be difficult.So in order to resist quantum computers, new cryptosystems should be explored that are not based on discrete logarithms problem or the large factor decomposition problem to protected information of cyberspace to be ensured in the upcoming Internet generation.(Shen et al., 2007).

According to IBM, the company has plans to develop systems with 1 million qubits as futuristic new class of computing abilities. Big Blue plans for its Condor quantum processor, coming in 2023, to have 1,121 qubits, a massive increase over the 27 and 53 qubits, respectively, in today's Falcon and Hummingbird chips. But it is an essential step to have more qubits without performance consideration. IBM, which names its quantum chips after birds, is upgrading its current Hummingbird chip to 65 qubits this year. The Eagle chip will have 127 next year, and Osprey will have 433 the year after.

"Think of quantum volume as the average of worst-case circuits run on any quantum computer," by Jay Gambetta, a research fellow and vice president in quantum computing at IBM. "The result means that if this 'worst case' is possible, quantum volume is a measure of the circuits' quality the higher the quality, the more complex circuits can be run on a quantum computer" (Hsu, 2020).

Quantum logic gates, operating on a number of qubits, are the building blocks of quantum circuits. There are many types of quantum gates, like H (Hadamard) gate, CX (Controlled-X) gate, ID (Identity) gate, U3 gate, U2 gate, U1 gate, Rx gate, Ry gate, Rz gate, X gate, Y gate, Z gate, S gate, Sdg gate T gate, Tdg gate, cH gate, cY gate, cZ gate, cRz gate, cU1 gate, cU3 gate, ccX gate, SWAP gate etc. Even custom gates can also be created for using in quantum circuits. Digital quantum computers use quantum logic gates to do computation. A quantum computer consists of the below mentioned blocks or chambers. Qubit Signal Amplifier Input Microwave Lines, Superconducting Coaxial Lines, Cryogenic Isolators, Quantum Amplifiers, Cryoperm Shield, Mixing Chamber. There are the two common terms in modern optimization aspects 'Heuristic' and 'meta-heuristic'. To use techniques to solve the optimization problems. 'Heuristic' means to discover certain solution by trial and error. Heuristic algorithms can attain to the optimum solutions within a given finite time, but it never assures its performance in achieving the best solution. To achieve more better and accurate solutions, meta-heuristic algorithms have been developed by making some improvements over heuristic algorithms.

The modern meta-heuristic algorithms work on the basis of certain randomization of the search process. In the subsequent subsections a number of modern optimization problem solving techniques have been discussed briefly with their limitations. These methods operate by considering the issues such as imprecision, partial truth, uncertainty and approximation which are often present in few real-world problems.

Modern techniques of resolving optimization problems. Genetic algorithms, simulated annealing, particle swarm optimization, differential evolution, ant colony optimization, bee-colony optimization, harmony search algorithm, bat-algorithm, Cuckoo search, neural network-based optimization, fuzzy optimization, etc. are available in literature, which are considered as modern methods of optimization problem solving.

When the complexity of optimization problems and amount of data involved rise, more efficient ways of solving optimization problems are needed. The power of quantum computing can be used for solving problems which are not practically feasible on classical computers, or suggest a considerable speed up with respect to the best known classical algorithm. This book enlightened on the basics of quantum computing and the quantum algorithms used for solving optimization problems. Few real-life optimization examples which can be resolved by quantum computing are Consumer products and retail companies tailoring marketing offers, financial services firms enhancing their risk optimization, Organizations developing employee work schedules, Universities scheduling classes, telecommunications companies upgrading their network infrastructure, Healthcare firms optimizing patient treatments and Governments improving air traffic control.

HISTORY OF QUANTUM COMPUTING AND QUANTUM CRYPTOGRAPHY

As quantum mechanics was developed between 1900 and 1925 and it remains the cornerstone on which chemistry, condensed matter physics, and technologies ranging from computer chips to LED lighting ultimately rests. Now Systems seemed be beyond the human ability to model with quantum mechanics. This is because simulating systems of even a few dozen interacting particles requires more computing power than any conventional computer can provide over thousands of years.

Serge Haroche, while a leader at the frontier of experimental quantum computing, continues to deride the vision of practical quantum computers as an impossible dream that can come to fruition only in the wake of some as yet unglimpsed revolution in physics.

Quantum computers were proposed in the 1980s by Richard Feynman and Yuri Manin. When Paul Benioff proposed a quantum mechanical model of the Turing machine (Benioff, 1980). Richard Feynman and Yuri Manin suggested after Paul Benioff quantum mechanical model that a quantum computer had the potential to simulate things that a classical computer could not. (Feynman, 1982; Manin, 1980), Quantum cryptography stems from the concept of quantum money, which was proposed by Wiesner in 1969. Limited by the level of technology in history, this novel and creative idea cannot be realized, which makes it remain unpublished until 1983 (Wiesner, 1983).

David Deutsch proposes the mathematical concept of the quantum Turing machine to model quantum computation in 1985. David Deutsch and Richard Jozsa in 1992 give the first such example. "The quantum computation solves the problem with certainty in exponentially less time than any classical deterministic computation." Ethan Bernstein and Umesh Vazirani show that quantum computers can be significantly faster than classical computers, even if the classical computer is allowed a small probability of error in 1993. Dan Simon shows that quantum computers can be exponentially faster in 1994. Peter Shor shows that quantum computers can factories large integers efficiently in 1994. Given an integer $N = p \times q$ for prime numbers p and q, Shor's algorithm outputs p and q. No efficient classical algorithm for this task is known. Shor's algorithm breaks the RSA public-key cryptosystem on which Internet security is based. Lov Grover gives a quantum algorithm which solves this problem using about $\sqrt{n}$ queries in 1996. The square-root speedup of Grover's algorithm finds many applications to search and optimization problems. Seth Lloyd proposes a quantum algorithm which can simulate quantum-mechanical systems in 1996. Peter Shor developed a quantum algorithm for factoring integers that had the potential to decrypt RSA-encrypted communications in 1994. Despite ongoing experimental progress since the late 1990s, most researchers believe that "fault-tolerant quantum computing is still a rather distant dream."

In recent years, investment into quantum computing research has increased in both the public and private sector. Google AI, in partnership with the U.S. National Aeronautics and Space Administration (NASA), claimed to have performed a quantum computation that is infeasible on any classical computer in 23 October 2019 (Elizabeth, 2019).

There are several models of quantum computers including the quantum circuit model, quantum Turing machine, adiabatic quantum computer, one-way quantum computer, and various quantum cellular automata. The most widely used model is the quantum circuit (Scott et al., 2019).

The most advanced quantum computers till 2007 have yet managed more than 16 qubits, which means that a useful quantum computer was far away. Quantum computers and the quantum theory had made advancement in recent decades.

Los Alamos and MIT researchers tried to use a single qubit in three nuclear spins in each alanine molecules in liquid form in 1998. Los Alamos National Laboratory scientists announced that they have succeeded to develop a 7-qubit quantum computer with a single drop of liquid in 2000 March. In 2001 Scientists from IBM and Stanford University successfully experienced Shor's Algorithm on a quantum computer. This Algorithm is used for finding the prime factors of numbers. They used a 7-qubit computer to calculate the factors of 15. The computer correctly calculated that the prime factors were 3 and 5. In 2005 Quantum Optics and Quantum Information Institute (University of Innsbruck) claimed that scientists are successful in creating the first Qubyte, or series of 8 Qubits, in which ion traps were used. Scientists in Waterloo and Massachusetts in 2006, found methods to control on a 12-qubit system. Quantum computation related control becomes more complex with the increase of Qubits. In 2007 Canadian startup company D-Wave created a 16- qubit quantum computer. The computer solved many pattern matching problems.

CURRENT AND FUTURE APPLICATION OF QUANTUM COMPUTING AND QUANTUM CRYPTOGRAPHY

Quantum cryptography provides security for various applications. The quantum key distribution (QKD) protocol in the noise-free channel. The QKD protocol in the noisy channel is used to simulate real situations in the future Internet. As finally theoretically security of quantum cryptography demonstrated but it have to make suitable for the Internet which leads to unavoidable challenges will exist in the future. But as experimentally shows that Sniffing detection of quantum cryptography, is suitable for future Internet. (Zhou et al., 2018) Question arises that Will quantum computers ever reliably best classical computers? A quantum computing future is unlikely, due to random hardware errors.

Machine learning technology to take advantage of the exponential computing speed-up that quantum technology promises, classical data needs to be efficiently loaded into a quantum system for execution. According to this research the progress against this challenge, highlighting an algorithm for the efficient loading of certain classes of heavily utilized functions, such as Gaussian and Probability distributions, used for generating these datasets. Challenging as this speed-up would be lost given the large amount of time it would take to load even a modestly sized dataset.

Recent progress through deep learning to design multi-qubit gates, Quantum dot silicon qubit is one of the many approaches being explored in the field of quantum computing are attractive for quantum scalability because of their small form factor. Running useful problems on commercial-scale quantum computers using this technology requires high-fidelity multi-qubit gates. This research demonstrates the successful use of a deep learning framework to simulate the design of high-fidelity multi-qubit gates for quantum dot qubit systems.

Branches of quantum machine learning focus on how quantum theory might inform the methods that computers use to learn, or the data they learn from, as well as fine-tuning the tools and techniques of classical machine learning in a quantum framework. While measurable outcomes are still mostly in the realm of theory, quantum machine learning does have everyday implications for ordinary people. It has long been predicted that the processing power of quantum computers could render current encryption techniques used in banking or other online transactions ineffective. More recently, quantum machine learning techniques such as annealing have shown business promise by optimising the yields of financial assets or the calculation of credit ratings. Quantum techniques in machine learning are also likely to become important in medical technology or drug design as the principles which underpin chemistry are fundamentally quantum. ProteinQure, a biotech company founded in 2017, already uses elements of quantum computation to engineer new therapies (Adams, 2019).

Accenture Labs explores the challenges of providing communication confidentiality in a post-quantum computer world, as well as the technologies that can help organizations prepare for this disruption. We look at both current generation (lattice-based cryptography, hash-based cryptography) and next generation solutions (quantum key distribution, quantum random number generation) for mitigating quantum computing attacks. Most importantly, we outline an approach for combining traditional cryptography with quantum cryptography to help provide unbreakable, end-to-end encryption with the ability to detect man-in-the-middle attacks.

Classic cryptography relies on the strength of the secret key to provide cryptographic security. Certain number theory problems—such as the Prime Factorization problem, the Discrete Log problem and Elliptic Curve methods—underpin current cryptographic schemes. These were chosen because it is computationally easy to combine two large numbers together; however, it is computationally difficult to go the opposite way and determine what the original numbers were if only given one.

Currently, there are no known mathematical shortcuts to these algorithms, meaning that every single possible combination (or brute force) must be tested to find the key number that will unlock the algorithm. Using current classical computation, and even with hardware accelerators, this could conceivably take hundreds of years. In contrast, one of the general classes of problems that quantum computers solve best is phase estimation, which can be described as identifying where two different frequencies overlap. Both the Prime Factorization problem and Discrete Log problem can be transformed into phase estimation problems. In 1994, Peter Shor showed that quantum computers could use quantum physics characteristics to efficiently solve these problems without relying on brute force, thereby rendering any information encrypted by our public key system vulnerable to decryption.

Quantum computing research has advanced to the point where a functional quantum computer capable of breaking current-grade cryptography will arrive within the next ten years. Accenture believes this inflection point will be much sooner, within the next eight years. To maintain secure communications and encryption, Global 2000 companies in every industry must begin now to refresh the technologies underpinning cryptography. This is the only way to prepare for a future filled with quantum computers that can break classical cryptography. In recent years, researchers have been working to create cryptographic schemes that preserve existing cryptographic infrastructure but swap in number theory problems that resist attacks by quantum computers. This would make it possible to replace just one small piece of the public key infrastructure the combined key space with quantum-resistant algorithms. Lattice based cryptography and hash based cryptography provide two options that will allow researchers to maintain the existing infrastructure that supports Diffie-Hellman key exchange and digital signing while still providing quantum cryptanalysis resistance.

Currently, countries such as Austria, China, Japan, Switzerland and the US are working to implement QKD to support one-time pad (OTP) generation. OTPs are large keys that are pre-shared between sender and recipient. Unlike other forms of cryptography in which keys are used multiple times, an OTP is a single use key to protect a single communication and must be as long as the communication itself. As the speed of QKD increases, QKD technology offers a means of securely transmitting OTPs. Using fiber optics and FPS 3000 technology, the current standard for communications transport is 100 Gbit/s in cordless and directionless networks. Current speeds of the quantum-based communications must be significantly increased prior to adoption. A collaboration between the University of Cambridge and Toshiba using the BB84 protocol demonstrated an exchange of secure QKD keys at 1 Mbit/s (over 20 km of optical fiber) and 10 Kbit/s (over 100 km of fiber) (Connor et al., 2018).

Quantum computing and quantum communication could impact many sectors, including healthcare, energy, finance, security, and entertainment. Recent studies predict a multibillion dollar quantum industry by 2030. However, significant practical challenges need to be overcome before this level of large-scale impact is achievable. The probabilistic nature of quantum theory is that quantum information cannot be precisely copied. From a security lens, this is game-changing. Hackers trying to copy quantum keys/ used for encrypting and transmitting messages would be foiled, even if they had access to a quantum computer, or other powerful resources.

Quantum computers are also ideally suited for solving complex optimization tasks and performing fast searches of unsorted data. This could be relevant for many applications, from sorting climate data or health or financial data, to optimizing supply chain logistics, or workforce management, or traffic flow.

Satellite-based quantum key distribution for encryption has been demonstrated, laying the groundwork for a potential quantum security-based global communication network.

"Just as quantum encryption is fundamentally different from current encryption methods based on mathematical complexity, quantum computers are fundamentally different from current classical computers. While small-scale quantum computers are operational today, a major hurdle to scaling up the technology is the issue of dealing with errors. Compared to bits, qubits are incredibly fragile. Even the slightest disturbance from the outside world is enough to destroy quantum information." (Ghose, 2020). Quantum Hacking Group in Norway is also working on quantum hardware to find flaws in them and propose Ways to achieve eavesdropping with aim to get absolute security via quantum systems.

According to PIB Delhi, recent news Quantum Communication between two DRDO Laboratories, "Quantum based communication offers a robust solution to sharing the keys securely. Defence Research & Development Organization (DRDO) undertook the project for development of this technology .A milestone of this project was achieved when DRDO developed Quantum Key Distribution (QKD) technology underwent trials in Hyderabad between two DRDO labs, DRDL and RCI, to show secure communication.

The technology is developed by CAIR, Bengaluru and DYSL-QT, Mumbai. Quantum Communication using time-bin Quantum Key Distribution (QKD) scheme was performed under realistic conditions. The setup also demonstrated the validation of detection of a third party trying to gain knowledge of the communication. Quantum based security against eavesdropping was validated for the deployed system at over 12kms range and 10dB attenuation over fibre optic channel.

Continuous wave laser source was used to generate photons without depolarization effect. The timing accuracy employed in the setup was of the order of picoseconds. The Single photon avalanche detector (SPAD) recorded arrival of photons and key rate was achieved in the range of kbps with low Quantum bit error rate. Software was developed for data acquisition, time synchronization, post-processing, determining Quantum bit error rate and extracting other important parameters".

LIMITATION OF QUANTUM COMPUTING

"Computing devices resembling the universal quantum computer can, in principle, be built and would have many remarkable properties not reproducible by any Turing machine": David Deutsch

Quantum computer is very complex to simulate classically. The difficulty has elicited recent trials on deep, random circuits that aim to demonstrate that quantum devices may already perform tasks beyond the reach of classical computing. According to Subhash Kak "a quantum computing future is unlikely, due to random hardware errors. The superposition vanishes when the experimenter interacts with the quantum state. Due to superposition, a quantum computer with 100 qubits can represent 2^{100} solutions simultaneously. For certain problems, this exponential parallelism can be harnessed to create a tremendous speed advantage. Some code-breaking problems could be solved exponentially faster on a quantum machine". Quantum annealing leads for narrow approach to quantum computing. Quantum systems are used to speed up optimization problems through qubits. Quantum computer based in Canada, D-wave system has built optimization systems that use qubits for this purpose, but according critics also claim that these systems are no better than classical computers.

In development of quantum computer, must be focus to remove numerous small random errors for appropriate working in all conditions. Such errors arise from the non-ideal circuit elements. Due to this type of errors may leads to lose coherency of the qubits in a fraction of a second. If random errors pertains in hardware system results will not be up to level and insignificant with degraded reliability. "The problem of noise is a serious challenge in the implementation of quantum computers". We will reach the goal of reliable, large-scale, error-tolerant quantum computers that can solve a wide range of useful problems. Different implementations of Quantum Computers have been developed with limited use and only for demonstration (Kak, 2019).

"Noise distortion can lead to information corruption. Current quantum computers are so noisy and error-prone that the information in its quantum state is lost within tens of microseconds through a mechanism called de-coherence and through faulty gates" (Somma, 2020).

The single-atom transistor could lead to building a quantum computer that works by controlling the electrons and thereby the quantum information, or qubits However the single-atom transistor does have one serious current limitation. It must be kept cold, at least as cold as liquid nitrogen, or minus 391 degrees Fahrenheit (minus 196 Celsius).

There has been significant progress in quantum computing, the field faces a number of challenges as there is difficulty of building a large-scale quantum computer, the difficulty of designing new quantum algorithms. The difficulty of applying existing quantum algorithms to practical problems.

Google announced in October 2019 that its quantum computer had done a computation in just 200 seconds, which it claimed that the world's fastest traditional supercomputer would have needed 10,000 years to solve. This meant that it had reached a milestone called quantum supremacy, even though a few days later, its rival IBM proved that it could have been done in hours with a modern supercomputer, which would make the quantum computer *only* 1,000 times faster.

The general consequences on fault-tolerant quantum computation when constraints on physical resources, such as limited energy input, result in physical error rates that grow as the computer grows. In this case, fault tolerance schemes can no longer reduce computational error to an arbitrarily small number, even if one starts below the so-called fault tolerance noise threshold.

A realistic situation is one where η depends on the total number of physical components (qubits and gates) N in the computer. One expects the resource needed to maintain a given quality of physical gate operations to scale with N, so a constraint on the total available resource will result in a fall in the resource per physical component as the computer scales up. This gives a consequential drop in the quality of the gate, or, equivalently, a rise in the physical error probability η. (Asiani et al., 2020).

"Whenever the limitations of quantum computing actualize, their action must in turn be isolated from the rest of the world. Also their handling, if possible, must take place in isolation. Accordingly, the limitations of quantum computing are termed natural" (Greiner, 1994).

Every detail in quantum computing belongs to the micro world. All the real and imaginary events must be probed and scrutinized in order to employ them in the quantum algorithms. All the theoretical components of a quantum algorithm must be put in a one to one correspondence or mapping with suitable real and/or imaginary events (Adeh, 2017).

LIMITATIONS OF QUANTUM CRYPTOGRAPHY

"A quantum computer with a few tens of quantum bits could perform in a few tens of steps simulations that would require Avogadro's number [6×10^{23}] of memory sites and operations on a classical computer": By Seth Lloyd

Quantum computers has the capability to break the encryption algorithms, as its use made the existing encryption algorithms vulnerable. For instance if some data is encrypted using a key establishment technique and then the data travelled via unsecure communication channel, puts the data and key into risk by the availability of quantum computer.

Quantum computing is the contemporary research area which is applied in many fields to enhance security. Quantum computing highly influence the field of cryptography. It is still unknown that whether the enormous scope, general purpose quantum computer ever built as a complete system or not (Dyakonov,2019).

In his study discussed the basic difference between traditional computers and quantum computers and discussed that sustained endeavor is going on to develop quantum computers. Moreover, when these computers obtained that will include lots of security mechanism of modern cryptographic systems. It is always advisable, while designing an extensive cryptographic system there is a need to investigate the quantum computing which is to be included in the system. The main focus of the study is to discuss the part of endangered with the availability of quantum computer, and the various consequences occur when system security is broken. The study also focusing on the methodology to replace cryptography implemented in every part of the system.

Limitations of Quantum computing and quantum Cryptography is a critical reference that provides knowledge on the basics of IoT infrastructure using quantum cryptography, the differences between classical and quantum cryptography, and the future aspects and developments in this field. As historical development of field of Quantum Cryptography, Bennett and Brassard propose to use quantum mechanics for secure distribution of cryptographic keys in 1984.Quantum key distribution demonstrated 1989 experimentally. The idea behind to use the principles of uncertainty and collapse to spot eavesdroppers of information. Quantum teleportation is proposed in 1993 with using entanglement and Quantum teleportation demonstrated experimentally in 1997. Practical deployment implication of Quantum Cryptography includes cryptographic's algorithms used in modern application feasibility for interface, sizing estimation and post quantum cryptography.

Post-Quantum Ciphers (PQC) is having different components from the classical public key cryptography. In PQC no key agreement is available which works on the principle of Diffie-Hellman algorithm. So, there is no requirement of 1:1 correspondence of tradition ciphers to the PQC domain. This section discusses some of the PQC categories used to encrypt the data. Cyberspace has become the most popular carrier of information exchange in every corner of our life, which is beneficial for our life in almost all aspects. With the continuous development of science and technology, especially the quantum computer, cyberspace security has become the most critical problem for the internet in near future. Quantum computational approaches expand upon classical methods for a number of dedicated tasks. Strong limitations on the power of quantum computation are known for many problems, it has been proven that quantum computation provides no significant advantage over classical computation. The extent of quantum computing's applicability is still being determined. It does not provide efficient solutions to all problems neither does it provide a universal way of circumventing the slowing of Moore's law. Quantum and visual cryptography-based security solutions by establishing a secure connection between communication partners, if any information theft is observed then the session is terminated.

In Lattice Cryptography, the Lattice is referred to the all integer set which is arranged as a linear group of basis vector set. The main problem in mathematics is the shortest vector problem which is used to observe non-zero vectors from the vector space which traverse with basis vector. Lattice cryptography is considered NP-hard type problem.

This book cover themes that span from the usage of quantum cryptography in healthcare, forensics, and more. While highlighting topics such as 5G networks, image processing, algorithms, and quantum machine learning, this book is ideally intended for security professionals, IoT developers, computer scientists, practitioners, researchers, academicians, and students interested in the most recent research on quantum computing.

Towards boosting quantum security over long distances, QKD has been demonstrated long distances transmission but problem persist regarding preserving security with high transmission rate. To overcome this limitation, Measurement Device-Independent –Quantum Key Distribution (MDI-QKD) transmission protocol was developed by Wang that uses photons with three characterized quantum states to encode data. Which is proposed an elegant "time-reversal" protocol which is based on the principle of entanglement swapping and to perform a Bell state measurement as a central idea. The standard MDI-QKD protocol can used in detection security breaches but perfect state preparation limits it in practice. MDI-QKD with uncharacterized patches state-preparation imperfections as countermeasures. As experimental setup for encoding and detection, the researchers showed that the new QKD approach could transmit keys over longer distances and at higher rates (10^{-7} /pulse key rate) .Theoretical calculations distance up to 200 kilometer.

According to Hash-Based Cryptography the ongoing danger of block chain innovation has restored center around. In light of the Merkle has trees, this methodology can be utilized as an option in contrast to customary computerized marks. The eXtended Merkle Signature Scheme (XMSS) has been distributed as an instructive record by the IETF as RFC 8391.

Through Code-Based Cryptography, Code-put together cryptography is based with respect to the trouble of interpreting a general straight code. The McEliece plot was presented in 1978 and depends on registering arbitrary straight changes of a mistake adjusting code's generator network, and just the private key holder knowing the variables of that framework (McEliece, 1978).

Super singular Elliptic Curve Isogeny Cryptography, reciprocals to encryption and mark conspires, a key understanding convention with forward mystery is prominently inadequate. In 2012, analysts demonstrated that super singular elliptic bends and super singular isogeny diagrams can be utilized to make a post-quantum Diffie-Hellman-type figure, yet these methodologies remain moderately beginning and unstudied in scholastic writing. NIST commenced a procedure to engage, estimate and regulate different quantum-resistant asymmetric-key cryptography in 2017, November (Khan et al., 2017).

IBM's Senior Vice President of Cloud and Cognitive Software has predicted quantum computers will become mainstream in the next five years. Even by Deloitte's more conservative estimates, the first commercial, general-purpose quantum computers are expected to appear in the 2030's. A post-quantum world is already within reach. A functional quantum computer capable of breaking our current cryptographic standards will be available by 2028.

Michael Freedman, Alexei Kitaev, and Zhenghan Wang showed that topological quantum field theories as "toy" models of quantum gravity, involving only two space dimensions and one time dimension that are equivalent in power to ordinary quantum computers. David Deutsch pointed out in a 1991 paper that we could use a similar idea to solve NP-complete problems in polynomial time. We would simply guess a possible solution (Scott, 2008).

More recently, researchers have shown that the same holds true for some problems used in cryptography. Such has been the fate of some of the best candidates for showcasing dramatic quantum speedups. Still, an understanding of the limitations of quantum computing has been helpful to the quest for new quantum algorithms.

"What we learned about NP-complete problems was a big setback, but now we have a better idea of which problems to focus on and what techniques couldn't possibly work," says Vazirani, the organizer of MSRI's fall 2002 program on quantum computing. Umesh Vazirani, a professor of computer science at the University of Calfornia, Berkeley (Robinson, 2003).

CONCLUSION

The main focus of the study is to discuss the part of threatened with the ease of use of quantum computer, and the various consequences occur when system security is broken. Limitations of Quantum computing and quantum Cryptography is a critical reference that provides knowledge on the basics quantum cryptography, the differences between classical and quantum cryptography, and the future aspects and developments in this field like IOT, Machine Learning, Data Analytics etc. The study also focusing on the methodology to replace cryptography implemented in every part of the system.

REFERENCES

Aaronson, S. (2008). *The Limits of Quantum Computers*. https://www.ime.usp.br/~pf/clippings/quantum/limitsqc-draft.pdf

Adeh, A. (2017). Natural Limitations of Quantum Computing. *International Journal of Swarm Intelligence and Evolutionary Computation, 6*, 1. doi:10.4172/2090-4908.1000152

Arapinis, M., Mancini, L., Ritter, E., Ryan, M., Golde, N., Redon, K., & Borgaonkar, R. (2012, October). New privacy issues in mobile telephony: fix and verification. In *Proceedings of the 2012 ACM conference on Computer and communications security* (pp. 205-216). ACM.

Arkko, J., & Haverinen, H. (2006). *Extensible authentication protocol method for 3rd generation authentication and key agreement (EAP-AKA)*. RFC 4187.

Arkko, J., Lehtovirta, V., & Eronen, P. (2009). Improved extensible authentication protocol method for 3rd generation authentication and key agreement (EAP-AKA). *Network Working Group Request for Comments, 5448*, 1–29.

Asiani, M. F., Chai, J. H., Whitney, R. S., Auffeves, A., & Ng, K. H. (2020). *Limitations in quantum computing from resource constraints.* arXiv:2007.01966v1 [quant-ph].

Benioff, P. (1980). The computer as a physical system: A microscopic quantum mechanical Hamiltonian model of computers as represented by Turing machines. *Journal of Statistical Physics, 22*(5), 563–591. doi:10.1007/bf01011339

Bennett, C. H., Brassard, G., Crepeau, C., Jozsa, R., Peres, A., & Wootters, W. K. (1993). Teleporting an unknown quantum state via dual classical and Einstein-Podolsky-Rosen channels. *Physical Review Letters, 70*(13), 1895–1899. doi:10.1103/PhysRevLett.70.1895 PMID:10053414

Boixo, S., Isakov, S. V., Smelyanskiy, V. N., Babbush, R., Ding, N., Jiang, Z., Bremner, M. J., Martinis, J. M., & Neven, H. (2018). Characterizing Quantum Supremacy in NearTerm Devices. *Nature Physics, 14*, 595.

Boixo, S., Isakov, S. V., Smelyanskiy, V. N., & Neven, H. (n.d.). *Simulation of Low-Depth Quantum Circuits as Complex Undirected Graphical Models.* arXiv:1712.05384.

Connor, DiValentin, Dukatz, & Farhady. (2018). *Cryptography in a Post-quantum World Preparing intelligent enterprises now for a secure future.* Cybersecurity R&D Accenture Labs.

Dyakonov, M. (2019). The case against quantum computing. *IEEE Spectrum, 56*(3), 24–29.

ElGamal, T. (1985). A public key cryptosystem and a signature scheme based on discrete logarithms. *IEEE Transactions on Information Theory, 31*(4), 469–472. doi:10.1109/TIT.1985.1057074

Feynman, R. (1982). Simulating Physics with Computers. *International Journal of Theoretical Physics, 21*(6/7), 467–488. doi:10.1007/BF02650179

Franklin, D., & Chong, F. T. (2004). *Challenges in Reliable Quantum Computing.* Nano, Quantum and Molecular Computing. doi:10.1007/1-4020-8068-9_8

Ghose, S. (2020). *Are You Ready for the Quantum Computing Revolution?* Academic Press.

Gibney, E. (2019). Quantum gold rush: the private funding pouring into quantum start-ups. *Nature, 574*(7776), 22–24. doi:10.1038/d41586-019-02935-4

Greiner, W. (1994). *Quantum mechanics an introduction.* MIT Press.

Grover, L. K. (1996). A fast quantum mechanical algorithm for database search. In *Proceedings of the twenty-eighth annual ACM symposium on Theory of computing* (pp. 212-219). Academic Press.

Grover, L. K. (1997). Quantum mechanics helps in searching for a needle in a haystack. *Physical Review Letters, 79*(2), 325.

Jónsson, B., Bauer, B., & Carleo, G. (n.d.). *Neural-Network States for the Classical Simulation of Quantum Computing.* arXiv:1808.05232.

Kak, S. (2019). *A quantum computing future is unlikely, due to random hardware errors.* https://theconversation.com/a-quantum-computing-future-is-unlikely-due-to-random-hardware-errors-126503

Khan, A. S., Abdullah, J., Khan, N., Julahi, A. A., & Tarmizi, S. (2017). Quantum-Elliptic curve Cryptography for Multihop Communication in 5G Networks. *International Journal of Computer Science and Network Security, 17*(5), 357–365.

Manin, Yu. I. (1980). *Vychislimoe i nevychislimoe* [Computable and Noncomputable]. Sov.Radio.

Markov, I. L., & Shi, Y. (2008). Simulating Quantum Computation by Contracting Tensor etworks. *SIAM Journal on Computing, 38*, 963.

McEliece, R. J. (1978). A public-key cryptosystem based on algebraic. *Coding Thv, 4244*, 114–116.

Mermin, D. (2006). Breaking RSA Encryption with a Quantum Computer: Shor's Factoring Algorithm. *Physics*, 481–681.

National Academies of Sciences, Engineering, and Medicine. (2019). *Quantum Computing: Progress and Prospects.* Washington, DC: The National Academies Press. doi:10.17226/25196

Paeckel, S., Khler, T., Swoboda, A., Manmana, S. R., Schollwck, U., & Hubig, C. (2019). Time-Evolution Methods for Matrix-Product States. *Ann. Phys. (Amsterdam), 411*, 167998.

Pakkin, S., & Coles, P. (2019). The Problem with Quantum Computers. *Scientific American.*

Peres, A. (2006). *Quantum Theory: Concepts and Methods.* Springer Science & Business Media.

Preskill, J. (1996). Quantum computing: pro and con. *ITP Conference on Quantum Coherence and Decoherence.*

Preskill, J. (2018). Quantum Computing in the NISQ era and beyond. *Quantum, 2*, 79. doi:10.22331/q-2018-08-06-79

Preskill, J. (2018). Quantum Computing in the NISQ Era and Beyond. *Quantum, 2*, 79.

Preskill, J. (2018). *Quantum Computing and the Entanglement Frontier.* arXiv:1203.5813.

Quantum Computing. (2018). *Progress and Prospects.* National Academies Press. doi:10.17226/25196

Rivest, R. L., Shamir, A., & Adleman, L. (1978). A method for obtaining digital signatures and public-key cryptosystems. *Communications of the ACM, 21*(2), 120–126. doi:10.1145/359340.359342

Robinson, S. (2003). Emerging Insights on Limitations of Quantum Computing, Shape Quest for Fast Algorithms. *SIAM News, 36*(1).

Rodrigo, C. M. (2020). *Trump budget proposal boosts funding for artificial intelligence, quantum computing.* The Hill.

SaiToh. (2013). A Multiprecision C++ Library for MatrixProduct-State Simulation of Quantum Computing: Evaluation of Numerical Errors. *Journal of Physics: Conference Series, 454*, 012064.

Schollwck, U. (2011). The Density Matrix Renormalization Group in the Age of Matrix Product States. *Ann. Phys. (Amsterdam), 326*, 96.

Shen, J., Zhou, T., Chen, X., Li, J., & Susilo, W. (2018). Anonymous and Traceable Group Data Sharing in Cloud Computing. *IEEE Transactions on Information Forensics and Security, 13*(4), 912–925. doi:10.1109/TIFS.2017.2774439

Shor, P. W. (1994). Algorithms for quantum computation: discrete logarithms and factoring. In *Proceedings 35th annual symposium on foundations of computer science* (pp. 124-134). IEEE.

Somma, R. (2020). *Are We Ready for Quantum Computers?* https://blogs.scientificamerican.com/observations/are-we-ready-for-quantum computers/#:~:text=Current%20quantum%20computers%20are%20so,progress%20toward%20more%20usable%20qubits

Tseng, Y.-M. (2007). An efficient two-party identity-based key exchange protocol. *Informatica (Vilnius), 18*(1), 125–136. doi:10.15388/Informatica.2007.168

Verstraete, F., Murg, V., & Cirac, J. I. (2008). Matrix Product States, Projected Entangled Pair States, and Variational Renormalization Group Methods for Quantum Spin Systems. *Advances in Physics, 57*, 143.

Vidal, G. (2003). Efficient Classical Simulation of Slightly Entangled Quantum Computations. *Physical Review Letters, 91*, 147902.

Vidal, G.A. J. Ferris and G. (2012). Perfect Sampling with Unitary Tensor Networks. *Physical Review B: Condensed Matter and Materials Physics, 85*, 165146.

White, S. R. (1992). Density Matrix Formulation for Quantum Renormalization Groups. *Physical Review Letters, 69*, 2863.

Wiesner, S. (1983). Conjugate coding. *ACM SIGACT News, 15*(1), 78–88. doi:10.1145/1008908.1008920

Zhou, Shen, Li, Wang, & Shen. (2018). *Quantum Cryptography for the Future Internet and the Security Analysis.* doi:10.1155/2018/8214619

Chapter 1
Quantum Cryptography:
Basic Principles and Methodology

Satish Rupraoji Billewar
Vivekanand Institute of Management Studies and Research, Mumbai University, India

Gaurav Vishnu Londhe
NMIMS Mumbai, India

Sunil Bahiru Ghane
Sardar Patel Institute of Technology, Mumbai, India

ABSTRACT

History repeats itself. Quantum cryptography has started a revolution of quantum computing and has repeated the days of Einstein's research paper on "Theory of Relativity," which changed the world's perceptions of physics completely written based on Newton's laws. Quantum cryptography is going to change the definition of computers right from scratch. The last century was witness of a space race between US and USSR. This century would be witness of quantum computing race between US and China. It has changed the dimensions of operating systems, software, hardware, databases, and applications. Quantum computers are in a phase to replace the conventional computers and they are reaching to the level called quantum supremacy. The chapter covers the details of the basic principles and work methodology of quantum cryptography, the contribution of various pioneers, advantages over classical cryptography, its applications, future scope, and limitations simultaneously. The chapter covers the contribution of leading countries and organizations in quantum revolution.

INTRODUCTION

Cryptography is the process to convert original text, conceal it in a disorganized way, and provide a protection password or a key by which the person having rights can only open it. Cryptography is the emergence of the implementation of ancient techniques to shroud the information. Quantum Cryptography brings scientific encryption to higher altitudes with the use of quantum physics principles like

DOI: 10.4018/978-1-7998-6677-0.ch001

Copyright © 2021, IGI Global. Copying or distributing in print or electronic forms without written permission of IGI Global is prohibited.

quantum mechanisms which encode and transmit the information securely in such a way that intruders cannot hack it. Quantum mechanism prepares the set of rules for secure transmission between sender and receiver (Goyal et al., 2011). The quantum mechanism is the base of the quantum cryptography process consists of two important elements.

Heisenberg Uncertainty Principle

In 1927, a German researcher Werner Heisenberg proposed Heinsenberg's principle of uncertainty which states that it is not possible to observe and calculate two properties at a time of an object and always shows uncertainty. For an instance, consider an object with the properties like position (x) and moving with the velocity (p) cannot be calculated simultaneously because it does not make sense to exist. A person's weight is not determined by his height. This idea works when we try to observe and calculate anything. The Heisenberg uncertainty prevents the intruder when applying this principle to protons because the proportions are affected by the polarity of the photon.

Photon Polarization Principle

This principle uses non-cloning methods to ensure that the attacker does not copy unique quantum bits. This creates a quantum state which cannot be recognized and distorts other information if anyone tries to measure the bit. Quantum cryptography is a solution for cryptographic functions that cannot be performed with classical cryptography. It is the safest solution to the problem in the key exchange process (Bhatt & Sharma, 2019).

The Contribution of the Pioneers

It seems that history is about to repeat itself for computers this time. Quantum cryptography began the evolution of quantum computers and remembered the history of a research paper written by Einstein's with the title "Theory of Relativity". The paper rewrote Newton's laws basic principles of physics and changed the world's understandings of physics. Quantum computer rewrites all computer concepts right from scratch. The computer is defined based on dimensions like software, hardware, database, and applications. But the Quantum computers are in the process of switching to older computers and gaining the level called Quantum Supremacy. This happened due to the contribution of its pioneers.

Quantum computing is known as 'quantum circuit' which works like programs, specifying a set of quantum machine operations to run. In the late 1960s, two researchers Stephen Weissner and Gilles Brassrd of Columbia University tried to solve the problems of classical cryptography very first time. They wrote a research paper for IEEE Information Theory Society which was rejected but then published in SIGACT News in the early 1980s.

Stephen Weissner and Gilles Brassrd proposed the idea of the Conjugate Code. Conjugate code is a way to encode and transmit two messages with two different forms. The concept of photon polarization is used in a linear and circular form where it is possible either to receive and decode messages on the safe and two stages secured channel. They titled the protocol "Quantum Key Distribution Protocol" which is widely known as the concept QKD. As the protocol was proposed in the year 1984, the method became famous as Bennett and Bassard 1984 (BB84) method.

As QKD is a two-stage protocol, it has certain limitations. The revised three-stage protocol is then proposed by an Indian-US-based computer scientist Subhash Kak in 2005 which describes a single photon transmission from sender to receiver. This is different from the previous QKD key exchange and explains the continuous and without break exchange of keys. This three-stage QKD protocol then becomes the base of next-generation computers.

HOW IS IT WORKING?

Quantum cryptography uses the concepts of quantum physics, which is secured against hacking to create a cryptosystem that cannot be defeated without the sender or recipient's knowledge of the messages. The word quantum itself refers to the simplest conduct of the smallest matter and energy particles.

Quantum cryptography, as one of the main aspects of its safety model, is distinguished from conventional cryptographic systems by relying more on physics than mathematics. The use of individual light particles/waves called photons and their inherent quantum properties in quantum cryptography are based on the construction of a cryptosystem – primarily because the quantum state of any system cannot be determined without disrupting the system. While other particles can be utilized theoretically, photons provide the qualities and actions required and provide the most promising means of communication for extremely high bandwidth, the expertise in fiber optic cables (Sharma & Thind, 2019).

Assume that the message between Gaurav (Sender), and Sunil (Receiver) can be exchanged safely by two individuals. Gaurav (Sender) sends a message to Sunil (Receiver) with a key. This is a random bit sequence transmitted via a scheme type that allows you to see a particular binary value (0 or 1) for the two separate start values.

Suppose this key is a stream of photons in a single direction, each of which consists of one bit of data (both 0 and 1). The oscillations can occur in any area of 360 degrees around any conceivable axis, but to make it more clear, we assume that the oscillations of these oscillations can be categorized into 4 basic states: UP/DOWN, LEFT/RIGHT, UPLEFT/RIGHTDOWN and UPRIGHT/LEFTDOWN.

In order for any photon bit to disperse, Gaurav (Sender) flips its polarisation scheme randomly between rectilinear and diagonal filters. This way, a single bit in whatever scheme it uses, either 1 or 0, can represent two polarizations.

When obtaining the photon key, Sunil (Receiver) requires either rectilinear or diagonal polarizer to calculate each photon bit: sometimes the right polarizer will be chosen, others the wrong polarizer will be chosen. Sunil (Receiver) selects polarizer randomly very similar to Gaurav (Sender). But it is uncertain to know about the wrong polarizer and cannot be explained what happens.

According to the Heisenberg Uncertainty Principle, it can be explained precisely what will happen to each photon, so the properties can be altered in calculating their behavior besides that if there are two properties of a system we want to measure, one prevents us from quantification. This theory states that it's very difficult to know what will happen to every photon. But we would guess what happens as a collective of them. Assume that the Sunil (Receiver) used for measurement of the UPLEFT and UPRIGHT/LEFTDOWN (diagonal) photon is a rectilinear polarizer. If this occurs, then the state of the photon will change to - half to UP/DOWN and a half to LEFT/RIGHT. But we cannot explain the state of transformation of individual photons. The fact is that in the real world, certain photons are blocked which cannot be explained by the theory.

Few photons are counted correctly by Sunil (Receiver) and some are counted incorrectly. Gaurav (Sender) and Sunil (Receiver) have built a channel for communication that is insecure and can be heard by others at this stage.

Now imagine we have an eavesdropper Satish, who wants to hear in, has the same polarizer as Sunil (Receiver), but also has to select randomly whether one of the photons must be used rectilinear or diagonally. Nevertheless, Sunil (Receiver) also faces the same issue when he picks the incorrect polarizer half the time. But it is important to Sunil (Receiver) to tell Gaurav (Sender) what sort of polarizer was used for each photon. It does not make any sense to Satish (Intruder) because he uses the incorrect detector for half the time and misunderstands some of the photons which makes the final key useless.

A different level of security is often indicated in the quantum cryptography of intrusion detection. Now both Gaurav (Sender) and Sunil (Receiver) would get to know that Satish (Intruder) wants to hear them.

METHOD OF QUANTUM COMMUNICATION

Two groups are used to describe quantum communication: a) direct quantum and b) quantum. The most straightforward way of recording the propagation of quantum signals in different locations is by using the direct model. Figure.1 (Tibbetts, 2019) demonstrates the Direct Quantum Communication Model.

Figure 1. Model of direct Quantum Communication

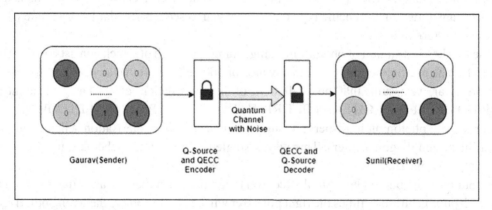

Figure 1 shows that Gaurav communicates with Sunil through a quantum channel. First, depending on the interaction with Sunil, Gaurav needs to construct a sequence of photons based on the direct transmission model. This knowledge also includes the processing of the encoder of a quantum source and the encoder QECC after the source output (Goyal et al., 2011).

In this process, Sunil receiver first produces the QECC code in the signal received and then integrates the quantum source code. The first quantum message is eventually sent to Sunil.

Quantum teleportation is another type of communication. Contrary to the normal communication form, the qubits can be wedged not only in the various orthogonal superposition systems. The objective of quantum teleportation is to create a quantum channel using a two-part high-density state. In this process, the message is then transmitted via a quantum procedure. Notice that the difference between direct and teleportation is the choice of networks. Figure 2 demonstrates the quantum teleportation model.

Figure 2. Model of Quantum Teleportation

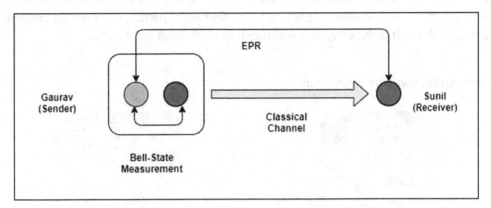

Quantum teleportation is the model where we present Gaurav who wants to use Sunil for a single-bit quantum elsewhere. The EPR pair is made up of the EPR capture source. Secondly, one particle is sent by the quantum channel to Gaurav and the other to the receiver Sunil (Goyal et al., 2011). Besides, Gaurav must also calculate particles in paired EPRs and retain the pending bits to transmit data. Again, Gaurav told Sunil about the calculation results. Finally, Sunil can obtain information from Gaurav and his EPR pair on the particles to be moved.

MISTRUSTFUL QUANTUM CRYPTOGRAPHY

The classic encryption branch, where parties do not trust each other is mistrustful encryption. Take an example of the collaboration between Gaurav (Sender) and Sunil (Receiver) in any computation involving such private feedback on both sides. But Gaurav (Sender) is not trusted by Sunil (Receiver) and Sunil (Receiver) is not trusted by Gaurav (Sender). Therefore a secure cryptographic task requires that Gaurav (Sender), once the calculation has been completed, can be assured that Sunil (Receiver) is not lying and Sunil (Receiver) has not tried Gaurav(Sender). Commitment schemes and robustly protected calculations are examples of mistrustful encryption activities. The area of mistrustful encryption is not a key distribution. Distrustful quantum cryptography using quantum systems studies the area of confounding encryption (Tibbetts, 2019).

QUANTUM COIN FLIPPING

Unlike a quantum key distribution., the method of Quantum Coin Flipping is used where the people the sender, and the receiver are transmitted message with a lack of trust. Participants interact and exchange information via qubit transmission through a quantum channel. For example, Gaurav (Sender) determines the random base and qubit sequence, then sends it to Sunil (Receiver). Sunil (receiver) then detects and writes the qubits. Having written down Sunil (Receiver) the qubits sent by Gaurav (Sender), he will give Gaurav (Sender) a guess as to the basis of her preference. Gaurav (Sender) announces whether or not Sunil (Receiver) has won or lost and then sends him the whole qubit sequence. During the process, fraud may occur as both sender and recipient have no confidence at any point. Quantum coin slipping is technically a secure way to communicate between two distrustful parties, however, the implementation of such criteria is difficult technically as it is difficult to implement practically.

Figure 3. Mistrustful quantum cryptography

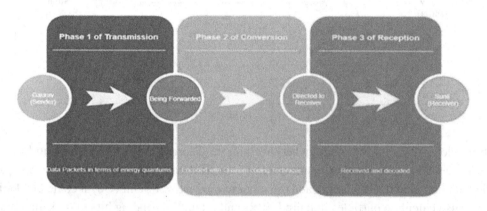

Figure 4. Quantum coin flipping

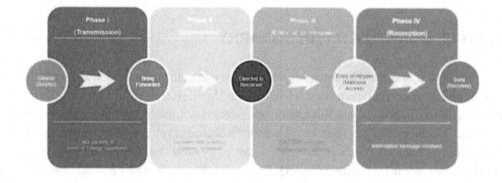

QUANTUM COMMITMENT

Apart from quantum coin flipping, when the parties with a lack of faith are involved, quantum commitment protocols are introduced. Gaurav (Sender) sends a specific value called "Commit" based on a commitment method so that Sunil (Receiver) should not be able to changes or learn that specific value unless Gaurav (Sender) reveals it Sunil (Receiver) (Campagna & Chen, 2015).

Figure 5. Quantum commitment

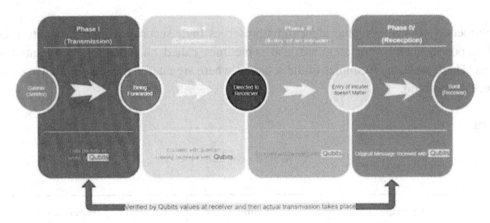

BOUNDED- AND NOISY-QUANTUM-STORAGE MODEL

This model is expected to restrict the amount of data an opponent can store in certain known continuous Q. Therefore the number of non-quantum data that the opponent can store is not reduced. One way to construct reliable quantum and quantum transmission protocols is to use the bounded quantum storage model (BQSM) (Sharma & Thind, 2019).

The quantum commitment and the obvious transmission protocols can be incorporated into the minimal quantum storage model. The parties share more than Q qubits (quantum bits) in this definition. Because all the information cannot be processed by even a disappointing group, it is appropriate to measure or discard a significant part of the data. The party that forces deception is to quantify a large portion of data to avoid the unlikely outcome of the protocol.

POSITION-BASED QUANTUM CRYPTOGRAPHY

The quantum cryptography position uses a geographical position as a player's credential. The geographical location is the only credential used to define location. The receiving party needs to read the message only if it is at that specific position. A player, Gaurav (Sender), has the simple job of position verification that he is located at a specified location. Chandran et al. have shown that position-verification by the colluding opponent is not possible except for the position asserted by the prover. Schemes are possible under various constraints on the adversaries.

DEVICE-INDEPENDENT QUANTUM CRYPTOGRAPHY

The researchers Mayers and Yao proposed a device-independent quantum cryptographic protocol with an idea that the parties cannot trust the devices used to transmit the sequence of qubits. A device-independent quantum cryptographic protocol is designed with a "self-testing" environment to detect malicious or unfit devices by using the statistical calculations of input and out given to the system. The researcher Roger Colbeck also suggested checking the trustful devices by using Bell test.

POST-QUANTUM CRYPTOGRAPHY

The phenomenon of cryptographic algorithms preserves their security against a quantum computer attack. The post-quantum computers are also sometimes called quantum-safe or quantum-resistant algorithms. There are many examples of the schemes where signature and encryption can be disturbed by the Shor's algorithm.

Analysis

Table 1.

Sr. No.	Methodology	Feature	Parameters
01	Mistrustful Quantum Cryptography concept	Quantum Codeing Techniques	Secure Computations, solve a loss-communication channel point-to-point repeater-less. A first efficient quantum repeater, characterised.
02	Quantum Key Distribution	Unconditional Security	Commitment schemes and secure computations
03	Coin Flipping	Intrusion Safe communication	Sequence of Qubits
04	Bounded and Noisy Quantum Storage Model(BQSM)	Noisy Storage, Requires the use of arbitrary imperfect quantum storage devices.	Quantum values
05	Position-Based Quantum Cryptography (PBQC)	Quantum tagging	Position at specific geographical location
06	Device Dependent Quantum Cryptography (DDQC)	Guarantees the security of an independent protocol system.	Entropy Accumulation Theorem (EAT)"
07	Post Quantum or Quantum Resistant	Signature and encryption schemes Quantum Resistant	ECC and RSA

APPLICATIONS OF QUANTUM SECURITY

Quantum-Encrypted Messaging and Video

To protect the world's data, communication with quantum-mechanically encrypted digital signals can be far safer than conventional signals. This is now possible due to the study of image sharing and the extremely secure video connection between satellite channels in China and Austria (Goel et al., 2007).

Quantum cryptography uses a set of bits (1s and 0s) called keys, similar to digital encryption, to encrypt and extract data. However, bits are classified in the quantum version as quantum regions – e.g. a state of photon polarization. The quantum pairs in the key are quantumly connected since the states of the pair depend on each other: the transmitter stores a qubit and transmits a qubit to the receptor (Bhatt & Sharma, 2019). Quantum mechanical laws forbid the physical capture and analysis of transmitted qubits without the sender and recipient detection.

QKD is a way to transmit a key that secretes the encrypted message as it is sent outside of the quantum protocol. Earlier QKD was seen between two remote locations with signals transmitted over many miles via optical cables, but simple signals transmitted via satellite relays could result in a reduction.

Jian-Wei Pan of the USTC recently recorded QKD on the laser beams between Chinese Xinglong and a low-orbit satellite called an orbit in Hefei and her colleagues. -Micius. -Micius. This satellite starts processing quantities and was launched by China in 2016. Furthermore, a QKD satellite link between Xinglong and Graz in Austria has been extended via Micius over 7,600 kilometers along with Anton Zeilinger and other members of the University of Vienna.

You can send different keys to the Xinglong and Graz stations, with laser pulses, each time they pass through. The transmitter says Gras-inserts the information using the Micius-Graz key, and Micius inserts the key in the Xinglong signal, encrypted with the Micius-Xinglong key.

Two fiber-optic networks between China and Austria sent two satellite images to the researchers showing cryptographical connections between Graz and Vienna and between Xinglong and Beijing. They sent the quantum philosopher Erwin Schrödinger (who served in Vienna) to Micius, a Chinese satellite philosopher, from Vienna to Beijing. There were 5 kilobytes of data on each disc.

Quantum Smart Cards

In quantum computers, security is depending on the fact that complex mathematical problems with computer processing power are not found. Eavesdroppers are especially able to understand at a descriptive pace even more complex mathematical issues with growing processing power(Dzau, 2019).

Stable encrypted documents can be archived for several years to eliminate any mathematical problems before computer needs have been met by the machine's capabilities. Researchers in the Los Alamos National Laboratory (LANL) has developed "QKarD," transformation technology that employs quantum mechanical laws and not complex mathematical encryption to resolve these concerns. The QKD method uses several individual photons to create private keys that can be shared in 2 or more classes.

Figure 6. QKarD Communication System

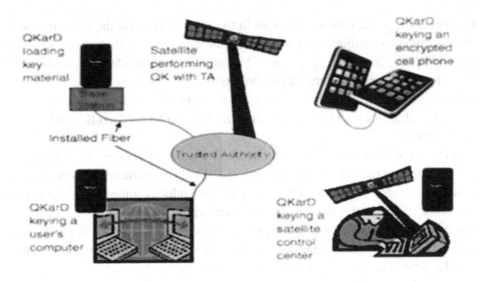

This encryption form, which is included in QKarD technology, guarantees high-quality protection regardless of the progress made in its use. QKarD is a small lightweight, easy-to-use wireless device. The user must insert the computer regularly into the primary authentication channel with a fingerprint and a pin. QKarD will then automatically transmit cryptographic quality passwords via an optical fiber to a trusted central authority (TA). Numbers are then saved to a computer-encrypted memory, encryption, authentication, and access control, which ensures secure connections to remote devices (free space).

IoT implementation of Quantum Cryptography

In quantum computers, IoT systems have plenty of room for a computer, user, or network protection. The new IoT architecture does not have a communication channel for eavesdropper acquisition. There may also be several attacks where only one virus can be used with a virus over the entire IoT network, and the rest of the devices are dependent on this system and stay in contact until detected. In this architecture, the error can only be identified later and suitable information can only be passed to any malicious organization. Some viruses will only harm systems if the systems are rebooted and industrial and commercial systems are not long upgraded. Thus several risk factors exist, and IoT systems are highly vulnerable to threats (Bhatt & Sharma, 2019).

The Quantum Computer can efficiently and at high speeds generate such large numbers. It is also very hard to guess the key and each system has its unique key. It's very hard to get the key to access and try to access the visual interface setup without being remembered. The key can therefore be secured and communication secure.

Safe Online Voting

In quantum computers, quantum cryptography can be used to avoid accidental cracking or data harm for Swiss voters. However, some electoral analysts caution that the current strategy does not take electoral risks into account.

On 21 October 2007, at the national elections in the State of Geneva, the transmission of findings from data centers from paper ballots to the state government database in Geneva is assured by quantum communication (Tibbetts, 2019). The goal, says Chancellor Robert Hensler, is to ensure that the information between log-in and retention are not compromised.

Quantum encryption connects quantum engines to create an encryption key, a secret series of 0s and 1s, that does not reveal the crime. In this processing, this key can be used to click and select a message at the end of the search.

In addition to optical fiber, a party gives the receiver a series of photons to create a quantum key. Each key photon is divided by a single indicator of 0 or 1. The encryption key is then a particular subset of these quantum elements – or qubits. If the eavesdropper includes some part of the key, the laws of quantum mechanics guarantee that photons are interfered with.

Quantum cryptography was first suggested in 1984, but the promotion of this idea took researchers decades. It was difficult to design the equipment needed to produce, maintain, and obtain single photons. It was also hard to prove that the security hypothesis works.

The three leaders in the field are BBN's technology in the United States; MagiQ in New York, United States; and ID Quantique in Geneva, Switzerland. All these firms, including banks and other financial institutions, have tried and tested quantum encryption systems.

Some analysts claim that military and intelligence firms use such devices as well. However, the Geneva elections are the first time it has been suggested by the government agency that it is using this technique.

FUTURE OF QUANTUM CRYPTOGRAPHY

There is a possibility that the earth could operate on quantum computers 20 or maybe 30 years from now. All our services work with quantum, which is linked to a limited amount of conventional computing on our local computers. The success of our services, organizations, and communities in general works quantum. We're not yet achieved with 100% confidence because, of course, there will be several fascinating shifts and turns along the way (Dzau, 2019).

On the other hand, the Government, including the majority of G20 members, has a strong interest in building a majority-based infrastructure. There are many ways of thinking about it: there are benefits of becoming a beginner and becoming a creator. The US also presses the envelope simultaneously. And he was the first person in the world to establish and attract the most successful in promoting technology, engineering, and basic science research when many other countries were distracted (Sharma & Thind, 2019).

Many governments worldwide want to embrace quantum physics, since it is the first race to go through it. There is certainly also an immense military need and it seems like most conflicts in the future will be one characteristic: terrorism. To try to slow down this sector, we will need good tools and analytics. It could also certainly see the significance of quantum computing.

Many countries have official policies. In China, the United States, and the European Union, some quantum policies, such as the EU, have not articulated development and philosophy: 'We believe the quantum is essential, and where we want to study it.

Future Security

The cyber wars will take the place of conventional war techniques. The information is becoming an asset and the hackers steal information, so it's a continuous task to protect it. More than 6,000 banks are headquartered in the United States with a total of 80,000 branches, about 6,000 hospitals, and thousands of insurance firms. These are all confidential (Zhou et al., 2018). These hidden keys are secured by endless mathematical ideas. When the giant "hears" when the knobs are transferred, they can be captured, manipulated, and exposed.

Quantum calculations that compromise the security of all major transfer methods are accepted. In the most common main exchanges, at least two different channel attacks break potentially strong exchange methods such as RSA-40963.

There are conventional cryptographic key methods of exchange that are in danger. There may have been a compromised fact that the RSA-1024, which once was commonly used for the exchange of keys between browsers and webserver; is no longer considered secure to use with a NIST, but the RSA-2048 is still approved.

Researchers use the called post-quantum cryptography to find ways to increase the safety of software-based key exchanges – ways to continue working until quantum computers are enough to break exchanges, dependent on the unexpressed argument that it is difficult to translate such technological numbers, it is not possible to copy them (formed) or at least to copy them completely. Comparing the structural dimensions of the fraction of these images, it can be seen that there is no sounding system listening so that the keys can be used safely.

Although quantum encryption is being called, we only trade encryption keys, so that researchers prefer to define this process by the term quantitative key distribution. Many nations believe that it is necessary to encrypt data safely, recognizing that even the greatest encryption today is at stake – may be in the future. QKD is the easiest way to secure encryption. Yes, there are issues with it but steady progress addresses these problems and gets us closer to a reality of long-haul and quantum d network infrastructure.

Does it imply that many security network applications are not interested in software-based methods? Of course, you do not always check the security costs for loss of your data, but a security solution must be assured in the assessment partly. Although post-quantum encryption and QKD in a particular application are adequately secured, QKDs is used when we know that our information is.

For years, QKD makes perfect sense if you have the data you want to secure. I am sure you can see this distributed across the world to safeguard this high value, long-term data. QKD is an excellent choice for high-value businesses and organizations.

The Future Internet

Cyberspace has become a common knowledge sharing provider in all aspects of our lives, helping almost every aspect of our wellbeing. Like science and technology, in particular quantum computing, progresses, internet security has recently become a major issue for the internet. Human society has entered a time of knowledge through the proliferation and rapid growth of the internet. Today it is difficult to isolate every group of people and every aspect of life from the network. In the 1990s, the idea of cyberspace on the Internet, social media, and interactive networking embodied many new ideas and circumstances.

The concept is currently used by strategic, security, government, military, industry, and business experts and analysts to describe the natural environment of global technology. The term also refers to Internet-related matters which enable people to engage in all forms of activities, including the transmission of ideas, exchange of information, support for the environment, business management, and development of art media, gaming, and political discourse. General web applications include cloud computing and customized complementary programs.

The problem of the protection of information is also a huge problem for cyberspace. pIT and business, on the other hand, have entered an unparalleled period of prosperity(Goyal et al., 2011). Internet security is significantly threatened by threats such as hackers and ransomware, as well as attacks by viruses. Furthermore, scientific and technical advances pose new challenges to communications protection. In the future of the Internet, cyberspace security should be protected because it brings together all information systems for people's survival. The growing security concern on the Internet is the first consideration of quantum cryptography.

Unconditional Protection

The major Internet communications providers today are cables and light networks. A producer of computers is Gaurav and Sunil, and Satish is a scavenger. Symmetric key cryptosystems and asymmetric key cryptosystems are divided into 2 types, symmetric and asymmetric. The security of both cryptosystems depends in large part on the complexity of the computer (Patil & Boda, 2016). The fast hardware construction and the new algorithms are however unparalleled challenges for the safety of traditional cryptosystems. Furthermore, the rapid growth of quantum computing in classical mathematics has produced more difficulties than in quantum physics. In 1994, for example, DLP and integer factorization problems were resolved.

In the 50s of the last century, Shannon, founder of knowledge theory, conducted a groundbreaking study on unconditional protection. In this analysis, unconditional safety requirements were given for the "one-time pad." This means that the encryption/decryption key is specifically set instead of a random fake number. And only once is this key used. Also, the length of the key is the same as the text and they function in bits with or especially with the text. However, the key distribution problem in a single pad was never solved. It is noteworthy that a quantum mechanical system can solve this main distribution problem. The model of the popular QKD protocol is shown in the figure 7.

Figure 7. Classical model of communication.

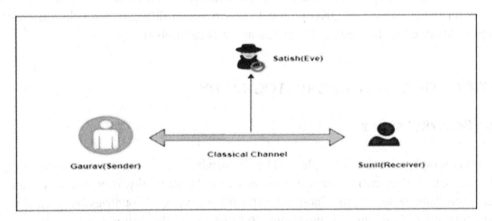

Figure 8. QKD protocol model.

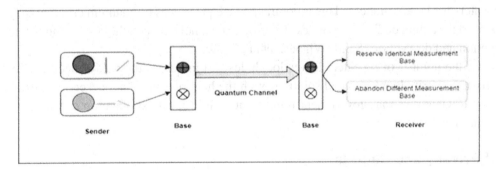

Sniffing Detection

In the figure, exchange information on the public channel for Gaurav and Sunil. To maintain security, the information is encrypted but the attacker cannot avoid listening to the channel. Furthermore, the eavesdropper cannot be identified by cable or fiber optic links because of the features of the system itself. The listener should use a multimeter or oscilloscope to track cable contact. The eavesdropper will obtain information on the signal segment of the lamp through a fiber optic link. Please note that loss of fiber is affected by natural factors including temperature and strain, thus reducing the loss of eavesdropping.

The eavesdropper would eventually be gained due to quantum teaching and cloning in quantum communication. In particular, if the unauthorized user monitors the quantum channel and chooses the same measurement basis as the 50-percent transmitter to acquire correct quantum information (Goyal et al., 2011). The eavesdropper is therefore available with a 50 percent probability of certain quantum information. Notice that the eavesdropper is likely to be detected with quantum-bit data.

Security of QKD

In QKD, there is a need to analyze the system by which channel keys are distributed to a silent channel to simulate real-life situations on the Internet. Also, a protocol to distribute quantum keys in the noise channel is still being sought (Goyal et al., 2011). The system reports quantum encoding and measurement results for the evaluation of QKD protocol security under different bases. In this process, both sides agree in advance that the vertical horizontal and vertical divisions are '1.'

LIMITATIONS OF QUANTUM CRYPTOGRAPHY

Defense Security issues

Quantum cryptography is in the initial phase. The complexity of the quantum cryptography algorithms makes them efficient. Data encryption is extremely safe and trustworthy. However, its complexity prevents legal users from navigating too. India and many other developed countries are researching various implementation areas of quantum cryptography. But they are in the testing level yet. But the research results will take a lot of time for full implementation of it. The fiber optic channels can provide uninterrupted secure transmission just up to 250km with a speed of just 16 bps. The network engineers are using repeaters for large distances. This is contrary to the principles of quantum cryptography because there is a need for a fully dedicated, wireless fiber-optic channel between the source and the destination for encryption and decryption (Sakthi Vignesh et al., 2009).

However, the number of repeaters leaves loopholes and increases the risk of hackers. Researchers are identifying security loopholes and solutions with the help of white-hat hackers. An article in MIT Technology Review says that government implementation of a robust quantum cryptography system will take another 20 years.

Loss of Privacy and Secrets

We are in an era of smart personal devices like cell phones, desktop computers, laptops, and many more. But the new quantum computing era is banging the door of our thinking of smart computing devices. Computers will be chipless and quantum computers will replace millions of desktop computers, laptops, and smart devices. Quantum cryptography refers to the idea of quantum computing in such a way that nobody is to have their personal computers or smart equipment. The leading quantum computing developers, including IBM and Microsoft, expect the advancement of quantum computing in the cloud services. The governments and big IT firms will own mammoth size clouds. There will not be the old ways to keep data and secrets on your computers or external hard drives. Very few governments and private companies have public information.

There has been controversy over the development in data security of quantum computers. But all the researchers have accepted the fact that power will be gathered by very few people. These people will likely have predominance in societies and they can misuse private data. The world is the witness of the Facebook-Cambridge Analytics data leak case of millions of users. Social media is fueling a revolution. People have a habit to socialize with their data.

Quantum Decoherence

According to the laws of quantum physics, the system is called coherent when different phase relation-ships are demonstrated in various states. This law will explain the electrons and form the mathematics of the wave function to define the quantum status of the quantum effect interpretations of a device. Thus this condition leads to a loss of information.

Classical computing is reliable, particularly when a great deal of functionality and reliability is required. It uses switches intolerance. If a switch fails, another switch triggers and gives error informa-tion. Quantum decoherence remains the main limitation of quantum computing. Researchers are taking efforts to develop decoherence at all levels to calculate results without troubling the processing at the same time. Quantum cryptography requires much similar research without compromising efficiency, rapid processing, and without knowing to the user at the same time.

Expensive and Time Consuming

Quantum encryption is in the preliminary stages. In contrast with classical cryptography, data encryption and decryption takes a long time. It is a modern technology, which takes time and requires dedicated infrastructure. While it benefits from its consistency in post-quantum encryption with existing networks, it anticipates major changes in all hardware, software, computers, and applications and must be specified from scratch by all entities.

Lack of Digital Signature and Certified Mail

Quantum cryptography has not enough key features to authenticate the sender to the receiver, like a digital signature or a certified mail. The digital signature can be used as part of the solution to the prob-lem of spoofing in complex applications like navigation satellite systems and Galileo and other Global Navigation Satellite Systems are working on implementation issues. The integrated digital signatures in the data stream authenticate data integrity and message origin.

To enforce a digital signature on a satellite-based framework for use in aviation, the signature would be short and cryptographically admissible for the next 30 years or more. Many state-of-the-art authentication systems are no longer feasible when quantum computing comes into operation, and an authentication scheme implemented in the satellite-based augmentation method must therefore be quantum-safe. The researchers are trying to understand the vulnerabilities caused by quantum cryptography and investigat-ing the solutions.

1.   Contribution of leading organizations

Science and Technology University of China (USTC)

Dr. Pan Jianwei, professor of science and technology at the Chinese University (USTC), described in an interview with the Massachusetts Institute of Technology (MIT) China's interest in being a superpower. China finances 400 million dollars to the army. The world has noticed the space race between the Soviet Union and the United States in the last century. This world will witness the race of quantum computers between the United States and China in this century (Washington Post, 2019).

Patinformatics, a market research company researched in 2018 and shown that China had twice the number of approved imports as much as the United States, which includes communications devices and cryptology.

The advancement of quantum technology has become a prime vision for China. India and many other countries are playing a major role in this field, but China is far ahead in the race of quantum computing. Micius, the quantum satellite is launched successfully by China. The satellite was used in a joint research study to link the video from Beijing to the Vienna states by quantum.

IBM

IBM is focusing on the manufacturing of commercial quantum computers. In its quantum computing technology, IBM announced IBM Q, which implements the operational prototype of 90 milliseconds of normal coherence and which can conduct quantum operations with 50 qubits or a quantum bits.

Recently, a patent analytics firm, Patinformatics, published a quantum patent landscape survey. It has shown that quantum computing patents are increasing with enormous speed. It underlines the dramatic growth of quantum patent rights published in the family, expected to increase from below 100 in 2014 to more than 400 published in 2017. The United States has been instrumental in a patent application in all countries (Patinformatics, 2018).

IBM is working aggressively to raise the quantum volume for the last three years. As a part of the roadmap, IBM is investing in critical hardware, device integration, and software innovations. Organizations in several sectors work with IBM to explore a wide range of quantum computing applications. The new solutions and faculties that could scarcely be thought about until recently are being looked at by carmakers, airlines, energy firms, health care providers, financial services companies, and world-class research organizations. IBM is providing the cloud access of the most advanced systems and software stack in support to these organizations. These projects demonstrate the potential of quantum computing to solve real world problems that are too complex for today's most efficient supercomputers.

Google with NASA

The US is a world leader in patents related to crucial parts of quantum computers, doing its complicated investment by IBM, Google, Microsoft, and other organizations. NASA announced a partnership with Google to explore the possibilities of a modern quantum processor. NASA is finding the prospects to use this technology in space missions in near future. Along with NASA, Google has shown that it can calculate the world's most complicated problems in seconds that take thousands of years to achieve by the biggest most advanced supercomputer. Google has achieved this benchmark which is called quantum supremacy (NASA, 2019).

NASA is finding the probabilities to use the techniques to support space missions, allowing more efficient mission schedules, simulating light and robust materials quantitatively for modern. Google's quantum processor experiments of Sycamore reflect quantum supremacy require for these projects.

The IEEE International Solid-Status Circuits Conference held in San Francisco in 2019. Google presented a custom circuit for quantum computing. The circuit will work within a cryogenic container that is less than 1 ° CK, a vital infrastructure movement for future expansion into quantum computer systems. Random quantum circuit results without a quantum processor are difficult, and theory involves the tasks above a certain amount that cannot even be carried out on the largest known supercomputer. It considers a test of more data units is necessary than atoms in the universe. This impossible task makes it the perfect test for quantum supremacy.

Google released a 72 qubit Bristlecone quantum processor. Google is running D-Wave quantum computers in the Quantum Artificial Intelligence Laboratory, hosted by NASA and the University of California Space Science Organization at NASA Ames Research Centre. D-Wave systems can measure 100 million times as fast as traditional computer chips. D-Wave machines have been exploring several computer applications including speech-image patterns, web search, planning and scheduling of projects, aviation, robotic missions to other planets, and mission control operations. D-Wave technology is used to reduce machine learning and human intelligence to lead in the emerging artificial intelligence sector to create its own quantum hardware.

Airbus

The Airbus Group is looking for quantum aerospace transformation computers. The Airbus Defense and Space Unit works on quantum cryptography to find the solutions to complex aerospace problems based on cloud computing.

Airbus reshapes existing quantum machines to aeronautical problems in particular those requiring vast quantities of data to be processed and stored, such as the sorting and analysis of satellite images or the creation of new ultra-lasting aircraft materials.

Airbus began Quantum Calculation Competition for solutions to a variety of designs and operational challenges of aircraft, including optimizing wing box construction, computer fluid dynamics, and the fuel efficiency of climbing aircraft routes.

Microsoft

The Microsoft QuArC community emphasizes the software architecture and algorithms for use in a scalable, defect-tolerant quantum computer, with excellent achievements in the fields of LIQUi > which is software architecture of quantum computing set of tools.

Microsoft announced in 2014 it was studying topological quantum computing on the UCSB campus in the area known as Station Q, intended to develop controlled, quantified state engineering. Station Q emphasizes the software and algorithms of the QuArC Community to construct a universally scalable, defect-tolerant quantum computer.

Microsoft has also taken steps to improve the quantum computing development layer. The Quantum Development Kit was released by Microsoft for developers who want to write Quantum Machine applications – the programming interface and language Q #. Microsoft introduced a network of quantum software and hardware of organizations from Microsoft Quantum Network which is downloaded the Q # script, compiler, and quantum simulator 100,000 times.

Nokia

Nokia is leading in the development of a quantum algorithm. Nokia is the motherhouse of Bell Laboratories. Many of its researchers Peter Shor and Luv Grover have developed pioneered quantum computing algorithms like the Shor's algorithm and the Grover algorithm. In 1994, Shor found that large-scale quantum computers could find the prime factors of huge numbers much faster than conventional computers, an attribute which could soon be undermined, and the new quantum computing area was boosted

Nokia is partnering with Lockheed Martin to explore the potential of quantum technology at Oxford University to improve machine learning and optimization. As the Morgan Stanley paper compared Bell Labs' quantum computing program with IBM, Google, and Microsoft, found be the "most credible" in all.

Intel

Intel is looking for the mass production of quantum computers. Intel pledged $50 million to provide engineering support for 10 years to QuTech, Delft University of Technology, and the Netherlands International Science Organization.

Intel built a 49-qubit top chip called Tangle Lake. Intel unveiled a quantum computer tool that will allow researchers to verify the proper functioning of quantum wafers before integrating into a complete quantum processor, which could save quantum computing researcher money and time and take a step towards a high volume quantum processor.

Toshiba

The Toshiba QKD platform provides digital keys for cryptographic fiber optic network applications. Toshiba has one of the world's largest quantum IP portfolios. Toshiba's Life Science Research Center encrypted and transmitted genome data via a quantum communication device to the Tohoku Medical Megabank Organization. It uses a 13.7 Mbps quantum key system.

Toshiba allied with the US Quantum Xchange developer to double the capabilities of its main quantum optical distribution network (Phio). The Phio project for various banks and asset management companies in New York City is currently being launched to help customers migrate and sustain data security.

Mitsubishi

Mitsubishi works on a safe encryption system for phone communications to keep the conversations secured and confidential. Mitsubishi Electric launched the world's first "one-time pad" app, a groundbreaking wireless encryption system to keep telephone calls secure.

The organization is exploring the implementation of a secure quantum network by taking in the National Institute of Information and Communication Technology project to assess mobile communications and communication devices.

British Telecommunications (BT)

British Telecommunications is researching the use of quantum properties to protect sensitive data. British Telecommunications works in cooperation with Toshiba Science ADVA Optical Networking, and the UK National Physical Laboratory of Science on quantum encryption to shield sensitive data from the transmission with no alterations in quantum status and to demonstrate that transmission is compromised. British Telecommunications developed a "quantum-safe" internet network spanning about 50 miles.

AT&T

AT&T aims to create a network for quantum communications. In May 2017, AT&T revealed its quantity networking technology to ensure secure interaction with the California Technology Institute. The United States Ministry of Energy and the NASA Jet Propulsion Laboratory are building the quantum network.

Alibaba

Alibaba Cloud opened a quantum computing facility for 11 qubit clouds for the implementation of security of data centers and artificial intelligence in E-Commerce.

REFERENCES

Bhatt, A. P., & Sharma, A. (2019). Quantum Cryptography for Internet of Things Security. *Journal of Electronic Science and Technology*, *17*(3), 213–220.

Campagna & Chen. (2015). *Quantum Safe Cryptography and Security: An introduction, benefits, enablers and challenges*. ETSI White Paper No. 8.

Dzau, V. J. (2019). *Quantum Computing: Progress and Prospects*. The National Academics Press.

Goel, R., Garuba, M., & Girma, A. (2007). Research Directions in Quantum Cryptography. *International Conference on Information Technology (ITNG'07)*, 1-6.

Goyal, A., Aggarwal, S., & Jain, A. (2011). Quantum Cryptography & its Comparison with Classical Cryptography: A Review Paper. *5th IEEE International Conference on Advanced Computing & Communication Technologies*, 428-432.

NASA. (2019). *Google and NASA Achieve Quantum Supremacy*. https://www.nasa.gov/feature/ames/quantum-supremacy/

Patil, P. A., & Boda, R. (2016). Analysis of Cryptography: Classical verses Quantum Cryptography. *International Research Journal of Engineering and Technology*, *3*(5), 1372–1376.

Patinformatics. (2018). *Quantum Computing Applications: A Patent Landscape Report*. Patinformatics, LLC. https://patinformatics.com/wp-content/uploads/2018/01/Quantum-Applications-Patent-Landscape-Report-Opt.pdf

Sakthi Vignesh, R., Sudharssun, S., & Jegadish Kumar, K. J. (2009). Limitations of Quantum & The Versatility of Classical Cryptography: A Comparative Study. *Second International Conference on Environmental and Computer Science*, 333-337.

Sharbaf, M. S. (2011). Quantum Cryptography: An Emerging Technology in Network Security. Loyola Marymount University, California State University, Northridge.

Sharma & Thind. (2019). A Quantum Key Distribution Technique Using Quantum Cryptography. *International Journal of Distributed Artificial Intelligence*.

Tibbetts. (2019). *Quantum Computing and Cryptography: Analysis, Risks, and Recommendations for Decisionmakers*. Center for Global Security Research, Lawrence Livermore National Laboratory.

Washington Post. (2019). *The quantum revolution is coming, and Chinese scientists are at the forefront*. https://www.washingtonpost.com/ business/2019/08/18/ quantum-revolution-is-coming-chinese-scientists-are-forefront/

Zhou, T., Shen, J., Li, X., Wang, C., & Shen, J. (2018). Quantum Cryptography for the Future Internet and the Security Analysis. Hindawi Security and Communication Networks. doi:10.1155/2018/8214619

Chapter 2
Fundamentals of Quantum Computing, Quantum Supremacy, and Quantum Machine Learning

Kamaljit I. Lakhtaria
Gujarat University, India

Vrunda Gadesha
Gujarat University, India

ABSTRACT

When we aim to demonstrate that a programmable quantum device can solve complex problems which cannot be addressed by classic computers, this fundamental goal is known as quantum supremacy. This concept has changed every fundamental rule of computation. In this chapter, the detailed concept of quantum computing and quantum supremacy is explained along with various open source tools and real-time applications of this technology. The major base concepts, quantum computing, the difference between classical and quantum computer on physical level, programing quantum device, and the experiment-quantum supremacy are explained conceptually. This chapter also includes an introduction of the tools Cirq and OpenFermion plus the applications like quantum simulation, error mitigation technique, quantum machine learning, and quantum optimization, which are explained with illustrations.

INTRODUCTION TO QUANTUM SUPREMACY

Scientists and physicists were pointing out about quantum computing science last 30 years, but the question with this innovation is "where is it useful? Is it worth investing time, money and resources in this?" To answer this, follow the good engineering practice; formulate decisive short-term goals that demonstrate whether the design is going in right direction. Thus to demonstrate that a programmable quantum device can solve a problem that no classical computer can solve; this experiment and demonstration is known

DOI: 10.4018/978-1-7998-6677-0.ch002

Copyright © 2021, IGI Global. Copying or distributing in print or electronic forms without written permission of IGI Global is prohibited.

as Quantum Supremacy. Many directions were discerned to overcome technical challenges inherent in quantum system to make a computer that is both programmable and powerful.

Here in the concept of quantum computers, the computer does not refer to Laptop, desktop, mobile phone or any such device which are prevalent in the current market. The word "Quantum Computer" is quite misleading as it contains the word "computer". Computer starting from the smallest device such as mobile phone to the largest device like super computer working on the same fundamental rules. These all the devices do work on classic bits. Where's Quantum Computer work on Qubits.

Scientists across the globe are working to demonstrate quantum supremacy. The famous scientist Hartmut Neven said about the experiment during the demonstration:

"The nice thing about Quantum supremacy is that, this is a very well defined engineering milestone" - Hartmut Neven [Engineering Director – Lead Google AI Quantum]

Hartmut Neven is clearly indicating the power of quantum supremacy, as it is the well-defined milestone. Thus, to achieve this; various people has contributed into the experiment. (Neven, 2020)

In a nut shell, this experiment shows that the experimental quantum computers can surpass the largest and best computers in the world. The processor which is created to achieve quantum supremacy is known as "Sycamore Processor". It processes 2^{53} states simultaneously.

According to the scientist Marrisa Gustina, this innovation is really exiting for mankind as it can be given to the researcher as a tool and they can come out with the best results.

Figure 1. The base concept of quantum computing

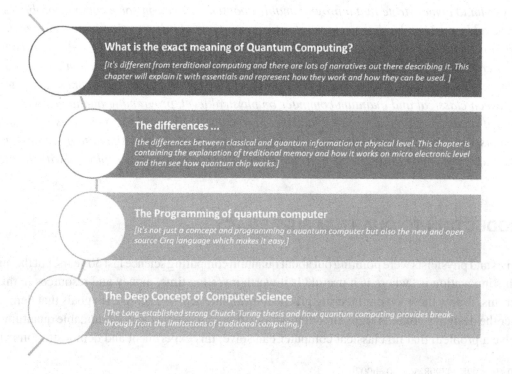

Base Concept: 1- What is the Exact Meaning of Quantum Computing?

Quantum Computing is been all over the news lately, but still this concept is still mysterious in the world of computer science, as we all consider the buzz word "Quantum" comes from the base of physics then how do it can form a technology with computer science?

If we refer the word meaning of "Quantum" it means "Volume", "Size", "Magnitude", "Degree of equation", "Quantity", and "Amount". These are the significance word meaning of the term "Quantum" used in the concept of physics in different scenario. The mystery comes to the mind when this term referred with "Computing".

Computing and "Volume", "Amount" or other significant meanings do not have any relation practically. Scientist has taken this challenge to make something very innovative to bring revolution in the field of computer science.

Thus the questions we have in our mind are:

- What does quantum mean in the context of computer hardware?
- What distinguishes a quantum computer from the regular one?
- What does the quantum computer looks like?
- How do we build it? And how it works?

Here these all questions are unpacked and explained with core theories. Scientists are trying to build devices that humans can interact with, control it and read out them. Devices; which behaves reliably according to a simple quantum model. In other words, the scientists are building quantum computing hardware.

Quantum hardware can be used as a tool from approaching certain kinds of computational problems. Thus scientists are targeting at both; to develop the hardware and to develop the algorithms to leverage this hardware. (Giustina, 2018)

What does Quantum Mean in the Context of Computer Hardware?

To get into this concept, the base theory is quantum mechanics. Consider any model, is physicist's tool to make predictions about what will happen when we put the universe into certain configuration and poke it in a certain way.

For example if you have never built long tower before, you might make a Lego Version before building it on full scale. Thus a Lego version can refer as model. Models can also be expressed in the language of mathematics. The most fundamental model of nature popular among us was developed in early 20th century and it is known as quantum mechanics. The word 'Mechanics' referred to the mechanism by which the things happen. The word 'quantum' referred to discrete quantities of energy or some other physical quantity. Within Quantum mechanics, energy comes in packets, which are called 'Photons'. The limitation is you cannot have fractional packets.

So, what is a quantum object? We think quantum object as being tiny and quantum leap is being large. However the term 'Quantum' does not dictate an object's size. Actually a quantum object is one that relets in a well-defined way to a single quantum of energy. (Sank, 2019)

Figure 2. Development in quantum computing

Figure 3. Example of is model

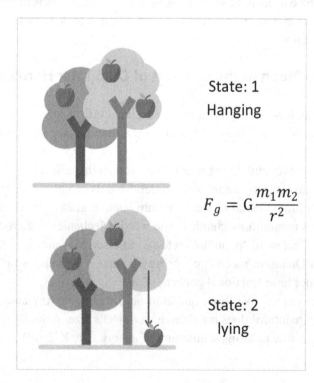

State: 1
Hanging

$$F_g = G\frac{m_1 m_2}{r^2}$$

State: 2
lying

Figure 4. Quantum Object - Energy

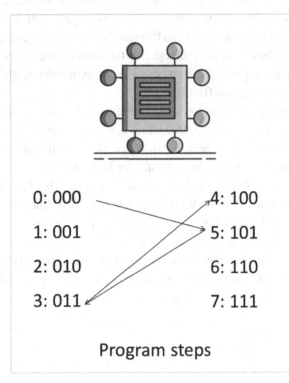

For instance, the photon is a quantum object. A photon is a single particle of energy. Similarly, atoms are quantum objects and an electron flying around an atomic nucleus may be exited into a higher orbit only by a particular quantum of energy. There is no half-way point between the lower orbit and the upper orbit. If the wrong energy is provided, there simply isn't a corresponding orbit for the electron to land in. *(Illustrated in figure 4)*

In a nutshell, a quantum object is one whose observable reflects that nature only offers energy in discrete packets. (Sank, 2019)

What Distinguishes a Quantum Computer from the Regular one?

In quintessence, quantum hardware lives in a richer world then its conventional counterpart. Let's consider a simple, abstract, quantum object which is entirely described by the fact that it can be in one of two different energy levels. Consider those levels '0' and '1'.

The classical bit of information can be assumed as switch; which can take either '0-state' or '1-state'. Because of the apparent similarity between our quantum and that classical bit of information, we call this quantum analog a quantum bit or Qubit. One peculiar feature about quantum mechanics is the ***existence of super positions***. A superposition is like a special mixture of the energy levels '0' and '1'; where the weight of each energy level is given by the complex constants C0 and C1. If we measure the energy of our Qubit, we will observe sometime 0, sometime 1; where the value of sometimes is given by the constants. An individual measurement will yield an outcome of '0' or '1'. There are no other options. But before the measurement occurs we know at most the chances of getting '0' or '1'. We can't know the actual outcome for sure until we measure it. Therefor when we want to talk about the energy state of the Qubit before we have made the measurement, we use this superposition to represent that the Qubit hasn't decided yet which outcome to display; even though the chances of getting each outcome are fixed. Now, even admitting that this superposition concept is little unusual. We can accept that it's easy enough to represent one Qubit, we can simply write with possible combinations of '0s' and '1s'. While thinking about more Qubits it increasingly gets difficult.

Suppose we add a second Qubit, if these were conventional switches; we could think about each switch independently, but Qubits are different. Just as one Qubit can be in a superposition state, two Qubits can share a superposition state, where for instance, the measurement outcome is unknown, but will certainly be the same for both objects or opposite for both objects.

For example *(Shown in below figure - 5)* here is a state where 'Blue Qubit' and 'Yellow Qubit' are together in a super position state. Here they are correlated to each other. Before the measurement, it cannot be known whether the 'Blue Qubit' will turn up '0' or '1'. In this case measuring the blue and yellow Qubits will always give opposite outcomes. This means that in order to fully describe two Qubits we need to consider C's for all possible measurement outcomes. Moving further, to describe 3 Qubits we need 8 C's; describing 4 Qubits takes 16 C's and so on. Every time we add another Qubit, it takes twice the information to describe the whole pile of them.

2 Qubits $C0 \rightarrow 0$ and $C1 \rightarrow 1$ 1 Qubit

Qubits 0 Bits

$C_0 \rightarrow 00, C_1 \rightarrow 01, C_2 \rightarrow 10, C_3 \rightarrow 11$

3 Qubits $C_0 \rightarrow 000, C_1 \rightarrow 001, C_2 \rightarrow 010, C_3 \rightarrow 011,$

$C_4 \rightarrow 100, C_5 \rightarrow 101, C_6 \rightarrow 110, C_7 \rightarrow 111$

4 Qubits $C_0 \rightarrow 0000, C_1 \rightarrow 0001, C_2 \rightarrow 0010, C_3 \rightarrow 0011, C_4 \rightarrow 0100, C_5 \rightarrow 0101, C_6 \rightarrow 0110, C_7 \rightarrow 0111,$

$\quad C_8 \rightarrow 1000, C_9 \rightarrow 1001, C_{10} \rightarrow 1010, C_{11} \rightarrow 1011, C_{12} \rightarrow 1100, C_{13} \rightarrow 1101, C_{14} \rightarrow 1110, C_{15} \rightarrow 1111$

Figure 5. super-positions grows exponentially with Qubits

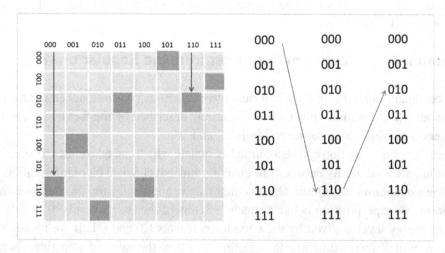

This is the **base concept or theory** which makes difference Quantum Hardware from other binary based devices. The number of **states increases exponentially** in the case of Qubits. The quantum system lives in a richer space, so that representing n-Qubits with a classical computer requires 2^n Numbers. But does this mean that quantum memory with 100 Qubits corresponds to a conventional memory with 2^{100} bits? Not so fast!

Quantum hardware is very effective at encoding and processing certain kind of information, but it cannot be efficiently mimic many useful aspects of its classical counterpart. When we say that a picture is worth 1000 words, we don't abolish words entirely in favor of pictures. Adding quantum hardware to our modern computing capabilities would be like adding pictures to a communication strategy that up to now used only words.

Figure 6. Pictures to a communication strategy

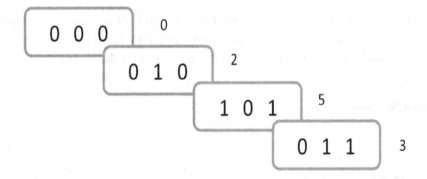

Figure 7. Quantum Lego Set

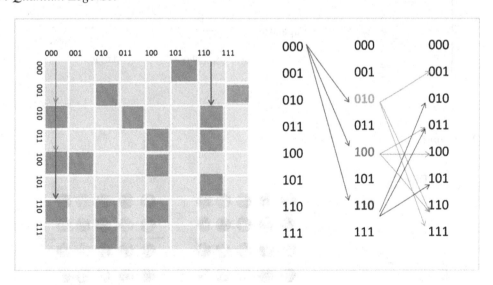

Based on this, think; what does quantum hardware do well? The exponentially growing complexity of quantum systems gives a clue about where quantum hardware could be useful. For example in the field of chemistry and materials development simulation of molecules could be a powerful technique to learn about the properties of a new molecule before fully synthesizing it in a lab.

However, our ability to simulate chemistry on computers is limited. And it is very difficult; chemistry is an application of quantum mechanics. Each electron we add to model doubles the number of parameters, crippling computers with expensive calculation already for very small molecules. Suppose instead that we could build chemistry models out of a quantum Lego set. Then the model would be built with the same physics that governs the system being modeled.

Infect chemistry and materials simulations have appeared as an appealing near-term problem to approach using quantum hardware. (Giustina, 2018)

What does the Quantum Computer Looks Like and how do we Build it?

Here let's take a first look at actual hardware shown in below figure. *(This hardware is built by Google).* The Qubits are resonant electrical circuits made of patterned aluminum on a silicon chip that slosh electrical current back and forth at two different energy levels to encode the quantum 0 and 1 states.

Figure 8. Quantum Hardware

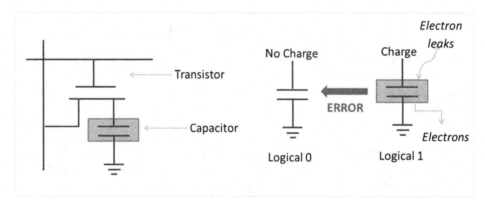

Figure 9. Quantum Chip

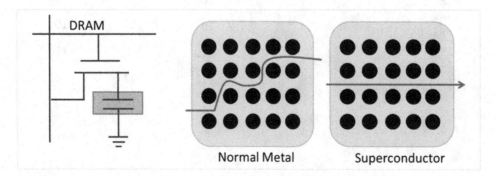

Here is a picture of Quantum Chip. Each chip features 72 Qubits. As shown in figure-9 the size of this chip is just about a quarter. The target is that each Qubit to behave as one single quantum object with two levels. Any other particle interacting with Qubit from its environment pulls it away from this two-level ideal. So creating a clean Qubit environment is a critical challenge. At the same time, we want to be able to control the Qubits efficiently, adding and removing quanta of energy and letting pairs of Qubits interact to exchange energy with each other on demand. These requirements seem to oppose each other. Ideal Qubit should be perfectly clean to interact with nothing. But then in specific cases, we want them to interact very strongly. This gives one insight into the tensions and challenges of building good quantum hardware.

A first step toward building clean Qubits is to build the Qubit circuits out of superconducting materials, which experience no electrical loss. Superconductors perform only at very low temperatures. We operate our Qubits in a cryostat at less than 50 millikelvin, just a fraction of degree above absolute zero. The cold temperatures and vacuum inside a cryostat also contribute to keeping the Qubit environment clean.

The cryostat consists of a series of nested plates and cans. The warmer stage is at the top, and it gets colder at the bottom. All the equipment in the central core of the cryostat is responsible for getting things cold. The hardware is installed around the edges and on the bottom, coldest plate. Each Qubit chip must be mounted in a package, which holds the chip at millikelvin temperature and bridges the gap between big cables and a small chip. To address the packages chip, electronics outside the cryostat send signals through cables in the cryostat. Each cable must carry electrical signals from room temperature all the way down to the coldest stage, while leaking only the smallest amount of heat. A large heat load would prevent the cryostat from reaching its millikelvin base temperature.

Figure 10. cryostat

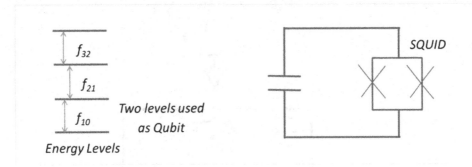

A collection of filters and amplifiers outfits each cable for its specific task. The electronics outside the cryostat are controlled by the code running on a computer. They generate precisely calibrated electrical signals, shaped pulses of microwave radiation, which are sent to control and read out Qubits. This entire system, from chip to cryostat, cables to code is required to run the quantum hardware.

So, with the first base concept 'the exact meaning of Quantum Computing' solved the questions in our mind such as what is quantum in terms of computer hardware, what distinguishes a quantum computer from the regular one, how does the quantum computer looks like, how do we build it and how it works.

Base Concept: 2- The Differences Between Classical and Quantum Information at Physical Level

Information is physical, written letters are carbon grains on paper, spoken words are vibrations of air molecules and computer bits are electric charge; each of these examples are sharing common limitation. They work under physics that was understood in the years of 1800s which is known as classical physics.

After that science has progressed and discovered new set of laws called quantum mechanics. There is a myth about quantum mechanics that; it only applies to microscopic objects like atoms. So how does the chip (figure-9) bring out quantum behavior?

So let's understand the base concept that how quantum bits are made and how they are. Physicist and computer scientist think in terms of states. So, according to the physical laws determine how nature goes from one state to another. We can see or observe the physical state and its transection, for example an apple is falling down from the tree, so its first physical state was 'hanging' on the tree, and after the gravitational force applied, it falls on the surface and its physical state changes from 'hanging' to 'lying'. Similarly in computer the state is the value of its memory bits. And computer program determine how the computer goes from one state to the next. For example when you hit the play button YouTube programs started manipulating your computer's memory to run a selected video. Where physics has physical states and natural laws, computer science has memory states and programs.

Figure 11. Physical States

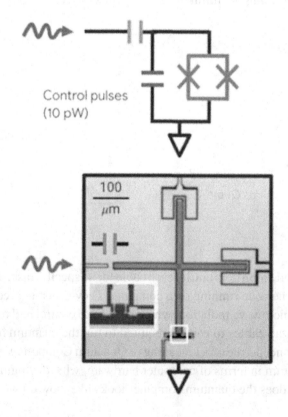

Figure 12. Computer Memory State

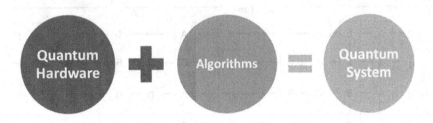

Think of the state of computer memory as a string of bits. For end bits there are two to the end possible strings. But because we are based in classical physics, the state of the computer is just one of these states at each point in time. On each step of classical algorithm, we go from one state to the next. For example the logic operation is shown in below figure; takes the state 0-0-0 to 1-1-0. If we were to apply same operation again the state moves from 1-1-0 to 0-1-0.

Figure 13. Logic Operation lookup table and computer states

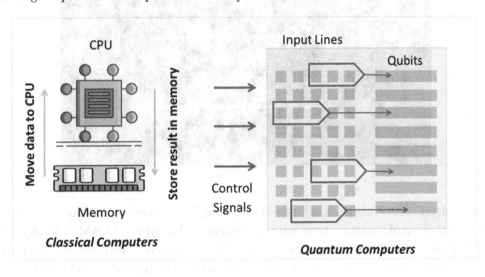

Compared to classical states, Quantum states are richer. They can have some weight in all possible classical states. Physicists call this situation as superposition. (Martinis, 2019)

Each step of quantum algorithm mixes the states into complex superposition. For example starting in 0-0-0, we go to a superposition of 1-0-0, 1-0-1 and 1-1-1. Then each of those three parts of the super post state branches out to even more states.

The extra complexity of quantum computers allows them to solve some problems faster than a classical computer ever could. Till now we have seen the computational difference between classical and quantum, but how do classical and quantum differ physically? How do we bring out quantum mechanics in our chip, which is so much bigger than the tiny atoms in which quantum mechanics was first discovered. (Martinis, 2019)

Figure 14. Quantum states

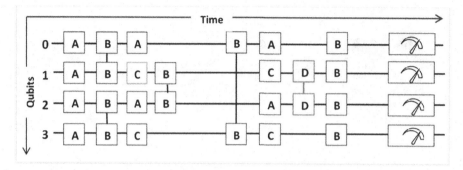

Figure 15. Logic Operation lookup table and computer states for superposition

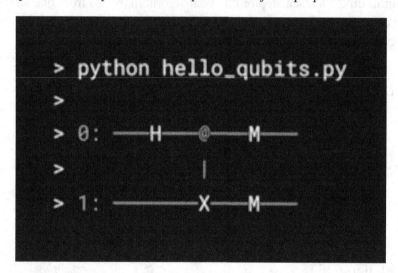

Let's take a detailed look at classical bits at the physical level; Classical computer bits are stored in the presence or absence of charge on a capacitor in a circuit called dynamic RAM or DRAM. If there is charge, it is logical 1, and if there is no charge, it's logical 0. In principal, we could just use the presence or absence of one electron as our logical bit, but in-fact there are more than 300,000 electrons has been used for the same. Thus, physical bits are noisy. Electrons are tiny and light, so they jiggle around and leak out of the DRAM. If we had only one electron and it were to leak out, out bit will change value, which is an error. By using lots of electrons, if few electrons leak out it will not harm our system, so this we can recover the error. DRAM circuits periodically check the logical level and replenish missing electrons. Encoding one logical bit in the state of so many physical bits gives classical information a level of reliability that we take for granted. We don't have to think about all those electrons bumping around when the programming conversation takes place. So, the question raised here is why can't we just put our DRAM into a quantum superposition of 0 and 1? Suppose we do have that superposition it will not be for long time. As soon as we do the first check to protect against the DRAM error, we have forced the bit into either 0 or 1, removing the quantum super position state. In fact, that collapse happens even without us checking for errors.

Figure 16. Classical Bits - DRAM

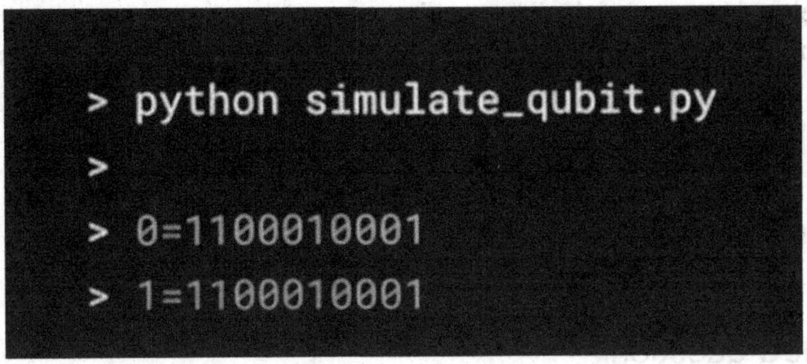

```
> python simulate_qubit.py
>
> 0=1100010001
> 1=1100010001
```

A single photon interacting with just one of our electrons can carry off information. When that happens, it's as if the photon observed the quantum state and the state collapses. This is its nature of observing and destroying our quantum states. Errors like this are unique to quantum information. In classical computing, it does not like that if somebody peeks at your bits, but that peek doesn't completely destroy them. Note that error occurs whenever nature observes any one of our physical bits, so while we normally stack up more physical bits for redundancy, that approach actually makes quantum error worse.

This is the main difficulty in quantum computation; the fundamental quantum constituents of matter are small and easily subjected to noise. But we can't brute force our way around that noise with redundancy because bigger systems are more subject to quantum errors.

The best technique discovered to solve this problem is superconducting Qubits. The circuits made with a huge number of electrons, but quantum errors are prevented using the technique called superconductivity. In regular metals, like with a conventional DRAM circuit, every individual electron does its own thing. As electrons move around, they can bounce off the positively charged ions of the metal, radiating vibrational waves that carry off quantum information about the electrons. This hectic, bustling cauldron of physical interactions generates lots of quantum errors and the information gets lost before we can use it. However, when certain metals are cool down, of quantum errors drops to almost 0.

Figure 17. Superconductivity

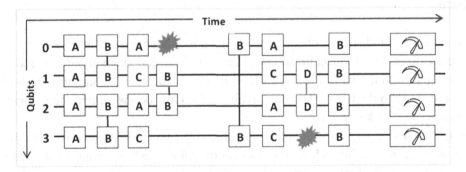

Our quantum bits are just electoral oscillators built from aluminum, which become superconducting when cooled to below 1 degree kelvin. The oscillators store tiny amounts of electrical energy. When the oscillator is in the 0 state, it has 0 volume of energy. When it is in the 1 state it has a single quantum of energy. The two states of the oscillator with 0 or 1 quantum of energy are the logical states of our quantum bit or Qubit.

Figure 18. Qubit: Quantum Resonator

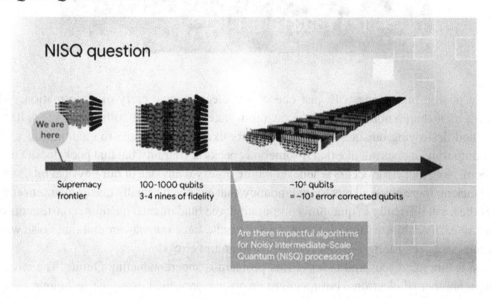

Figure shows super conducting Qubit along with its circuit diagram. The crosses indicate 'Josephson tunnel junctions' which are nonlinear superconducting inductors. We pick the resonance frequency of our oscillators to be about 6 gigahertz, which sets the energy difference between the 0 and 1 state. That is a low enough frequency that we can build control electronics from readily available commercial parts, but also high enough that the ambient thermal energy doesn't scramble the oscillation and introduce errors.

Architecture

After understanding the fundamental of computation it's important to understand how superconducting Qubit architecture differs from conventional computers. In a conventional computer memory and logic processing are separated into the RAM and CPU. When we want to do a computation, we first move the data from the RAM to the CPU. Then the circuits in the CPU do the computation, and finally, the resulting data is written back to RAM.

In Quantum Computing with superconducting Qubits, we cannot effort the errors that would come from moving the data around. Instead, we build a grid of Qubits, each one connected to its neighbors. The Qubit stay put and we do logic operations by sending control signals into individual Qubits or pairs of Qubits.

Figure 19. Superconducting microwave circuit

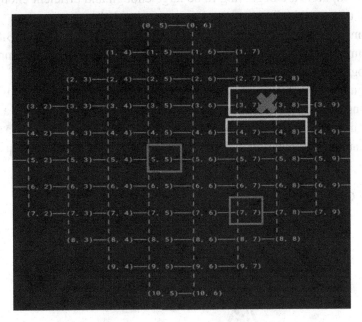

Figure 20. Architecture: Classical V/S Quantum

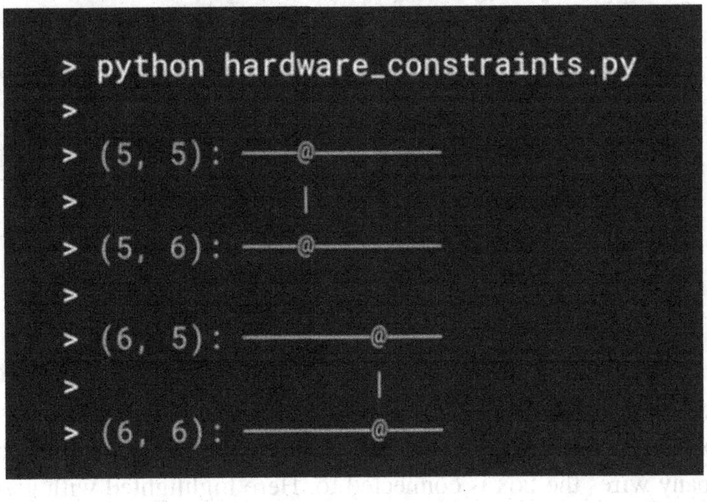

```
> python hardware_constraints.py
>
> (5, 5):  ——@——
>              |
> (5, 6):  ——@——
>
> (6, 5):        ——@——
>                   |
> (6, 6):  ——————@——
```

So, this base concept make us clear about the fact that information is physical, we understood the physical incarnation of classical and quantum computer bits. We also understood the quantum errors and superconductivity. (Martinis, 2019)

Base Concept: 3- The Programming of Quantum Computers

After understanding the previous two base concepts, we can say that a quantum computer is a new type of computer that stores and acts on information in its quantum form. Now we are entering into an exciting era where quantum computers are beginning to be large enough and efficient enough to execute tasks in less than a second that would take years to execute on a normal computer.

The quantum computer made of superconducting circuits with 72 Quantum Bits. Researchers can use this chip to attempt to achieve a task that can be solved in years on supercomputer. The quantum computer can be programmed using an open source framework called **Cirq**.

A quantum computer stores its information using Qubits; the information in this Qubits is then maneuvered around using the lows of quantum physics. To describe an algorithm on a quantum computer 'the quantum circuit model' can be used. The quantum circuit model is essentially a diagram describing how to perform a quantum computation. Following figure shows the example of quantum circuit.

Figure 21. Quantum Circuit

The above sheet is just looks like a sheet of music from left to right. Each of the Qubits in a quantum computer corresponds to a single horizontal wire in the quantum circuit. Here this circuit operates on four Qubits. The boxes in the figure correspond to quantum gates are applied to one or more Qubits, depending on how many wires the box is connected to. Here highlighted with green is a single Qubit gate. And highlighted with orange is a two Qubit gate. Quantum gates are instructions to send control signals to the quantum computer to perform a certain quantum action on Qubits.

Finally highlighted in blue is a part which has instructions for reading out the quantum information. This corresponds to quantum gates that perform measurements and turn quantum bits into classical bits. If we have a quantum circuit diagram, we can use this to send microwave pulses and instructions to our quantum computing hardware. This will execute the quantum gates and then read out the result of the circuit.

The quantum circuit diagrams are simple to look at them, but when we deal with large and complex programs it becomes very challenging to draw the circuit diagram. To solve this issue, researchers have developed frameworks or programming languages to write more traditional looking programs that represent the quantum circuits.

Here we are going to learn the basic fundamentals of the open framework **cirq**. This is a python framework. This means you can use all the goodness of python in helping to write quantum program.

The central object in cirq is a circuit object. So to create new circuit we can write following code. Another key set of objects are Qubits. So we have defined two Qubits with simple names. Now we can perform some quantum gates on these Qubits. We applied hadamard gate denoted by H to one of the Qubits, followed by a two Qubit controlled NOT or CNOT gate between both the Qubits. Finally let's measure the quantum bits. (Bacon, 2019)

```
import cirq
circuits = cirq.Circuits()
(q0, q1) = cirq.LineQubit.range(2)
circuit.append ([cirq.H(q0), cirq.CNOT(q0, q1)])
circuit.append([cirq.measure(q0), cirq.measure(q1)])
print(circuit)
```

Think; after this program what circuits have we produced? We can simply use 'print' to see the circuit. We can use ASCII-diagrams to see the quantum circuits.

Figure 22. ASCII-diagram - quantum circuit

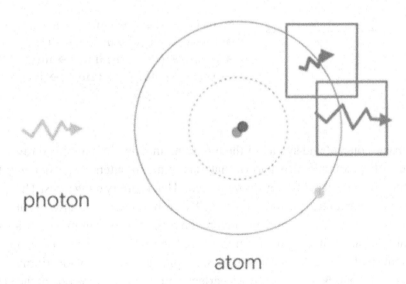

```
import cirq
circuits = cirq.Circuits()
(q0, q1) = cirq.LineQubit.range(2)
circuit.append ([cirq.H(q0), cirq.CNOT(q0, q1)])
circuit.append([cirq.measure(q0), cirq.measure(q1)])
```

```
sim = cirq.Simpulator()
results = sim.run(circuit, repetation=10)
print(result)
```

Here we see the H gate for a Hadamard, followed by the controlled NOT gate with the '@' symbol and the 'x' symbol. The measurements are represented by 'M'. Once the construction of circuits is completed we can perform the simulation of the circuit. (Bacon, 2019)

Here we run the circuit 10 times and see the measurement results. Measurement results in quantum computers don't always give the same value of bits. One run of the circuit may result in the output being 0, and another in it being 1. Here we see that the measurement results differ for each run of the simulation. Cirq also contains an interface for running the quantum circuit against actual quantum hardware.

Figure 23. Result of simulation

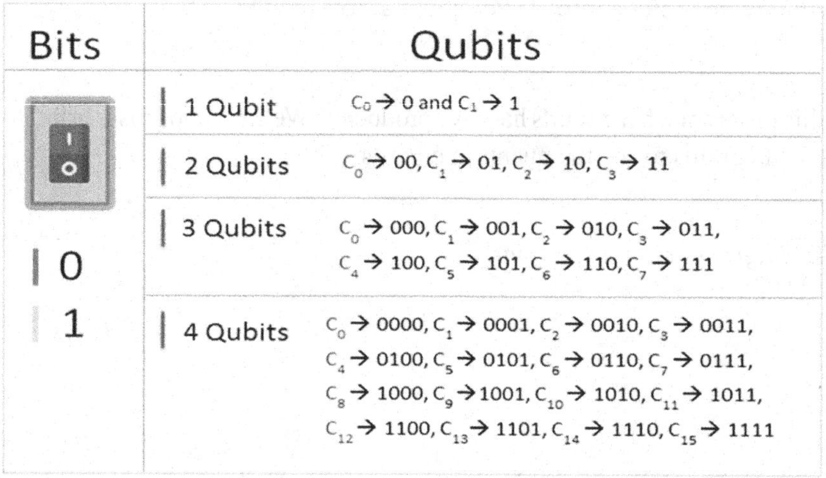

Bits	Qubits	
	1 Qubit	$C_0 \rightarrow 0$ and $C_1 \rightarrow 1$
	2 Qubits	$C_0 \rightarrow 00, C_1 \rightarrow 01, C_2 \rightarrow 10, C_3 \rightarrow 11$
0	3 Qubits	$C_0 \rightarrow 000, C_1 \rightarrow 001, C_2 \rightarrow 010, C_3 \rightarrow 011,$ $C_4 \rightarrow 100, C_5 \rightarrow 101, C_6 \rightarrow 110, C_7 \rightarrow 111$
1	4 Qubits	$C_0 \rightarrow 0000, C_1 \rightarrow 0001, C_2 \rightarrow 0010, C_3 \rightarrow 0011,$ $C_4 \rightarrow 0100, C_5 \rightarrow 0101, C_6 \rightarrow 0110, C_7 \rightarrow 0111,$ $C_8 \rightarrow 1000, C_9 \rightarrow 1001, C_{10} \rightarrow 1010, C_{11} \rightarrow 1011,$ $C_{12} \rightarrow 1100, C_{13} \rightarrow 1101, C_{14} \rightarrow 1110, C_{15} \rightarrow 1111$

So, after the basic concept and syntax of the programming, here the light is thrown on writing large quantum programs. For example, it is known that quantum computers can efficiently factor numbers, something that breaks modern public key cryptography. That is pretty dangerous. The quantum computers are very far from being able to perform this task. This is because essentially, quantum computers can only perform so much quantum computation before the quantum computation falls apart.

Consider again the quantum circuit shown in above figure. Every gate that you apply in this circuit corresponds to some pretty complicated electronics, shaping and setting of electromagnetic fields to the quantum computer. These pulses are not always perfect, and so every single one of the gates you perform has some effective chance of falling. In addition to not being able to execute gates exactly, quantum computers also have a problem just doing nothing. That is, if you leave Qubit around, over time, the quantum information stored in them will decay away. This process is known as **de-coherence**. In the next step, while waiting to execute the next gate, one of our Qubits has failed due to de-coherence. These modern quantum computers don't perform exactly as we specify in the circuit model. This problem is known as **noise in quantum computer**. Because of noise, the size of quantum computation is limited, in both the terms. (a) The number of Qubits and (b) the number of operations we perform on these Qubits. If these computers are noisy, we can never build a really large quantum computer. But in order to do it, we apply the protocol called **quantum error correction**. In this, we do not focus on error correction; but it is a procedure for turning a bunch of noisy Qubits into a fewer number of much less noisy Qubits. These quantum computers cannot perform arbitrary large or a long quantum computation, an important question is, what can these modern quantum computers do? This is known as **NISQ era**. NISQ stands for **N**oisy **I**ntermediate **S**cale **Q**uantum. This is used to distinguish today's quantum computers from future error corrected quantum computers. Are there algorithms of practical value in the NISQ era? This is the unfold question for the universe till now.

Figure 24. Noise and De-coherence in Quantum Computers

The quantum computer built in current scenario can exceed the capabilities of classical computers, which is so-called **supremacy frontier**. The world is entering into the era where there is potential for important discovery. Cirq is focused on NISQ computers and not on quantum error corrected computers.

```
device = cirq.google.bristlecone
print(cirq.google.bristlecone)
```

To program for NISQ algorithms needs to be aware for the idiosyncrasies of the hardware upon which the quantum computation can run. Hardware is not abstracted away in Cirq. In Cirq, this is captured by device objects. Following is the example for device object. *(Bristlecone Device)* (Bacon, 2019)

Printed Out, it gives a representation of the layout of the Qubit on the device. We can see it is a strange grid of Qubits. The Qubits are represented by pluses. The lines between the Qubits represented the fact the only adjacent Qubits can be subjected to a two Qubit gate. For example we can perform a two Qubit gate between these **green** highlighted Qubits, but not with the Qubits highlighted in **Red** as they are too far apart to directly interact. Another subtlety of the Bristlecone device is that there are important constraints on when you can simultaneously perform two Qubit gates. If we apply two gates together then you cannot simultaneously apply a two Qubit gate to any of the adjacent Qubits of these gates. Because the hardware is not abstracted away in Cirq, we can use the device objects directly when building our quantum program to enforce these constraints.

Figure 25. NISQ era

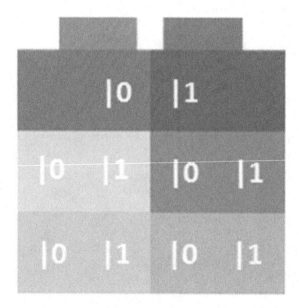

Figure 26. layout of the Qubit on the device

```
circuit = cirq.circuit(device=device)
a0, a1 = cirq.gridqubit(5,5), cirq.gridqubit(5,6)
b0, b1 = cirq.gridqubit(6,5), cirq.gridqubit(6,6)
circuit.append ([cirq.CZ(a0,a1), cirq.CZ(b0,b1)])
print(circuit)
```

For example here we try to perform two, two Qubit 'Z gates' at the same time on adjacent Qubits. But because we have passed this in the device object to the circuit, it is aware of the Bristlecone constraint. Thus we can see the following output when we print-out the above circuit. We can see that the circuit has correctly moved on of the CZ's to a later time slice in order to avoid violating the constraint.

Figure 27. Two Qubit Z-gates

Cirq is an open source project license under apache2 license. Following are the steps of installation the Cirq.

1. Run the commend: pip install Cirq *(most properly configured environment)*
2. Update often. Cirq is alpha released. (It is under constant and active change)

So, this is the brief introduction of the base concept of programming the NISQ computer. Further in this chapter we are going to understand the 4th base concept that is the deep concept of computer science, where the quantum supremacy is explained. (Bacon, 2019)

Base Concept: 4- The Deep concept of computer science and Quantum Supremacy

Quantum supremacy is an experiment done by the IT leads. The latest experimental quantum processor produced has 72 Qubits on a single chip. We can test quantum circuits using this device called Bristlecone with the goal of reducing errors. By their nature, quantum gates have a probability of errors, and errors can cross quantum circuits. As we calibrate quantum circuits we bring down the probability of error. We simulate quantum circuits with traditional computers to benchmark and calibrate quantum circuits. As we work to reduce the probability of errors, simulation gets exponentially harder. This means that it gets too computationally intensive even for a super computer to keep up. From this we get the name *'Quantum Supremacy'* for this experiment. (Boixo, 2019)

This has to do with a **strong Church-Turing thesis** in computer science. Traditional computers from abacus to laptops implement equivalent operations or classical gates, although a modern computer is much faster.

The strong Church-Turing thesis says that all universal computers are equivalent in this way, and can simulate each other efficiently. But according to quantum computing, the strong Church-Turing thesis is false. Quantum Computers can solve problems exponentially faster than other universal computers. So the basic concept is if we want to prove that we reach to quantum supremacy, we need to break the strong Church-Turing thesis. Imagine a Qubit can be like an arrow pointing to some direction on a sphere. Quantum Gates are operations on Qubits. Similar to classical gates, we often depict quantum gates as boxes with the input on one side and the output on the opposite side. In a quantum circuit, we apply layers of gates, on per clock cycle. A measurement at the end of the circuit produces the string of beats.

For the quantum supremacy experiment, we choose the quantum gates at random. Following is the first program for quantum computers. Crucially, in this case we have the strongest critical evidence against the strong Church-Turing thesis. It takes exponential time to simulate a random quantum circuit with a classical computer. According to quantum mechanics, every practical can also act as a wave and this applied to Qubits. The quantum state of a quantum computer contains an exponential number of waves or computational paths. This is the property that we are testing. The output state of a random quantum circuits looks like the speckles of a laser.

Following figure shows figure print of quantum circuit. For some bit strings, the computational paths interfere constructively, and the intensity of the output probability grows. For others, the computational paths interfere destructively, and the output probability decreases.

Simulating interface of the exponential number of computational paths in the quantum circuit takes exponential time. We can check if we obtain the correct fingerprint in the experiment, and measure the probability of error. First we get around a million bit strings from the quantum computer. This takes few seconds. Then we use an expensive classical simulation to check if those bit strings have high probability. In this case, the error rate is low, and the experiment has succeeded. The implication will be that quantum computers seem to be breaking strong Church-Turing thesis. As we reduce errors further, we expect to see a similar exponential speed up for a practical problem. (Boixo, 2019)

Tools and Frameworks

Understanding the concept and to apply them is quite challenging. Thus the concept of Quantum computers and quantum supremacy is cleared with illustrations and examples, but what to do if we practically want to apply these fundamentals on actual hardware with programming?

Following open-source frameworks are specifically designed for developing novel quantum algorithms to help solve near-term applications for practical problems. (Sergio Boixo, 2018)

- OpenFermion
- Cirq

A. OpenFermion

OpenFermion is the first open source platform for translating problems in chemistry and materials science into quantum circuits that can be executed on existing platforms. OpenFermion is a library for simulating the systems of interacting electrons (fermions) which give rise to the properties of matter. Prior to OpenFermion, quantum algorithm developers would need to learn a significant amount of chemistry and write a large amount of code hacking apart other codes to put together even the most basic quantum simulations. While the project began at Google, collaborators at ETH Zurich, Lawrence Berkeley National Labs, University of Michigan, Harvard University, Oxford University, Dartmouth College, Rigetti Computing and NASA all contributed to alpha releases.

One way to think of OpenFermion is as a tool for generating and compiling physics equations which describe chemical and material systems into representations which can be interpreted by a quantum computer. The most effective quantum algorithms for these problems build upon and extend the power of classical quantum chemistry packages used and developed by research chemists across government, industry and academia. Accordingly, we are also releasing OpenFermion-Psi4 and OpenFermion-PySCF which are plugins for using OpenFermion in conjunction with the classical electronic structure packages Psi4 and PySCF.

The core OpenFermion library is designed in a quantum programming framework agnostic way to ensure compatibility with various platforms being developed by the community. This allows OpenFermion to support external packages which compile quantum assembly language specifications for diverse hardware platforms. We hope this decision will help establish OpenFermion as a community standard for putting quantum chemistry on quantum computers. To see how OpenFermion is used with diverse quantum programming frameworks, take a look at OpenFermion-ProjectQ and Forest-OpenFermion - plugins which link OpenFermion to the externally developed circuit simulation and compilation platforms known as ProjectQ and Forest. The following workflow describes how a quantum chemist might use OpenFermion in order to simulate the energy surface of a molecule.

- The researcher initializes an OpenFermion calculation with specification of:
  - An input file specifying the coordinates of the nuclei in the molecule.
  - The basis set (e.g. cc-pVTZ) that should be used to discretize the molecule.
  - The charge and spin multiplicity (if known) of the system.
- The researcher uses the OpenFermion-Psi4 plugin or the OpenFermion-PySCF plugin to perform scalable classical computations which are used to optimally stage the quantum computation. For

instance, one might perform a classical Hartree-Fock calculation to choose a good initial state for the quantum simulation.

- The researcher then specifies which electrons are most interesting to study on a quantum computer (known as an active space) and asks OpenFermion to map the equations for those electrons to a representation suitable for quantum bits, using one of the available procedures in OpenFermion, e.g. the Bravyi-Kitaev transformation.
- The researcher selects a quantum algorithm to solve for the properties of interest and uses a quantum compilation framework such as OpenFermion-ProjectQ to output the quantum circuit in assembly language which can be run on a quantum computer. If the researcher has access to a quantum computer, they then execute the experiment. (Neven, 2020)

B. Cirq

Cirq is a software library for writing, manipulating, and optimizing quantum circuits and then running them against quantum computers and simulators. Cirq attempts to expose the details of hardware, instead of abstracting them away, because, in the Noisy Intermediate-Scale Quantum (NISQ) regime, these details determine whether or not it is possible to execute a circuit at all. Cirq is currently in alpha.

Over the past few years, quantum computing has experienced a growth not only in the construction of quantum hardware, but also in the development of quantum algorithms. With the availability of Noisy Intermediate Scale Quantum (NISQ) computers (devices with ~50 - 100 Qubits and high fidelity quantum gates), the development of algorithms to understand the power of these machines is of increasing importance. However, a common problem when designing a quantum algorithm on a NISQ processor is how to take full advantage of these limited quantum devices—using resources to solve the hardest part of the problem rather than on overheads from poor mappings between the algorithm and hardware. Furthermore some quantum processors have complex geometric constraints and other nuances, and ignoring these will either result in faulty quantum computation, or a computation that is modified and sub-optimal.

APPLICATIONS

Following are few near-term application developed by Technology giant Google and released officially. *(Neven, 2020)*

A. Quantum Simulation

The design of new materials and elucidation of complex physics through accurate simulations of chemistry and condensed matter models are among the most promising applications of quantum computing.

B. Error Mitigation Techniques

To develop methods on the road to full quantum error correction that has the capability of dramatically reducing noise in current devices. While full-scale fault tolerant quantum computing may require considerable developments, we have developed the quantum subspace expansion technique to help utilize techniques from quantum error correction to improve performance of applications on near-term devices.

Moreover, these techniques facilitate testing of complex quantum codes on near-term devices. We are actively pushing these techniques into new areas and leveraging them as a basis for design of near term experiments.

C. Quantum Machine Learning

Development on hybrid quantum-classical machine learning techniques on near-term quantum devices is in progress. For this, studying universal quantum circuit learning for classification and clustering of quantum and classical data is necessary. World also interested in generative and discriminative quantum neural networks that could be used as quantum repeaters and state purification units within quantum communication networks, or for verification of other quantum circuits.

D. Quantum Optimization

Discrete optimizations in aerospace, automotive, and other industries may benefit from hybrid quantum-classical optimization, for example simulated annealing, quantum assisted optimization algorithm (QAOA) and quantum enhanced population transfer may have utility with today's processors.

CONCLUSION

After the super computers we are entering into the new era of quantum computers which works on Qubits. These Qubits can carry both 0 and 1 states together and grow the states exponentially which is known as superposition. This system can compute the problem within fraction of seconds which classic computers may take years to compute. We have popular frameworks like Cirq and OpenFermion which can give large platform to researchers and developers. Few years down the line the era of quantum computing will completely change the point-of-view of computers and computation in all the fields.

REFERENCES

Bacon, D. (2019, February 25). *Applied Science: Quantum: Google Research*. Retrieved from Google Research: https://youtu.be/16ZfkPRVf2w

Boixo, S. (2019, March 4). *Applied Science: Quantum: Google Research*. Retrieved from Google Research: https://youtu.be/gylmjTOUfCQ

Giustina, M. (2018, December 10). *Google Research*. Retrieved from https://research.google.com: https://youtu.be/k-21vRCC0RM

Martinis, J. (2019, October 23). *Google AI Blog*. Retrieved from ai.googleblog.com: https://ai.googleblog.com/2019/10/quantum-supremacy-using-programmable.html

Neven, J. R. (2020). Decoding Quantum Errors Using Subspace Expansions. *Nature Communications*, 636. PMID:32005804

Pednault Edwin, J. A. (2019, October 22). *Cornell University*. Retrieved from arxiv.org: https://arxiv.org/abs/1910.09534

Sank, D. (2019, February 7). *Google Research*. Retrieved from https://research.google.com: https://youtu.be/uPw9nkJAwDY

Sergio Boixo, S. V. (2018). Characterizing quantum supremacy in near-term devices. *Nature Physics*, 595-600.

Chapter 3
Quantum Cryptography:
In Security Aspects

S. Venkata Lakshmi
https://orcid.org/0000-0001-7965-6552
Sri Krishna College of Engineering and Technology, India

Sujatha Krishnamoorthy
Wenzhou-Kean University, China

Mudassir Khan
https://orcid.org/0000-0002-1117-7819
King Khalid University, Saudi Arabia

Neeraj Kumar
https://orcid.org/0000-0002-6674-0584
Babasaheb Bhimrao Ambedkar University, Lucknow, India

Varsha Sahni
CT India, India

ABSTRACT

Cryptography is used for the secure communication in which two parties are involved. The most popular cryptographic issue is the transmission of confidential messages. The privacy is maintained using the cryptographic protocol. The security of quantum cryptography relies more on physics including quantum mechanics and statistics rather than on solving mathematical problems. A well-known application of quantum cryptography is quantum key distribution (QKD) that is used to establish communication by generating cryptographic keys. Moreover, it is based on the Heisenberg uncertainty principle that ensures the security and prevents from eavesdropping. Basically, quantum cryptography with faint laser pulses, polarization coding, phase coding, and frequency coding have been discussed.

DOI: 10.4018/978-1-7998-6677-0.ch003

Copyright © 2021, IGI Global. Copying or distributing in print or electronic forms without written permission of IGI Global is prohibited.

1. INTRODUCTION

Information Technology and Communication has undergone development remarkably in the past years. To secure the communication among the parties from adversary the technique that is used is called as Cryptography. Main aim of Cryptography is to ensure Confidentiality (Third party cannot interpret the message or data that is sent between intended users), Authentication (Message is received from authentic user), Integrity (Message is not altered in between). This is achieved by sending secret message that requires the creation of the key that is sent to the other party. This key can be stolen or can be copied by the third party. Public key Cryptography can involve complex mathematical calculation that makes the process slower. To overcome these limitations and to make the communication more secure quantum Cryptography is used. Quantum cryptography was built in late 1960, when conjugate coding was written by Stephen Wiesner. Quantum Cryptography is an approach to transmit the information securely by applying the concept of quantum physics. Mathematical cryptography algorithms like RSA and elliptic curve cryptography are widely used today. There is a lack of security in these algorithms. There is a threat to sensitive information that needs high degree of security by these prevailing mathematical cryptosystems. The security of quantum cryptography relies more on physics including quantum mechanics and statistics rather than on solving mathematical problems. Well known application of quantum cryptography is quantum key distribution (QKD) that is used to establish communication by generating cryptographic keys. Moreover, it is based on Heisenberg Uncertainty principle that ensures the security and prevents from eavesdropping. Even if there is any case of eavesdropping of key that occurs by adversary, the two parties communicating with each other can come to know easily about this due to some discrepancies. QKD device comprise of photon transceiver along with electrical component. There are various limitations of QKD as well like the range is limited from 50 to 100 km as photons are easily lost during communication. Quantum Computing follows the principles of superposition, entanglement and quantum mechanics. Superposition refers to as making new moves while processing information. Quantum Superposition states that 2 particles can be at distinct locations at the same time. It is not feasible to observe it in real world as it exists in subatomic particles. Entangled particles refer to the state where the particles cannot be defined or described individually, without the consideration of other particles. In Quantum mechanics qubits are used rather than simple bits on which quantum cryptography is highly dependent on.

2. LITERATURE SURVEY

- Aditya et al. (2005) discussed on quantum cryptography and how it contribute to a defense-in-depth strategy to reduce the efforts of malicious hackers. There are various weaknesses in modern digital cryptosystems that are explained which involves complex calculations that are slow. These weaknesses are overcome by quantum cryptography that is based on the fundamental and unchanging principles of quantum mechanics. Quantum Key Distribution example is demonstrated that explain the secure distribution of keys. Desirable Characteristics of QKD are discussed that involves Confidentiality, Authentication, Rapid Key Delivery, Robustness, Location Independence and its Resistance to traffic Analysis. Different Systems have implemented Quantum Cryptography like DARPA Quantum Network, MagiQ Technologies. Quantum cryptography involves a suite of specialized protocol involving Sifting, Error Correction, Privacy amplification, Authentication.

- Kulkarni et al. (2012) discussed Classical Cryptography that is used to send secret messages that include Symmetric and Asymmetric Cryptography. Advantages of Quantum Cryptography are demonstrated. Quantum entanglement phenomenon is explained in which the quantum of two or more objects has to be described with reference to each other. Quantum Key Distribution, the application of Quantum Cryptography is discussed. Quantum Cryptography integration in 802.11 networks is described where three aspects of security mechanisms are explained: Authentication, encryption key establishment and encryption algorithm.

- Hughes et al. (1995) explained the goals of Cryptography. Procedure of key distribution is discussed how it is transmitted securely by quantum cryptography. Uses of One time pad is explained as it is unbreakable but it faces the problem like key generation, distribution and management issues. B92 QKD protocol is described. The outstanding feature of quantum mechanics is that pre-existing values are not revealed that allow it to be more secure. Its Practical Implementation is done using single-photon polarization states. There are many factors affecting data rate and error rate of the system. Many methodologies improving the rate are discussed in this paper.

- Brassard et a. (2000) discussed the security of Quantum key distribution over classical schemes. Losses and dark counts are discussed. Different error mechanisms are explained. Parametric down conversion is used as a signal source to make it secure by increasing the distance but it also have some limitations like range, reduction of dark counts in order to increase the distance. Quantum repeaters can be used for secure transmission and can cover any amount of distance without compromising with the security.

- Fedorov et al. (2018) discussed desktop modular QKD scheme that is secure and assemble complex schemes. Here plug and play scheme is implemented in which optical pulses are processed with higher frequency but in plug and play scheme various limitations are there such as polarization fluctuation problems as optic pulses pass the quantum channel twice. The given scheme has various advantages that are discussed like flexibility, usability, and robustness.

Table 1. Comparative Study of literature survey

Research Paper	Description	Limitations
Quantum Cryptography	Various advancement in the field of Quantum Cryptography is discussed that how it provides security by providing confidentiality, authentication etc. How Quantum Cryptography is implemented is discussed with the help of DARPA Quantum Network and MagiQ Technology.	Main limitation in DARPA Quantum Network that is used for implementing Quantum Cryptography is limited geographic reach.
Research Directions in Quantum Cryptography and Quantum Key Distribution	Quantum Cryptography is discussed with the concept of Quantum entanglement. Quantum key Distribution is discussed in which BB84 protocol is used. Key Management and encryption algorithms are discussed like TKIP and CCMP.	In spite of these algorithms used in Quantum Cryptography still it can be broken by Quantum Computers.
Educational Potential of Quantum Cryptography and Its Experimental Modular Realization	Quantum key Distribution for education purpose and scientific research is proposed. Many workshops can be carried for students in universities by desktop device. Another device Plug & Play QKD has been tested in different circumstances.	Desktop modular QKD system is costly and its cost can be reduced in future by further modifications. Polarization fluctuation problems can occur in that has to be solved.
Security Aspects of Practical Quantum Cryptography	It shows that QKD can be secured with the experiments implemented using WCP using appropriate parameters for the expected photon number, which are considerably lower than those used today.	Limited geographic reach is the problem faced in the experiments that can be overcome by use of quantum repeaters
Quantum Cryptography	Quantum key distribution, One time password are discussed. B92 QKD protocol is explained. Practical Implementation is explained using single-photon polarization states	There are many factors affecting data rate and error rate of the system that can be improved

3. QUANTUM KEY DISTRIBUTION

The reason for key circulation is for two clients "Alice" and "Bounce," who share no mystery data at first, to concede to an arbitrary key, which stays mystery from an foe "Eve," who listens in on their correspondences. In conventional cryptography and data hypothesis it is underestimated that computerized correspondences can generally be latently checked, so the busybody learns their whole substance, without the sender or recipient staying alert that any listening in has occurred. On the other hand, when advanced data is encoded in rudimentary quantum frameworks, for example, single photons, it gets conceivable to create an interchanges divert whose transmissions can't on a basic level be dependably perused or duplicated by a busybody uninformed of certain data utilized in framing the transmission. The busybody can't increase fractional data about such a transmission without upsetting it in an irregular and wild manner prone to be recognized by the channel's genuine clients.

The fundamental quantum key dissemination conventions starts with Alice sending an irregular succession of the four authoritative sorts of spellbound photons to Bob. Weave at that point picks arbitrarily and freely for every photon (and autonomously of the decisions made by Alice, obviously, since these decisions are obscure to him at this point) regardless of whether to quantify the photon's rectilinear or roundabout polarization. Bounce at that point reports freely which sort of estimation he made (yet not the aftereffect of the estimation), and Alice lets him know, again freely, regardless of whether he made the right estimation (i.e., rectilinear or roundabout). Alice and Bob at that point concur freely to dispose of all piece positions for which Bob played out an inappropriate estimation. So also, they consent to dispose of bit positions where Bob's finders neglected to distinguish the photon by any means - a genuinely regular occasion with existing locators at optical frequencies. The polarizations of the rest of the photons is deciphered as bit 0 for even or on the other hand left-round, and bit 1 for vertical and right-roundabout. The subsequent parallel string ought to be shared mystery data among Alice and Bob, gave that no listening in on the quantum channel has occurred. The aftereffect of the abovementioned steps is alluded to as the quantum transmission (or at times the crude quantum transmission to underline that it was acquired right off the bat all the while). In the basic protocol, Alice and Bob next test for eavesdropping by publicly comparing polarizations of a random subset of the photons on which they think they should agree.

1. Alice sends an arbitrary succession of photons enraptured even (*- -,), vertical ($), right-round (~) what's more, left-round (~);
2. Bounce quantifies the photons' polarization in an irregular succession of bases, rectilinear (+) and round (0).
3. Consequences of Bob's estimations (a few photons may not be gotten by any means).
4. Weave reveals to Alice which premise he utilized for every photon he got;
5. Alice reveals to him which bases were right;
6. Alice and Bob keep just the information from these accurately estimated photons, disposing of all the rest.
7. This information is deciphered as a twofold arrangement as per the coding plan ~ = C~ = 0.

Figure 1. Basic quantum key distribution protocol

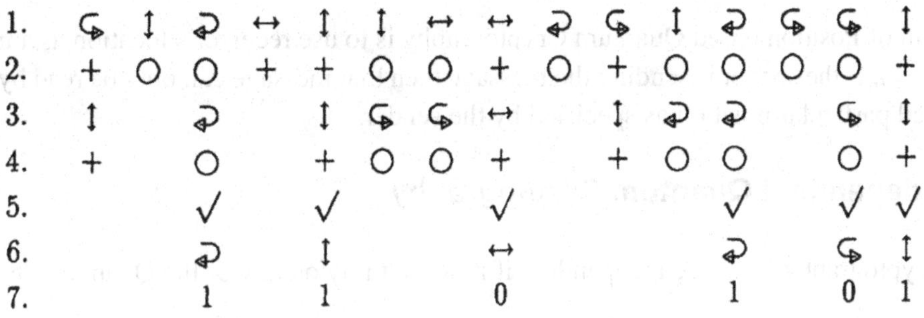

1.	↙	↕	⤵	↔	↕	↕	↔	↔	⤵	↙	↕	⤵	↙	↙	↕
2.	+	○	○	+	+	○	○	+	○	+	○	○	○	○	+
3.	↕		⤵		↕	↙	↙	↔		↕	⤵	⤵		↙	↕
4.	+		○		+	○	○	+		+	○	○		○	+
5.			√		√		√				√			√	√
6.			⤵		↕		↔				⤵			↙	↕
7.			1		1		0				1			0	1

4. CRYPTOGRAPHY

Converting a message to secret message to hide a message from adversary is called Cryptography. The message is encrypted before transmitting it to receiver so that it cannot be intercepted by an eavesdropper. The original message is called Plain text whereas the encrypted message is known as Cipher Text. For Cryptography algorithms such as Encryption and Decryption algorithms are used and Cipher key is used

Encryption: $c = E(K, m)$

Decryption: $p = D(K, m)$

where c stands for cipher text, p for plain text, K for Key, m for message, E for encryption and d for decryption.

Symmetric Encryption: If there is common secret key used by sender and receiver to encrypt the message. It is referred as Symmetric Encryption.

Asymmetric Encryption: It uses 2 keys (Public key and Private Key).Message encrypted by one kind of key can be decrypted by other key. Public key is known to everyone and the private key is known only to him. To ensure Confidentiality message is encrypted by sender using receiver's public key so that it can only be decrypted by the receiver with his private key. On the other hand to ensure Authentication message is encrypted by sender using sender's public key so that receiver can decrypt it with sender's public key and can be sure that message has been received from authentic user only.

Many Cryptosystems around symmetric encryption have been developed; one of them that are un-breakable and secure is called as One Time Pad. It is the improvement of Vigenere Cipher. There is no relationship between Plain Text and Cipher Text that makes it more secure. New key is used for every new message, the key word is not repeated the key length is equal to that of message and random letters are used in the key. It is accomplished by time pad that is why it is called One Time Pad. But it also has some limitations such as distribution of key pad is difficult. If encrypted message is lost it could create a problem as key pads should be identical and if it is lost they will no longer remain identical for future messages.

Position Based Quantum Cryptography

The main aim of Position based Quantum Cryptography is to use receiver's location as a main base for communication. If the sender is sending the message then that message can only be read by the receiver at that desired particular position as specified by the sender.

Device Independent Quantum Cryptography

Quantum Cryptography is device independent if it doesn't rely on any of the Quantum devices.

Post Quantum Cryptography

Various Cryptographic methodologies along quantum computers are used against adversary, this methodology is known as Post Quantum Cryptography. This Post Quantum Cryptography is needed as many popular algorithms can be broken using different algorithms.

5. QUANTUM CRYPTOGRAPHY WITH FAINT LASER PULSES

Exploratory quantum key dissemination was shown without precedent for 1989 (it was distributed as it were in 1992 by Bennett et al. 1992a). From that point forward, huge advancement has been made. Today, a few gatherings have demonstrated that quantum key conveyance is conceivable, even outside the lab. On a basic level, any two-level quantum framework could be utilized to execute QC. By and by, all executions have depended on photons. The explanations that their connection with the earth, likewise called decoherence, can be controlled and directed. What's more, scientists can profit by all the devices created in the previous two decades for optical media communications. It is impossible that different transporters will be utilized in the not so distant. Contrasting diverse QC-arrangements is a troublesome assignment, since a few models must be considered. What makes a difference at long last is obviously the pace of adjusted mystery bits (refined piece rate, Rdist) that can be sent and the transmission separation. One would already be able to take note of that with present and not so distant future innovation, it will likely not be conceivable to accomplish paces of the request for gigahertz, these days normal with regular optical correspondence frameworks (in their thorough paper distributed in 2000, Gilbert and Hamrick talk about viable techniques to accomplish high piece rate QC). This suggests encryption with a key traded through QC is to be constrained to profoundly private data. While the assurance of the transmission separation and pace of discovery (the crude piece rate, Rraw) is direct, assessing the net rate is somewhat troublesome. Despite the fact that on a basic level mistakes in the bit grouping follow just from altering by a malignant busybody, the circumstance is somewhat unique in all actuality. Disparities in the keys of Alice and Bounce additionally consistently happen as a result of exploratory defects. The mistake rate (here called quantum bit blunder rate, or QBER) can be effectively decided. So also, the mistake rectification strategy is somewhat basic. Mistake remedy prompts a first decrease of the key rate that relies firmly upon the QBER. The genuine issue comprises in evaluating the data got by Eve, an amount fundamental for protection intensification. It doesn't as it were rely upon the QBER, yet in addition on different variables, similar to the photon number measurements of the source, or the way the decision of the estimation premise is made. In addition, in a down to business approach, one may likewise acknowledge limitations on Eve's innovation, constraining her methodologies and accordingly likewise the data she can get per blunder she presents. Since the productivity of security enhancement quickly diminishes when the QBER builds, the refined bit rate relies significantly upon Eve's data and subsequently on the presumptions made. One can characterize as the greatest transmission separation, the separation where the refined rate arrives at zero. This idea generates to evaluate the QC system from a physical point.

A.   Quantum Bit Error Rate

The QBER is defined as the number of wrong bits to the total number of received bits30 and is normally in the order of a few percent. In the following we will use it expressed as a function of rates:

$$QBER = \frac{N_{\text{wrong}}}{N_{\text{right}} + N_{\text{wrong}}} = \frac{R_{\text{error}}}{R_{\text{sift}} + R_{\text{error}}} \approx \frac{R_{\text{error}}}{R_{\text{sift}}} \tag{1}$$

where the sifted key corresponds to the cases in which Alice and Bob made compatible choices of bases, hence its rate is half that of the raw key. The raw rate is essentially the product of the pulse rate frep, the mean number of photon per pulse μ, the probability tlink of a photon to arrive at the analyzer and the probability η of the photon being detected:

$$R_{\text{sift}} = \frac{1}{2} R_{\text{raw}} = \frac{1}{2} q f_{\text{rep}} \mu t_{\text{link}} \eta \tag{2}$$

The factor q (q≤1, typically 1 or 1 2) must be introduced for some phase-coding setups in order to correct for noninterfering path combinations. One can distinguish three different contributions to Rerror. The first one arises because of photons ending up in the wrong detector, due to unperfect interference or polarization contrast. The rate Ropt is given by the product of the sifted key rate and the probability popt of a photon going in the wrong detector:

$$R_{opt} = R_{sift} P_{opt} = \frac{1}{2} q f_{rep} \mu t_{link} P_{opt} \eta \tag{3}$$

This contribution can be considered, for a given set-up, as an intrinsic error rate indicating the suitability to use it for QC. We will discuss it below in the case of each particular system. The second contribution, Rdet, arises from the detector dark counts (or from remaining environmental stray light in free space setups). This rate is independent of the bit rate31. Of course, only dark counts falling in a short time window when a photon is expected give rise to errors.

$$R_{\text{det}} = \frac{1}{2} \frac{1}{2} f_{\text{rep}} P_{\text{dark}} n \tag{4}$$

where pdark is the probability of registering a dark count per time-window and per detector, and n is the number of detectors. The two $\frac{1}{2}$ -factors are related to the fact that a dark count has a 50% chance to happen with Alice and Bob having chosen incompatible bases (thus eliminated during sifting) and a 50% chance to arise in the correct detector. Finally error counts can arise from uncorrelated photons, because of imperfect photon sources:

$$R_{acc} = \frac{1}{2}\frac{1}{2} p_{acc} f_{rep} t_{link} m\eta \tag{5}$$

This factor appears only in systems based on entangled photons, where the photons belonging to different pairs but arriving in the same time window are not necessarily in the same state. The quantity pacc is the probability to find a second pair within the time window, knowing that a first one was created32 . The QBER can now be expressed as follows:

$$QBER = \frac{R_{opt} + R_{det} + R_{acc}}{R_{sift}}$$
$$= p_{opt} + \frac{p_{dark} \cdot n}{t_{link} \cdot \eta \cdot 2 \cdot q \cdot \mu} + \frac{p_{acc}}{2 \cdot q \cdot \mu} \tag{6}$$
$$= QBER_{opt} + QBER_{det} + QBER_{acc}$$

We analyze now these three contributions. The first one, QBERopt, is independent on the transmission distance (it is independent of tlink). It can be considered as a measure of the optical quality of the setup, depending only on the polarisation or interference fringe contrast. The technical effort needed to obtain, and more important, to maintain a given QBERopt is an important criterion for evaluating different QC-setups. In polarization based systems, it's rather simple to achieve a polarisation contrast of 100:1, corresponding to a QBERopt of 1%. In fiber based QC, the problem is to maintain this value in spite of polarisation fluctuations and depolarisation in the fiber link. For phase coding setups, QBERopt and the interference visibility are related by

$$QBER_{opt} = \frac{1-V}{2} \tag{7}$$

A visibility of 98% translates thus into an optical error rate of 1%. Such a value implies the use of well aligned and stable interferometers. In bulk optics perfect mode overlap is difficult to achieve, but the polarization is stable. In single-mode fiber interferometers, on the contrary, perfect mode overlap is automatically achieved, but the polarisation must be controlled and chromatic dispersion can constitute a problem.

The second contribution, QBERdet, increases with distance, since the darkcount rate remains constant while the bit rate goes down like tlink. It depends entirely on the ratio of the dark count rate to the quantum efficiency. At present, good single-photon detectors are not commercially available for telecommunication wavelengths. The span of QC is not limited by decoherence. As QBERopt is essentially independent of the fiber length, it is the detector noise that limits the transmission distance.

Finally, the QBERacc contribution is present only in some 2-photon schemes in which multi-photon pulses are processed in such a way that they do not necessarily encode the same bit value.

B.   Polarization Coding

Encoding the qubits in the polarization of photons is a characteristic arrangement. The main showing of QC by Charles Bennett and his associates (Bennett et al. 1992a) utilized this decision. They understood a framework where Alice and Bob traded swoon light heartbeats delivered by a LED and containing short of what one photon by and large over a separation of 30 cm in air. Despite the little scope of this analysis, it importantly affected the network as in it demonstrated that it was most certainly not irrational to utilize single photons rather than old style beats for encoding pieces. A run of the mill framework for QC with the BB84 four states convention utilizing the polarization of photons is appeared. Alice's framework comprises of four laser diodes. They radiate short old style photon beats ($\approx$ 1ns) spellbound at −45ο, 0ο, +45ο, and 90ο . For a given qubit, a solitary diode is set off. The beats are then constricted by a set of channels to diminish the normal number of photons well under 1, and sent along the quantum channel to Alice. It is fundamental that the beats remain captivated for Bob to have the option to remove the data encoded by Alice. The polarization mode scattering may depolarize the photons, gave the deferral it presents between both polarization modes is bigger than the rationality time. This sets an imperative on the kind of lasers utilized by Alice. When arriving at Bob, the beats are removed from the fiber. They travel through a lot of waveplates used to recuperate the underlying polarization states by repaying the change initiated by the optical fiber. The beats arrive at then a symmetric beamsplitter, actualizing the premise decision. Sent photons are broke down in the vertical-level premise with a polarizing beamsplitter and two photon checking locators. The polarization condition of the reflected photons is first pivoted with a waveplate by 45ο (−45ο to 0ο). The photons are then examined with a second arrangement of polarizing beamsplitter and photon checking indicators.

C.   Phase Coding

Encoding the estimation of qubits in the stage of photons was first referenced by Bennett in the paper where he presented the two-states convention (1992). It is in fact a characteristic decision for optics authorities. State readiness and examination are then performed with interferometers, that can be acknowledged with single-mode optical filaments parts. It presents an optical fiber variant of a MachZehnder interferometer. It is made out of two symmetric couplers – what could be compared to beamsplitters – associated to one another, with one stage modulator in each arm. One can infuse light in the set-up utilizing a nonstop and traditional source, and screen the force at the yield ports. Given that the cognizance length of the light utilized is bigger than the way confuse in the interferometers, impedance edges can be recorded. Taking into account the $\pi/2$-stage move experienced upon reflection at a beamsplitter, the impact of the stage modulators (φA what's more, φB) and the way length contrast (ΔL), the force in the yield port named "0" is given by:

$$I_0 = \overline{I} \cdot \cos^2\left(\frac{\phi_A - \phi_B + k" L}{2}\right) \tag{8}$$

where k is the wave number and I the intensity of the source. If the phase term is equal to $\pi/2 + n\pi$ where n is an integer, destructive interference is obtained. Therefore the intensity registered in port "0" reaches a minimum and all the light exits in port "1". When the phase term is equal to $n\pi$, the situation is reversed.

D.   Frequency Coding

Stage based frameworks for QC require stage synchronization and adjustment. As a result of the high recurrence of optical waves (roughly 200 THz at 1550 nm), this condition is hard to satisfy. One arrangement is to utilize selfaligned frameworks like the "plug&play" set-ups talked about in the past segment. Prof. Goedgebuer and his group from the University of Besancon, in France, presented an elective arrangement (Sun et al. 1995, Mazurenko et al. 1997, M'erolla et al. 1999; see additionally Molotkov 1998). Note that the title of this segment isn't totally right in the feeling that the estimation of the qubits isn't coded in the recurrence of the light, yet in the relative stage between sidebands of a focal optical frequency. A source emanates short beats of traditional monochromatic light with precise recurrence ωS. A first stage modulator PMA adjusts the period of this shaft with a recurrence $\Omega \ll \omega S$ what's more, a little tweak profundity. Two sidebands are along these lines created at frequencies $\omega S \pm \omega$. The stage modulator is driven by a radio-recurrence oscillator RFOA whose stage ΦA can be changed. At last, the shaft is lessened so that the sidebands contain substantially less than one photon for each beat, while the focal pinnacle stays old style. After the transmission interface, the bar encounters a subsequent stage balance applied by PMB. This stage modulator is driven by a second radio-recurrence oscillator RFOB with a similar recurrence Ω and a stage ΦB. These oscillators must be synchronized. In the wake of going through this gadget, the shaft contains the first focal recurrence ωS, the sidebands made by Alice, and the sidebands made by Weave. The sidebands at frequencies $\omega S \pm \Omega$ are commonly lucid and accordingly yield impedance. Sway would then be able to record the obstruction design in these sidebands, after expulsion of the focal recurrence and the higher request sidebands with an otherworldly channel.

E.   Free space line-of-sight applications

Since optical fiber channels may not generally be accessible, a few gatherings are attempting to grow free space view QC frameworks, proficient for instance to disperse a key between building's housetops in a metropolitan setting. It might obviously solid difficult to recognize single photons in the midst of foundation light, yet the first tests exhibited the chance of free space QC. Moreover, sending photons through the climate likewise has favorable circumstances, since this medium is basically not birefringent. It is then conceivable to utilize plain polarization coding. What's more, one can guarantee a high channel transmission over huge separations by picking cautiously the frequency of the photons. The environment has for instance a high transmission "window" in the region of 770 nm (transmission as high as 80% between a ground station and a satellite), which happens to be viable with business silicon APD photon tallying modules (discovery efficiency as high as 65% and low commotion). The frameworks produced with the expectation of complimentary space applications are in reality fundamentally the same as. The fundamental difference is that the producer and collector are associated with telescopes pointing at one another, rather than an optical fiber. The commitment of foundation light to mistakes can be kept up at a sensible level by utilizing a mix of timing segregation (occurrence windows of normally a couple of ns), unearthly filtering (≤ 1 nm obstruction filters) and spatial filtering (coupling into an optical fiber). This can be delineated with the accompanying basic count. Let us guess that the isotropic ghostly foundation brilliance is $10-2$ W/m2 nm sr at 800 nm. This compares to the unearthly brilliance of an unmistakable apex sky with a sun height of 77o (Zissis and Larocca, 1978). The dissimilarity θ of a Gaussian shaft with range w0 is given by $\theta = \lambda/w0\pi$. The result of bar (telescope) cross-area and strong point, which is a consistent, is hence $\pi w2\ 0\pi\theta2 = \lambda2$. By increasing the brilliance by $\lambda2$, one gets the phantom force thickness. With an impedance filter of 1 nm width, the force on the locator is $6\cdot10-15$ W, comparing to $2\cdot104$ photons every second or $2\cdot10-5$ photons per ns time window. This amount is roughly two significant degrees bigger than the dull tally likelihood of Si APD's, yet viable with the prerequisites of QC. Other than the exhibition of free space QC frameworks relies significantly upon air conditions and air quality. This is tricky for metropolitan applications where contamination and mist concentrates debase the straightforwardness of air. The first free space QC explore over a separation of in excess of a couple of centimeters 40 was performed by Jacobs and Franson in 1996. They traded a key over a separation of 150 m in a lobby enlightened with standard fluorescent lighting and 75 m outside in brilliant sunlight without exorbitant QBER. Hughes and his group were the first to trade a key over more than one kilometer under open air evening conditions (Buttler et al. 1998, and Hughes et al. 2000a). All the more as of late, they even improved their framework to arrive at a separation of 1.6 km under sunshine conditions (Buttler et al. 2000). At last Rarity and his colleagues played out a comparative test where they traded a key over a separation of 1.9 km under evening conditions (Gorman et al. 2000). Remember that Bennett and his associates played out the first exhibition of QC more than 30 cm in air (Bennett et al. 1992a). Before quantum repeaters become accessible and permit to beat the separation restriction of fiber based QC, free space frameworks appear to offer the main opportunities for QC over separations of in excess of two or three handfuls kilometres. A QC connection could be built up between ground-based stations and a low circle (300 to 1200 km) satellite. The thought is first to trade a key kA among Alice and a satellite, utilizing QC, close to set up another key kB among Bob and a similar satellite. At that point the satellite freely declares the worth $K = kA \oplus kB$ got after a XOR of the two keys ($\oplus$ speaks to here the XOR administrator or proportionally the twofold expansion modulo 2 without convey). Weave takes away then his key from this incentive to recoup Alice's vital ($kA = K \ominus kB$) [41]. The way that the key is known to the satellite administrator might be at first sight seen as an impediment. Yet, this point may on the opposite be a positive one for the improvement of QC, since governments consistently prefer to keep control of correspondences! In spite of the fact that this has not yet been illustrated, Hughes just as Rarity have assessed - taking into account their free space tests - that the difficulty can be aced. The fundamental difficulty would originate from bar pointing - remember that the satellites will move as for the ground - and meandering actuated by turbulences. So as to diminish this last issue the photons would practically speaking presumably be sent down from the satellite. Environmental turbulences are to be sure essentially focused on the first kilometer over the earth surface. Another likelihood to make up for shaft meander is to utilize adaptative optics. Free space QC tests over separations of the request for 2 km establish significant strides towards key trade with a satellite. As indicated by Buttler et al. (2000), the optical profundity is undoubtedly like the effective air thickness that would be experienced in a surface-to-satellite application.

F.   Multi-users implementations

Paul Townsend and associates explored the use of QC over multi-client optical fiber networks (Phoenix et al 1995, Townsend et al. 1994, Townsend 1997b). They utilized a latent optical fiber network design where one Alice – the organization administrator – is associated with numerous organization clients. The objective is for Alice to build up a verifiably secure and novel key with each Bob. In as far as possible, the data communicated by Alice is accumulated by all Bobs. In any case, on account of their quantum conduct, the photons are effectively steered at the bar splitter to one, and just one, of the clients. Utilizing the twofold Mach Zehnder configuration examined above, they tried such a course of action with three Bobs. By and by, in light of the way that QC requires an immediate and low weakening optical channel among Alice and Bob, the likelihood to execute it over huge and complex organizations seems restricted.

6. EAVESDROPPING

A. Problems and Objectives

After the qubit trade and bases compromise, Alice and Bob each have a filtered key. In a perfect world, these are indistinguishable. Yet, all things considered, there are in every case a few mistakes and Alice and Bob must apply some traditional data handling conventions, similar to blunder revision and security amplification, to their information. The first convention is important to get indistinguishable keys, the second to get a mystery key. Basically, the issue of listening in is to find conventions which, given that Alice and Bob can just quantify the QBER, either gives Alice and Bob a provenly secure key, or stops the convention and illuminates the clients that the key conveyance has fizzled. This is a fragile inquiry, truly at the crossing point between quantum material science and data hypothesis. All things considered, there isn't one, yet a few listening in issues, contingent upon the exact convention, on the level of romanticizing one concedes, on the innovative force one expect Eve has and on the accepted fidelity of Alice and Bob's gear. Let us quickly stress that the total examination of listening in on quantum channel is by a long shot not yet finished. In this part we survey a portion of the issues and arrangements, with no case of numerical thoroughness nor complete front of the immense and quick advancing writing. The overall target of listening in examination is to find extreme and handy verifications of security for some quantum cryptosystems. Extreme implies that the security is ensured against whole classes of listening in assaults, regardless of whether Eve utilizes the best of the present innovation, yet any possible innovation of tomorrow. They appear as hypotheses, with obviously expressed suppositions communicated in numerical terms. Conversely, viable confirmations manage some real bits of equipment and programming. There is in this way a pressure among "extreme" and "useful" evidences. Undoubtedly, the first ones courtesy general dynamic suppositions, though the subsequent ones focus on physical usage of the overall ideas. By the by, it merits targeting finding such verifications. Notwithstanding the security issue, they give enlightening exercises to our overall comprehension of quantum data. In the ideal game Eve has immaculate innovation: she is just restricted by the laws of quantum mechanics, however not in the least by the present innovation 47. Specifically, Eve can't clone the qubits, as this is incongruent with quantum elements, yet Eve is allowed to utilize any unitary communication between one or a few qubits and a helper arrangement of her decision. In addition, after the collaboration, Eve may keep her assistant framework unperturbed, specifically in complete confinement from nature, for a subjectively significant time-frame. At long last, subsequent to tuning in to all the public conversation among Alice and Bob, she can play out her preferred estimation on her framework, being again restricted uniquely by the laws of quantum mechanics. In addition, one expect that all blunders are because of Eve. It is enticing to accept that a few mistakes are because of Alice's and Bob's instruments and this most likely bodes well by and by. In any case, there is the threat that Eve replaces them with greater instruments. In the following area we expand on the most pertinent differences between the above ideal game (ideal particularly from Eve's perspective!) and genuine frameworks. Next, we re-visitation of the glorified circumstance and present a few listening in techniques, beginning from the least difficult ones, where express equations can be recorded and finishing with an overall unique security evidence. At last, we disk viable listening in assaults and remark on the multifaceted nature of genuine framework's security.

B. Idealized vs. Real Implementation

Alice and Bob utilize innovation accessible today. This minor comment has a few ramifications. To begin with, all genuine parts are blemished, so that the qubits are arranged and identified not actually in the premise depicted by the hypothesis. Additionally, a genuine source consistently has a finite likelihood to create more than one photon. Contingent upon the subtleties of the encoding gadget, all photons convey the equivalent qubit. Thus, on a fundamental level, Eve could quantify the photon number, without irritating the qubit. Review that in a perfect world, Alice ought to produce single qubit-photons, for example each legitimate qubit ought to be encoded in a solitary level of opportunity of a solitary photon. On Bob's side the circumstance is, first, that the efficiency of his indicators is very restricted and, next, that the dull checks (unconstrained tallies not delivered by photons) are non-unimportant. The restricted efficiency is similar to the misfortunes in the quantum channel. The examination of the dull tallies is more fragile and no total arrangement is known. Minimalistically, Lu¨tkenhaus (2000) accept in his investigation that all dim tallies give data to Eve. He additionally prompts that at whatever point two finders fire all the while (by and large because of a genuine photon and a dull tally), Bob ought not dismissal such occasions however material science may be pick an incentive at arbitrary. Note likewise that the different commitments of dull check to the all out QBER rely upon whether Bob's decision of premise is executed utilizing a functioning or an aloof switch. Next, one for the most part accept that Alice and Bob have altogether checked their hardware and that it is working as per the specifications. This isn't specific to quantum cryptography, yet is a serious sensitive inquiry, as Eve could be the real producer of the gear! Traditional crypto-frameworks should likewise be deliberately tried, similar to any business devices. Testing a crypto-framework is anyway fragile, on the grounds that in cryptography the customer purchases confidence and security, two characteristics difficult to evaluate. D. Mayers and A. Yao (1998) proposed to utilize Bell imbalance to test that the hardware truly obey quantum mechanics, yet even this isn't completely palatable. Surely, and strikingly, one of the most inconspicuous escape clauses in all present-day trial of Bell disparity, the identification proviso, can be misused to create a simply traditional programming emulating all quantum relationship (Gisin and Gisin 1999). This represents indeed how close down to earth issues in QC are to philosophical discussions about the establishments of quantum material science! At long last, one needs to expect that Alice and Bob are totally segregated from Eve. Without such a supposition the whole game would be aimless: obviously, Eve isn't permitted to investigate Alice's shoulder! However, this rudimentary supposition that is again a nontrivial one. Imagine a scenario where Eve utilizes the quantum channel interfacing Alice to the rest of the world. In a perfect world, the channel should join an isolator 48 to shield Eve from focusing light into Alice's yield port to inspect the inside of her research facility. Be that as it may, all isolators work just on a finite transfer speed, thus there ought to likewise be a filter. In any case, filters have just a finite efficiency. we consequently expect that Alice and Bob are separated from Eve.

9. CONCLUSION

Quantum cryptography is a fascinating illustration of the dialog between basic and applied physics. It is based on a beautiful combination of concepts from quantum physics and information theory and made possible thanks to the tremendous progress in quantum optics and in the technology of optical fibres and of free space optical communication. Its security principle relies on deep theorems in classical information theory. However, quantum cryptography provides security as compared to classical cryptography but it also has limitations like high cost implementation, in terms of distance. Improvements will be made in terms of technical advances. A quantum repeater usage in future can be there to overcome the problem of distance and can be used for secure transmission. Secure Communication is important in every field and is the most important criteria that should be kept in mind while communicating. The methods used by the quantum cryptography take classical cryptography as the base that is why the problem of security arise as it can be broken by quantum computers. Thus post-quantum cryptography can be used as the methods used in it cannot be broken by quantum computers.

REFERENCES

Aditya & Rao. (2005). Quantum cryptography. *Proceedings of Computer Society of India.*

Ardehali, M., Chau, H. F., & Lo, H.-K. (1998). *Efficient Quantum Key Distribution.* quant-ph/9803007.

Aspect, A., Dalibard, J., & Roger, G. (1982). Experimental Test of Bell's Inequalities Using Time-Varying Analyzers. *Physical Review Letters*, *49*(25), 1804–1807. doi:10.1103/PhysRevLett.49.1804

Bechmann-Pasquinucci, H., & Gisin, N. (1999). Incoherent and Coherent Eavesdropping in the 6-state Protocol of Quantum Cryptography. *Physical Review A*, *59*(6), 4238–4248. doi:10.1103/PhysRevA.59.4238

Bechmann-Pasquinucci, H., & Peres, A. (2000). Quantum cryptography with 3-state systems. *Physical Review Letters*, *85*(15), 3313–3316. doi:10.1103/PhysRevLett.85.3313 PMID:11019329

Bechmann-Pasquinucci, H., & Tittel, W. (2000). Quantum cryptography using larger alphabets. *Physical Review A*, *61*(6), 062308–1. doi:10.1103/PhysRevA.61.062308

Bell, J. S. (1964). On the problem of hidden variables in quantum mechanics. Review of Modern Phys., 38, 447-452.

Bennett, C. H. (1992). Quantum cryptography using any two nonorthogonal states. *Physical Review Letters*, *68*, 3121–3124.

Bennett, C. H., & Brassard, G. (1984). Quantum cryptography: public key distribution and coin tossing. *Int. Conf. Computers, Systems & Signal Processing*, 175-179. doi:10.1103/PhysRevLett.68.3121

Bennett, C. H., & Brassard, G. (1985). Quantum public key distribution system. *IBM Technical Disclosure Bulletin, 28,* 3153–3163.

Brassard, G. (2000). Security aspects of practical quantum cryptography. In *International conference on the theory and applications of cryptographic techniques.* Springer. 10.1109/IQEC.2000.907967

Fedorov, A. K. (2018). Educational potential of quantum cryptography and its experimental modular realization. In *Proceedings of the Scientific-Practical Conference" Research and Development-2016.* Springer. 10.1007/978-3-319-62870-7_9

Hariharan, P., & Sanders, B. C. (1996). Quantum phenomena in optical interferometry. *Progress in Optics, 36,* 49–128. doi:10.1016/S0079-6638(08)70313-5

Hughes, R. J., Alde, D. M., Dyer, P., Luther, G. G., Morgan, G. L., & Schauer, M. (1995). Quantum cryptography. *Contemporary Physics, 36*(3), 149–163. doi:10.1080/00107519508222149

Huttner, B., Imoto, N., Gisin, N., & Mor, T. (1995, March). Quantum cryptography with coherent states. *Physical Review A, 51*(3), 1863–1869. doi:10.1103/PhysRevA.51.1863 PMID:9911795

Jaynes, E. T., & Cummings, F. W. (1963). Comparison of quantum and semiclassical radiation theories with application to the beam maser. *Proceedings of the IEEE, 51*(1), 89–109. doi:10.1109/PROC.1963.1664

Kim, J., Benson, O., Kan, H., & Yamamoto, Y. (1999). A single-photon turnstile device. *Nature, 397*(6719), 500–503. doi:10.1038/17295

Kulkarni & Harihar. (2012). Research directions in quantum cryptography and quantum key distribution. *International Journal of Scientific and Research Publications, 2,* 6.

L¨utkenhaus, N. (1999). Security of quantum cryptography with realistic sources. *Acta Physica Slovaca, 49,* 549–556.

L¨utkenhaus, N. (1999). *Security against individual attacks for realistic quantum key distribution.* Los Alamos Archives quant-ph/9910093.

L¨utkenhaus, N. (2000). Dim coherent states as signal states in the BB84 protocol: Is it secure? In P. Kumar, G. Mauro D'Ariano, & O. Hirota (Eds.), *Quantum Communication,Computing, and Measurement 2* (pp. 387–392). Kluwer Academic/Plenum Publishers.

Marand, C., & Townsend, P. D. (1995, August). Quantum key distribution over distances as long as 30 km. *Optics Letters, 20*(15), 1695–1697. doi:10.1364/OL.20.001695 PMID:19862127

Mayers. (1996). Quantum key distribution and string oblivious transfer in noisy channels. In *Advances in Cryptology: Proceedings of Crypto'96, Lecture Notes in Computer Science,* (Vol. 1109). Springer-Verlag.

Chapter 4
Security and Privacy Aspects Using Quantum Internet

Nilay R. Mistry

https://orcid.org/0000-0001-5683-3499

Gujarat Forensic Sciences University, India

Ankit Y. Dholakiya

Gujarat Forensic Sciences University, India

Jay P. Prajapati

Gujarat Forensic Sciences University, India

ABSTRACT

Quantum internet is an innovative approach to secure communication. Quantum internet is the next revolution in technology that enables the devices to perform operations that are beyond the classical internet. Quantum internet with quantum cryptography is one of the best solutions for secure data communication. Quantum internet uses the fundamental laws of quantum physics, which make it secure against sophisticated network attacks. In this research, the authors described quantum cryptography, which enhances the secure transmission over quantum internet using cryptographic protocols. These protocols use random bits transformations, which prevent attackers to make out the patterns of random bits transformations. Also, they introduced the conceptual OSI model for quantum internet, which makes it easy to understand the working of the quantum internet at different layers. Quantum internet can be implemented in intelligence network, satellite communication, critical infrastructure, etc. This can mark a significant change in secure communication.

I. INTRODUCTION

The Internet is the collection of networks that uses Internet Protocol suite for communication as well as a nice medium to connect with the entire world. However, this Classical Internet is vulnerable to Eavesdropping, Masquerading, and Sniffing of data. Due to such vulnerabilities like this, the Classical

DOI: 10.4018/978-1-7998-6677-0.ch004

Copyright © 2021, IGI Global. Copying or distributing in print or electronic forms without written permission of IGI Global is prohibited.

Internet is not safe from sophisticated Cyber Attacks. So, to overcome these vulnerabilities it is a necessity to develop a network that is more secure as compared to the Classical Network. Quantum Internet is a novel approach for communication as well as securely access the Internet. The development of Quantum Internet is inspired by the concept of Quantum Computing and the vulnerabilities exist in the Classical Internet. Quantum is the smallest amount of entity that can be excitation of quantized wave or field, as a photon and also it could be used as a physical entity in an interaction. This interaction is possible with the help of Quantum bits which are also known as Qubits. So, a Qubit is a unit that is used to measure Quantum Information. To transfer Quantum Information over Quantum Channel an approach is used called Quantum Teleportation. This can be achieved through entanglement of photons / information which is known as swapping of information / photons, in simple terms. The phenomenon of entanglement forms the basis of a quantum internet. There are some fundamental differences between a future quantum internet and therefore the internet that we see today. Stephanie Wehner said that two quantum bits are often 'entangled' Such entanglement is sort of a connection this is often very different to things for classical link layer protocols where we typically just send signals. therein case, there's no sense of connection inbuilt at a fundamental level. (Quantaneo, 2019)

Quantum Internet may be able provide reasonable level of security by utilizing the mentioned terms and principles. In this chapter we will cover each of the above-mentioned topics as well as introduced OSI reference model for Quantum Internet which will be helpful to understand the Quantum communication flow. The basics of the quantum communication based on Quantum physics principles which are "Heisenberg Uncertainty Principle" and "No cloning theorem" are well explained in this chapter. The goal of Quantum internet security can be achieved through Quantum cryptography, which have been described here as an essential element of securing Quantum communication which will overwhelm weakness into the classical internet. Although a fully comprehend quantum network is still a far-off vision, recent breakthroughs in transmitting, storing and manipulating quantum information have convinced some physicists that a simple proof of principle is imminent. (Anathaswamy A., 2020)

A. Quantum Bit

Quantum bit (or Qubit) is a unit that represents Quantum information on Quantum Internet. The term "qubit" was introduced by Ben Schumacher in a "intriguing and valuable conversations" with Bill Wootters paper published in 1995. (Whurley, 2017) There is the number of elemental particles like electron or photon that can be used in Quantum Computer and their charge represents 0 and/or 1 which are known as Qubit. In the Classical Internet, the Classical bit has two possible states, either 0 or 1 at a time. On the contrary, the Quantum Internet possesses two states of Qubit, 0 and 1 simultaneously. So, two Qubits can contain information about four states. In general, the state of a Qubit is described by:

$$|\psi\rangle = \alpha|0\rangle + \beta|1\rangle$$

Where α and β are probability amplitudes and can in general both be complex numbers and ψ is Qubit.

This type of phenomenon of Qubit known as a state of superposition. Quantum Information can be in a variety of forms such as (i)The Polarization State of Photon, (ii) The Spin of an Electron and (iii) Excited State of an Atom.

For example, if two Qubits contains information about four states than a machine with "n" Qubits can be in a superposition of 2^n states at the same time. In this case, 2^n states can be analyzed in a single operation. The standard 64-bit computer would take around 400 years to cycle through all its possible values. An array of qubits can use superposition to represent all 2^{64} possible values at once, allowing a quantum computer to solve problems that are practically impossible for standard computers. (Whurley, 2017)

B. Quantum Teleportation

Quantum Network allows the transportation of Quantum Information between different Quantum Systems. Thus, a Quantum Communication Channel relies on the Quantum Network can transmit Quantum Information using the concept of Quantum Mechanics known as Quantum Teleportation. Quantum Teleportation offers a reliable and efficient way to transmit Quantum Information over the Quantum Network. It offers the most promising mechanism for future Quantum Internet along with secure communication and a distributed computational power that significantly exceeds that of the Classical Internet. Quantum teleportation's biggest application will likely be as a means of encrypting information. Because the two photons communicate with each other by entanglement, there's no way for an outsider to read them. As such, quantum teleportation can be defined as "the instantaneous transfer of a state between particles separated by a long distance". (Scharping N., 2020)

Recently physicists achieved Quantum Teleportation between computer chips for the first time. They demonstrated the two-chip teleportation experiment, where the individual quantum state of a particle is transmitted across the 2 chips after a quantum measurement is performed. This utilizes the behavior of quantum physics, which simultaneously collapses the entanglement link and transfers the particle already on the receiver chip. Using this measurement, researchers were able to run experiments during which the fidelity reached 91 percent, as in most of the information was accurately transmitted and logged. Physicists have conducted a follow-up research on the same experiment, which then resulted in low data loss, high stability of teleportation and high level of control. (Nield D., 2019)

C. Quantum Entanglement

Quantum Entanglement is a phenomenon in which Qubits interacts with each other in such a way that it seems like swapping of atoms. Quantum entanglement occurs when two particles become inextricably linked, and whatever happens to one immediately affects the other, regardless of how far apart they are. Hence it is the 'spooky action at a distance' described by Albert Einstein. Entanglement generally refers to different particles having correlated quantum states. For example, the spin of two (physically separated) electrons being antiparallel. (Macdonald F., 2019) Entanglement became the basis for Quantum Information processing and also used in Quantum Cryptography, Quantum Teleportation, Quantum Error Correction Codes, and Quantum Computation. Quantum Entanglement works with the spin of Quantum which is -1/2 and +1/2. Physicists working on new ways of securing quantum encrypted messages are exploiting the fact that, at the quantum scale, a given qubit can only be entangled with one other qubit; this unique trait is referred to as monogamy of entanglement. (Phys Org, 2019)

Let's think of particle A and particle B is in opposite directions. But the original particle had a Quantum spin of 0 but they have to add up to 0 so if one may have a spin of -1/2 then the other is +1/2. This relationship defines that the two particles are entangled. (Jones A. Z., 2016, Kurzyk D., 2012)

Figure 1. Quantum Entanglement

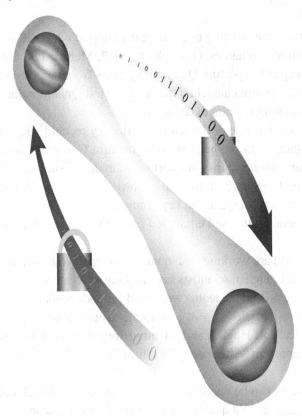

If one particle is found spinning in one direction, then the other particle instantaneously and immediately changes its spin in a corresponding manner dictated by the entanglement. For example, "Alice" and "Bob" share a pair of particles which are in one of two quantum states, "0" and "1." These particles are prepared in an entangled state in which a measurement of the state of Alice's particle is correlated with the measured state of Bob's particle, no matter how far apart they are. (Macdonald F., 2019)

D. Quantum Dot Technology

A Quantum Dot is a human-made nanoparticle that has semiconductor properties. They're tiny, ranging in size from 2 to 10 nanometers, with the size of the particle dictating the wavelength of light it emits, and therefore the color. When Quantum Dots are hit with a light source, each dot emits a color of a specific bandwidth: Larger dots emit light that is skewed toward red, and progressively smaller dots emit light that is skewed more toward green.

Quantum Dots are usually applied to a sheet of film that sits as a layer in that "sandwich" in front of the LED backlight that's used to illuminate a Liquid Crystal Display (LCD). The light passes through the LCD display stack, with the Quantum Dot color filter layer enhancing and enabling the LCD to reveal a wider and more saturated range of colors than would otherwise be possible.

II. LITERATURE REVIEW

A dream of security experts is the creating of a Quantum Internet which allows secure communication based on the laws of Quantum Mechanics. (Kurzyk D., 2012, Mehrdad S., 2009) Almost 25 years ago researchers discovered a way of teleporting Quantum systems from one place to another place without physically moving it. Recently, China launched the world's first Quantum Satellite named Mozi, on 16 August 2016 for testing Quantum Communication in space.

The Mozi has been selected as one of the ten revolutionary technologies that changed the world in 2016 by Scientific American. With the help of this Quantum Communication, China will be able to provide high-level communication security support to many areas such as islands in the South China Sea, Chinese Embassies and Consulates in foreign countries, and Naval Vessels. To transmit Quantum Keys to earth, the satellite requires a Quantum key communicator, a processing unit, a laser communicator, Quantum Entanglement emitter and entangled source which are already assembled in it. (Lloyd S., Shabrias M. S., 2000)

Scientists around the world are working on a quantum internet to communicate by teleportation. In addition to that, Chinese and Canadian scientists say that they have successfully implemented a structure of teleportation across the city. Both the teams were working independently and have teleported almost identifiable version of micro-particles known as Photons using cables across Calgary in Canada and Hefei in Anhui province. Richard Hughes and a team of researchers at Los Alamos National Labs in New Mexico have been running an "Alternative Quantum Internet," and have been doing so for roughly two-and-a-half years.

In the quantum world, data can be encoded in the state of qubits, which can be created in quantum devices like a quantum computer or a quantum processor. And the quantum internet, in simple terms, will involve sending qubits across a network of multiple quantum devices that are physically separated. (Leprince-Ringuet D., 2020) Last year in 2015 a team at the National Institute of Standards and Technology in the US reported that they had achieved Quantum Teleportation over a Fiber optical network more than 100 kilometers in length, but the cable was coiled within a Laboratory. Scientists have also teleported photons through the air over 100 kilometers, but the technology can only be used at night and in remote areas because too many of the particles are generated by other sources including natural light. (Knapp A., 2013)

The research put a step forward in the development of "Quantum Internet" which is a futuristic particle-based information system that could be much more secure as compare to the existing form of digital communication. The researchers claim that this Quantum Communication is "hack-proof".

This year in 2020, Xiao-Hui Bao at the University of Science and Technology of China and his colleagues have now smashed a record by entangling two quantum memories over 22 kilometers of fiber-optic cable installed underground.

Their quantum memories were each fabricated from about 100 million extremely cold rubidium atoms during a vacuum chamber. The quantum state for each system of atoms was entangled with the state of one photon, and thus the researchers sent those photons through the fiber-optic cables. When a specific observation called a Bell measurement was performed on the two photons simultaneously, the quantum memories with which the photons were paired before the measurement became entangled to at least one another. In the end of 2019 Physicists have been able to demonstrate quantum teleportation between two computer chips for the first time. To achieve their result, the team generated pairs of entangled photons, encoding quantum information in a way that ensured low levels of interference and high levels of accuracy. Up to four qubits – the quantum equivalent of classical computing bits – were linked together. This measurement utilizes the strange behavior of quantum physics, which simultaneously collapses the entanglement link and transfers the particle state to another particle already on the receiver chip. The researchers were then able to run experiments in which the fidelity reached 91 percent – as in, almost all the information was accurately transmitted and logged. (Nield D., 2020)

During a different experiment, Bao and his team entangled quantum memories across 50 kilometers. This experiment was conducted using cables that were not installed within the underground but just coiled up within the lab. the top goal of this work is to create a quantum repeater that will receive and re-transmit quantum information in an order, that it shall be sent over long distances, eventually building up a secure internet of quantum information. (Crane L., 2020)

In November 2020, research group from Dutch QuTech, is leading a project that will lead to a Quantum Network across Amsterdam. The project with telecom operator KPN, SURF and OPNT will focus on connecting different quantum processors, a significant distance apart, across the Randstad area of the city. This TKI (Top consortium for Knowledge and Innovation) project would connect quantum processors to each other via optical channels to exchange quantum bits, or qubits, to enable distributed processing. Working with these partners, they expect to have taken significant steps towards a quantum network by the end of the TKI project. Quantum communication networks are expected to evolve over time towards a global quantum network, and this would allow secure communication; position verification; clock synchronization; computation using external quantum computers; and more. Among other things, the project is intended to lead to new techniques, insights and standards that will bring a quantum network closer. (Flaherty N., 2020)

A team of scientist at University of Bristol have found a scalable process, connecting eight devices on a Quantum Network. This was the largest research on entanglement-based Quantum Communication Network. Scientist have conducted this research at a city-wide level. According to scientist, this would be a next step towards connecting cities with Quantum Network.

To understand this research let us take problem statement of walkie-talkie. In walkie-talkie, one set talks another. Now, if a person wants to send a message to third person, that person have to listen on one walkie-talkie and repeat it to second walkie-talkie. So, if there are eight people wanted to communicate, they would require 56 walkie-talkies. This means one for each of the seven others in the network.

However, scientist of Bristol University has found a workaround this problem by performing wavelength multiplexing. In simple terms, split the light based on its colour (i.e., wavelength) which will provide many entangled states. Then distribute these wavelengths to various users which if done simultaneously, then everyone can talk to everyone else. (Banerjee C., 2020)

Physicists at the Technical University of Munich (TUM) have announced a dramatic leap forward in the methods used to accurately place light sources in atom-thin layers. That fine positioning has been one block in the movement towards quantum chips.

Breakthroughs in the manipulation of light are making it more likely that we will, in due course, be seeing a significantly faster and more secure Internet. Adoption of optical circuits in chips, for example, to be driven by quantum technologies could be just around the corner.

Previous circuits on chips rely on electrons as the information carriers. However, by using light instead, it's possible to send data at the faster speed of light, gain power-efficiencies and take advantage of quantum entanglement, where the data is positioned in multiple states in the circuit, all at the same time.

Roughly, quantum entanglement is highly secure because eavesdropping attempts can not only be spotted immediately anywhere along a circuit, due to the always-intertwined parts, but the keys can be automatically shut down at the same time, thus corrupting visibility for the hacker.

The school says its light-source-positioning technique, using a three-atom-thick layer of the semiconductor molybdenum disulphide (MoS2) as the initial material and then irradiating it with a helium ion beam, controls the positioning of the light source better, in a chip, than has been achieved before. They say that the precision now opens the door to quantum sensor chips for smartphones, and also "new encryption technologies for data transmission." Any smartphone sensor also has applications in IoT.

The TUM quantum-electronics breakthrough is just one announced in the last few weeks. Scientists at Osaka University say they've figured a way to get information that's encoded in a laser-beam to translate to a spin state of an electron in a quantum dot. They explain, in their release, that they solve an issue where entangled states can be extremely fragile, in other words, petering out and not lasting for the required length of transmission. Roughly, they explain that their invention allows electron spins in distant, terminus computers to interact better with the quantum-data-carrying light signals. The achievement represents a major step towards a 'quantum internet,' the university says. (Nelson P., 2019)

III. SECURITY IN QUANTUM INTERNET

In this era of Digitization, everyone is connected to the Internet. But no one is concerned about the security of data. Users have to take security as a prime concern while accessing the data through the Internet. Without taking security precautions important data, credentials, personally sensitive information, banking related information may leak over the Internet and criminals can use that information to gain benefits out of it. These things matter to a criminal whose intention is to harm someone. Through Eavesdropping or Man in the Middle Attack, Communication level/Internet Security can be compromised. This is where the concept of Quantum Internet may help to achieve the precautionary level of security over the Internet.

Quantum Communications are secure because of any interference with them is detectable. The basic idea here is that the act of measuring a quantum object, such as a photon, that is always dynamic. Due to the dynamic nature of Quantum, it is very difficult for an attacker to deal with data communicated over the Internet. Because the photon changes its state consecutively which may not be identified by an attacker. So, any information transmitted in the form of single photons over Quantum Channel will self-destruct, in the case of an attempt to access or tamper with any unauthorized user/device. This functionality allows the user to send a "one-time pad" over a Quantum Channel which can then be used for secure communication using classical communication. (Fernholz T., 2016)

Security in Quantum Internet relies on two main principles of Quantum Physics, which are,

1) The Heisenberg Uncertainty Principle
2) The No-Cloning Theorem

3)   ***The Heisenberg Uncertainty Principle:*** The principle states that any of a variety of mathematical inequalities asserting a fundamental limit to the precision with which certain pairs of physical properties of a particle, known as complementary variables, such as position x and momentum p, can be known. In other words, the more precisely the position is determined, the less precisely the momentum is known in this instant, and vice versa. The Heisenberg Uncertainty Principle is a fundamental theory in quantum mechanics that defines that it is not possible to measure multiple quantum variables simultaneously.

Figure 2. Quantum Internet (Hensley B., Terhorst J., 2016)

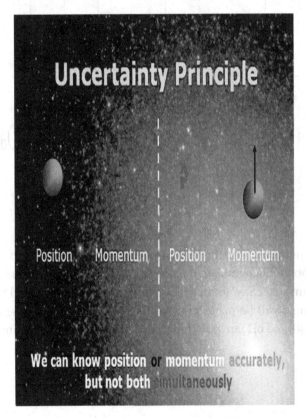

It is hard to conceptualize not being able to know exactly where a particle is at a given moment. It seems inherent that if a particle exists in space, then we can point to where it is; however, the Heisenberg Uncertainty Principle clearly shows otherwise. This is because of the wave-like nature of a particle. (LibreTexts, Chemistry, 2020) Let us assume that Δx is position and Δp is momentum, so according to the Heisenberg Uncertainty Principle,

Δx Δp > ℏ/2

Where Δ refers to the uncertainty in that variable and h is Planck's constant.

Note that the two uncertainties are multiplied together in equation (1), and the result must be greater than some number. This means that, although Δq can be as small as you like as long as Δv is large enough, or vice versa, they cannot both be arbitrarily small.

Figure 3. Classical Internet

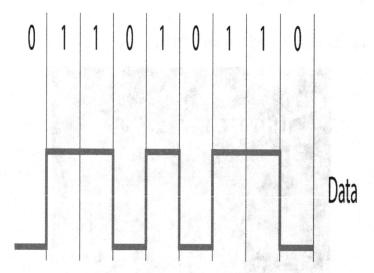

4)   **The No-Cloning Theorem:** The theorem says that it is impossible to create an identical copy of an arbitrary unknown Quantum state since the world of Quantum has some law that restricts copying one Quantum state. Say, for instance, if somehow, one managed to copy a Quantum state, then also minor change will be made so, it will never be as same as the original Quantum state. Let us assume that a|0⟩ and b|1⟩ are possible state of a photon can be defined as an original state on Quantum Channel,

$|s\rangle = a|0\rangle + b|1\rangle$

Now, the state of a photon at the end of transmission must be,

$|s\rangle|s\rangle = ((a|0\rangle + b|1\rangle)) (a|0\rangle + b|1\rangle)))$

Unfortunately, when an intruder tries to clone the state of a photon on Quantum Channel at given time t, it will be cloned as,

$|e\rangle = a|00\rangle + b|11\rangle$

So, it is impossible to create a copy of a state of any photon during transmission. (Wootters W. K., Zurek W. H., 2016)

To summarize both the principles let us understand by following example:

An organization is transmitting information in the form of specially crafted stream of photons representing 0s and 1s. If anyone tries to eavesdrop or intercept, he/she unintentionally modifies the photons being transmitted. This notifies the rightful recipient regarding the tampering. As a final layer of security, the beam of photons does not encode the actual secret message, it just contains an encryption key. Hence, if part of the key is intercepted, the sender and recipients would be able to detect the altered photons and discard that part of the key. Once both sender and recipients have transmitted enough photons, the shared key is used to encrypt the message, which can be transmitted over public communication channel. (Crane L., 2020)

However, despite of the mentioned groundbreaking facilities that Quantum Internet may provide, there are some limitations as well in the present generation which limits the building and working of Quantum Internet:

1. Devices and the space that may be used to establish Quantum Network, is costly.
2. Accuracy of the photons / data transmitted is yet to reach 100% ratio (Data loss prevention during transmission)
3. Nocturnal curse – The term is explained as a phenomenon where-in the transmission of photons is restricted to nighttime only. Because during day light transmission collides with the light particles which may result in loss of transmission.

IV. QUANTUM CRYPTOGRAPHY

Quantum Cryptography is introduced because of the shortcomings of the Classical Cryptography Methods, in which communicating nodes share random bit-stream based on a predefined mathematical algorithm, called keys. (Mehrdad S., 2009) These keys are vulnerable to attacks. These vulnerabilities might allow an intruder to intercept or modify the data during transmission likewise Man in the Middle.

In Classical Cryptography, data is being protected by encryption algorithms such as RSA, DES, MD5, SHA-1, HMAC, and AES, etc. Even though these algorithms may provide security, but it will not be able to provide an acceptable level of secure communication. Since these algorithms are vulnerable to attacks like keys can be easily compromised by Brute Force deciphering, by espionage from within a company or by hacking using Sniffing techniques.

In contrast to Classical Cryptography, Quantum Cryptography keeps the data secret since it follows the Laws of Quantum Mechanics. The entire basis of Quantum Cryptography relies on two main principles which are the "No-Cloning Theorem or Photon Polarization Principle" and "The Heisenberg Uncertainty Principle" which depicts that, the state of a quantum object cannot be read or intercept due to its high entropy. Thus, any information transmitted in the form of photons over Fiber channels will self-destruct when hacking attempts detected. For example, the voice may be distorted, or video may be edgy, or data may be converted to raw format.

The main goal of Quantum Cryptography is to provide high-level security. In Quantum Cryptography, encryption can be provided by using Quantum Key Distribution (QKD) to the sender and receiver. US-based agency DARPA conducted an experiment on Quantum Cryptography for end-to-end secure communication via high-speed Quantum Key Distribution. Through the experiment, the agency has tested sophisticated Cyber Attacks over Quantum Channel. The network was built by BBN Technologies,

Harvard University and Boston University and the deployment is possible in standard telecom Fiber. In DARPA Quantum Communication Network, keys that are provided by Quantum Cryptography completely replaced the existing encryption keys. (Elliott C., 2002)

Figure 4. Quantum Key Distribution Management

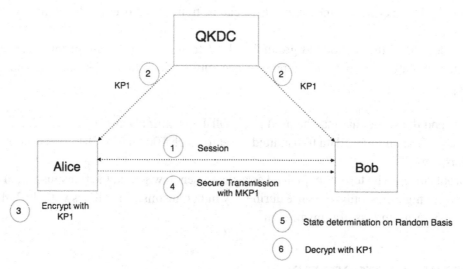

1. Establishes a Session between Alice and Bob.
2. KP1(Random Bits) distributed to Alice and Bob From QKDC.
3. Alice Encrypts the message with KP1.
4. Encrypted message sent to Bob.
5. Bob checks the random basis of KP1.
6. Bob decrypts the message using the state of KP1 determined in Step-5.

Quantum Key Distribution provides more secure communication rather than Classical Key Distribution. It will establish a Quantum Key Agreement by generating a shared key for the sender and receiver. For this kind of distribution, it uses QKA Protocol by using entanglement swapping. (Morales G., 2015) The main difference between both key distribution technique is complexity. Most Classical Key Distribution technique works upon mathematical complex calculation but that can be cracked or breached by reverse calculation techniques. Through the Quantum Key Distribution technique, key distribution is performed using the concept of photon polarization which may be tough to reassemble or compromise. It uses BB84 Protocol which was the first Quantum Cryptography protocol that transmits Qubits from sender to receiver via Quantum Communication Channel. (Ch. H., Brassard, G., 1984) This protocol encodes the information in such a way that it will not allow the illegitimate user to recover the information with 100% reliability. BB84 protocol may allow a higher-key generation rate and remain secure over long distances as compared to classical key distribution protocols. (Shore P. W., Preskill J., 2000) For example, Alice and Bob are transmitting information over Quantum Channel. Alice has encoded random bits {0,1} with a random basis {0/1, +/-} and transmits to Bob. Before that, a shared key will be generated which is used in encoding and decoding. Now on the other side, Bob receives those encoded bits of information and measures them on the random basis used by Alice. In between, if Eve tries to sense the bits than successfully sent bits are being sacrificed, which indicates the presence of an intruder. (Daniels K., Marcellino C.,)

Figure 5. Intercept and Resend attack in Quantum Cryptography (Wikipedia 2017)

Alice's random bit	0	1	1	0	1	0	0	1
Alice's random sending basis	+	+	X	+	X	X	X	+
Photon polarization Alice sends	↑	→	↘	↑	↘	↗	↗	→
Eve's random measuring basis	+	X	+	+	X	+	X	+
Polarization Eve measures and sends	↑	↗	→	↑	↘	→	↗	→
Bob's random measuring basis	+	X	X	X	+	X	+	+
Photon polarization Bob measures	↑	↗	↗	↘	→	↗	↑	→
PUBLIC DISCUSSION OF BASIS								
Shared secret key	0		0			0		1
Errors in key	√		✗			√		√

Here the indications used in figured are explained as below

Figure 6. Indications of Signs

Basis	0	1	Degree of Polarization
Rectilinear (+)	↑	→	0° or 90°
Diagonal (x)	↗	↘	45° or 135°

As shown in the figure, at first Alice sends some bits of data to Bob, using a random basis with its appropriate polarization state. In between Eve tries to measure the random basis of those data to set polarization state accordingly and sends it to Bob. Now, what happens is, the data bits, as well as polarization states, will be transformed into a different form as compare to its original form. So, both Eve and Bob will get raw data bits, which provokes an error when compared to Shared Secret Key.

In context with Classical Cryptography, Quantum Cryptography is difficult to crack, simple to use, it requires less processing resource in the encryption-decryption operation and can be used to detect eavesdropping in Quantum Key Distribution.

A. Device-Independent Quantum Cryptography

In general communications networks, it is often seen that two computers do not communicate directly. There are always some intermediate measurement devices that help the message to go from the source to the destination. Now in such a case, we cannot trust the third-party devices to be completely safe and secure. They may be tampered with by some malicious entity or by the developers themselves. Also, the risk of side-channel attacks is to be worried. The device-independent quantum key distribution aims at modifying the original quantum key distribution to be safe in case of untrusted third-party devices. The aim of quantum key distribution is for two computers, Alice and Bob, to share a common cryptographic key through communications over public channels. It is known that the BB84 protocol (the quantum cryptographic protocol) is safe even under the channel noise and possible detector faults at the end of Bob, with the assumption that the apparatus used at Alice's side are perfectly working to produce photons. But when we work in reality, this assumption does not hold good because there are high possibilities of faulty apparatus at Alice's side, too, which could hamper the security of the private string shared by Alice and Bob for communications.

For the solution of this problem, we need some devices which have the capabilities of self-testing. After passing these tests the device is said to be secure for communications. Also, cross-checking the polarizations and their probability distributions can be a solution. There are various implementations for the solution of these problems. (Sharma A., Bhatt A. P., 2019)

B. Quantum Cryptography Implementation with IoT

IoT devices have many loopholes in terms of the security of the devices, users, or the network. The current classical architecture of the IoT does not provide any provisions to detect the eavesdropper in the communications channel. Also, there can be some attacks wherein only one device in the whole IoT network can be infected with some virus and other devices trust the infected device and continue communications until it is detected. The fault might not be detected until a late time point and by then a sufficiently large amount of information could be transmitted to any malicious entity. Some viruses may affect the systems in a manner that they can only be removed by rebooting the systems and the industrial and enterprise systems are not rebooted for a very long time. Hence, there are multiple different points of vulnerability and IoT systems are highly susceptible to attacks. Here, we study the possible solution of IoT security through quantum cryptography.

A very basic aspect of the quantum cryptography is a quantum key distribution which is discussed above. The best feature in the quantum key distribution is the ability of the channel to detect the presence of any eavesdropper in the architecture of the system. This is in sharp contrast to classical algorithms for cryptography.

There are several variations of the quantum cryptographic protocol, BB84, but the main problem in the physical implementation of these protocols is the maximum distance that can be traveled by the photons. Photons are essentially light particles, and they can easily be distorted by the environmental or natural calamities. The photons need to travel a very long distance in cases where the IoT networks are wide and stretch across many cities/countries. Here, quantum computing fails to do so. Also, quantum devices are very big, bulky, and expensive. These cannot be afforded by every organization. The existing quantum key distribution protocol is designed to work with only 2 devices. This is not possible in actual IoT systems which connect hundreds of devices together to communicate.

So, to cure these problems we can give a solution wherein we combine both the classical and quantum approaches. One solution is proposed, which keeps the current semiconductor chips but uses quantum techniques to create a long and unique cryptographic key for each device. This can be done using quantum random number generation (QRNG), which generates a noise source with a high level of randomness. Quantum computing is capable of generating such large numbers quite efficiently and at a fast speed. Thus, it will be very difficult to guess the key and each device will have its unique key. The only way to get the key is to access the physical device configuration and trying to do so without getting noticed is very difficult. Hence, the key can be secured, and the communications can be safe. Additionally, the device-independent quantum cryptography can be used to ensure that the manufactured devices are trustworthy. (Sharma A., Bhatt A. P., 2019)

V. OSI REFERENCE MODEL FOR QUANTUM INTERNET

Computer networks are intended to use for communication and information sharing between two devices. In the network, data travels through multiple nodes, to make sure that the data reaches its destination. Those nodes having predefined rules to ensure security and accuracy of data that is known as Protocols. In the Classical Internet, these protocols play a crucial role in communication. These protocols group together and makes communication model. One such communication model is known as the OSI (Open System Interconnection Communication) Model, which was developed by an organization named ISO (International Organization for Standardization) in 1980. (Skill Gurukul, 2014)

Till the date, there are very few and a basic level of protocols are introduced for Quantum Internet. So, there should be some security efficient models or protocols required for Quantum Internet. Through which communication can be done between end-users. For instance, think of an OSI Model for Quantum Internet to understand the flow of Quantum Communication. To comprehend the vision of Quantum Internet more precisely, let's inherit the concept of the OSI Reference Model into it.

As shown in the above figure there are seven layers in the Quantum OSI Model, which are responsible for transmitting Qubits containing information, between end-systems. Each layer plays a different role in which, the top four layers are implemented by end-systems while the bottom three layers are implemented by all the nodes in the path. Every layer has a protocol through which it can communicate with each other as well as a corresponding layer in another system. A detailed overview of all the layers is as below.

1) *Physical Layer:* Basically, the physical layer describes the architecture of the transmission channel. In other words, it provides a medium for the transmission of Quantum Information via Fiber Optics Cable and Quantum Network Interface. These are the Interfaces that enable the generation and manipulation of Qubits at both ends. So, when Qubits enters into the Fiber optics medium, it will be converted into an optical source through Pulse Code Modulation. Now, this optical source is the data that is traveling in the Fiber optics medium. On the other hand, at the receiving side, it will be again converted into Qubits through Signal Restorer. For example, Fiber Optic Cable as a

wired medium to form electrical signals into the optical source or vice-versa and Radio waves as a wireless medium in a free space network.

2) ***Data Link Layer:*** The Data link layer mainly responsible for end-to-end delivery of Qubits from source to destination and to deliver them entanglement of Qubits is required. Hence in this layer entanglement plays a phenomenal role by making the interaction of Qubits in such a way that Quantum State of each Qubit cannot be determined. These entangled Qubits then formed into photon energy packets that contain the data to be transmitted. This layer also provides the functionality of error detection and error correction. On the contrary, the Quantum Computer itself has the built-in functionality of error detection and correction. (Hsu J., 2015)

Figure 7. OSI Reference Model

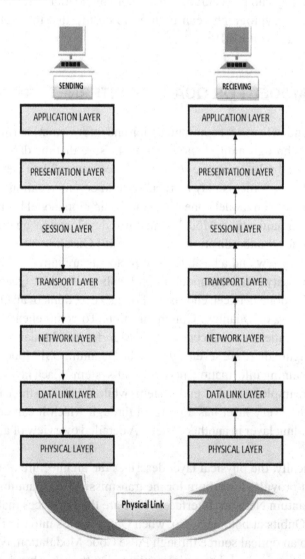

3) *Network Layer:* The Network Layer provides the functionality of path determination with the use of logical addressing which helps them to route towards an adequate destination over a network. It also organizes the energy packets when they enter into the network layer and reassemble them to the original state at the time of delivering to a destined point. The protocol of this layer may provide a reliable way of delivering the message, but it is not necessarily guaranteed to be reliable.

4) *Transport Layer:* This layer mainly deals with the reliability like encryption/decryption, reduces congestion by performing maintenance of energy packets that are currently in a flow. It can use Quantum Tunneling protocols to encrypt the data at the transport layer. The Transport layer divides the packets into segments to teleport energy packets to their suitable destination. It also provides a sequence number to each segment which helps energy packets to track and get reassemble at the network layer. This functionality ensures the complete data transfer between two nodes.

5) *Session Layer:* The session layer plays an essential role in the communication as well as maintaining the flow of energy packets in the network since it creates an environment and controls the interaction between two communicating parties. So, that application on either end can exchange data within that session. It also tries to maintain the integrity of communication as long as possible. The session layer also provides the service of synchronization, so when any dispute occurs on a Quantum System during data transmission, it can be retrieved from checkpoints.

6) *Presentation Layer:* The presentation layer provides the facility of data representation, security encryption and also converts the state of Qubits to network formatted code. This layer projects the photons to the destination, where based on probability it will find the correct state. When the state will be determined it will merge them with another pair of Qubits and then the data will be decrypted.

7) *Application Layer:* Application layer provides a platform through which user and data interaction are possible. The user frequently interacts with this layer through the Quantum Device. At first, the Quantum Device will identify the communicating source and destination, then it will look for available resources and, in the end, it will synchronize the communication between them. So, decrypted data will be presented in this layer via high-level APIs.

VI. ADVANTAGES OF QUANTUM INTERNET

- Quantum Internet provides a secure way of communication-based on Quantum Mechanics, which plays a major role in security.
- High-speed data transmission is possible due to the use of an optical source.
- A Cyber Attack like MITM (Man in the Middle Attack) can be prevented because of the principle of Quantum Mechanics.
- Unlike the Classical Internet, Quantum Internet is not using the mathematical algorithm which leads to less usage of the computational resource.
- The omnipresent nature of Qubits enables the Quantum System to process the data simultaneously, which provides an unexpected level of efficiency in Quantum Internet.

VII. APPLICATIONS OF QUANTUM INTERNET

- Quantum Internet can be used for secret data sharing in Government Sectors such as Defense Agency and Law Enforcement Agency.
- In the future, the Quantum Internet can be used in IoT devices since it is secure and un-hackable.
- Also, it might be applicable in Space Research Organization to secure satellite communication.
- Furthermore, in the future, it can be used to reduce Cyber Attacks by implementing them globally.

VIII. LIMITATIONS OF QUANTUM INTERNET

We have implemented the concept of Quantum Internet using fundamental laws of Quantum Mechanics to provide a high-level of security by replacing classical internet with it. Despite the advantages, we have mentioned there are some limitations to Quantum Internet.

- Distance is the main constraint in the Teleportation of Quantum Information as to the date it is possible for more than 100 kilometers (Elliott C., 2002) using fiber optics as a wired medium. Even though we use Quantum Repeater, it is possible to enhance the distance to an extent, after that it is not possible.
- As per this research work, implementation of the Quantum Internet in the wireless medium is somewhat complex because of the "Nocturnal Curse" phenomenon that has restricted the data transmission activities to night-time as during daylight it might collide with light particles.
- There are no sufficient protocols available for Quantum Communication, so the development of protocols is required in the future.

IX. CONCLUSION

Classical Internet is vulnerable to sophisticated Cyber Attacks which might have security and privacy issues. So, the phenomenon of Classical Internet can be mitigated with the use of Quantum Internet because it is defensive. Quantum Internet prevents data communication from being intercepted by an intruder. Due to Quantum Mechanics laws, Quantum Internet allows secure communication over the Quantum channel. An additional level of security can be provided using Quantum Cryptography because Quantum Key Distribution uses random bit-stream and polarization to send information over the Quantum Channel. Apart from that, we have introduced the OSI Reference Model for Quantum Internet which defines the flow of Quantum Internet at different layers. As a result of this research, usage of Quantum Internet along with Quantum Cryptography may lead to the secure internet soon. In addition to that, Quantum Internet is beneficial to Government Sectors, Law Enforcement Agencies, Corporate and Critical Infrastructures against sophisticated Cyber Attacks.

REFERENCES

Ananthaswamy, A. (2019). *Scientific American, The Quantum Internet Is Emerging, One Experiment at a Time*. https://www.scientificamerican.com/article/the-quantum-internet-is-emerging-one-experiment-at-a-time/

Banerjee, C. (2020). *The Times of India, Indian-led research team brings quantum internet closer to reality*. https://timesofindia.indiatimes.com/india/indian-led-research-team-brings-quantum-internet-closer-to-reality/articleshow/79470191.cms

Brassard, G. (1984). Quantum Cryptography: Public Key Distribution & Coin Tossing. *IEEE Conference on Computer, Systems, and Signal Processing.*

Crane, L. (2020). *New Scientist, Record-breaking quantum memory brings quantum internet one step closer*. https://www.newscientist.com/article/2233317-record-breaking-quantum-memory-brings-quantum-internet-one-step-closer/

Daniels, K., & Marcellino, C. (n.d.). *Security of Quantum Cryptography using Photon for Quantum Key Distribution*. Physics C191C.

Elliott, C. (2002, July). *New Journal of Physics: Building the Quantum Network*. BBN Technologies.

Fernholz, T. (2016, Aug. 20). *China's new Quantum Satellite will try to teleport data outside the bounds of space and time*. Quantum Supremacy.

Flaherty, N. (2020). *eeNews Europe, Quantum network for Amsterdam*. https://www.eenewseurope.com/news/quantum-network-amsterdam

Goyal, A., Aggarwal, S., & Jain, A. (n.d.). Quantum Cryptography and its Comparison with Classical Cryptography: A Review Paper. *5th IEEE Conference on Advanced Computing and Communication Technology.*

Hensley, B., & Terhorst, J. (2016, Sept. 13). *Heisenberg Uncertainty Principle*. Chemistry 2, Period 8.

Hsu, J. (2015). *Google Tests First Error Correction in Quantum Computing*. IEEE Spectrum, (March), 4.

Hutchinson, A. (2008). *Popular Mechanics, Lasers Could Send World's Most Secure Messages Through Space*. https://www.popularmechanics.com/space/satellites/a3597/4279669/

Jones, A. Z. (2016). *What is Quantum Entanglement*. Thought Co.

Knapp, A. (2013). *Los Alamos, Scientists Build a prototype Quantum Network*. www.forbes.com

Kurzyk, D. (2012). Introduction to Quantum Entanglement. Institute of Mathematics, Silesian University of Technology.

Leprince-Ringuet, D. (2020). *ZDNet, What is the quantum internet? Everything you need to know about the weird future of quantum networks*. https://www.zdnet.com/article/what-is-the-quantum-internet-everything-you-need-to-know-about-the-weird-future-of-quantum-networks/

LibreTexts. (2020). *Chemistry, Heisenberg's uncertainty principle.* https://chem.libretexts.org/Bookshelves/Physical_and_Theoretical_Chemistry_Textbook_Maps/Supplemental_Modules_(Physical_and_Theoretical_Chemistry)/Quantum_Mechanics/02._Fundamental_Concepts_of_Quantum_Mechanics/Heisenberg%27s_Uncertainty_Principle

Lloyd, S. & Shabrias, M. S. (2000). *Teleportation and Quantum Internet.* Massachusetts Institute of Technology.

Macdonald, F. (2019). *Science Alert, Scientists Just Unveiled The First-Ever Photo of Quantum Entanglement.* https://www.sciencealert.com/scientists-just-unveiled-the-first-ever-photo-of-quantum-entanglement

Mehrdad, S. (2009). Quantum Cryptography: A New Generation of Information Technology Security System. *Sixth International Conference on Information Technology: New Generations*, 1644-1647.

MIT Technology Review. (2013, May 6). *Government Lab Reveals It has Operated Quantum Internet for over Two Years.* Author.

OSI Model: The 7 Layers Explained. (2014, April 12). *Skill Gurukul.*

Morales, G. (2015). Luna, Quantum Communication Protocols based on Entanglement Swapping. Computer Science Department, CINVESTAV - IPN, Mexico City, Mexico.

Nelson, P. (2019). *Network World, Breakthroughs bring a quantum internet closer.* https://www.networkworld.com/article/3432509/breakthroughs-bring-a-quantum-internet-closer.html

Nield, D. (2019). *Science Alert, Physicists Just Achieved The First-Ever Quantum Teleportation Between Computer Chips.* https://www.sciencealert.com/scientists-manage-quantum-teleportation-between-computer-chips-for-the-first-time

Nield, D. (2019). *Science Alert, Physicists Just Achieved The First-Ever Quantum Teleportation Between Computer Chips.* https://www.sciencealert.com/scientists-manage-quantum-teleportation-between-computer-chips-for-the-first-time

Pirandola, S., & Braunstein, S. L. (2016, April). Physics: Unite to Build a Quantum Internet. *Nature Photonics.*

Quantaneo. (2019). *Delft University of Technology, World's first link layer protocol brings Quantum Internet closer to reality.* https://www.quantaneo.com/%E2%80%8BWorld-s-first-link-layer-protocol-brings-quantum-internet-closer-to-a-reality_a152.html

Quantum Key Distribution, Intercept and Resend. (2017). In *Wikipedia.*

Scherping, N. (2016, Sept. 20). *Discover Magazine, Quantum Teleportation Enters the Real World.* https://www.discovermagazine.com/the-sciences/quantum-teleportation-enters-the-real-world

Sharma, A., & Bhatt, A. P. (2019, September). Science Direct, Quantum Cryptography for Internet of Things Security. *Journal of Electronic Science and Technology, 17*(3). Retrieved November 28, 2020, from https://www.sciencedirect.com/science/article/pii/S1674862X19300345

Shore, P. W., & Preskill, J. (2000). Simple Proof of Security of the BB84 Quantum Key Distribution Protocol. *Physical Review Letter, 85*(2), 441.

Springer, P. O. (2019). *Quantifying how much quantum information can be eavesdropped.* https://phys.org/news/2019-01-quantifying-quantum-eavesdropped.html

Vas, G. (n.d.). *Economic Theory of Network.* Temple University.

Whurley, S. (2017). *7 things you need to know about Qubits.* https://superposition.com/2017/10/05/seven-things-need-know-about-qubits/

Wootters, W. K., & Zurek, W. H. (2016, Nov. 14). *The No Cloning Theorem.* Department of Physics, Williams College.

Chapter 5
Quantum Algorithms:
Application Perspective

Renata Wong

ⓘ https://orcid.org/0000-0001-5468-0716
Nanjing University, China

Amandeep Singh Bhatia

Chitkara University Institute of Engineering and Technology, Chitkara University, Patiala, India

ABSTRACT

In the last two decades, the interest in quantum computation has increased significantly among research communities. Quantum computing is the field that investigates the computational power and other properties of computers on the basis of the underlying quantum-mechanical principles. The main purpose is to find quantum algorithms that are significantly faster than any existing classical algorithms solving the same problem. While the quantum computers currently freely available to wider public count no more than two dozens of qubits, and most recently developed quantum devices offer some 50-60 qubits, quantum computer hardware is expected to grow in terms of qubit counts, fault tolerance, and resistance to decoherence. The main objective of this chapter is to present an introduction to the core quantum computing algorithms developed thus far for the field of cryptography.

INTRODUCTION

In recent years, quantum computing has become an area of high interest for both the academia and the industry. Although some companies such as IBM and Microsoft have made available quantum devices of up to 16 qubits and with varying qubit layouts, the era of quantum computing that would involve a number of qubits that facilitates useful and scalable quantum applications lies still well ahead. Once quantum computers become physically possible and economically viable, though, it is believed that they will be able to outperform classical devices, both in terms of the required space as well as time, by utilizing such quantum mechanical phenomena as superposition, entanglement and, equally importantly, destructive and constructive interference. It is clear however that quantum computers will not solve computationally

DOI: 10.4018/978-1-7998-6677-0.ch005

Copyright © 2021, IGI Global. Copying or distributing in print or electronic forms without written permission of IGI Global is prohibited.

unsolvable problems such as the halting problem. They might though be useful for certain problems for which classical algorithms are currently unable to provide efficient solutions.

The potential for quantum computing to become an important discipline was realized in 1994 with the emergence of Shor's algorithms for integer factorization and discrete logarithms (Shor, 1994). Shor's were the first quantum algorithms that offered a promise of a direct commercial usage especially in the field of cryptography. In 1996 quantum search algorithm (Grover) was proposed, which thanks to its simplicity proved to be applicable as a subroutine in many other quantum algorithms, such as quantum counting (Brassard, Høyer and Tapp, 1998) or protein structure prediction (Wong and Chang, 2020). While Shor's algorithms have applications in asymmetric cryptography, Grover's algorithm can be used to tackle symmetric keys.

The possibility of a practical development of quantum computers was given a boost with the publication by Arute et al. (2019) of their results of boson-sampling (Aaronson and Arkhipov, 2013) experiments on a noisy 53-qubit quantum device. These experiments are widely held as the first successful attempt at demonstrating that quantum mechanical computing methods might indeed be faster than classical ones for certain problems, despite the fact that no practical problem was solved by these experiments.

Quantum computing is intended to improve the computational performance of hard problems. As cryptographic algorithms are designed around assumptions of computational hardness of such problems as large prime number factorization, lattice problems such as lwe (learning with errors) (Regev, 2009), or that, more generally, $P \neq NP$. Quantum algorithms other than Shor's and Grover's might as well prove useful in handling information security issues.

The discorvery of the three quantum algorithms mentioned above has led to the development of the field of post-quantum cryptography (Bhatia and Zheng, 2020). It seeks to counteract against the potential threat of currently unbreakable classical codes being eventually broken by the quantum technology. Within the post-quantum cryptographic research, it is believed that certain lattice-based cryptographic optimization schemes will be insurmountable by quantum-mechanical methods (Peikert, 2016), (Bhatia and Kumar, 2019).

Table 1. Unexhaustive list of some of the most significant quantum algorithms developed thus far for cryptography

Quantum Algorithm	Proposed by
Integer factorization	(Shor, 1994)
Discrete logarithms	(Shor, 1994)
Unstructured search	(Grover, 1996)
Pell's equation & principal ideal	(Hallgren, 2002)
Shortest lattice vector	(Kuperberg, 2005)
Linear systems of equations	(Harrow, Hassidim and Lloyd, 2009)

In this chapter, the authors present the quantum algorithms that are currently the most relevant to quantum cryptography, as well as some of those that constitute advances in quantum computing and might thus one day be found to the applicable in cryptographic schemes due to the hardness of problems they optimize. The list of described algorithms is given in Table 1. For a broader selection of quantum algorithms, not only for cryptography, the reader is referred to the Quantum Algorithm Zoo (Jordan). A general familiarity with quantum notation on the part of the reader is assumed. A good introduction to quantum computing and core quantum algorithms can be found in Nielsen and Chuang (2010).

QUANTUM ALGORITHM FOR INTEGER FACTORIZATION

Shor's algorithm for integer factorization is a randomized polynomial-time procedure that provides an almost exponential speed-up over the existing classical algorithms for the problem. The most efficient known classical algorithm for factorization of large numbers is the number field sieve (lenstra, lenstra, manasse and pollard, 1990), which in order to factor an integer of length $\log_2 n$ bits into its prime factors requires asymptotic time $\exp\left(c(\log n)^{1/3}(\log\log n)^{2/3}\right)$. Where c is a constant. In comparison, Shor's quantum factorization takes asymptotically $O\left((\log n)^2(\log\log n)(\log\log\log n)\right)$ steps quantumly as well as some polynomial time in $\log n$ classically for the conversion of quantum output to classical. Shor's algorithm belongs to the complexity class bqp, which stands for bounded-error quantum polynomial time and that the algorithm outputs the correct answer with a small probability of error.

The strong belief that integer factorization is computationally intractable, made it became the basis of several cryptosystems, including the RSA asymmetric cryptography protocol (Rivest, Shamir & Adleman, 1978), (Bhatia & Kumar, 2018) one of the most widely used present-day public-key protocols.

Shor's algorithm does not factor a number n into its prime factors directly but relies instead on the result by Miller (1976) which stipulates that factorization can be done indirectly by reducing the problem to finding the order of an element x in the multiplicative group modulo n $(\mathbb{Z}/n\mathbb{Z})^{\times}$. The order is the least integer r such that $x^r \equiv 1 (\text{mod } n)$. From this congruence relation follows that $r \leq n$.

The general procedure is as follows:

1. PICK A RANDOM NUMBER x.
2. Compute $x^0 \equiv 1(\text{mod } n)$, $x^1 \equiv 1(\text{mod } n)$, $x^2 \equiv 1(\text{mod } n)$, through $x^r \equiv 1(\text{mod } n)$ to find r.

To that end, realise that r is the period of the function $f_x(k) = x^k(\text{mod } n)$. Given that $x^r \equiv 1(\text{mod } n)$ it follows that

$$f_x(n+r) = x^{n+r}(\text{mod } n) = x^n x^r(\text{mod } n) = x^n(\text{mod } n) = f_x(n)$$

and the function f_x is periodic. Moreover, all $f_x(k)$ are distinct with $0 < k < r$.

3. Compute $\gcd\left(x^{r/2} - 1, n\right)$.

Since $\left(x^{r/2} + 1\right)\left(x^{r/2} - 1\right) = x^r - 1 \equiv 0(\text{mod } n)$. It follows that $\gcd\left(x^{r/2} - 1, n\right)$ cannot be computed if r is odd, and that it does not result in a non-trivial divisor if $x^{r/2} \equiv -1(\text{mod } n)$. If, on the other hand, r is even then $\left(x^{r/2}\right)^2 \equiv 1(\text{mod } n)$ and $\left(x^{r/2}\right)^2 - 1 \equiv 0(\text{mod } n)$. From this it follows that at least one of $\gcd\left(x^{r/2}+1,n\right)$ and $\gcd\left(x^{r/2}-1,n\right)$ must be a nontrivial factor of n. Greatest common divisor can be computed classically in polynomial time by the Euclidean algorithm. The probability of the period being even is at least $\dfrac{1}{2}$.(Dasgupta, Papadimitriou & Vazirani, 2011).

Example: the problem is illustrated on an example for $n=21$. This is the largest number that has been factored on a quantum computer at the time of writing (Lopez, Laing, Lawson, Alvarez, Zhou, & O'brien, 2012). In accordance with the steps given above:

1. Pick, e.g., $x=2$.
2. Compute $2^0 \equiv 1 (\mathbf{mod} 21), 2^1 \equiv 2 (\mathbf{mod} 21), 2^2 \equiv 4 (\mathbf{mod} 21), 2^3 \equiv 8 (\mathbf{mod} 21), 2^4 \equiv 16 (\mathbf{mod} 21), 2^5 \equiv 11 (\mathbf{mod} 21),$ $2^6 \equiv 1 (\mathbf{mod} 21)$, etc. The period $r=6$.
3. since r is even, the following calculations are made: gcd(8+1.21)=3 and gcd(8–1.21)=7 both 3 and 7 are prime factors of 21.

In the above procedure, step 2 is carried out using a quantum device. The quantum part makes use of two quantum registers holding integers represented in binary and some auxiliary qubits as a workspace that will be reset to 0 after each subroutine. The initial state of both registers is $|0\,|\,0\rangle$. Next, given x and n. Find q such that $n^2 \le q < 2n^2$ where q is a power of 2 and set the first register in the uniform superposition representing numbers $a(\mathbf{mod}\ q)$ to obtain the state

$$\frac{1}{\sqrt{q}}\sum_{a=0}^{q-1}|a\,|\,0\rangle$$

then, compute $x^a(\mathbf{mod}\ n)$ in the second register

$$\frac{1}{\sqrt{q}}\sum_{a=0}^{q-1}|a\,|\,x^a\left(\mathbf{mod}\ n\right)\rangle$$

as specified in Shor (1994), this can be done along the classical method

```
power:= 1
for i = 0 to b-1
        if ( a_i == 1 . then
                power:= power * x^{2^i} (mod n) .                 endif
    endfor
```

Next, quantum fourier transform (Knuth, 1981) is performed on the first register mapping it to the following state

$$\frac{1}{\sqrt{q}} \sum_{c=0}^{q-1} e^{\frac{2\pi iac}{q}} \, |c\rangle$$

where the fourier transform matrix contains (a,c) entries of the form

$$\frac{1}{\sqrt{q}} e^{\frac{2\pi iac}{q}}$$

after the transformation has been performed, which can be done in polynomial time (Shor, 1997), the quantum registers are in the state

$$\frac{1}{q} \sum_{a=0}^{q-1}\sum_{c=0}^{q-1} e^{\frac{2\pi iac}{q}} \, |c \,|\, x^a \,(\bmod n)\rangle.$$

Upon measuring the first register, the value of c is observed that corresponds to a potential period r. Repeating the computation $O(\log \log r)$ times facilitates a high probability of observing the right period (Shor, 1997).

Fowler (2012) has estimated that a factorization of a 2000-bit number - which corresponds to some 600 decimal digits - using Shor's algorithm would require around 3×10^{11} sequential toffoli gates, around a billion qubits and 26.7 hours to complete. In comparison to that, a classical factorization of a 768-bit number conducted by Kleinjung *et al.* (2010) using the number field sieve factoring method (Lenstra, 1993) involved more than 10^{20} operations and around 2 years to carry out using hundreds of computers.

In 2017, another quantum algorithm for integer factorization was proposed that makes use of existing classical factorization algorithms for finding small prime factors and accelerates them using quantum techniques. The algorithm is called geecm and stands for "Grover plus eecm". It applies Grover's algorithm to the classical ecm with elliptic Edward curves to more efficiently search through the elliptic curves over $(\mathbb{Z}/n\mathbb{Z})$ .it has been reported to be "often much faster than Shor's algorithm and all pre-quantum factorization algorithms" (Bernstein, Heninger, Lou and Valenta, 2017). As the authors point out, Shor's algorithm for integer factorization is inferior to factorization algorithms based on ring operations with respect to finding small prime factors.

QUANTUM SEARCH ALGORITHM

Grover's quantum algorithm (Grover, 1994) facilitates search for an item in an unstructured database and requires about $\frac{\pi}{4}\sqrt{n}$ much time on a quantum computer as compared to n time it would take on its classical counterpart and a database of n entries. As pointed out by brassard (1997), Grover's method of amplitude amplification could be used to break classical cryptographic systems such as the, at that time in the 1990s, widely used data encryption standard (des). To that end, Grover's algorithm could be used to speedup the key lookup for an intercepted ciphertext, given that the database could be encoded in quantum memory. As it delivers a quadratic temporal improvement, it cannot however be as fast as Shor's algorithms. Des is obsolete today due to its relatively short key length of 56 bits and has been superseded by the advanced encryption standard (aes), which involves a symmetric-key algorithm and keys of up to 256 bits in length. In principle, Grover's algorithm can find multiple solutions. However, for the use in cryptography usually one single solution is desired and for that reason the authors will focus on the version of the algorithm that assumes such a single solution.

Consider an unsorted database of n entries. These entries can be encoded using $N=\log_2 n$ qubits in superposition. The algorithm avails itself of an oracle that determines which entry α if the one is looking for and outputs the respective value assigned to that entry. Let f be the function that maps every entry x in the database to either 1 or 0 in such a way that f(x)=1 if and only if x=α. Then, assume that the oracle is a unitary transformation that maps state $|x\rangle$ to $(-1)^{f(x)}|x\rangle$ if and only if $f(x)=1$. In other words, the oracle flips the sign of the marked element α.

Conceptually, the algorithm consists in two operations – amplitude inversion and inversion about the mean - that are repeated in succession $\pi\sqrt{n}/4$ times. Suppose that the quantum system (database) is in a uniform superposition. This means that the amplitudes of all entries are all the same, as indicated below

$$\frac{1}{\sqrt{n}}\sum_{x=0}^{n-1}|x\rangle.$$

Amplitude inversion involves the oracle flipping the sign as specified above, i.e., the amplitudes of all the entries but α are unchanged, while the amplitude of entry α becomes negative:

$$\frac{1}{\sqrt{n}}\sum_{x=0}^{n-1}(-1)^{f(x)}|x = \frac{1}{\sqrt{n}}\sum_{x=0,x\neq\alpha}^{n-1}|x - \frac{1}{\sqrt{n}}|\alpha\rangle.$$

Inversion about the mean (the average of all amplitudes) will subsequently result in increasing the amplitude of α. While at the same time decreasing the amplitudes of all other elements. Inversion about the mean corresponds to transforming each amplitude a as follows

$$a \to 2\bar{a}-a, \bar{a} = \frac{1}{n}\sum_{x=0}^{n-1}a.$$

If the number of steps $\pi\sqrt{n}/4$ has not been reached, another sequence of amplitude inversion and a subsequent inversion about the mean is performed. Again, the first operation will flip the sign of the amplitude of the marked element α while keeping the amplitudes of all other elements unaffected. Afterwards, inversion about the mean will make the amplitude of α even larger than in the previous step. And so on.

As the amplitude of the marked element will be much larger than the amplitudes of the remaining elements, upon measuring the system, one is likely to obtain the correct result α with the probability of failure being O(*1*/n) only.

QUANTUM ALGORITHM FOR DISCRETE LOGARITHMS

The discrete logarithm problem is the basis of such asymmetric cryptographic systems as diffie-hellman key exchange (dh) and elliptic curve cryptography (ecc). The difficulty in breaking these systems boils down to the difficulty of establishing the smallest integer $r = \log_g x$ of x such that $g^r \equiv x \pmod p$ given p and g. Here, p is a prime, $0 \le r < p-1$. And g is a generator such that $1, g, g^2, \ldots, g^{p-2}$ .comprise all the nonzero residues modulo p of the cyclic multiplicative group $\left(\mathbb{Z} / p\mathbb{Z} \right)^{\times}$.

The fastest known classical algorithm that solves the discrete logarithm problem requires $\exp(O((\log p)^{1/3} (\log \log p)^{2/3}))$ time (Gordon, 1993). Shor's algorithm for finding the discrete logarithm (Shor, 1994) is a randomized quantum algorithm with an asymptotic time complexity polynomial in the input size and probability of success of at least 3/4.

Example: consider the multiplicative group $\left(\mathbb{Z} / 7\mathbb{Z} \right)^{\times}$ and let $x=2$ while $g=3$. Then the smallest integer such that $3^r \equiv 2 \pmod 7$ is $r=2$.

The algorithm uses three quantum registers. In the first step, an integer q must be found that corresponds to a power of 2 and for which holds that $p < q < 2p$. Then, the first two registers $|a\rangle$ and $|b\rangle$ are put in the uniform superposition modulo $p-1$. Which results in the following state (tracing out the third register)

$$\frac{1}{p-1} \sum_{a=0}^{p-2} \sum_{b=0}^{p-2} |a|b$$

Next, in the third register the value $f = g^a x^{-b} \pmod p$ is computed leading to

$$\frac{1}{p-1} \sum_{a=0}^{p-2} \sum_{b=0}^{p-2} |a|b| g^a x^{-b} \pmod p \rangle$$

subsequently, apply the quantum fourier transform to map values $|a\rangle$ onto $|c\rangle$. And $|b\rangle$ onto $|d\rangle$. This transformation produces the following changes to the first two registers

$$\frac{1}{q} \sum_{c=0}^{q-1} \sum_{d=0}^{q-1} e^{\frac{2\pi i (ac+bd)}{q}} |c|d\rangle$$

the entire quantum state has the form

$$\frac{1}{q(p-1)} \sum_{c=0}^{q-1} \sum_{d=0}^{q-1} e^{\frac{2\pi i (ac+bd)}{q}} |c|d| g^a x^{-b} \pmod p \rangle$$

since $g^a x^{-b} = g^{a-b \log_g x} = g^{a-br}$. Some of the values in the last register will correspond to $g^k (\bmod\ p)$ for $k \equiv a - rb (\bmod\ p)$. Not all the pairs $|c\ |\ d\rangle$ fulfill these conditions. Hence, upon measuring the first two registers, a pair of numbers is obtained that may or may not constitute a desired result. The two conditions that determine whether an output is desired or not are rather complex. Here they are given for the sake of completeness in the form specified by Shor (1997):

$$\left|\{T\}_q\right| = |T - jq| = \left|rc + d - \frac{r}{p-1}\{c(p-1)\}_q - jq\right| \leq \frac{1}{2}$$

$$\left|\{c(p-1)\}_q\right| \leq \frac{q}{12}.$$

where j is the closest integer to T/q and $\{w\}_q$ is the residue of $(w(\bmod\ q))$. If both above conditions hold, the pair (a,b) is said to be "good". The probability of observing each of the "good" states c is at least $(p-1)/20q^2$.

Subsequently, the discrete logarithm r can be deduced from a sample of c is for which the first of the above conditions holds by dividing the condition by q to obtain

$$-\frac{1}{2q} \leq \frac{d}{q} + r\left(\frac{c(p-1) - \{c(p-1)\}_q}{(p-1)q}\right) \leq \frac{1}{2q}(\bmod\ 1)$$

the quantum part of the calculation needs to be repeated only a polynomial number of times in order to determine r. Every time a measurement is made, a pair is obtained of the form (c_i, d_i). Where $d_i = -rc_i (\bmod\ p-1)$. If c_i and $p-1$ are coprime, i.e., $\gcd(c_i, p-1)=1$. Then the multiplicative inverse of $c_i (\bmod\ p-1)$ can be found by using Euclid's algorithm. Then, the discrete logarithm r of x can be recovered by computing $r = -c_i^{-1} d_i$. However, if c_i is not coprime to $p-1$ then it is not possible to uniquely determine the exponent r from the state $|c_i\ |\ d_i\rangle$. The probability of observing $\gcd(c_i, p-1)$ is $1/\log \log(p-1)$. Therefore, in order to determine r with a high probability the algorithm will need to be run repeatedly $O(\log \log p)$ times (Jozsa, 2001). The time complexity for finding the discrete logarithm is the same as for factoring integers on a quantum computer: $O\left((\log n)^2 (\log \log n)(\log \log \log n)\right)$.

In cryptography the multiplicative group is commonly chosen such that p is prime. The quantum discrete logarithm however can handle any positive integers as well though under the condition that $(\mathbb{Z}/n\mathbb{Z})^\times$ is a multiplicative cyclic group or e.g. The field used has a cyclic multiplicative group. This condition stems from the fact that discrete logarithms are defined with regard to multiplicative cyclic groups. In general, $(\mathbb{Z}/n\mathbb{Z})^\times$ is not a group for arbitrary n due to the lack of multiplicative inverses.

THE HIDDEN SUBGROUP PROBLEM

Shor's approach to integer factorization and discrete logarithms is based on reducing the task to a special case of a problem known as the hidden subgroup problem (hsp). The difference between the two tasks shor tackled is the different parametrization by the group. For integer factorization the group $G = \mathbb{Z}$. While for discrete logarithms $G = \mathbb{Z}_{p-1} \times \mathbb{Z}_{p-1}$. The problem can be stated as follows. Given a function f on a group G. Find the subgroup $H \leq G$ of G such that for every element $g \hat{\in} G$ holds that $f(gh)=f(g)$ where $h \hat{\in} H$.

The hsp turns out to be the foundation of several quantum algorithms that could be used to break the existing cryptographic systems once quantum computers become a reality and the hsp with a particular parametrization could be solved efficiently. For example, no efficient quantum algorithms exist yet for the dihedral and symmetric groups (Montanaro, 2016).

The existence of a quantum algorithm for the hsp with the dihedral groups with a polynomial time complexity would imply the possibility of solving the shortest lattice vector problem (svp) in polynomial time. Given a specific norm, svp aims to find the shortest non-zero vector in a vector space V. The problem in its various formulations and with different norms is in general np-hard ((Ajtai, 1998), (Van Emde Boas, 1981)) and as such makes a basis for such cryptosystems as Ajtai-Dwork (Ajtai & Dwork, 1997) or ntru. Both of them are known to be resistant to attacks using Shor's algorithms.

Having a polynomial time quantum algorithm that solves the hsp parametrized by a symmetric group, on the other hand, would enable efficient solutions to the graph isomorphism problem that determines whether two given graphs are isomorphic to each other. This could be potentially used in e.g. An identification scheme in which an agent a sends a mapping i to an agent b in order for the agent b to check whether the agent a is the right party in a communication protocol, i.e., possesses the correct isomorphic mapping i.

The best currently known classical algorithm for graph isomorphism is due to Babai and Luks (1983) and has an asymptotic runtime complexity of $2^{O\left(\sqrt{n \log n}\right)}$ where n specifies the number of graph vertices. There is no efficient quantum algorithm for the problem. In contrast, a small controversy has played out in 2015-2016 upon the announcement by Babai (2016) to have devised a quasi-polynomial classical algorithm for graph isomorphism. Following the discovery of some errors in Babai's proof, the author has revised the paper in the following year. It appears however that the revision hasn't been published yet. Should it be the case that the classical algorithm can indeed be executed efficiently, it would preclude the use of it in any future cryptographic systems, thereby making any potential efficient quantum algorithm for the problem obsolete for the domain.

The hidden subgroup problem is an eminent example of a structure in a problem that can be taken to one's advantage while designing a quantum algorithm. This is why problems related to cryptography that are based on the hsp achieve exponential speedup over their classical counterparts. The existence of such a structure makes it possible to limit the number of inputs (Beals, Buhrman, Cleve, Mosca & de Wolf, 2001). Such an underlying structure is not present in the general formulation of the unstructured search problem, which is tackled by Grover's algorithm. In fact, lower bounds have been proven for many problems that preclude any algorithms for those problems attaining an exponential improvement over the corresponding classical cases. It has been shown that Grover's algorithm is optimal (Bennett, Bernstein, Brassard & Vazirani, 1997) for the problem of unstructured search. Hence, reducing the number of required queries from $\pi \sqrt{n} / 4$ would negatively impact the probability of observing the right state.

SHORTEST LATTICE VECTOR

The problem of finding the shortest vector (svp) in a lattice is an instance of the hidden subgroup problem parametrized by the dihedral group. A dihedral group is the group of symmetries of a regular polygon in the plane, denoted by D_n where n refers to the number of sides in the respective regular polygon. It is known of such polygons to possess $2n$ different symmetries, namely n rotations and n reflections.

In the hsp formulation for the svp, the hidden subgroup is generated by a reflection. The svp aims to find the shortest non-zero vector in a lattice. Ajtai-dwork cryptosystem mentioned above, as well as another public key cryptosystem proposed by Regev (2003) are both based on the hardness assumption of the svp and will be affected if an efficient quantum algorithm existed to solve it.

Almost all known quantum algorithms that run exponentially faster than the best classical algorithms solving the same problem are special instances of the hsp on abelian groups. Some instances of non-abelian groups for which efficient quantum algorithms are known include the nil-2-groups (Ivanyos, Sanselme & Santha, 2007), solvable groups (Watrous, 2001) and normal subgroups (Hallgren, Russell & Ta-Shma, 2003). It is not clear though whether they could be applied to cryptography.

Dihedral groups are in general non-abelian. In fact, D_1 and D_2 are the only commutative dihedral groups. No efficient classical solution to the problem is known. On the quantum side, there exists a quantum algorithm (Kuperberg, 2005) that has subexponential (but superpolynomial) complexity for both time and space: $2^{O\left(\sqrt{\log n}\right)}$.

In (Regev, 2004) a relationship has been established between the hidden subgroup problem and the shortest vector problem by determining that a solution to the svp can be obtained under the assumption that there exists an algorithm for the hsp on the dihedral group. Hence, the quantum algorithm by Kuperberg can be applied to improve the speed of breaking cryptographic systems based on svp, even though it in all likelihood will not be able to break the codes in a significant manner.

The conventional presentation of a dihedral group is

$$D_n = \left\langle r, f \mid r^n = f^2 = \left(fr\right)^2 = 1\right\rangle$$

it has two generators r and f. r refers to the counter clockwise rotation by an angle $2\pi/n$ radians, while f stands for a flip about some fixed axis, with every two axes or reflection located π/n radians apart from each other. 1 stands for the group's identity element, which corresponds to n rotations, or 2 reflections, or a sequence of a reflection and a rotation, followed by another reflection and a rotation. An element of the form r^s is a rotation, while an element of the form fr^s is a reflection. Parameter s is the slope of the reflection fr^s. Any element g of the dihedral group can be written in the form $f^t r^s$. Sometimes also represented as (s,t). Orders t and s are defined as elements of different modulo groups, namely

$$s \in \mathbb{Z}/n\mathbb{Z}, \; t \in \mathbb{Z}/2\mathbb{Z}.$$

Therefore, $n+1$ qubits altogether are required to represent both t and s. With t needing n qubits and s needing 1 qubit.

The subgroups of a dihedral group can be either cyclic or dihedral. Ettinger and Høyer (1999) reduced this general dihedral hsp, in which the subgroup could be any of the two types, to the hsp where the hidden subgroup is a dihedral group of the form $H = \langle (1,s) \rangle$. Which corresponds to the generator being fr^s for some $s \hat{I} \{1,\ldots,n-1\}$. Thus, Kuperberg assumes for his algorithm, without loss of generality, that the hidden subgroup of D_n is of this form and that the period $n=2^N$.

The hidden subgroup problem for the dihedral group reduces to finding the slope s of a hidden reflection fr^s (Kuperberg, 2005). Let s be expressed as a binary number. The main idea behind Kuperbergs algorithm is to recursively determine all the bits in the number s. This corresponds to first finding the parity of s for D_n and then finding the parities for subgroups isomorphic to $D_{n/2}$. In each recursion step, one bit of information is recovered, namely the least significant bit of s. This procedure recovers the entire binary representation of s in n iterations.

The group D_n has two subgroups isomorphic to $D_{n/2}$.

$$F_0 = r^2, f, \ F_1 = \langle r^2, fr \rangle$$

with r^2 and f. And r^2 and fr being the respective group's generators. If s has even parity, the hidden subgroup is a subgroup of the former. If s has odd parity, the hidden subgroup is a subgroup of the latter.

The algorithm starts with an oracle $h: D_n \otimes X$ that maps the group elements into the elements of the finite pure state

$$|X = \frac{1}{\sqrt{|X|}} \sum_{x \in X} |x\rangle$$

where $X \subset D_n$ is an unstructured set. This register will hold the output of the algorithm. Next, apply the circuit U_h that implements the oracle to the group elements g to obtain

$$U_h |g = |g| h(g)\rangle$$

h is a function that hides a subgroup $H \leq D_n$. This means that h is constant on the right cosets of H. While taking on a distinct value for each different right coset. Disregarding the register $|X\rangle$ .for the time being, the result of applying the oracle is a mixed state

$$\rho_{G/H} = \frac{1}{|G|} \sum |H a\rangle \langle H a|.$$

Where $|Ha\rangle$ .is a randomly chosen coset [1]. Let the coset be $(0,z)H$. Then, the state corresponding to this coset is

$$|(0,z)H = \frac{1}{\sqrt{2}} (|0, z + |1, s+z\rangle).$$

Using samples of this state it is possible to determine the value of s. The sampling is performed by applying the quantum fourier transform to the second register over $\mathbb{Z}/n\mathbb{Z}$ and results in the following quantum state

$$\left(I \times QFT\right)\left|(0,z)\right.H = \frac{1}{\sqrt{2n}}\sum_k\left(\omega_n^{kz}\left|0,k\right. + \omega_n^{k(s+z)}\left|1,k\right.\right).$$

With $\omega = \dfrac{2\pi i}{n}$. Which can be written separately for each register as the tensor product

$$\frac{1}{\sqrt{2}}\left(\left|0\right. + \omega_n^{ks}\left|1\right.\right)\otimes\frac{1}{\sqrt{n}}\sum_k\omega_n^{kz}\left|k\right.$$

let the state in the first register be called

$$\left|\psi_k\right. = \frac{1}{\sqrt{2}}\left(\left|0\right. + \omega_n^{ks}\left|1\right.\right)$$

Kuperberg then proposes to combine the states for different k to produce states with values that could be then evaluated to obtain the value of s. Such a desirable state would be for example

$$\left|\psi_{n/2}\right. = \frac{1}{\sqrt{2}}\left(\left|0\right. + (-1)^s\left|1\right.\right)$$

measurement in the

$$\left|+\right. = \frac{1}{\sqrt{2}}\left(\left|0\right. + \left|1\right.\right),\ \left|-\right. = \frac{1}{\sqrt{2}}\left(\left|0\right. - \left|1\right.\right)$$

basis would reveal the least significant bit of s. To that end, Kuperberg combines states by means of the controlled pauli-x operator, which flips the bit of the second qubit if and only if the value of the first qubit is 1:

$$\left|\psi_m,\psi_l\right. = \frac{1}{\sqrt{2}}\left(\left|0\right. + \omega_n^{ms}\left|1\right.\right)\otimes\frac{1}{\sqrt{2}}\left(\left|0\right. + \omega_n^{ls}\left|1\right.\right) = \frac{1}{2}\left(\left|0,0\right. + \omega_n^{ls}\left|0,1\right. + \omega_n^{ms}\left|1,0\right. + \omega_n^{s(m+l)}\left|1,1\right.\right)$$

$$\frac{1}{2}\left(\left|0,0\right. + \omega_n^{ls}\left|0,1\right. + \omega_n^{ms}\left|1,1\right. + \omega_n^{s(m+l)}\left|1,0\right.\right) = \frac{1}{2}\left(\left(\left|0\right. + \omega_n^{s(m+l)}\left|1\right.\right)\left|0\right. + \left(\omega_n^{ls}\left|0\right. + \omega_n^{ms}\left|1\right.\right)\left|1\right.\right)$$

the last form can then be separeted into

$$\frac{1}{2}\left(\left|\psi_{m+l}\right\rangle|0\rangle + \omega_n^{ls}\left|\psi_{m-l}\right\rangle|1\rangle\right)$$

upon measuring the second register, the first register will be either $\left|\psi_{m+l}\right\rangle$ or $\left|\psi_{m-l}\right\rangle$. Both outcomes happen with the probability 1/2. By iterating this qubit extraction, a desired state $\left|\psi_{n/2}\right\rangle$ can be generated. For that purpose, Kuperberg constructs a sieve that starts with $2^{\Theta\left(\sqrt{n}\right)}$ qubits and, in each stage, two qubits $\left|\psi_k\right\rangle$ and $\left|\psi_l\right\rangle$ are found such that k and l share at least $\sqrt{n}$ of the next least significant bits. Discard all qubits that don't fulfil this condition and cannot thus be paired. Measure the second register and discard it if the corresponding first register is $\left|\psi_{m+l}\right\rangle$. If the sieve has depth $\Theta\left(\sqrt{n}\right)$. It will produce the desired state with a high probability.

PELL'S EQUATION AND PRINCIPAL IDEAL PROBLEM

Pell's equation is a diophantine equation of the form $x^2-dy^2=1$ where d is a positive square-free integer. In cartesian coordinate system, the equation is visualized as a hyperbola. Coordinates x and y are solutions to the equation whenever the curve reaches a point for which both coordinates are integers. The number of possible solutions to Pell's equation is infinite thus making it a problem harder than that of integer factorization. In fact, integer factorization reduces to finding solutions to Pell's equation, while a reduction in the other way is not known (Buchmann & Williams, 1989). Moreover, the problem of solving Pell's equation reduces to solving the principal ideal problem (Buchmann & Williams, 1989). The hardness of the principal ideal problem lies at the core of the Buchmann-Williams key-exchange cryptosystem.

Classically, Pell's equation is solved using continued fractions, where approximations of the continued fraction of $\sqrt{d}$ lead to the solution. However, not every approximation will give the solution and approximating over many terms in the continued fraction may be necessary in order to obtain one.

Despite having an infinite number of solutions, it is sufficient to obtain the smallest solution (x_1, y_1) called the fundamental solution, meaning that $x_1 + \sqrt{d}y_1$ is smallest. Lagrange (1768) showed that every other solution can then be easily constructed from the fundamental solution by exponentiation. $x_1 + \sqrt{d}y_1$ can be exponentially large in d and so requires exponential time in the input size $\log d$ to write it down. To circumvent this difficulty, a regulator R of the fundamental solution is defined as

$$R := \ln\left(x_1 + \sqrt{d}y_1\right)$$

R can be written down using $O(\log d)$ bits. R is an irrational number and can be computed to arbitrary precision. The fastest algorithm for a classical computer runs in sub exponential time $O\left(e^{\sqrt{\log d}} poly(n)\right)$. Quantumly, polynomial $O\left(poly(\log d) poly(n)\right)$ running time is achievable, with error probability $1/poly(\log d)$ (Hallgren, 2002). Hallgren's algorithm solves a closely related problem, which is finding the regulator of the ring $\mathbb{Z}\left[\sqrt{d}\right] = \left\{x + y\sqrt{d} : x, y \in \mathbb{Z}\right\}$.

Hallgren's algorithm consists of two conceptual steps. In the first step, the regulator is encoded as the period r of a periodic function over $\mathbb{R}$. In the second step, this period is computed taking into consideration that it may constitute an irrational number.

Let d be given as above. The quadratic number field $\mathbb{Q}\left[\sqrt{d}\right]$ is defined as

$$\mathbb{Q}\left[\sqrt{d}\right] = \left\{ x + y\sqrt{d} : x, y \in \mathbb{Q} \right\}.$$

It follows that $\mathbb{Z}\left[\sqrt{d}\right] \subset \mathbb{Q}\left[\sqrt{d}\right]$. Furthermore, an operation of conjugation is defined as below:

$$\overline{x + y\sqrt{d}} := x - y\sqrt{d}.$$

With this it follows that for any solution $\xi \in \mathbb{Z}\left[\sqrt{d}\right]$ to Pell's equation the following condition applies:

$$\xi\bar{\xi} = x^2 - y^2 d = 1.$$

An element of a ring having its multiplicative inverse belonging to the ring as well is called a *unit*. The smallest unit u is called the fundamental unit. From the above equality it follows that the multiplicative inverse of ξ $\xi^{-1} = \bar{\xi}$ and that $\bar{\xi} \in \mathbb{Z}\left[\sqrt{d}\right]$. Hence, ξ is a unit of the ring $\mathbb{Z}\left[\sqrt{d}\right]$. The following proposition relates units to solutions to Pell's equation:

Proposition 1: $\xi = x + y\sqrt{d}$ .is a unit in the ring $\mathbb{Z}\left[\sqrt{d}\right]$ if and only if $\xi\bar{\xi} = x^2 - dy^2 = \pm 1$.

The set of all units of $\mathbb{Z}\left[\sqrt{d}\right]$ is $\left\{ \pm u^n : n \in \mathbb{Z} \right\}$. As u generates all other units, it is sufficient to find u in order to find the fundamental solution. After obtaining the fundamental unit, all the solutions of Pell's equation can be found. Namely, if $u = x + y\sqrt{d}$ and it holds that $x^2 - y^2 d = 1$ then the units correspond to the solution of Pell's equation. If, on the other hand, it holds that $x^2 - y^2 d = -1$ then the solutions to Pell's equation are obtained by taking powers $2n$ of u.

With the above, the regulator can be redefined to $R = \ln u$. In order to define a periodic function f that encodes the regulator as its period, the notion of a principal ideal must be introduced. An ideal I if a ring R is a subset of R that is closed under multiplication and under integer linear combinations. A principal ideal is an ideal that is generated by a single element $\alpha \hat{I} R$, i.e., it is of the form αR.

The task of computing regulators must now be converted into the task of computing periodicity. This can be done by observing that the function that maps ξ to the principal ideal ξR $f(\xi) = \xi\mathbb{Z}\left[\sqrt{d}\right]$ is periodic with period u. Since ξ is a unit, it is generated by the fundamental unit u, *i.e.*, $\xi = u^k$ *for* some $k \in \mathbb{Z}$. Therefore, the function $g(k) = u^k \mathbb{Z}\left[\sqrt{d}\right]$ has period r. While formally justified, there are issues with representing the values this function takes. Therefore, Hallgren uses the notion of a reduced ideal instead. Due to a rather high level of technicality, the authors refer the reader to the original paper by Hallgren as well as to an exposition by Jozsa (2003). For the purpose of this chapter, the authors assume that the period r *h*as an encoding.

The second conceptual step taken by Hallgren was to estimate the period r by using a modified version of the quantum phase estimation algorithm to account for the possibility that r is an irrational number. The quantum period finding subroutine was previously used by Shor in his quantum algorithm for factorizing integers into their prime factors. Here, the authors refer the reader to (Jozsa, 2003).

Besides a protocol to calculate the solutions to Pell's equation, Hallgren's paper also proposed a quantum algorithm for solving the principal ideal problem (PIP), which makes use of the same notions as the algorithm for solving Pell's equation. The existence of a polynomial-time quantum algorithm for PIP has significant implications for the Buchmann-Williams and the Diffie-Hellman (1976) key-exchange systems, which are based on the assumption that PIP is classically hard. Hallgren's algorithm for PIP is rather complex and for that reason it has been left out of this chapter. For details, the reader is referred to (Hallgren, 2002).

SYSTEMS OF LINEAR EQUATIONS

Solving systems of linear equations is one of the most important problems in science and engineering. The task entails finding a vector $|x\rangle$ for a given matrix A and input vector $|b\rangle$ such that $A|x\rangle = |b\rangle$. The fastest classical algorithm for this task is by gaussian elimination and takes $O(n^3)$ time, where n is the number of varibles in the linear system. Gaussian elimination finds the exact values of vector $|x\rangle$.

In juxtaposition to that, the time complexity of classical algorithms can be reduced in situations when the solution l*x* is a statistical approximation rather than an exact solution, and often also under the additional requirement for the matrix to be sparse. The quantum version of the problem is due to harrow, Hassidim and Lloyd (2009) and the algorithm is usually referred to as hhl. As an machine learning algorithm, it also provides an approximation of $|x = \sum_i x_i |i\rangle / \|x\|$ with the values of $|x\rangle$ encoded in the amplitudes x_i. This particular case can be approximated classically in $O\left(n\sqrt{\kappa}\right)$ time, where κ is the system's condition number2 Quantumly, an exponential improvement can be achieved thanks to the algorithms logarithmic run time $O(\kappa 2 l^\circ g \, n/\epsilon)$ with ϵ being the desired error.

There are serious drawbacks though regarding the hhl algorithm. It turns out that the postulated exponential speed-up can be achieved only under certain conditions (Aaronson, 2015). Firstly, the quantum state $|b\rangle$ must be easy to prepare. Some of easily preparable states include $|0\rangle$, $|1\rangle$ and their superpositions. There is however no general way of preparing an arbitrary state. Secondly, the condition number κ of matrix A must not be too big. And thirdly, the operation e^{iA} can be efficiently applied. For that, the sparseness of the matrix A is usually a sufficient condition. As stated in Aaronson (2015), with these constraints, the hhl algorithm is unlikely to be useful for the actual problem of solving linear systems of equations. Rather, it may be applicable as a subroutine for other algorithms.

The workings of the hhl algorithm are as follows. It takes a Hermitian matrix $A \in \mathbb{R}^{n \times n}$ and a vector $b \in \mathbb{R}^n$ as input. Matrix A has n eigenvalues λ_1 through λ_n and n *c*orresponding eigenvectors v_1 through vn. Represent the vector b *i*n the eigenbasis of matrix A.

$$|b = \sum_{i=1}^{n} \beta_i |v_i\rangle$$

if A is non-singular then there exists an inverse A^{-1}. This redefines the problem of finding $|x\rangle$ to applying $A^{-1}|b\rangle$. Applying A^{-1} corresponds to multiplying $|b\rangle$ with $1/\lambda i$.

To obtain the eigenvalues λi The hhl algorithm utilizes the quantum phase estimation algorithm (Kitaev, 1995), which is one of the core techniques in quantum computing. Given a unitary U and an eigenvector $|\psi\rangle$ of U. Phase estimation outputs an approximation of the associated eigenvalue θ in polynomial time:

$$U|\psi = e^{2\pi i,} |\psi\rangle$$

for the case of hhl, the unitary matrix is e^{iA} and the assumption is that it can be applied efficiently, otherwise the perceived exponential speed-up will vanish (Aaronson, 2015).

Let the eigenvalue be stored in the second register:

$$\sum_{i=1}^{n} \beta_i |v_i |\lambda_i\rangle.$$

In the next step, a new qubit, initialized to $|0\rangle$. Is added to the system and its state rotated by an angle of at most $1/\lambda i$

$$\sum_{i=1}^{n} \beta_i |v_i |\lambda_i\rangle \left(\frac{1}{\lambda_i} |0 + \sqrt{1 - \frac{1}{\lambda_i^2}} |1\rangle \right)$$

the phase estimation operation can be uncomputed, which allows one to ignore the state of the second register. Moreover, the state can be separated as follows in accordance with the value of the third register:

$$\sum_{i=1}^{n} \frac{\beta_i}{\lambda_i} |v_i |0 + \sum_{i=1}^{n} \beta_i \sqrt{1 - \frac{1}{\lambda_i^2}} |1\rangle$$

comparing this state to the represenation of vector $|b\rangle$ it is possible to read out the state of vector $|x\rangle$ in the first register for which the third register is $|0\rangle$.

$$|x = \sum_{i=1}^{n} \frac{\beta_i}{\lambda_i} |v_i$$

however, in order to completely characterize the state with all of the n amplitudes, multiple runs of the algorithm are required.

State $|1\rangle$ in the third register is undesired. Therefore, one hopes to measure the third register and observe a $|0\rangle$. In such a case, the first register will "collapse" to the desired representation for $|x\rangle$ specified above. To improve the probability of reading $|0\rangle$ upon measuring the third register, amplitude amplification can be used, which is a generalization of the quantum search algorithm ((Brassard & Høyer, 1997), (Grover, 1998)).

Despite being one of the most important developments in quantum algorithms since Shor's and Grover's contributions, the constraints under which the hhl algorithm will be able to achieve its potential performance highlight eminently the difficulty of developing quantum algorithms. It appears that while some improvements are indeed possible, they are not easy to find. This holds especially for the desired exponential speed-up.

CONCLUSION

In the present chapter, the authors presented a total of six algorithms with applications or a potential to be applied in quantum cryptography. An underlying mathematical problem, namely the hidden subgroup problem, has been described as the basis of many of the quantum algorithms for cryptography discovered thus far. At this stage of quantum computing research, it appears that breaking cryptosystems might well be one of the fields that quantum algorithms will prove most successful in. The topic of this chapter might feel mathematically challenging at times. Specially, a solid understanding of linear algebra would be an advantage while reading the descriptions of the algorithms.

REFERENCES

Aaronson, S. (2015). Read the fine print. *Nature Physics*, *11*(4), 291–293. doi:10.1038/nphys3272

Aaronson, S., & Arkhipov, A. (2013). The computational complexity of linear optics. *Theory of Computing.*, *9*(1), 143–252. doi:10.4086/toc.2013.v009a004

Ajtai, M. (1998).The shortest vector problem in L2 is NP-hard for randomized reductions. *Proceedings of the Thirtieth Annual ACM Symposium on Theory of Computing*, 1-10.

Ajtai, M., & Dwork, C. (1997). A public-key cryptosystem with worst-case/average-case equivalence. *Proceedings of the Twenty-Ninth Annual ACM Symposium on Theory of Computing*, 284-293. 10.1145/258533.258604

Arute, F., Arya, K., Babbush, R., Bacon, D., Bardin, J. C., Barends, R., Biswas, R., Boixo, S., Brandao, F. G. S. L., Buell, D. A., Burkett, B., Chen, Y., Chen, Z., Chiaro, B., Collins, R., Courtney, W., Dunsworth, A., Farhi, E., Foxen, B., ... Martinis, J. M. (2019). Quantum supremacy using programmable superconducting processor. *Nature*, *574*(7779), 505–510. doi:10.103841586-019-1666-5 PMID:31645734

Babai, L. (2016). Graph isomorphism in quasipolynomial time. In *Proceedings of the 48th ACM STOC* (pp. 684-697). ACM.

Beals, R., Buhrman, H., Cleve, R., Mosca, M., & de Wolf, R. (2001). Quantum lower bounds by polynomials. *Journal of the Association for Computing Machinery, 48*(4), 778–797. doi:10.1145/502090.502097

Bennett, C. H., Bernstein, E., Brassard, G., & Vazirani, U. (1997). Strengths and weaknesses of quantum computing. *SIAM Journal on Computing, 26*(5), 1510–1523. doi:10.1137/S0097539796300933

Bernstein, D. J., Heninger, N., Lou, P., & Valenta, L. (2017). Post-quantum RSA. In *Proceedings of the International Workshop on Post-Quantum Cryptography* (pp. 311-329). 10.1007/978-3-319-59879-6_18

Bhatia, A. S., & Kumar, A. (2018). *McEliece Cryptosystem Based On Extended Golay Code.* arXiv preprint: 1811.06246.

Bhatia, A. S., & Kumar, A. (2019). Post-Quantum Cryptography. *Emerging Security Algorithms and Techniques,* 139.

Bhatia, A. S., & Zheng, S. (2020). Post-Quantum Cryptography and Quantum Cloning. In *Quantum Cryptography and the Future of Cyber Security* (pp. 1–28). IGI Global.

Brassard, G. (1997). Searching a quantum phone book. *Science, 275*(5300), 627–628. doi:10.1126cience.275.5300.627

Brassard, G., & Høyer, P. (1997). An exact quantum polynomial-time algorithm for Simon's problem. In *Proceedings of Fifth Israeli Symposium on Theory of Computing and Systems* (pp. 12-23). IEEE Computer Society Press. 10.1109/ISTCS.1997.595153

Brassard, G., Høyer, P., & Tapp, A. (1998). Quantum counting. In K. G. Larsen, S. Skyum, & G. Winskel (Eds.), *Automata, Languages and Programming* (pp. 820–831). Springer. doi:10.1007/BFb0055105

Buchmann, J. A., & Williams, H. C. (1989). A key exchange system based on real quadratic fields. In G. Brassard (Ed.), Advances in Cryptology—CRYPTO '89. Academic Press.

Dasgupta, S., Papadimitriou, C. H., & Vazirani, U. (2011). *Algorithms.* McGraw-Hill.

Diffie, W., & Hellman, M. E. (1976). New directions in cryptography. *IEEE Transactions on Information Technology, 22*(6), 644–654. doi:10.1109/TIT.1976.1055638

Ettinger, M., & Høyer, P. (1999). On quantum algorithms for noncommutative hidden subgroups. In *Annual Symposium on Theoretical Aspects of Computer Science* (pp. 478-487). 10.1007/3-540-49116-3_45

Fowler, A. G., Mariantoni, M., Martinis, J. M., & Cleland, A. N. (2012). Surface codes: Towards practical large-scale quantum computation. *Physical Review A, 86*(3), 032324. doi:10.1103/PhysRevA.86.032324

Gordon, D. M. (1993). Discrete logarithms in GF(p) using the number field sieve. *SIAM Journal on Discrete Mathematics, 6*(1), 124–139. doi:10.1137/0406010

Grover, L. K. (1996). A fast quantum mechanical algorithm for database search. In *Proceedings of the 28th Annual ACM symposium on Theory of computing* (pp. 212–219). ACM. 10.1145/237814.237866

Grover, L. K. (1998). Quantum computers can search rapidly by using almost any transformation. *Physical Review Letters*, *80*(19), 4329–4332. doi:10.1103/PhysRevLett.80.4329

Hallgren, S. (2002). Polynomial-time quantum algorithms for Pell's equation and the principal ideal problem. *Symposium on the Theory of Computation STOC*. 10.1145/509907.510001

Hallgren, S., Russell, A., & Ta-Shma, A. (2003). The hidden subgroup problem and quantum computation using group representations. *SIAM Journal on Computing*, *32*(4), 916–934. doi:10.1137/S009753970139450X

Harrow, A. W., Hassidim, A., & Lloyd, S. (2009). Quantum algorithm for linear systems of equations. *Physical Review Letters*, *103*(15), 150502. doi:10.1103/PhysRevLett.103.150502 PMID:19905613

Ivanyos, G., Sanselme, L., & Santha, M. (2007). An efficient quantum algorithm for the hidden subgroup problem in nil-2 groups. *Algorithmica*, *62*(1-2), 480–498. doi:10.100700453-010-9467-0

Jordan, S. (n.d.). *The Quantum Algorithm Zoo*. Retrieved March 10, 2020, from https://quantumalgorithmzoo.org

Jozsa, R. (2001). Quantum factoring, discrete logarithms and the hidden subgroup problem. *Computing in Science & Engineering*, *3*(2), 34–43. doi:10.1109/5992.909000

Jozsa, R. (2003). *Notes on Hallgren's efficient quantum algorithm for solving Pell's equation*. Technical report, quant-ph/0302134.

Kitaev, A. Y. (1995). *Quantum measurements and the Abelian stabilizer problem*. Retrieved March 15, 2020 from arxiv.org, quant-ph/9511026

Kleinjung, T. (2010). Factorization of a 768-Bit RSA Modulus. *Advances in Cryptology – CRYPTO 2010. LNCS, 6223*, 333–350.

Knuth, D. E. (1981). The Art of Computer Programming, Vol. 2: Seminumerical Algorithms. Addison-Wesley.

Kuperberg, G. (2005). A subexponential-time quantum algorithm for the dihedral hidden subgroup problem. *SIAM Journal on Computing*, *35*(1), 170–188. doi:10.1137/S0097539703436345

Lenstra, A. K., Lenstra Jr., H. W. (1993). The Development of the Number Field Sieve. *LNM, 1554*.

Lenstra, A. K., Lenstra, H. W., Manasse, M. S., & Pollard, J. M. (1990). The number field sieve. In *Proceedings of the 22nd Annual ACM Symposium on Theory of Computing* (pp. 564-572). ACM.

Lopez, E. M., Laing, A., Lawson, T., Alvarez, R., Zhou, X.-Q., & O'Brien, J. L. (2012). Experimental realisation of Shor's quantum factoring algorithm using qubit recycling. *Nature Photonics*, *6*(11), 773–776. doi:10.1038/nphoton.2012.259

Miller, L. (1976). Riemann's hypothesis and tests for primality. *Journal of Computer and System Sciences*, *13*(3), 300–313. doi:10.1016/S0022-0000(76)80043-8

Montanaro, A. (2016). Quantum algorithms: an overview. *NPJ Quantum Information*, *2*, 15023.

Nielsen, M. A., & Chuang, I. L. (2010). *Quantum Computation and Quantum Information*. Cambridge University Press. doi:10.1017/CBO9780511976667

Peikert, C. (2016). A decade of lattice cryptography. *Foundations and Trends in Theoretical Computer Science*, *10*(4), 283–424. doi:10.1561/0400000074

Regev, O. (2003). New lattice based cryptographic constructions. *Proc. 35th ACM Symp. on Theory of Computing*.

Regev, O. (2004). Quantum computation and lattice problems. *SIAM Journal on Computing*, *33*(3), 738–760.

Regev, O. (2009). On lattices, learning with errors, random linear codes, and cryptography. *Journal of the Association for Computing Machinery*, *56*(1), 1–40.

Rivest, L., Shamir, A., & Adleman, L. (1978). A method of obtaining digital signatures and public-key cryptosystems. *Comm. Assoc. Comput. Math.*, *21*, 120–126.

Shor, P. W. (1994). Algorithms for quantum computation: discrete logarithms and factoring. In *Proceedings of 35th Annual Symposium on Foundations of Computer Science* (pp. 124–134). Santa Fe, NM: IEEE.

Shor, P. W. (1997). Polynomial-time algorithms for prime factorization and discrete logarithms on a quantum computer. *SIAM Journal on Computing*, *26*(5), 1484–1509.

Van Emde Boas, P. (1981). *Another NP-complete partition problem and the complexity of computing short vectors in a lattice*. Technical report 8104, University of Amsterdam.

Watrous, J. (2001). Quantum algorithms for solvable groups. In *Proceedings of 33rd ACM STOC* (pp. 60-67). ACM.

Wong, R., & Chang, W.-L. (2020). *Quantum algorithm for protein structure prediction in two-dimensional hydrophobic-hydrophilic model on square lattice*. Under review.

ENDNOTES

1   A coset *Ha* is the set generated from the subgroup *H* by multiplying all elements in it by *a*.
2   The condition number is the ratio between the matrix's largest and smallest eigenvalue: $\lambda m_{ax}/\lambda mi_n$.

Chapter 6
Post–Quantum Lattice–Based Cryptography:
A Quantum–Resistant Cryptosystem

Aarti Dadheech

Institute of Technology, Nirma University, India

ABSTRACT

Quantum cryptography is a branch of cryptography that is a mixture of quantum mechanics and classical cryptography. The study of quantum cryptography is to design cryptographic algorithms and protocols that are against quantum computing attacks. In this chapter, the authors focus on analyzing characteristics of the quantum-proof cryptosystem and its applications in the future internet. Lattice-based cryptography provides a much stronger belief of security, in that the average-case of certain problems is equivalent to the worst-case of those problems. With the increase in cryptanalytic attacks conventional cryptographic schemes will soon become obsolete. As the reality of quantum computing approaches, these cryptosystems will need to be replaced with efficient quantum-resistant cryptosystems. We need an alternate security mechanism which is as hard as the existing number theoretic approaches. In this chapter, the authors discuss the security dimension of lattice-based cryptography whose strength lies in the hardness of lattice problems and also study its application areas.

INTRODUCTION

For a long history, we always tend to seek a safe way to exchange messages between each other, and prevent the others from gaining uninvited access to confidential information. Many mechanisms have been invented for this purpose in different time period. Historically, the study of cryptography focused on the design of systems that provide secret communication over an insecure channel. For example, people in Egypt's Old Kingdom carved non-standard scripts into stones to keep messages secure.

Recently, individuals, corporations, and governments have started to demand privacy, integrity, authenticity, and reliability in all sorts of communication, from e-commerce to discussions of national secrets. Therefore, the need for secure commercial and private communication has been led by the In-

DOI: 10.4018/978-1-7998-6677-0.ch006

Copyright © 2021, IGI Global. Copying or distributing in print or electronic forms without written permission of IGI Global is prohibited.

formation age, which began in 1980s. Mathematical cryptography secretly used after World War I, when cryptosystems were widely used between armies. One of the most famous cryptosystem that influenced the world is the Germany's Enigma during the World War II. Cryptography has been an area of complex mathematical study for centuries that analyzes protocols that prevent third parties from reading private messages. Now, cryptography might better be defined as the design of systems that need to withstand any malicious attempts to abuse them.

A mechanism that exchanges information secretly is called a Cryptosystem. Such systems consist of two main algorithms: an encryption algorithm, which allows one entity to encode or "scramble" data, and a decryption algorithm, which allows another entity to decode or "unscramble" data. Each of these algorithms has an input called a key, which dictates some aspect of the algorithm's behavior. Before 1975, all cryptosystems are the Symmetric Cryptography, which required the sender and the receiver to agree on the same secret key. The Enigma Machine, for example, is a symmetric cryptography. In 1977, Rivest, Shamir and Adleman introduced to public the RSA Public Key cryptosystem, which was the first time that the concept of Public Key Cryptography (Diffie & Hellman,1976) circulated in the research community. In this cryptosystem sender and receiver uses two different keys; one for encryption and one for decryption. It solves the key distribution and scalability problems associated with symmetric systems. After the RSA cryptosystem, many Public key Cryptography were proposed, for example, the ElGamal Cryptosystem, the ECC Cryptosystem, and the GGH Cryptosystem and so on. Most common algorithms like RSA and Diffie Hellman key exchange scheme are computationally secured schemes and are based on the hard problem of factorizing a large number and solving the discrete logarithm problem respectively but with the invention of Shor's algorithm, it would solve both these hard problems in polynomial time using quantum computers, if built. A quantum computer making use of large qubit registers that can put the RSA and DH algorithms out of practice as theoretically, Shor's algorithm (Bernstein et al., 2009) with large number of quantum gates of quantum computer can solve the factorization problem in $logN^3$ time approximately which is a polynomial factor. This would put the entire internet domain at risk along with usage of user data at major risk. As the reality of quantum computing approaches, these cryptosystems will need to be replaced with efficient quantum-resistant cryptosystems.

There are important classes of algorithms which are considered to be quantum attack resistant based on the underlying problems.

- **Hash-based cryptography**; based on one-way functions that map bit-strings of an arbitrary length to short fixed-length bit strings. It is based on the usage of hash trees coupled with one time signature schemes
- **Code-based cryptography**; based on error-correction codes to detect and correct bit errors when messages are transmitted over an unreliable channel,
- **Lattice-based cryptography**; based on high dimensional lattices and presumed hardness of lattice problems
- **Multivariate quadratic (MQ) cryptography**; based on solving multivariate (many unknown variables) quadratic equations over the finite field (large quadratic tuples, cyclic rings, etc.) is NP-hard. This has been one of the most recently developed classes of algorithm.

Lattice-Based cryptography is one of the most important classes. There are problems based on lattices that are NP-hard and have no known efficient quantum solutions, unlike both the integer-factorization and discrete logarithm problems that have known quantum solutions. Hence there are two motivations for this thesis, one is with respect to protecting the user data and the other is selecting lattice-based cryptography among the classes of algorithms that are supposed to be post-quantum attacks resistant. This thesis uses lattice theory to study the GGH Public key cryptosystem, which uses a trapdoor one-way function of finding closest vectors in a lattice. The security of GGH cryptosystem is relying on the difficulty of lattice reduction. We use this scheme to secure the users' data. We also analyze this scheme and apply some method to improve this scheme so that attacks on it can be prevented.

We showed in experiments that proposed method was also a feasible method to prevent attack on GGH cryptosystem in general cases. In this work, we will explore various ways to improve the practicality of lattice-based cryptosystems (GGH Encryption scheme) in terms of space complexity and user data protection.

CHAPTER OUTLINE

The structure is as follow. In Chapter section 1, an introduction to lattice theory and some basis definitions that were used in this work are given. In section 2, we present an in-depth literature survey of existing cryptographic systems which promise to enable secure statistical computation on encrypted data in presence of quantum computers. In section 3, we give an overview of the cryptosystem by Oded Goldreich, Shaft Goldwasser and Shai Halevi followed by attack presented by Nguyen on this scheme and explain the security related to the choice of secret parameters. section 4 describes the various parameters and methods by which GGH cryptosystem can be protected against attack and presenting some solutions to make the system more reliable. In section 5 we implemented the new improvised algorithm. The efficiency and security of the proposed cryptosystem are also assessed in this chapter. Finally, at last we summarize the facts.

LATTICE THEORY

Lattice-based cryptography is a new approach towards cryptographic protection of data in computer systems. It is a counterpart of more commonly known, thoroughly tested and smoothly-working traditional algorithms (such as RSA, AES), which seem so far to fulfill their purpose more than adequately. A most appealing property of lattice based cryptography is that there are resilient to cryptanalysis, in presence of quantum computers.

Lattices were first studied by mathematicians Joseph Louis Lagrange and Carl Friedrich Gauss. In 1996, Miklos Ajtai and Micciancio discussed the use of lattices as cryptography primitive. The security assurances given by lattice-based cryptography provide a much greater confidence in the long-lasting security of cryptosystems built using hard lattice problems for two reasons. Firstly, many problems in lattice-theory are proven to be NP-Hard (Micciancio, 2001)(i.e. at least as hard as the hardest problems in NP). Secondly, the security of many lattice problems has a worst-case to average-case reduction (Paeng et al., 2003). This reduces the requirement of a cryptosystem's security proof to a proof of average-case hardness due to this worst-case to average-case reduction.

Definition

A lattice is defined informally as the set of all integral linear combinations of a set of basis vectors in an n-dimensional vector space. It follows that from a geometrical perspective, this produces a set of regular, repeating points of a set pattern. Similarly, it also follows that such a lattice can be defined by an infinite number of bases. Multiple bases defining the same lattice are said to exhibit lattice equality. A formal definition can be seen below:

Definition: A lattice $\mathcal{L}$ is a discrete sub-group of $\mathbb{R}^n$ or equivalently the set of all the integral combinations of n linearly independent vectors $b_1 \ldots b_n$ over $\mathbb{R}$.

$$\mathcal{L}\left(b_{1,\ldots,}b_n\right) = \left\{ \sum_{i=1}^{n} x_i b_i : x_i \in \mathbb{Z} \, for \, 1 \leq i \leq n \right\} \cdot \bullet$$

The set of vectors $b_1, \ldots, b_n$ are called a basis for the lattice. A basis can be represented by the matrix $B = [b_1, \ldots, b_n] \in \mathbb{R}^{n \times n}$ having the basis vectors as column.

- The lattice generated by a matrix $B \in \mathbb{R}^{n \times n}$ an be defined as $\mathcal{L}(B) = \{Bx : x \in \mathbb{Z}^n\}$, where Bx is the usual matrix-vector multiplication.

A lattice $\mathcal{L}$ is a set of points in the n dimensional Euclidean space R^n with a strong property of periodicity. For example, Figure 1.1 shows a lattice defined by basis $[b_1, b_2]$. Every lattice point can be defined in terms of b_1 and b_2. For example, points $e_1 = 2 b_1 - b_2$ and $e_2 = b_2 - b_1$.

Figure 1. Lattice $\mathcal{L}$ of High orthogonality-defect basis$[b_1 b_2]$, Low orthogonality-defect basis $[e_1 e_2]$

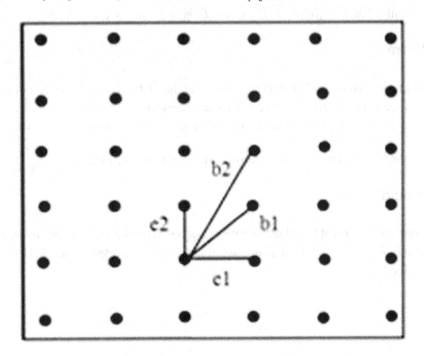

For dimensions 2 or greater, every lattice has an infinite number of bases. If two bases generate the same lattice, then the absolute value of the determinant of each basis is same, and there exists a unimodular matrix U that transforms either basis to the other. That is, in Figure 1.1 for bases B_b and B_e if $\mathcal{L} B_b = \mathcal{L} B_e$, then |det($B_b$)| = |det($B_e$)|, and B_b, B_e. A matrix is unimodular if it is a square integer matrix with determinant ±1. Unimodular matrices have the property that they are invertible in $\mathbb{Z}$.

Some bases are easier to work with than others. The lattice in Figure 1.1 is defined by two different bases: [b_1, b_2] and [e_1, e_2]. The basis B_e in Figure 1.1 has a low orthogonality defect because its vectors are nearly orthogonal. This is considered a "good" basis as it can be used to solve certain variants of lattice problems very efficiently. Usually, the private keys are "good" basis. The basis B_b in Figure 1.1 has a high orthogonality defect because its vectors are far from orthogonal. This is considered a "bad" basis because there are no known methods that can use it to solve lattice problems efficiently. For that obvious reasons, bad basis are used as the public key (Yoshino & Kunihiro, 2012).

LATTICE PROPERTIES

Rank

The rank of a lattice is defined as the number of linearly independent vectors in any basis for that lattice. A full-rank lattice is defined as a lattice where the number of linearly independent vectors in any basis of this lattice is equal to the dimension in which the lattice is embedded. The lattice $\mathcal{L}$ B) is full rank if $n=m$ i.e. if B spans the entire vector space.

Determinant

For a rank n lattice $\mathcal{L}$ its determinant denoted by det($\mathcal{L}$ is defined as the n-dimensional volume of $\mathcal{L}$ (.). Mathematically, det($\mathcal{L} = \sqrt{det\left(B^T B\right)}$ when $\mathcal{L}$ .is full rank, det($\mathcal{L}$|det(B)|.

Euclidean Norm

This norm comes from Pythagoras' theorem, stating that the distance between two points is the square root of the sum of the axial distances squared. This can be extended to an arbitrary, finite-dimensioned vector space by squaring each of the axial dimensions and taking the square root of the sum.

Let b be a vector of $\mathbb{R}^n$. The Euclidean norm is the function • defined by $b_2 = \sqrt{\sum_{i=1}^{n} |b_i|^2}$.

1.2.1.1 Hadamard Ratio

It can be use as one measurement to judge the qualities of bases produced by lattice reduction algorithm. Given a basis $B=\{b_1, b_2, \ldots, b_n\}$ and the n dimensional lattice $\mathcal{L}$ generated by B, the Hadamard Ratio of the basis B is defined as:

$$\mathcal{H}(B) = \left(\frac{\det(\mathcal{L})}{b_{12} \cdot b_{22} \ldots \cdot b_{n2}} \right)^{\frac{1}{n}}$$

where represents the Euclidean Norm of $\cdot$.

The range of Hadamard Ratio is:

$$0 < \mathcal{H}(B) \leq 1.$$

The more orthogonal a basis B is, the closer to 1 its Hadamard Ratio $\mathcal{H}(B)$ is.

Unimodular Matrices

If a basis B can be transformed by a multiplication with a transformation matrix U such that the new basis B' yields the same lattice as the original basis B (ie. $B' = U\,B$, $\mathcal{L}_B \equiv \mathcal{L}_{B'}$), we refer to this transformation U as a unimodular transformation (Ajtai, M,1998). A unimodular transformation matrix is defined as an integer matrix, whose inverse is also integer. This implies the following properties:

1. U must be integral.
2. U must be square.
3. $\det(U)$ must be exactly $\pm$.

As such, any basis of a lattice can be transformed to any other basis for the same lattice through a multiplication with a single unimodular transformation matrix. Any multiplication of a lattice basis with a unimodular matrix will produce a new basis that generates the same lattice. In fact, lattice equality is only achieved if there exists such a unimodular transform between bases. Due to the determinant of a unimodular matrix being $\pm$, it is clear that the choice of basis will not affect the lattice determinant.

Hermite Normal Form

A particularly convenient basis for some applications is the Hermite Normal Form (HNF). A basis B is in HNF if it is upper triangular, all elements on the diagonal are strictly positive, and any other element $b_{i,j}$ satisfies $0 \leq b$, $j < b_j$. It is easy to see that every integer lattice $\mathcal{L}$ B) has a unique basis in Hermite Normal Form, denoted HNF(B). Moreover, given any basis B for the lattice, HNF(B) can be efficiently computed. HNF(B) does not depend on the particular basis B but it is uniquely defined by the lattices $\mathcal{L}$ (B) generated by B. See A.1 in Appendix for its algorithm.

$$\forall 1 \leq i,j \leq n \quad H_{i,j} \begin{cases} = 0 & if & i > j \\ \geq 0 & if & i \leq j \\ < H_{j,j} & if & i < j \end{cases}.$$

Furthermore, the HNF of a lattice basis is unique for the lattice (Plantard et al., 2009) i.e. any basis representing the same lattice will have the same HNF decomposition.

Orthogonality Defect

Let B be a non-singular n x n matrix. Then the orthogonality defect of B is defined as the product of the basis vector lengths divided by the parallelepiped volume. It is a measure of nearly orthogonal.

$$\text{Orth-defect}(B) = \frac{\prod_i b_i}{\det(B)}.$$

LATTICE PROBLEMS

An important characteristic of lattices is the fact that they can have different bases producing the same lattice. The determinants of all these bases have the same value. Regarding lattices, vectors with minimum length are interesting. There are two important problems related with lattice: the *Shortest Vector Problem* and the *Closest Vector Problem*.

1.   The Shortest Vector Problem(SVP)

Find a shortest nonzero vector in a given lattice $\mathcal{L}$ i.e., search for a vector $v \in \mathcal{L}$ that minimizes the Euclidean norm v.

2.   The Closest Vector Problem(CVP)

Given a lattice $\mathcal{L}$ and a vector $w \in \mathbb{R}^m$, normally $w \notin \mathcal{L}$, find a vector $v \in \mathcal{L}$ that is closest to w among all points of $\mathcal{L}$ i.e., find a $v \in \mathcal{L}$ that minimizes the Euclidean norm $w-v$.

According to the hardness problems related with cryptography, we are more interested in algorithms for finding a lattice vector closest to a given arbitrary target vector, when we study the GGH cryptosystem or other lattice based cryptosystems. Target vector is a vector not belonging to that lattice. Solving SVP always accompanies with the algorithms of solving CVP.

Algorithmic Solution for Lattice problems

Gram-Schmidt Orthogonalization

The Gram-Schmidt Orthogonalization algorithm is an iterative approach to orthogonalizing the vectors of a basis. The procedure takes a nonorthogonal set of linearly independent vectors $v_1, v_2, \ldots, v_n$ and constructs an orthogonal basis of vectors $u_1^*, u_2^*, \ldots, u_n^*$.

Figure 2. Gram-Schmidt orthogonalization

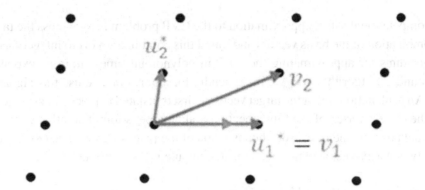

The first vector v_1 of a given basis B is taken as a reference and the second vector v_2 is projected on to an (n-1)-hyperplane perpendicular to v_1. The third vector v_3 is projected onto a (n-2)-hyperplane perpendicular to the plane described by v_1 and v_2. This process continues in an iterative fashion until all degrees of freedom are exhausted.

We define the Gram-Schmidt vectors $u_1^*, u_2^*, \ldots, u_n^*$ .by:

$$u_i^* = b_i - \sum_{j=1}^{i-1} \mu_{i,j} u_j^*, \qquad where \quad \mu_{i,j} \bullet \frac{b_i, u_j^*}{u_j^*, u_j^*}$$

LLL

It is a lattice reduction algorithm that produces a lattice basis of "short" vectors. With the Gram-Schmidt orthogonalization in higher dimensions, Lenstra, Lenstra, and Lovasz proposed an approximation algorithm of basis reduction in higher dimensions in 1982, which is called LLL basis reduction algorithm. The LLL algorithm gives us an approximation within an exponential factor of the actual shortest vector in polynomial time. Technically, LLL can be defined as follow:

Definition: Let $\{b_1, b_2, \ldots, b_n\}$ be a basis for a n-dimensional Lattice $\mathcal{L}$ and $\{u_1^*, u_2^*, \ldots, u_n^*\}$ be the orthogonal basis generated and we have $\mu_{i,j} \cdot \dfrac{b_i, u_j^*}{\|u\|^* \|u\|^*}$ be say $\{b_1, b_2, \ldots, b_n\}$ is a LLL reduced basis if it satisfies two conditions:

1. $\forall i \neq k, \mu_{i,j} \leq \dfrac{1}{2}.$

2. For each i, $\mu_{i+1}^* + \mu_{i,i+1} u_i^* \geq \dfrac{3}{4} u_i^*$

Babai's Round-Off

A simple and computationally-fast approximation to the CVP problem is to express the target vector as a linear, real combination of the basis vectors and round this combination off to integer factors. In 1986, Babai gave algorithms for approximating the CVP in polynomial time within an exponential factor, known as the round-off algorithm see A.2 in Appendix for algorithm. We use this algorithm in GGH Cryptosystem. An explanation is that the target vector is first translated to place it inside the fundamental parallelotope, the closest vertex of the fundamental parallelotope is found and this vertex is translated back to its original position and returned. The inversion of the matrix R, which is $O(n^3)$ is costly part of algorithm. The two matrix-vector multiplications to compute v costs only $O(n^2)$.

Cryptosystem Construction Using CVP

We present some cryptosystems whose common feature is that they all rely on computational problems in lattices for their security. The subject of lattice based cryptography is very active and there have recently been new ideas that revolutionized the field. Below are such cryptosystems:

GGH

Inspired by the results of Ajtai, Oded Goldreich, Shaft Goldwasser and Shai Halevi published a cryptosystem based on CVP in 1997, a lattice-analogy of McEliece cryptosystem. The system is known as Goldreich-Goldwasser Halevi cryptosystem or simply GGH. Their practical proposition of a cryptosystem was attacked and broken by Nguyen in 1999. However, the general idea is still viable, as can be seen by the many variants of the basic GGH cryptosystem that have been proposed since. It uses a trapdoor one-way function that is relying on the difficulty of lattice reduction. The cryptosystem depends on two (public) parameters: n $\in \mathbb{N}$ the dimension and $\sigma \in \mathbb{N}$ a security parameter. First, choose a random basis R of short vectors for an n -dimensional lattice as private basis. Then reduces the R into bad basis and generate and publish another basis B, serving as public key. For GGH scheme to work, one must be able to solve CVP with R i.e with "good basis" but not with B (bad basis). It follows that one needs to multiply R by suitable Unimodular matrices. As a result, the entries in B tend to be much larger.

The Micciancio Cryptosystem

In 2001, Micciancio proposed some major improvements of the speed and the security of GGH. In this scheme, the public key is of a Hermite Normal Form (HNF). Such a HNF basis is not only compact in storage requirements, it also seems to be more difficult to transform to a "good basis" compared to other bases. Furthermore, the HNF of a lattice (and hence the public key of the Micciancio cryptosystem) is unique and can be computed from any lattice basis in polynomial time. The HNF public keys gives space complexity advantages as the resulting public key is much smaller than those proposed by GGH. Rather than Babai's Round Off method as suggested by Goldreich et al., Micciancio suggested the use of Babai's Nearest-Plane method to address the CVP. However, implementations of this algorithm are extremely slow. It is possible however to adapt this cryptosystem to use Babai's Round-Off method and in doing so, much faster decryption speeds are seen, providing that the matrix inverse is precomputed.

Unfortunately, the storage requirement for this matrix inverse is extremely large and practicality is again limited.

Applications of Lattice based Cryptography

With the increase of varied computing paradigms, the necessity of getting their security definitions has become a true threat for the pc scientists. As technological services like Cloud Computing, Internet of Things, Quantum computation etc. demand highly encrypted software-defined networks for communications. In IoT, the normal cryptographic measures seem to fail because the IoT space demands larger number of keys. So as to handle this increased generation of the key by classical cryptographic measures demanded development of some standard lightweight cryptographic schemas with increased agility and performance. This development calls out for Lattice-based public key cryptosystem and hence becomes a neighborhood of interest for its implementation. Likewise, for cloud computing the channel or the software-defined network which it demands, got to have high agility and performance, should be energy-efficient and must be of low delay. This couldn't achieved by classical cryptosystems, which furthermore demands a replacement system, capable enough to run quite one cryptic algorithm with full agility and efficiency. After these diverse an application of Lattice-based cryptosystems, lattice cryptosystem is applied on areas where security is that the utmost priority.

GGH CRYPTOSYSTEM

Description of the System

In 1996, Oded Goldreich, Shafi Goldwasser, and Shai Halevi introduced a new Public key cryptographic system based on the hardness of solving CVP in a high dimension lattice called the GGH cryptosystem. Comparing with traditional cryptosystems such as RSA, ElGamal and Diffie-Hellman, the GGH cryptosystem is surprisingly simple but born with high performance taking advantage of matrix operations of modern computers. Besides, GGH is hard to break even in average case. Since the complexity of solving CVP has been proved to be NP-hard on average cases, the GGH cryptosystem is designed to be a novel encryption and decryption mechanism based on hardness of solving CVP.

GGH is the lattice-analog of the McEliece cryptosystem based on algebraic coding theory. In both schemes, a ciphertext is the addition of a random noise vector to a vector corresponding to the plaintext. The public key and the private key are two representations of the same object (a lattice for GGH, a linear code for McEliece). Their practical proposition of a cryptosystem was attacked and broken by Nguyen in 1999. However, the general idea is still viable. The Goldreich–Goldwasser–Halevi (GGH) cryptosystem is an asymmetric cryptosystem based on lattices. GGH cryptosystem makes use of the fact that the closest vector problem can be a hard problem. It uses a trapdoor one-way function that is relying on the difficulty of lattice reduction. The idea included in this trapdoor function is that, given any basis for a lattice, it is easy to generate a vector which is close to a lattice point, for example taking a lattice point and adding a small error vector. But returning from this erroneous vector to the original lattice point, a special basis is needed.

Algorithm

The cryptosystem depends on two parameters $n \in \mathbb{N}$, the dimension and $\sigma \in \mathbb{N}$ the security parameter. Given a target point and a lattice with two different bases, namely the *Private key* and the *Public key*. The Private key is a nearly orthogonal basis B_{good} and the Public key B_{bad} is a bad basis that is far away from being orthogonal. According to the Babai's rounding off algorithm, for the target point, the good basis B_{good} can find the correct closest lattice point with a high possibility, but B_{bad} cannot solve CVP in the lattice. In such way, the data will be transferred successfully with security.

Key Generation

To initiate a GGH cryptosystem, Party A begins with constructing a Private key, which will be kept secretly throughout the information exchanging process. In order to achieving this, he selects a full-column rank integer matrix:

$$R = k.I_n + Q$$

where $k = \sqrt{n.l}$, $l4$ and **Q** is a random perturbation matrix with entries from $\{-l, \dots, l\}$. The public key B was then obtained by applying sufficiently many elementary column operations to **R**.

Party A then randomly generates an integer n-by-n unimodular matrix **U**, which satisfies equation $\det(\mathbf{U}) = \pm 1$. To construct the unimodular matrix **U**, Party A can randomly generate a sequence of elementary matrices and multiply them together. Hence a new matrix B can be created by computing B = U.R where U is "random" unimodular matrix and $\mathbf{B}^{-1}$ is easily to be discovered. Then the integer matrix **B** can be chosen as the Public key and be published to audience.

Encryption

Now, assuming the message matrix as $m \in \mathbb{Z}^n$ and randomly chosen error matrix as $e \in \{\pm\sigma\}$, the cipher matrix c is calculated as below and Party A sends the following ciphertext to Party B: c=m.B+e.

Particularly they encoded message *m* to a vector e with coefficients $e_i = \{\pm 3\}$ which does not belong to the lattice. Then this encoded message is send through channel.

Decryption

Use the good basis to find the closest vector in the lattice of the encrypted ciphertext message *c*. The closest vector of the encrypted message c is the random vector *e*. To decrypt this cipher c, the calculations are performed according to the following equations:

$$round\left(c.R^{-1}\right) = round\left(\left(m.B+e\right)R^{-1}\right)$$

$$= m.U.R.R^{-1} + round\left(e.R^{-1}\right).$$

$$= m.U + round\left(e.R^{-1}\right)$$

The Babai's rounding technique will be used to remove the error term as it is a small value. Finally, Party B computes the original message m as follows: $\boldsymbol{m=m.U.U^{-1}}$.

The decryption process will work correctly when $\boldsymbol{round(e.R^{-1})=0.}$ The algorithm is shown in Table 3. below. In this process the value of n and σ are public parameters.

Table 1. The GGH Cryptosystem

Party A	Party B
Key Generation	
1. Choose a nearly orthogonal basis **R** as Private Key; 2. Choose an Unimodular matrix **U**; 3. Compute a Bad basis **B=R*U**; **4.** Publish **B** as the Public Key	
Encryption	
	1. Choose a message **m** 2. Choose an error vector $e \in \{\pm\sigma\}n$ 3. Use A's Public Key to encrypt m: **c=mB+e** 4. Send the ciphertext c to Party A
Decryption	
1. Use the Private Key R and Babai's rounding off algorithm to decrypt the closest vector of c by removing error vector. **2.** Compute round(**c*R^{-1}**) to get message.	

Flow Chart

See Figure 3.

Security

If a third person listened the ciphertext c the only basis available to him is the Public key B, which is a hardly orthogonal basis for the lattice L. Let consider it the task of determining the plaintext given only the ciphertext. Correctly performing this task amounts to solving an instance of CVP, for example, the eavesdropper, given only $c=mB+e$ needs to first find mB which the vector in the lattice is closest to c. And there is no known polynomial time algorithm to solve CVP exactly with bad basis, or to approximate it to within a polynomial factor. Therefore, the closest vector she decodes is far away from the exact closest point c. Hence, the plaintext decrypted is incorrect. It is easy to find the closest vector with a "good basis" but difficult to do so with a "bad basis". The original information m keeps safe.

Second note that by construction, the public basis B has high orthogonality defect and the private basis R has low orthogonality defect. Thus in order to determine the private key given only the public key, an eavesdropper would again need to solve an instance of hard problem. It is easy to compute a "bad basis" from a "good basis", but it is difficult to compute a "good basis" from a "bad basis".

Figure 3. Flowchart of GGH cryptosystem

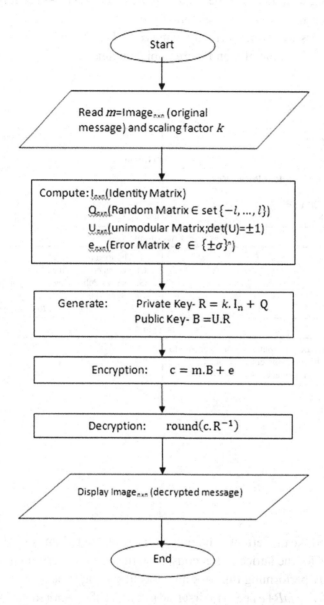

Example

This example taken a matrix of size 2x2 as input and run GGH Encryption and Decryption algorithm on it.

1. **Key Generation**

Let $L \subset R^2$ be the lattice with basis matrix R (Private key) $= \begin{pmatrix} 9 & -3 \\ 4 & 10 \end{pmatrix}$.

Public Key B = U*R $= \begin{pmatrix} -1 & 23 \\ 39 & 21 \end{pmatrix}$.

2.   **Encryption**

Let the message be m = $\begin{pmatrix} 0.7625 & 0.7273 \\ 0.5976 & 0.7315 \end{pmatrix}$ and take e = $\begin{pmatrix} -3 & 3 \\ -3 & 3 \end{pmatrix}$ (this is encryption with σ =

3). Then ciphertext will be: c = m.B + e = $\begin{vmatrix} 25.2358 & 35.5996 \\ 22.5207 & 32.9097 \end{vmatrix}$.

3.   **Decryption**

To decrypt, compute round(c.R^{-1}).

D=c.R^{-1} $\approx \begin{pmatrix} 0.7625 & 0.7273 \\ 0.5976 & 0.7315 \end{pmatrix}$.

Hence, the value of D = = m and we recover the original message.

ATTACKS

Computing a Private Key

In the first attack, third person uses the reduced basis B and simply run a lattice basis reduction algorithm to perform the same rounding off technique as Party A uses in the decryption procedure with the private basis R. The vector third person obtains will be an approximation to the correct message vector, and can be used as a starting point for an exhaustive search for the message. According to experiments cited in [4], in dimensions up to 80 this attack works well since the LLL algorithm tends to perform very well in practice, but in higher dimensions the attack quickly becomes infeasible since a measure of the work required grows exponentially with the dimension.

Computing Information about the Message

For the second attack we exploit the fact that $c=m.B+e$ where e is a vector with small entries. A naive attack is to try all values of the error vector e until $c-e$ lies in the image. A more subtle idea is to compute c and try to deduce possible values for some entries of $e.B^{-1}$. To defeat this attack one should not naively encode the message as a vector m $\in Z_n$. Instead, one should use an appropriate randomized padding scheme.

Nguyen's Attack

Phong Nguyen, in his paper showed some major flaw in the design of the GGH scheme. His "leaky remainder" attack exploited the specific form of the error vector, allowing recovering the plaintext remainders: $c + \sigma \equiv mB^{-1} \pmod{2\sigma}$. This simplified the CVP instance, making plaintext recovery tractable. The following are the weaknesses discovered by Nguyen:

Weakness 1: Short error vector

GGH error vectors are significantly shorter than the lattice vectors, making GGH CVP instances much easier than general CVP instances.

Weakness 2: Special form of error vector

The choice of the error vector $e \in \{\pm\sigma\}$ in the original GGH cryptosystem made it extremely vulnerable to attack. This $\sigma = (\sigma, \sigma,..., \sigma) \in Zn$ can reveal partial information about the plaintext.

Weakness 3: "Leaky Remainder" Attack

Nguyen noted that the error vector from the ciphertext could be remove with a well-chosen modulus. By adding σ to every element of the ciphertext, the error vector changes from $\{-\sigma, \sigma\}^n$ to $\{0, 2\sigma\}^n$. The error vector can then be completely removed by reducing modulo 2σ. The crucial observation is that if c is a GGH ciphertext then we can solve c + $\sigma \equiv$ mB^{-1} (mod 2σ) for m as $m_\circ$. The natural approach to resist Nguyen's attack is to choose error vectors with a more general range of entries (e.g.

$$e_j \in \left\{-\sigma, -\left(\sigma-1\right),...,-1,0,1,...,\sigma\right\} for 1 \leq j \leq n .$$

IMPROVISED METHODOLOGY

Description of the System

Even though the GGH cryptosystem may be provably secure, after careful analysis of it, we found that it has significant drawbacks, like, high space complexity with large public key size, information leakage about the original message by its ciphertext and randomly chosen short error vector. All these shortcomings of GGH scheme prevent its widespread adoption.

In improvised cryptosystem, we describe a simple technique that can be used to substantially reduce the public key and ciphertext size of kind of cryptosystem proposed by GGH using the Hermite Normal Form (HNF). Public key is generated as Hermite normal form of Private key.

To overcome the information leakage problem of GGH cryptosystem, the new cryptosystem uses pixel permutation method on cipherimage, produced by GGH encryption algorithm. The pixels of the ciphered image will be shuffled so that no information about the original message will be leaked from new generated cipherimage. We therefore formulate a new lattice-based cryptosystem which is more secure than the GGH cryptosystem. In addition with GGH Encryption and GGH Decryption function, new cryptosystem consist of two additional functions to improve the security of system. Encryption algorithm is consisting pixelPermutation() function and Decryption algorithm consisting of reconstruct() function.

In new cryptosystem a more general range of entries (e.g.

$$e \in \left\{-\sigma, -\left(\sigma-1\right),...,-1,0,1,...,\sigma\right\}$$

unlike $e \in \{\pm\sigma\}$ of error vectors are chosen to resist Nguyen's "leaky remainder" attack. The increased efficiency of the new cryptosystems allows the use of bigger values for the security parameter, while keeping the size of the key even below the smallest key size for which lattice cryptosystems were supposed to be hard to break.

We design this new scheme specifically to provide more security to user information while still maintaining a similar structure to existing cryptosystems. Specifically, this involved consideration in the design for encryption and decryption using "pixelPermutation" and "reconstruct" technique discussed later. This new cryptosystem is based on the work done by Goldreich et al. and Micciancio but is more secure and has lesser memory storage when implemented on common hardware platforms. Block diagram of Proposed scheme can be seen in Figure 4.

Figure 4. The block diagram of the Proposed Cryptosystem

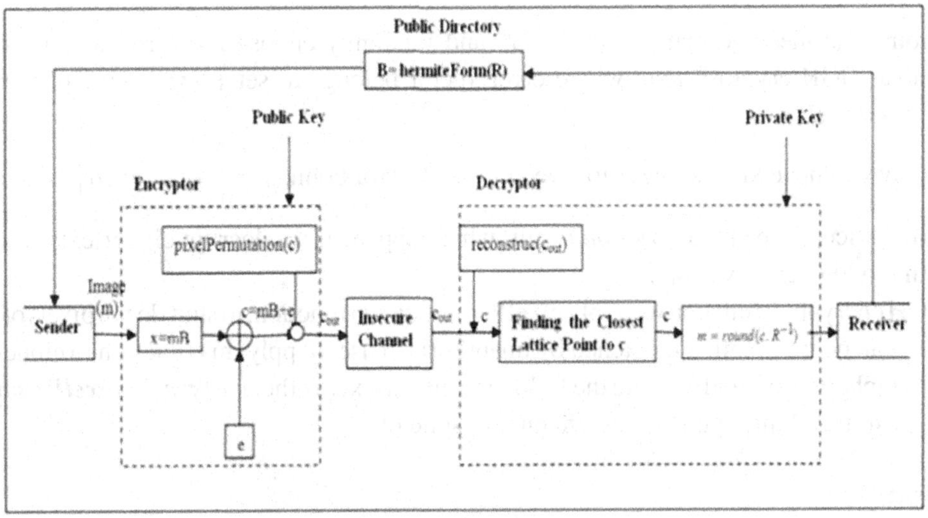

Algorithm

Proposed cryptosystem also depends on two parameters $n \in \mathbb{N}$ the dimension and $\sigma \in \mathbb{N}$ the security parameter. The Private key is a nearly orthogonal basis B_{good} and the Public Key B_{bad} is a bad basis that is far away from being orthogonal. B_{bad} is Hermite Normal Form of B_{good}. Encryption and Decryption algorithm of new cryptosystem is embedded with pixelPermutation() and reconstruct() functions respectively along with GGH encryption and decryption functions to prevent information leakage. In this way, the data will be transferred securely

Key Generation

The key generation process of Proposed cryptosystem is same as GGH cryptosystem. We begin with constructing a Private key, a full-column rank integer matrix: where , and **Q** is a random perturbation matrix with entries from .

We then compute the Hermite normal form of Private key **R** and get a unique Public key **B** of corresponding lattice. Hence a new matrix B can be created by computing

B = hermiteForm(R)

Then the integer matrix **B** published to audience.

Encryption

Now, assuming the message matrix as $m \in \mathbb{Z}^n$ and randomly choose the error vector from the set $\{-\sigma,...,\sigma$ unlike GGH cryptosystem, where error vector belongs to set $\{\pm\sigma\}$. The cipher matrix c is calculated as: $c=m.B+e$.

Particularly we encoded message m to a vector e with error bounds $= \left\{\frac{1}{2},1,2,4,8\right\}$, which does not belong to the lattice, to see the impact on result, what happens if we decrypt ciphertexts which are encrypted with too high error vectors.

After GGH encryption function we apply pixelPermutation() function, to shuffle the pixels of cipherimage so that it leak no information if listened by unauthorized user. Apply this function to ciphertext c and generate new ciphertext c$_{out}$ and we send the following ciphertext to other party: $c_{out}=pixelPermutation(c)$

Now, c_{out} will travel through insecure channel in spite of c.

Decryption

To decrypt the cipher c_{out} first reconstruct() function is applied on it to get the ciphertext c. This c_{rec} will be same as , which is generated in GGH encryption scheme.

$$c_{rec} = reconstruct\left(c_{out}\right).$$

Then to decrypt, the calculations are performed according to the following equations:

$$round\left(c_{rec}.R^{-1}\right) = round\left(\left(m.B+e\right)R^{-1}\right).$$

The Babai's rounding technique will be used to remove the error term $e.R^{-1}$ is it is a small value. The algorithm is shown in Table 4 below:

Table 2. The Proposed Cryptosystem

Party A	Party B
Key Generation	
5. Choose a nearly orthogonal basis **R** as Private Key; 6. Compute Bad basis **B=hermiteForm(R)** **7.** Publish **B** as the Public Key	
Encryption	
	5. Choose a message **m** 6. Choose an error vector **e** 7. Use A's Public Key to encrypt m: **c=mB+e** 8. Compute: $\mathbf{c_{out}}$**=pixelPermutation(c)** **9.** Send the ciphertext c_{out} to Party A
Decryption	
3. Reconstruct the cipher $\mathbf{c_{rec}}$**=reconstruct(**$\mathbf{c_{out}}$**)** 4. Compute round(c_{rec}*R^{-1}) to find the original message	

Flow Chart

See Figure 5.

Security

If a third person try to determine the plaintext given only the ciphertext with the help of the Public key B then there is no known polynomial time algorithm to solve CVP exactly, but in GGH some information about the original message get leaked from cipher *c* with the help of only public key. In proposed scheme, with the help of pixel permutation technique the pixels of the ciphertext *c* generated by GGH encryption algorithm, get shuffled and new ciphertext c_{out} is generated. Therefore, the closest vector the third person decodes from c_{out} is far away from the exact closest point *c* and leaks no information about the original message. The original information *m* keeps safe.

In GGH cryptosystem, any multiplication of a lattice basis with a unimodular matrix will produce a new basis that generates the same lattice. New cryptosystem uses a HNF basis, which is not only compact in storage requirements as will be shown in later sections of coming chapter. It is also provably the hardest basis to transform to a "good basis" compared to other bases . Furthermore, the HNF of a lattice (and hence the public key) is unique,

In new cryptosystem, it is no longer necessary to choose the error vector from the set $\{\pm\sigma\}$, but rather from the set $\{-\sigma,\ldots,\sigma$, which makes the system no longer vulnerable to Nguyen's attack.

Example

This example taken a matrix of size 2x2 as input message and run new Proposed Encryption and Decryption algorithm on it.

Figure 5. Flowchart of Proposed cryptosystem

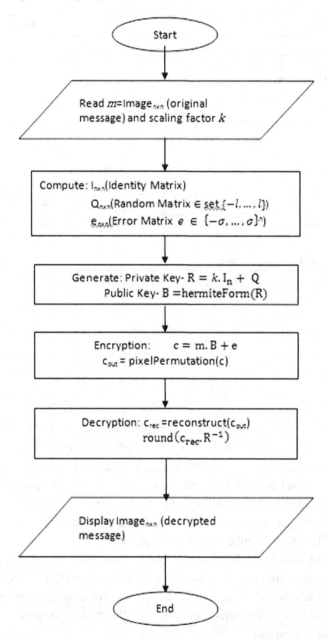

1.   Key Generation

Let $L \subset R^2$ be the lattice with basis matrix R

$$R(\text{Private key}) = \begin{pmatrix} 9 & -3 \\ 4 & 10 \end{pmatrix}.$$

Public Key $B = \text{hermiteForm}(R) = \begin{pmatrix} 1 & -23 \\ 0 & 102 \end{pmatrix}$.

2. Encryption

Let the message be $m = \begin{pmatrix} 0.7625 & 0.7273 \\ 0.5976 & 0.7315 \end{pmatrix}$ and take $e = \begin{pmatrix} 1 & -2 \\ -3 & 0 \end{pmatrix}$ (this is encryption with $\sigma = 3$). Then ciphertext will be:

$$c = m.B + e = \begin{pmatrix} 1.7625 & 54.6428 \\ -2.4024 & 60.8701 \end{pmatrix}.$$

Perform random permutation of ciphertext c and generate new cipher c_{out}

$$c_{out} = \text{pixelPermutation}(c) = \begin{pmatrix} 54.6428 & -2.4024 \\ 1.7625 & 60.8701 \end{pmatrix}.$$

3. Decryption

To decrypt, one first recover the actual ciphertext c out of c_{out} and then computes original message.

$$C_{rec} = \text{reconstruct}(c_{out}) = \begin{pmatrix} 1.7625 & 54.6428 \\ -2.4024 & 60.8701 \end{pmatrix}.$$

$$D = c_{rec}.R^{-1} \approx \begin{pmatrix} 0.7625 & 0.7273 \\ 0.5976 & 0.7315 \end{pmatrix}.$$

Hence, the value of $D == m$ and we recover the original message.

Limitation

- Despite of secure against all types of attack the proposed cryptosystem has significant time complexity drawback. As it uses HNF to produce Public key from Private Key to improve the storage complexity. Public key generation takes more time in improvised cryptosystem than GGH cryptosystem.
- The New scheme is proposed for squared grayscale images only.
- Due to additional functions in encryption and decryption algorithm of new scheme the time taken for execution also increases to some extent. Inclusion of these functions makes the scheme more secure and reasonably practical.

CONCLUSION AND FUTURE WORK

Conclusion

Lattice problems are interesting as it is based on the worst case scenario in the reduction of middle cases. The basic problems are NP-hard. Lattice problems are useful for signature and encryption programs and hash functions. Complete homomorphic encryption, many maps have important research areas in the field of quantum resistant processes. In this work, we have proposed a novel approach to prevent the "remaining leaky" attack of the GGH cryptosystem system. That is, to use the proposed new function to update the encryption phase text based on the HNF Community key and delete the new text using the new scripting function.

We first introduced the concepts of lattices and bases in a chapter. The GGH cryptosystem was then introduced in section 3. Theoretical schemes like lattices offer strong security proof but use impractically large key sizes for general use. The proposed approach was described in section 4 with GGH vulnerabilities solutions. And finally, we have completed the initial work. The proposed algorithm works much better locally and is safer than the GGH algorithm. The implementation has shown a very positive effect in terms of space complexity, with much better performance than traditional GGH methods. But the main generation of the proposed system was moving very slowly. Although the standard Hermite form is completely protected and works well in space, it is very expensive to calculate. We tested the effectiveness of the proposed scheme by encrypting and deleting values with vector errors and the results are as expected.

Future Work

The lattice function can be extended to several applications such as IoT, Embedded Devices, Cloud computing, etc. You can also upgrade to the slow-moving public key generation issue which has been a major problem. One good field where the use of lattices is mandatory is embedded devices. They only look at the credibility of the options and do not agree on who gets the call. Therefore, by simply interrupting the selection of all the system is often exploited. So the need for a cryptographic hashing algorithm arises. Similarly, by machine learning, AI and Neural Network where the whole system depends on the integrity of the choice. In addition, there is a wide range of Computer Networking and Web-Technology where encryption is the basic requirement for everything to work. The growing growth of technology and the many potential opportunities make us wonder where technology will go in the future. So you should encrypt our data / stuff into the best deal now. So we assume, this technology based on thigh-based cryptography will turn these threats into fantasy.

REFERENCES

Ajtai, M. (1998). The Shortest Vector Problem in L2 is NP-hard for Randomized Reductions. *Proc. thirtieth Annual ACM Symposium on Theory of Computing -STOC*, 10–19 10.1145/276698.276705

Babai, L. (1986). On Lovaśz lattice reduction and the nearest lattice point problem. *Combinatorica*, 6(1), 1–13. doi:10.1007/BF02579403

Bernstein, D. J., Buchmann, J., & Dahmen, E. (2009). *Post-Quantum Cryptography*. Springer. doi:10.1007/978-3-540-88702-7

Diffie, W., & Hellman, M. E. (1976). New Directions in Cryptography. *IEEE Transactions on Information Theory, 22*(6), 644–654. doi:10.1109/TIT.1976.1055638

Goldreich, O., Goldwasser, S., & Halevi, S. (1997). Public-key Cryptosystems from Lattice Reduction Problems. In *Proc. 17th Annual International Cryptology Conference on Advances in Cryptology (CRYPTO '97)*. Springer-Verlag.

Goldreich, O., Goldwasser, S., & Halevi. (1997). Eliminating decryption errors in the Ajtai-Dwork cryptosystem. *Lecture Notes in Computer Science, 1294*, 105–111.

Hooshmand, R. (2015). *Improving GGH Public Key Scheme Using Low Density Lattice Codes*. Available: https://eprint.iacr.org/2015/229

Kumar, V. (2014). *Text Encryption using Lattice-Based Cryptography. IOSR Journal of Computer Engineering* , 16.

McEliece, R. (1978). *A public-key cryptosystem based on algebraic number theory*. Technical report, DSN Progress Report 42-44, Jet Propulsion Laboratory.

Micciancio, D. (2001). Improving Lattice Based Cryptosystems Using the Hermite Normal Form. In Cryptography and Lattices. CaLC 2001, Lecture Notes in Computer Science, vol 2146. Springer. doi:10.1007/3-540-44670-2_11

Nguyen, P. Q. (1999). Cryptanalysis of the Goldreich-Goldwasser-Halevi Cryptosystem. *LNCS, 1666*, 288–304.

Paeng, S. H., Jung, B. E., & Ha, K. C. (2003). *A Lattice Based Public Key Cryptosystem Using Polynomial Representations. In Proc. Public Key Cryptography — PKC 2003* (Vol. 2567). Springer.

Plantard, T., Rose, M., & Susilo, W. (2009). Improvement of lattice-based cryptography using CRT. *Proc. QuantumComm'09*, 275-282.

Rose, M. (2011). *Lattice-Based Cryptography: A Practical Implementation* (M.Sc. thesis). School of Computer Science and Software Engineering, University of Wollongong, New South Wales, Australia.

Shor, P. W. (1994). Algorithms for quantum computation: discrete logarithms and factoring. *Proc. 35th Annual Symposium on Foundations of Computer Science*, 124-134. 10.1109/SFCS.1994.365700

Sokouti, M., Zakerolhosseini, A., & Sokouti, B. (2016). Medical Image Encryption: An Application for Improved Padding Based GGH Encryption Algorithm. *The Open Medical Informatics Journal, 10*(1), 11–22. doi:10.2174/1874431101610010011 PMID:27857824

Yoshino, M., & Kunihiro, N. (2012). Improving GGH cryptosystem for large error vector. *International Symposium on Information Theory and its Applications ISITA*, 416-420.

Chapter 7

Quantum Cryptography for Securing IoT–Based Healthcare Systems

Anand Sharma

iD https://orcid.org/0000-0002-9995-6226

Mody University of Science and Technology, Lakshmangarh, India

Alekha Parimal Bhatt

Capgemini IT India Pvt. Ltd., India

ABSTRACT

IoT-based healthcare is especially susceptible as many IoT devices are developed without keeping in mind the security issue. In addition, such smart devices may be connected to global networks to access anytime, anywhere. There are some security challenges like mobility, computational limitation, scalability, communication media, dynamic topology, and above all the data confidentiality in storage or in transmission. There are some security protocols and methodology which is used in IoT-based healthcare systems like steganography, AES cryptosystems, and RSA cryptographic techniques. Therefore, it is necessary to use quantum cryptography system to make sure the security, privacy, and integrity of the patient's data received and transmitted from IoT-based healthcare systems. Quantum cryptography is a very fascinating domain in cyber security that utilizes quantum mechanics to extend a cryptosystem that is supposed to be the unbreakable secure system.

1. INTRODUCTION

The proliferation of physical objects connecting to the Internet leads to a novel paradigm called "Internet of Things (IoT)."

The Internet of things is an emerging global Internet-based information infrastructure in which associated physical objects furnished with sensors, actuators, and processors communicate with one another to serve an important purpose. The 'thing' in Internet of Things can alluded as an individual or any device

DOI: 10.4018/978-1-7998-6677-0.ch007

Copyright © 2021, IGI Global. Copying or distributing in print or electronic forms without written permission of IGI Global is prohibited.

that has been relegated an IP address. The Internet of Things (IoT) is characterized as a paradigm which is presently situated as the true stage for ubiquitous sensing and customized service delivery. Internet of Things has been characterized by various authors, yet at the most crucial level it tends to be depicted as a network of devices connecting with one another by means of machine to machine (M2M) communication, empowering collection and exchange of data. It guarantees another data foundation wherein all items around us are associated with the Internet, having the ability to communicate with each other with minimal conscious interventions (Guo, Zhang, Yu et al, 2013). By its computing and networking capabilities, today the Internet has contacted pretty much every edge of the globe and is influencing human life in incomprehensible manners.

The Internet of Things (IoT) is being used in pretty much every part of life today, despite the fact that this reality is frequently obscure and not publicized. The fuse of IoT into regular procedures will keep on expanding. IoT permits individuals and devices to interface at whenever, and anyplace, with anything and anybody, in a perfect world are associated with a network to facilitate worldwide exchange to accomplish complex errands that require a high level of insight and intelligence and delivery of intelligent and relevant services (Perera et al., 2013). These IoT devices are outfitted with actuators, sensors, handsets, processors, transceivers and storage units. The IoT infrastructure comprises of heterogeneous, addressable and readable virtual and physical objects that can convey over internet, where every unit is skillful to produce or consume intelligent services. Lately, scientific advancement is estimated by smart sensor device that are introduced in the virtual and physical domain of IoT to go about as or for the benefit of individuals. With this innovative and progressive extension, it is presently workable for our day by day objects to know about our needs: what we like or need and when and where we need them.

Rather than an official meaning of IoT in 2016, NIST published an article titled "Networks of 'Things'" to quantify the shortfall of having an ordinary IoT definition (Voas, 2016). In that article, five natives were introduced for any network of "things." The primitives are sensors, aggregators, communication channels, *e*-Utilities and decision trigger.

A. Working of IoT

In a classical IoT system devices and services are the key component where they are establishing connection among them and change as per the requirement. In and IoT System first the data have been collected from device then it will be preprocessed and communicated for the intelligent decision or servie.

- Data Collection: The data is collected by actuators and sensor devices, which helps in communicating the physical world. There are a number of sensors are available for example The accelerometer - for motion sensing, gyroscope – for orientation, thermometer- for temperature, camera – for visual capturing, barometer- for atmospheric pressure, magnetometer – for magnetic fields detection, proximity sensor - for calculation of distance, chemical sensors- for chemical and biochemical substances
- Data Preprocessing: The data collected by the actuators and sensor devices then preprocessed at the specific sensor or some different proximate device. Sensors have to be process intelligently to derive valuable inferences from it.
- Data Communicaton: Now, after the processing of collected data, some intelligent action is required on the source inferences. The character of actions may be diverse. For making intelligent decision the processed information can be send to other smart devices or some server. The IoT

sensors' communication is mostly wireless since they are usually installed at different geographically locations. There are various methodologies by which the sensors are communicating for example Wireless Sensor Networks Near Field Communication, Bluetooth Low Energy, Zigbee, Low Power WiFi and so on.

B. Layered Architecture

As the IoT is collection of various heterogeneous device connected to each other, the connections and working of these devices is defined by the layered architecture. There are no single and final consensuses are available on layered architecture. There are many architecture have been proposed by many researches but the classical architecture is three-layered architecture (Mashal et al., 2015).

- Perception Layer: It is a physical, known as a device layer which is used for sensing and producing information. It works like people's ears, eyes and nose. It senses some physical parameters and has the responsibility for identifying other smart. The sensors are selected based on application requirement.
- Network layer: it is like transmission layer which is responsible to connect other smart things, devices, and network servers to each other. It acts like a bridge between application layer and perception layer. Its features are also used for processing and transmitting the data collected from the physical objects through sensors.
- Application Layer: It is responsible for the application service delivery to the user in which IoT has deployed. The application and services may be changeable for every application because services are depended on the sensors' collected information.

C. Integration with Big Data and Cloud Computing

As it has been seen in nearly all of the cases, a large generated data are mentioning the requirement of the big data system for storage, analysis and building intelligent services. And for the large storage and communication it is required to be associated with cloud computing. The layered architecture of the IoT gives communication among devices, network infrastructure and cloud infrastructure. Cloud computing and big data helps IoT for advance analytics and monitoring of IoT devices. In a cloud and big data enabled IoT infrastructure, applications can be deployed to process and analyze the collected data rapidly and make intelligent decisions instantly. Cloud computing working as a workplace for IoT and big data where IoT is the producing the data and big data is analyzing it for intelligent decisions. The union of the inter-disciplinary IoT, big data and cloud computing influence new possibilities of decision support system.

D. Healthcare Systems

Healthcare nowadays is costlier than ever, the population is on a rise and also new diseases are seen every few months. With the introduction of IoT integration with healthcare systems, now these facilities are lighter on the pockets and more accessible. The combining of IoT with healthcare systems has revolutionized the way our healthcare works. Healthcare services are now very easily accessible to each and every one, and also quality of life has improved significantly.

For countries like Africa with low access to medical facilities and sparse distribution of doctors, eHealth systems prove to be a boon.

Various advancements like real time monitoring of body vitals like blood pressure, sugar levels, heart rate, etc. to identify any risk factors, remote medical assistance, alerts reduce the cost of routine checkups significantly and help healthcare workers make informed decisions.

Where on one side eHealth systems have many benefits, technologies are usually prone to malicious attacks. There have been numerous incidents where IoT systems have been attacked and data have been stolen. Data security is a huge risk. As IoT devices transmit data in real time, cyber criminals can hack into the systems to steal the data like patient's ID and medical records and later use them to buy drugs and sell in a black market.

2. APPLICATIONS OF IoT

Along with the incredible enlargement in the variety and number of sensors connected to the Internet, the IoT has been emerging into Smart Home, smart cities, Smart vehicular networks, healthcare, Smart grid, agriculture, and other enterprises. Internet of Things is a technology trend that is on a sharp rise these days.

There are a huge number of areas and domains where intelligent applications and services have been developed. There are several applications of IoT in various different sectors. Some examples are given here:

A. Home Automation

The IoT applications have emerged in Smart homes. The sensors and communication technologies are making the home smarter. In smart home different sensors have been deployed which automate the application as per the users' requirement for automated and intelligent services. Turning OFF / ON any electronic gadget, intelligently and automatically is the best example of it. It also helps in automating the daily routine tasks. By using motion sensor it can provide security to the user. Temperature sensors and fire sensor can also be deployed for home automation.

Smart Home concept refers to the automation of different household appliances and devices. An example can be Air Conditioning system which can be controlled through SMS, when an SMS indicating ON is sent to the AC it turns on, similar for turning it off. Another example is smart lighting systems which can adjust the brightness, color intensity, etc. of the lights according to the weather, mood, etc.

B. Smart City

A city can be a smart city by deploying the IoT applications and services like smart transportation system- in which the traffic lights can be managed by sensors and their intelligent processing, smart parking system- in which the free space for parking is checked while entering, Smart Water Systems- to deal with water scarcity and intelligent distribution of water and waste management-monitoring of environment.

In traffic management smart cameras are installed on the traffic signals which can detect if someone is violating the traffic rules (like exceeding the speed limit, or travelling without helmet on 2-wheeler vehicle), capture their image, and search up the particular person's details using the license plate and he/she has to pay the due fine. This method accommodates for the absence of traffic inspectors on the traffic signals.

C. Smart Grid

The IoT enabled power grids are getting intelligent and smart enough to make the power system as smart grid. To make the generation, transmission, distribution and conservation smarter the smart grid utilized the intelligence at each and every step.

D. Supply Chain

IoT helps to abridge real life procedure in enterprises, commerce and their managerial systems (Ferreira et al., 2010). The goods like raw materials, packaged product and intermediate product in the supply chain can be easily tracked by the IoT enabled tracking systems from the place of manufacture industries to the distributor.

E. Human Life and Entertainment

Entertainment plays a key role in people's life. There are many application and services that keep tracking the human activities. "Opportunistic IoT" (Guo, Zhang, Wang et al, 2013) refers to data sharing among gadhets based on availability and movement of contacts. Personal gadgets like wearables, mobile phones and tablets have sensing and transmission capabilities. Individuals' can search and communicate among themselves. "Circle Sense" (Liang & Cao, 2013) is an application, utilizing various types of sensors data to detect the social activities of individual. There is another IoT based technology "Affective computing" (Picard & Picard, 1997), which recognizes, stimulates, understands and responds to the human beings emotions "Logmusic" (Lee & Cho, 2014), is an entertainment application, which recommends music depending upon the time, weather and location.

F. Smart Agriculture and Environment

Some parameters such as humidity, soil information and temperature are imperative for agricultural development. Farmers are using sensors to measure such parameters in the field.

Greenhouses Production (Zhao et al., 2010) is an service of IoT in agriculture for automated irrigation. Environmental parameters like humidity, temperature, and soil information, are collected in run time and forwarded to a application server for analysis. The intelligent results are then utilized to get better yield and crop quality.

G. Baby Monitors

Baby monitoring systems are very essential these days where both the parents are working. This system is integrated with camera, voice module, and artificial intelligence which can monitor the baby's surroundings and can alert the parents on the mobile application of something is not right.

H. Wearables

Wearables are very trending application of IoT. These are devices that are mostly integrated with watches (smart watches) or are standalone as fitness bands. These devices are capable to measuring and monitoring parameters like heart rate, step counts, calories burnt, etc. Also, these devices can be paired with smart phones to control the smart phones from smart watches.

I. Healthcare

IoT devices can be integrated with healthcare services to make them more fast and accessible. Examples can be devices that continuously transmit high risk patient data to the hospitals. This can be very important in monitoring the health of patients that suffer from heart diseases, hypertension or other chronic illness. If the device senses that the patient's body vitals are below a certain level, it can trigger an alert to the relatives and call an emergency service like ambulance. Also data collection can be done for research and analysis.

J. Smart Cars

Smart cars refer to the cars that have a wide-ranging network of many sensors, embedded software, and antennas. These help in making decisions regarding speed, accuracy, and avoid accidents on the road. Also, these cars are further being developed into autonomous vehicles where there will be no human intervention required to drive the car.

3. IoT IN HEALTHCARE

Healthcare is an indispensable part of human life. Regrettably, the gradually increase in populace and the associated increase in sickness is introduced noteworthy sprain on healthcare systems. Obviously, a resolution is necessary to decrease the strain on healthcare systems at the same time providing high-quality treatment and care to patients. Research in this area has shown that the IoT has a prospective resolution to lessen the pressures on healthcare systems. In this section, the IoT in healthcare system is highlighted and explored.

A. IoT Sensors for Healthcare

The IoT has been recognized as a key module of a healthcare system founded on such developments of sensors or devices which can sense, assess and monitor the various medical parameters in the body (Bui & Zorzi, 2011). These IoT enabled healthcare sensors can aspire at a patient's health monitoring when they are away from hospital. Afterward, they can present real time data to the doctor, patient, or the relatives. Mc Grath and Scanaill (McGrath & Scanaill, 2013) have shown the variety of sensors that can be used for monitoring. There are various wearable sensor devices available which are ready with medical sensors that are competent of sensing diverse parameters like the pulse, heart rate, body temperature, blood pressure and respiration (Pantelopoulos & Bourbakis, 2010).

- Pulse Sensors
Possibly the usual read imperative sign, pulse can be utilizes to detect a huge assortment of crisis circumstances, like pulmonary embolisms, cardiac arrest, and vasovagal syncope. Pulse sensor has been broadly researched, for both the purposes, medical and fitness tracking.

- Blood Pressure
BP (Blood pressure) is often measured beside the other medical parameters. a known risk factor of high BP is hypertension for cardiovascular disease, including heart attack.

- Body Temperature Sensors
The next vital sign is body heat temperature, which might be utilized to identify fevers, heat stroke, hypothermia and so on. As, body temperature is a helpful diagnostics measure that would be incorporated in a IoT based healthcare system.

- Respiratory Rate Sensors
Next important sense is respiratory rate, the breaths count per minute. Because to the significance of respiration, many researchers have developed various sensors. Monitoring respiration might aid in the recognition of circumstances like asthma attacks, apnea episodes, tuberculosis, lung cancer and so on.

- Pulse Oximetry Sensors
It sense the oxygen level in the blood. Like blood oxygen, blood pressure level is not a fundamental sign, but does provide an indication of respiratory system and can aid in diagnostics of hypoxia conditions.

- Neural Sensors
It is used for sensing signals from neurons in the brain to understand the brain state and train it for improved concentration and focus. The neurons electronically communicate and generate electric field, which can be measured as frequencies. Further, based on the frequency, waves may be classified into alpha, beta, gamma, theta, and delta waves. The brain is wandering in thoughts or calm, can be detected based on brain wave. This is called as neurofeedback (Gruzelier, 2014), which can be taken in real time and can be utilized to train the brain to mange stress, focus, and encompass better mental health.

B. IoT Sensor to aid

- Hearables
Hearables are hearing aid devices which have completely changed the way people who suffer from hearing loss relate with the outside world. It has the provisions to filter, even out and append layers to real-world sounds so that the people with hearing loss can get real life hearing experience.

- Ingestible sensors
These are special pills which have sensors embedded in them. When these pills are ingested, they can monitor our body from the inside. It can monitor whether the patient has taken the medicine

and what effects the medicine is having in the patient's body. It is a boon for patients with ailments like diabetes, blood pressure, heart diseases.

- Mood elevating devices
  These are mood improving devices which help in enhancing our mood. These devices can be worn over our head and they can send soothing currents to our brain which can help in releasing of calming chemicals thereby elevating the mood.

- Medical assistance through drones
  Drones can be used for emergency services. First aid kits can be delivered through drones at any specified location in minimum time.

- Computer vision
  This technology helps the visually impaired people to move around while detecting and helping them avoid the obstacles.

- Body vitals charting
  These devices are implants on the patient's body and they can monitor parameters like blood pressure, heart rate, sugar levels, etc. This helps the medical professionals by saving a lot of time. It can also help the patient by saving their visits to the doctor just to get these vitals measured. The doctors can get routine updates and can prescribe the medicines to the patients accordingly. Also, when the patient is showing some danger signs the doctor can initiate emergency procedures and send ambulance for the patient to reach the hospital on time.

C. IoT Solutions for Healthcare

The IoT has the potential and plays an important role to transform healthcare systems in a variety of healthcare applications, from supervision of chronic diseases, preventing disease to make hospital network smarter. The IoT based healthcare systems includes clinics, hospitals and other care amenities which sense, collect, and use data by combining the major business and technical trends of automation, mobility and data analytics to get better patient care delivery. The data collected from these IoT based healthcare devices and sensors can then be analyzed by the health care organization for the following purposes.

- Enhanced patient care
  Patients who requires close attention could be closely monitored by offering novel or improve care services and delivery using IoT-driven sensing. The medical sensors collect various parameters and utilize cloud server to store and analyze the information and revert intelligent decision to healthworker for further care.

- Personalized patient care
  By Learning more about patients' preferences and requirements concurrently enhance the quality of personalized care and experience care through steady attention.

- Optimize patient care
  The collected data can be utilized to develop new solutions and services that improve efficiency and reduces the operating cost by eliminating the requirement for a health-worker to vigorously engage in data collection and analysis

- Remote monitoring
  There are individuals' who don't have access to healthcare may suffer. But tinny, powerful IoT sensors are making it possible to those individuals'. These systems can be utilized to capture patient medical data, analyze the data and then share it with health-worker who can give proper medical recommendations.

- Early prevention / intervention
  Healthy people could take advantage of IoT- based healthcare system by monitoring their daily health parameters and activities. For example, a senior citizen who is living alone, can detect an interruption in everyday activity or fall and report it to family members or emergency responders. For other example, an athlete such as a biker or hiker could benefit from such a solution at any age.

- Make hospital networks smarter
  by actively monitoring the significant infrastructure, deployment of information technology and automating the healthcare system the hospital network can be made smarter.

4. IoT DEPLOYMENT ISSUES IN HEALTHCARE SYSTEMS

IoT develops an inter-connected environment of heterogeneous objects and platforms by dealing both physical and virtual world together. This section covers the challenges which has been faced while IoT deployment in healthcare systems. (Chaqfeh & Mohamed, 2012; Razzaque et al., 2016).

A. Interoperability and Compatibility

As IoT is being considered a collection of heterogeneous device and platforms, there is an issue regarding interoperability. The deployment of different software and hardware component may not work properly. It is depended on whether the correct component has been chosen, the component has the proper reliability and the specification and infrastructure of the system.

B. Scalability

This concern started from an expectation that a huge amount of devices are communicated as a part of the system. The services to connect all of them are frequently comparatively economical and therefore make a chance to functionality inflate. That makes complexity to increase gradually, causing intricacy for checking and performance.

C. Measurement

By the lack of IoT measures and metrics it is difficult to deploy IoT-based healthcare system. Measures and metrics are the key factors. There are only few measures and metrics available to integrators and adopters.

D. Synchronization

This concern generated by the distributed computing behavior of IoT systems. The distributed computing system has different activity and computations happening concurrently. In healthcare system there can be huge activities and computations occurring simultaneously, and those activities and computations must require some synchronization.

E. Excessive Data

The anxiety is irresistible amounts of data that get produced, collected and processed in a system. It is essential to analyze all data to make an intelligent decision. Mostly IoT systems have a rapidly and dynamic workflow. There is a possibility to have huge inputs sources such as sensor devices, peripheral databases, the clouds, and other outside subsystems. The likelihood of not providing the integrity of huge data is a big concern.

F. Design Complexity

IoT based healthcare faces a foremost measure because of design complexity for both its network as well as applications. The applications or services must be with lesser complexity and must not need additional knowledge for activities by its users.

5. SECURITY IN IoT BASED HEALTHCARE SYSTEMS

With the beginning IoT applications are typically related to individuals' personal life. In IoT based healthcare systems, the exchange of medical data and information becomes a daily routine. Due to the advancement, security and privacy are major concern for all types of IoT applications (Sharma et al., 2017). For example, medical data might be theft, deleted, tampered, or insecurely transmitted, permitting it to be used by adverse parties. Therefore, security and integrity of the medically sensetive data issues need to be addressed in all such IoT systems. This can be achieved by classical cryptography approach depending on the requirements and needs of an application. The system should have been developed with theses cryptographically mechanisms to guarantee the issues and integrity of patient's data, along with user authentication and access control mechanism. Security management of internal threats and policing are also required as security mechanism (Kamm¨uller et al., 2017).

A. Vulnerabilities in IoT Based Healthcare Systems

Like classical information security, IoT security is not a small problem, it requires the mechanism to counter this problem. Utilization of different applicability and difference in deployment mode, the privacy and security are of extremely required. As an alternative, it should be predictable that the security issue of IoT is based upon standardization. Mostly the threats occur because of insufficient mechanism of security feature. Some vulnerability is there that stay undetected due to the inattention of security mechanism (Li et al., 2016). These Vulnerabilities are explored on the basis of attack mode and assessment of application, hardware, protocol, organization or software (Amit et al., 2013).

- Insecure protocols
- Insecure infrastructure
- Inefficient data encryption and transport
- Common managing interface
- Firmware insecurity
- XSS (Cross-site scripting)
- Unauthenticated scans
- Process isolation
- User policies and patching

These are some example by the exploration on loopholes and vulnerabilities at the different level of IoT-based healthcare systems.

B. Security Frameworks for IoT Based Healthcare Systems

Here in this section the various security frameworks have been explored.(Park & Shin, 2017) (Ma et al., 2018).

- Encryption and Hashed Based Security
  As the classical information security there must be some mechanism to provide the security in IoT system. In the system the information is travelling through insecure channels also, for that purpose some encryption and hash function based mechanism is required to secure information from the attackers.

- Access Control and Authorization-based Mechanisms
  As the IoT has a huge number of sensors and devices. These sensors require an identity for authorization and accessibility to communicate among themselves. Consequently, support and security of those devices is subjected to the management of personal data as well particular services This type of mechanism provides securing the users by limiting the control over the usability of components and services. The strength of this mechanism depends upon the novelty of architecture were the devices dependent on other devices to connect and communicate.

- Secure Authentication-based Framework

Authentication of the devices and users is of extremely important and crucial. All the services and data are to be given to authenticated users only. The authentication guarantees the safety of authenticated and legitimate users by giving a safe communication mode.

- Risk-Assessment-based Adaptive Framework
  A framework that is obliging to decrease the security challenges is a Risk-Assessment-based Adaptive Framework. It observes the complete system with regular intervals to identification of potential conflicting and to find changes through detection modeling. These frameworks guesses the attack type to pre-identify any potential risks and predicts the loss in leveraging services.

- Services-based Framework
  Security of a network has been affected by the service type. Some of the services require light-frameworks while others require quick processing frameworks

- Reputation and Anomaly Detection Based Mechanism
  To detect the misbehavior of user and Identification of false users or services, in an IoT system, collaboration of nodes mechanism is proposed. It is accountability of security mechanism to identify communities and users by the maintenance of reputation table and the watchdog mechanism. such a classified mechanism are executed by inspection the correctness of a user or device against the predefined policies of precise operations.

In this section a number of security mechanisms have been explored but due to the advancement in computing power at the adversary side, these security mechanisms are easily breakable. For this reason, It is required that the deployment of IoT system is done in ultra-reliable formations. Further, such cryptographic protocols are required by which the security implications, assessment, and threat modeling can be done against adversary during the functioning of IoT devices. For that purpose the quantum cryptography is deployed in IoT based healthcare system.

C. Security Breaches in IoT Based Healthcare Systems

These days, the networks are globally extended and information is sent from many devices to many other. Information exchange has increased significantly. Important data and information are now being stored in devices and are transmitted through various channels to various locations.

As information plays such a fundamental role, the computer systems are being targeted by the cyber criminals to either steal the crucial information or to disturb the significant information system for some personal gain. Information channels are also being targeted the same way.

Classical cryptographic algorithms provide a set of techniques to make sure that the malicious intentions of the cyber criminals are disillusioned and in turn ensure that the actual end users have access to all the information in an uninterrupted manner. Here in this section the authors discuss the ways in which security can be compromised in healthcare systems working with IoT systems/devices.

There have been numerous security breaches when IoT devices are used in healthcare systems. The main reasons why IoT devices are so vulnerable to these breaches are:

- IoT devices are developed on obsolete software and old versions of operating systems that make them more prone to attack.
- IoT devices are more progressively storing and collecting large amounts of data due to which they are an attractive and easy target for cyber criminals.
- IoT devices act as a straightforward entry point for attackers wanting to move across across an IT network and get access to more critical information. Another way the systems can be attacked is by shutting them down altogether causing a heavy loss to the organization.

Healthcare data security breaches often render highly critical information, from personally identifiable information such as ID numbers, names, and patients' medical histories.

The IoT devices used in healthcare operate on very low resources, low power, limited computational memory and the security mechanisms have to be integrated within these limitations which are a tough task and hence complexity has increased.

These days medical equipments like MRI machines, Sonography machines are connected to a network to transfer the reports and images. Cyber criminals can hack the systems easily or attack the systems with ransom ware as these systems generally use older, less secure versions of operating systems. Medical equipments combined with IoT are the most vulnerable devices for cyber attacks as compared to all the other IoT devices.

The healthcare devices in the previous section can be hacked as:

- Hearables can be hacked to transmit wrong signals which could lead to distress to the person wearing them.
- If ingestible sensors are attacked that may lead to very bad consequences as it may lead to triggering wrong medicines at the wrong position inside the body.
- Medical drones can be hacked to change the route so that emergency help doesn't reach the patient in time
- Body vitals charting devices can be hacked and the transmitted information can be intercepted and used for wrongful purposes.

D. Classical Cryptography Techniques and their Disadvantages

- Steganography

Steganography is a cryptographic technique which is used to hide the content by embedding it in something else giving the notion that no content is present at all. In an image various parameters like pixel values, brightness, and filter settings can be changed in order to encode some information in it. The person seeing the image can never make out that there is some hidden information in the image.

In medical systems, electronic patient records can be embedded in images and stored/transferred with a good level of security.

Loophole in Steganography: cyber criminals can intercept the images and replace them with malicious images which when accessed by anyone can infect their device with virus or ransomware. Cyber criminals will put more prominence on making it tough to detect and trace the malware back to its origin.

- DES (Data Encryption Standard) Algorithm

DES is a symmetric block cipher cryptographic approach. The data blocks are encrypted in size of 64 bits. The encryption and decryption key has 56 bit. Initially the key consists of 64 bits but every 8th bit is removed (not used by encryption algorithm) making it 56 bits long. The algorithm works as: initially the 64 bit plaintext goes through a preliminary permutation that shuffles the bits to produce the permitted output. Output of the final round is of 64 bits that are a function of input plain text and key. The left and right halves of input are swapped to produce another output. Finally this output is passed through inverse permutation (used before) to get a 64 bit cipher text. After that for each round, a subkey Ri is created by combination of left circular shift and permutation. Data block size is 64 bit; the rounds will be 16. Hence, it will use dissimilar subkeys for each round. And the number of subkeys will be 16.

Loophole in DES algorithm: It is possible to break this algorithm with rigorous brute force attack on modern processors using parallel processing capabilities, so this algorithm is not used anymore for any crucial systems.

- AES (Advanced Encryption Standard) Algorithm

AES algorithm is a replacement of the DES algorithm. It is also a symmetric block cipher cryptographic algorithm. The data blocks are encrypted in size of 128 bits. Keys can be of 128, or 192, or 256 bits. AES treats 128 bits plaintext as 16 bytes data blocks. Number of rounds depends upon the size of key: 128 bits, 10 rounds; 192 bits, 14 rounds; 256 bits, 14 rounds.

The algorithm works as:

The 16 bytes of input is substituted according to a fixed table. The output is a matrix of size 4x4. Each row is then shifted to left: don't shift the first row, shift 2nd row by 1, shift 3rd row by 2, shift 4th row by 3. Now columns are mixed using a mathematical function which takes one column as input and outputs a transformed column. Now the 128 bits (16 bytes) are XORed with 128 bits of key. The process is repeated for the required number of rounds.

Loophole in AES algorithm: It uses algebraic structures that are too simple and every block is encrypted in the same fashion. This can be a very big advantage for a hacker if he/she decodes the pattern of encryption.

- RSA (Rivest–Shamir–Adleman) Algorithm

RSA algorithm is an asymmetric cryptographic algorithm. It consists of two keys: private key and public key. The public key is given to everyone whereas the private key is kept with the client who decrypts the message. The public key consists of 2 numbers in which one is a multiplication of a very large prime numbers. The private key is also determined from the same 2 prime numbers. The only way these keys can be compromised is if someone can factor the large number. The strength of encryption increases exponentially with the size of numbers.

Loophole in RSA algorithm: the basic loophole in this algorithm is that the security can be compromised if the numbers are factorized and prime numbers are determined. But if the numbers are very large it can be a very cumbersome task for a classical computer. So RSA is considered to be very secure. But we will see in further topics how this loophole can be exploited to break this secure crypto algorithm.

6. QUANTUM CRYPTOGRAPHY

Cryptography is known as a scientific approach of secret message sharing. It is used to develop and execute techniques of private message sharing between two parties along with the presence of a third party. Further the Quantum cryptography (QC) is one of the most vigorous cryptographic approaches consists on the sharing of a common secret key by using the polarization of photon with a secure channel between the parties; QC is depended upon consistent and fundamental of quantum mechanics principles. The method shows that the level of security is depending upon complexity of the key and the protection of the used channel and not the complexity of the algorithm's process. QC concerned in 20th century, is depended on quantum mechanics principle and on the principle of photon polarization and Heisenberg Uncertainty principle.

Heisenberg's uncertainty principle says that it is nearly not possible to measure the quantum state without disturbing the system. That can only be measured in a specific measurement time and with a particular polarization. This concept is a key factor in opposing the adversary attempt in a system which is QC enabled.

The second important principle of QC is photon polarization. It describes that the photon particle can be oriented or polarized in a particular direction so that a filter can detect the said photon in a particular polarization else it will be destroyed.

In QC, 'qubit' is known as a bit of quantum information(Bhatt et al., 2018). In QC the photon is characterize based upon the polarization plane, ranging from 0° to 180°with horizontal and vertical orientation.

The QC was developed by C. H. Bennet and G.Brassard in 1984 as fraction of a study between information and physics(Bennett & Brassard, 1984). It is the unstoppable photons associated with Heisenberg Uncertainty principle that makes QC a tempting option for guarantee the security of data.

QC does not send or receive any message signal in its place it is only utilized to generate and for distribution of key. The key generation is depending upon the how and how much photon have been received by a recipient [25

The way the private key cryptosystems work is based on sharing of private keys between the sending and receiving parties so that the message can be encrypted and decrypted correctly. Let the sending party be 'A' and receiving party be 'B'. 'A' encode the message with a private key and sends the message to 'B'. Now, 'B' will need the private key 'A' used in order to decrypt the message. Here comes the main issue: how to exchange the keys so that they are not intercepted by a malicious eavesdropper and used to read the message? Here, the concept of Quantum Cryptography comes into use. Let's see how:

We have been using classical computers everyday for our daily tasks and experiencing its benefits in several ways. However, there are some challenges that are beyond the scope of classical computers to solve as they don't have enough computing power and resources. So, to solve some of those problems, we can use Quantum Computers.

Our classical computers rely on 0 and 1 bits to store and maneuver data and information, whereas Quantum computers use Quantum bits (or, Qubits) derived from the quantum mechanical laws to work with data.

Qubits can be in a coherent superposition of multiple states simultaneously. And the superposition can be broken in 0 or 1 if measured.

Quantum Cryptography is a field of cryptography that uses the laws of Quantum mechanics to develop a system that has the maximum security. No one can intercept the system without getting noticed by either of the parties involved in the transfer of secure data. This property of Quantum mechanics is based on several facts such as:

- The particles are uncertain in nature and exist as a superposition of two or more valid states.
- Photons are generated randomly in one of two quantum states.
- Quantum property can never be measured without disturbing or changing it.
- Only some of the properties of a particle can be cloned, not the whole particle.

Quantum Entanglement is another property which plays an important role in Quantum Cryptography. Entanglement of particles describes a relationship among their primary properties. Quantum Entanglement occurs when two particles become inseparably linked and whatever changes happen to one particle immediately affects the other particle regardless of the distance they are separated by. Entanglement is broken when entangles particles decohere through interaction with environment like measurement through outside interception. This property can help us detect if anyone is maliciously intercepting the network.

Quantum cryptographic systems also use the well known Heisenberg Uncertainty Principle which says that measuring a Quantum system disturbs it and gives incomplete information about the system. This in turn alerts the users of some kind of eavesdropping on the communication channel.

One of the most common cryptographic algorithms today (RSA algorithm) uses the property of prime factorization of large numbers to derive the keys. Factorizing large numbers is a very cumbersome and time taking task for the classical computers which can very easily be accomplished by the quantum computers using the Shor's algorithm.

A. Shor's Algorithm

Shor's algorithm is a quantum approach for factoring a large number N. It has $O((\log N)^3)$ time complexity and $O(\log N)$ space complexity.

Current cryptographic algorithms like RSA work on a basic principle where the key is a multiplication of 2 very large prime numbers. No classical algorithm exists yet which can solve the factorization of large numbers in polynomial time. So currently RSA is believed to be unbreakable.

Shor's algorithm is probabilistic in nature. It generates the accurate answer with a good probability and repetition of the algorithm improves the performance.

It works on 3 principles:

- Modular arithmetic
- Parallelism in Quantum computers
- Quantum Fourier Transform (QFT)

7. QUANTUM KEY DISTRIBUTION

Quantum Key Distribution is secure method of communication which is based on the laws of Quantum mechanics. Using QKD, the parties involved in information exchange can produce a random private key which is only known to them, and use that for encryption and decryption of messages to be transferred.

There are various QKD protocol developed by the researchers. Some are using single state polarization and some are entangled photon to generate the secret key. Because of the need of channel's security to keep the channel secure from attackers, the QKD with BB84 protocol is utilized. The QKD approach can transmit over 144 Km trough free space when it is executed in 5G-IoT [26]. Additionally, this protocol includes two various kinds of channels which can be utilized in a 5G wireless communication [27]: the main sort is the Quantum channel and its job is the exchange of the regular polarization of light's key, and the second sort is the ordinary channel which empowers the communication between the two parties and the exchange of the encoded data.

Subsequently, the QKD doesn't avoid Man in the middle attack, so the adversary can use spoofing to mask himself as an authorized collector at that point can peruse the traded information, however with the deployment of some authentication techniques, for example, counter based it can be prevented [28].

An important quantum phenomenon that QKD uses is the ability to detect the eavesdropper due to disturbance in quantum system because of the measurement of the photons. It also uses the phenomenon of Quantum Entanglement and Quantum Superposition to transfer the information securely over a communication channel.

Quantum Entanglement is the phenomenon where the particles have a relationship between their fundamental properties. They are governed by the same wave function and the changes occurring in one particle are reflected in a complementary (opposite in nature) way to the other particle.

Quantum Superposition is a phenomenon where two or more Quantum states can be added to produce a new Quantum state that will be valid. Conversely, every Quantum state can be represented as a superposition of two or more valid and distinct Quantum states.

Let us assume two parties: Alice and Bob. Let Alice be the sender and Bob be the receiver. In QKD the information is usually encoded in single photons.

The protocol described below was developed by Charles Bennett and Gilles Brassard in 1984 and hence this protocol is famously known as the BB84 protocol.

Alice can choose to encode the bit sequences in one of the following polarizations: horizontal polarization, vertical polarization, +45° or -45°. The horizontal and vertical polarizations are called as rectilinear schemes, the +45° and -45° polarizations are called as diagonal schemes. The horizontal and +45° represents the binary bit 1 and the vertical and -45° represents the binary bit 0. Here, when an external attempt to intercept is made the photon polarizations change resulting in change in the final measurements, so intruder is detected.

Alice uses the four polarizations randomly while sending the photon stream to Bob. The photons reach Bob and he then uses either rectilinear (+) or diagonal (X) bases to read the polarizations of the photons. Bob doesn't know the bases Alice used and hence he randomly guesses any one of the beam splitters- rectilinear or diagonal. Now after all the photos have been sent Bob tells Alice (thorugh a public channel) which bases he has used for photon measurement and Alice compares them with the bases she used while sending the photons. The photons measured by Bob using the wrong base are discarded and the other ones are kept and these photons become the key for communication. Finally Alice and Bob cross check their keys by adding the bits; both should either get an odd calculation or even calculation.

This key can only be used once. Hence it is called one-time-pad (OTP).

Now if there was any eavesdropper in Alice and Bob's communication, he would have measured the photons and once measured the photon states will have changed. One can never read/measure a photon and just forward it without any changes without being detected, so Alice and Bob will know that security has been compromised.

The mechanism described above can be depicted as follows:

Table 1. Quantum Key Distribution Protocol

Alice's bit sequence	1	0	1	1	0	0	1	1	0	0	1	1	1	0
Bob's detection	+	X	+	+	X	X	+	+	X	+	X	X	+	+
Bob's measurements	1	0	0	1	0	0	1	1	0	0	0	1	0	0
Key	1	- -	- -	1	0	0	- -	1	0	0	- -	1	- -	0

There is another very famous Quantum Cryptography protocol developed by Artur Ekert in 1991 known as the E91 protocol. This protocol uses the entangled photon pairs to secure the communication channel. The entangled pairs of photons are created and distributed between Alice and Bob such that both of them get either of the photon from the entangled pair. When Alice and Bob measure the photons with vertical or horizontal bases they get the same answers with 100 percent probability. Also when they both use complementary bases they will get the same answers with the same 100 percent probability. But the results are random and Alice can never make out whether Bob has vertical polarization or horizontal polarization. When the eavesdropper tries to intercept and measure the photons the polarization gets disturbed and this can be detected by Alice and Bob. So this is also a secure protocol that will prevent interception in communication channel.

8. QC IN IOT-BASED HEALTHCARE SYSTEMS

IoT based healthcare has many applications as already discussed in the previous sections. Healthcare is a very critical field of application where very important data are transmitted from one device to the other[29]. Unfortunately this is the field with the least secure connections and networks. If cyber criminals get hold of these data records they can exploit them in various different malicious ways. If a patient's health record gets leaked to a cyber criminal it can lead to identity theft, insurance fraud, wrongful acquisition of drugs and selling in black market, etc. So it is very important to protect these data.

As we saw in previous sections that classical cryptography is not 100 percent secure and unbreakable. Quantum cryptography can break the classical algorithms quite easily and all the secure data can be leaked easily[30]. So, to prevent this from happening we can apply the Quantum cryptography protocols in the medical devices and equipments.

Devices like body vitals tracking devices, ingestible sensor pills, etc. are required to be safe guarded against attacks.

Take an example of body vitals tracking device: This device continuously monitors the body parameters like heart rate, blood pressure, sugar levels, etc. and transmits the data continuously to the hospital. If it was intercepted, the eavesdropper can read all the data being transmitted and can change the data which may either lead to a fatal condition not being reported or the doctor prescribing a wrong dose of medication which could eventually be fatal for the patient.

Also, hospital equipments like Sonography machines are now enabled with technologies which can transfer the captured images to a computer for faster record processing. If this transfer is intercepted, the eavesdropper can access the crucial medical images and use them for insurance frauds or for his/her own benefit in a wrong way.

So it is increasingly important to secure the transmissions from these devices.

The authors' proposed method is to integrate the healthcare devices with quantum cryptography protocols [31].

The devices can implement the BB84 protocol explained in the previous section and establish a secure channel for communication.

Let us take the example of hospital equipment like Sonography machine. When the machine wants to transfer the images and data records to the computer, the machine can encrypt the data or photons using either the horizontal, vertical, +45° or -45° polarizers and send the data to the computer. The computer can then randomly choose either rectilinear beam splitter or diagonal beam splitter. Then the coinciding photons between the machine and the computer are kept as the secret key for communication. This way the communication can be secure[32].

Another example is of body vitals tracking device. Usually the device communicates with a smart phone application which in turn transfers the data to the medical center (in some cases there can be direct communication from device to the medical center, but let us consider the mentioned scenario here). So here, 2 channels are required to be secured: one from device to the smart phone and other from the smart phone to the medical center receiver, as interception can happen at any of the channels. Now the smart phone works as both the transmitter and receiver so it has to perform both the actions. First the device establishes a secure key with the smart phone according to the BB84 protocol and sends the body vitals' data. Then the smart phone establishes a secure connection with the medical center receiver according to the BB84 protocol and forwards the data.

Next example is of the ingestible sensor pills. These are the pills that go into the patient's body and monitor if the patient is taking regular medication and if the medication is working properly in the body. This pill is currently not approved for human use but soon it will be out for human consumption. This pill will then use a three layer communication: it will transmit the data to a wearable patch (because it is difficult to integrate the support for communication with a smart phone in a small sized pill), which will transmit the data to smart phone, which will finally transmit the data to the medical center receiver. So now there will be three paths for communication and three paths will need to be secured. The wearable patch as well as the smart phone will now act as both senders and receivers. The BB84 protocol will be followed between the pill and the wearable patch, the wearable patch and the smart phone, and the smart phone and the medical center receiver.

These are some ways in which Quantum cryptography can be used in healthcare devices. Thus crucial medical records can be secured.

9. ADVANTAGES OF QC IN IoT-BASED HEALTHCARE SYSTEMS

The QC is theoretical unbreakable approach which can secure the medical data in the IoT-based healthcare system. To enable secure IoT-based healthcare system, all devices, users, applications and services within the system are QC enabled.

In adding together to IoT containment, QC security mechanism provide layered security across multiple levels of the network. At the lower physical perception layer the device and user are kept secure by

QC as it is can be used for authentication and authorization purpose. That means only limited persons those are authentic and authorized to access the data is permitted to use the medical data.

Next at the network layer, QC protected the medical data while transmission by provide the secure channel. It protect network from adversary, potential back doors, embedded malware and vulnerabilities.

Further at the application layer the QC protocols provide the security by identifying malicious user, activity, and services, detection of anomaly, limiting bandwidth and blocking the unwanted user and achieve QoS[33].

With the application of Quantum cryptography in eHealth systems we can achieve many benefits. First and the most important benefit is that communication will become secure and non-interceptable. As the communication will be secured, the data and information being transmitted will be 100 percent correct which can help the patients in getting correct treatment; it can help the doctors better understand the patient's condition and ailment and help them recommend proper treatment and medications. Also, when the data is used for research and analysis it will yield better results and help in the growth of our medical systems so that we can be ready for any diseases that might attack in the future.

We can take an example of the most recent pandemic which started in the late 2019: Sars-Cov-2 or Covid-19. Tracking device can be installed on some of the infected patients of all age groups which can help the medical professionals and researchers in understanding the way the virus works inside the human body and behavioral patterns can be deduced from this data. Tracking devices can also be placed on the recovered patients and analysis can be done on how their bodies react after the deadly virus is removed and many important conclusions can be derived about the nature of the virus.

We can say that as the classical cryptographic algorithms work on the basis of assumptions that are computationally unproven they are not said to be completely secure whereas Quantum cryptography uses the laws of Quantum mechanics and Physics, so it is much more reliable and secure than classical algorithms.

The QC gives the overall security to IoT-based healthcare system. The followings are some additional measures which QC provides along with the security of sensitive data.

- Data Integrity

The QC is capable to provide the data integrity in IoT-based healthcare system. Data integrity is very much essential regarding the medical data because bases on this data only the intelligent medical decision are taken.

The integrity and quality data involves lots of parameters like, accuracy, availability, fidelity, and confidence that the data cannot be tampered or corrupted with. These concerns are taken care by QC in IoT-based healthcare system.

- Reliability

Reliability is a key concern for IoT–based healthcare systems. It ensure that the system is working perfectly for any given context and environment. QC gives guarantee for reliability by ensuring secure information of the context and environment.

- Certification

QC provides the certification without any conflict. QC resolves the problem regarding the selection of certificate provider. With the satisfactory answers to these questions, it is improbable that QC can offer the certification that is required by IoT adopters.

- Credential management

By keeping the credentials like sensitive data and keys which are essential for secure communication, safe and secure, QC provide the credential management mechanism. The security and privacy of devices against network-based vulnerability is ensured by credential management.

10. CHALLENGES OF QC IN IoT-BASED HEALTHCARE SYSTEMS

There are a few challenges when Quantum cryptography is considered. First is that a commercially usable quantum computer has not yet been designed, so these algorithms cannot be applied to the IoT devices as of now. And integrating the quantum components on such small scale devices can take some time. Quantum computers are very difficult to build and program. Hence they have a high error rate such as noise and faults.

In future developments, we can expect some new protocols and algorithms for the quantum computers so that the error rates are reduced and commercial quantum computers can become a reality.

Quantum computing in future can be very much useful in developing vaccines for new found diseases within days. Presently the vaccine making procedure can take years because the molecules are made in the laboratory and then tested against various parameters. Molecules are made without any predictions beforehand. And we can only know the results after the tests. After the testing too, it is not possible to predict the future complications these molecules could create. With the help of quantum computing we can simulate the molecules with the help of already present databases and the data collected from tracking of patients (as mentioned in the previous section). Vaccines can be made within a number of days along with almost all the predictions of the future complications.

11. CONCLUSION AND FUTURE WORK

The most awaited IoT uprising in healthcare system is already in progress, as shown in this work. These mechanism and techniques is just the tip of the recognizable iceberg, as new circumstances and situations continue to appear to measure the urgent requirement of accessible and affordable, care. In the intervening time, It has been seeing that the IoT approaches of automation and security mechanism continue to be recognized.

IoT security mechanism especially in healthcare application should support the huge data storage and computations because of data generated by the various devices are huge. This is, unfortunately, not always feasible. However, there are some IoT devices which have sufficient capabilities, like for storing, processing and communicating capabilities. The important patient data records, medical images, details, etc. are to be protected the most. Because if these things are leaked any malicious cyber criminal can take wrong advantage like faking medical records for medicines, insurance frauds, blackmailing the owner/organization for money in return for the sensitive medical records, creating fatal conditions for a patient, etc. To avoid this we need to secure the communication channels so that they are not intercepted in between the transfer of data. The problem that were recognized are also somewhat prejudiced by the outlook of the healthcare data since information was produced by them to take the intelligent medical decision. Approaches for IoT-based healthcare data security offer an exciting research field producing solutions that harmonize security mechanism and protocols for application and services.

Classical cryptographic algorithms are not powerful enough to prevent the systems against the attacks. The algorithms may seem secure now but they are just based on the unproven solvability of the logic by the classical computers.

When the authors talk about Quantum Cryptography, they mention how easily classical cryptography can be broken by the quantum cryptography protocols. Also, the authors discuss how the IoT devices in the healthcare sector can be secured with the help of applying the quantum cryptography algorithms in the IoT devices. This way the devices can be secured 100 percent against any interception in the networks.

For example, in the post-quantum era, that is vulnerable against cryptoanalysis done by quantum computer, security would have a key issue because all the classical cryptographic approaches will be replaced by quantum cryptography. Even the exchange and distribution of cryptographic keys for wireless communication would be based on QC.

By exploring various approaches and techniques to secure IoT data, it has been concluded that QC is very much appropriate for the IoT-based healthcare system. Applying QC in IoT will further enter in to all significant application of connected smart environment. In near future, IoT applications will be pervasive and the security issue of that application will be measured by QC. Under such critical secure setting, QC is supposed to be ubiquitous.

REFERENCES

Amit, Y., Hay, R., Saltzman, R., & Sharabani, A. (2013). *Pinpointing security vulnerabilities in computer software applications.* US Patent 8,510,842.

Bennett, C. H., & Brassard, G. (1984). *Quantum cryptography: Public key distribution and coin tossing. IEEE Intl. Conf. Computers, Systems and Signal Processing.*

Bhatia & Sumbaly. (2014). *Framework For Wireless Network Security Using Quantum Cryptography.* Academic Press.

Bhatt, A. P., Babuta, T., & Sharma, A. (2018, February). Quantum information processing and communication: Asian perspective. *Intl. Journal of Computer and Mathematical Sciences, 7*(2), 616–621.

Bhatt, A. P., & Sharma, A. (2019, September). Quantum Cryptography for Internet of Things Security. *Journal of Electronic Science and Technology, 17*(3), 213–220.

Bui, N., & Zorzi, M. (2011). Health care applications: a solution based on the internet of things. In *Proceedings of the 4th International Symposium on Applied Sciences in Biomedical and Communication Technologies (ISABEL '11).* ACM. 10.1145/2093698.2093829

Chaqfeh, M. A., & Mohamed, N. (2012). Challenges in middleware solutions for the internet of things. *Proceedings of the 13th International Conference on Collaboration Technologies and Systems (CTS '12),* 21–26. 10.1109/CTS.2012.6261022

Chen, C. Y., Zeng, G.-J., Lin, F. J., Chou, Y. H., & Chao, H.-C. (2015, October). Quantum Cryptography and Its Applications over the Internet. *IEEE Network*, *29*(5), 64–69. doi:10.1109/MNET.2015.7293307

Chen, S., Xu, H., Liu, D., Hu, B., & Wang, H. (2014, April). A Vision of IoT: Applications, Challenges, and Opportunities with China Perspective. *IEEE Internet of Things Journal*, *1*(4), 349–359. doi:10.1109/JIOT.2014.2337336

Ferreira, P., Martinho, R., & Domingos, D. (2010). Iot-aware business processes for logistics: limitations of current approaches. *Proceedings of the Inforum Conference*, *3*, 612–613.

Gruzelier, J. H. (2014). EEG-neurofeedback for optimising performance. I: A review of cognitive and affective outcome in healthy participants. *Neuroscience and Biobehavioral Reviews*, *44*, 124–141. doi:10.1016/j.neubiorev.2013.09.015 PMID:24125857

Guo, B., Zhang, D., Wang, Z., Yu, Z., & Zhou, X. (2013). Opportunistic IoT: Exploring the harmonious interaction between human and the internet of things. *Journal of Network and Computer Applications*, *36*(6), 1531–1539. doi:10.1016/j.jnca.2012.12.028

Guo, B., Zhang, D., Yu, Z., Liang, Y., Wang, Z., & Zhou, X. (2013). From the internet of things to embedded intelligence. *World Wide Web (Bussum)*, *16*(4), 399–420. doi:10.100711280-012-0188-y

Kamm¨uller, F., Kerber, M., & Probst, C. W. (2017). Insider threats and auctions: Formalization, mechanized proof, and code generation. *Journal of Wireless Mobile Networks, Ubiquitous Computing and Dependable Applications*, *8*(1), 44–78.

Khan, S., Abdullah, J., Khan, N., Julahi, A. A., & Tarmizi, S. (2017). *Quantum-Elliptic curve Cryptography for Multihop Communication in 5G Networks. IJCSNS International Journal of Computer Science and Network Security*.

Lee, M., & Cho, J.-D. (2014). Logmusic: context-based social music recommendation service on mobile device. In *Proceedings of the ACM International Joint Conference on Pervasive and Ubiquitous Computing (UbiComp '14)* (pp. 95–98). 10.1145/2638728.2638749

Li, J., Li, J., Xie, D., & Cai, Z. (2016). Secure auditing and deduplicating data in cloud. *IEEE Transactions on Computers*, *65*(8), 2386–2396. doi:10.1109/TC.2015.2389960

Liang, G., & Cao, J. (2013). CircleSense: a pervasive computing system for recognizing social activities. In *Proceedings of the 11th IEEE International Conference on Pervasive Computing and Communications (PerCom '13)* (pp. 201–206). IEEE.

Ma, C., Kulshrestha, S., Shi, W., Okada, Y., & Bose, R. (2018). E-learning material development framework supporting vr/ar based on linked data for iot security education. In *International Conference on Emerging Internetworking, Data & Web Technologies* (pp. 479–491). Springer. 10.1007/978-3-319-75928-9_43

Mashal, I., Alsaryrah, O., Chung, T.-Y., Yang, C.-Z., Kuo, W.-H., & Agrawal, D. P. (2015). Choices for interaction with things on Internet and underlying issues. *Ad Hoc Networks*, *28*, 68–90. doi:10.1016/j.adhoc.2014.12.006

McGrath, M. J., & Scanaill, C. N. (2013). *Body-worn, ambient, and consumer sensing for health applications. In Sensor Technologies*. Springer.

Pantelopoulos, A., & Bourbakis, N. G. (2010). A survey on wearable sensor-based systems for health monitoring and prognosis. *IEEE Transactions on Systems, Man and Cybernetics. Part C, Applications and Reviews*, *40*(1), 1–12. doi:10.1109/TSMCC.2009.2032660

Park, K. C., & Shin, D.-H. (2017). Security assessment framework for iot service. *Telecommunication Systems*, *64*(1), 193–209. doi:10.100711235-016-0168-0

Perera, C., Zaslavsky, A., Christen, P., & Georgakopoulos, D. (2013). Context aware computing for the internet of things: A survey. *IEEE Communications Surveys and Tutorials*, *16*(1), 414–454. doi:10.1109/SURV.2013.042313.00197

Picard, R. W., & Picard, R. (1997). *Affective Computing* (Vol. 252). MIT Press.

Razzaque, M. A., Milojevic-Jevric, M., Palade, A., & Cla, S. (2016). Middleware for internet of things: A survey. *IEEE Internet of Things Journal*, *3*(1), 70–95. doi:10.1109/JIOT.2015.2498900

Sharma, A., Ojha, V., & Goar, V. (2010, May). Security aspect of quantum key distribution. *International Journal of Computers and Applications*, *2*(2), 58–62. doi:10.5120/625-885

Sharma, V., Lee, K., Kwon, S., Kim, J., Park, H., Yim, K., & Lee, S.-Y. (2017). *A consensus framework for reliability and mitigation of zero-day attacks in iot* (Vol. 2017). Security and Communication Networks.

Spiller, T. P. (1996, December). Quantum Information Processing: Cryptography, Computation, and Teleportation. *Proceedings of the IEEE*, *84*(12), 1719–1746. doi:10.1109/5.546399

Sufyan. (n.d.). *Defeating Man-in-the-Middle Attack in Quantum Key Distribution*. Academic Press.

Voas, J. (2016). *Networks of Things, NIST Special Publication (SP) 800-183*. National Institute of Standards and Technology.

Xu, F., Curty, M., Qi, B., & Lo, H. (2015, March). Measurement-Device-Independent Quantum Cryptography. *IEEE Journal of Selected Topics in Quantum Electronics*, *21*(3).

Zhao, J.-C., Zhang, J.-F., Feng, Y., & Guo, J.-X. (2010). The study and application of the IOT technology in agriculture. *Proceedings of the 3rd IEEE International Conference on Computer Science and Information Technology (ICCSIT '10)*, 462–465.

Chapter 8
Quantum Security for IoT to Secure Healthcare Applications and Their Data

Binod Kumar

https://orcid.org/0000-0002-6172-7938

JSPM's Rajarshi Shahu College of Engineering, India

Sheetal B. Prasad

SRM Institute of Science and Technology, India

Parashu Ram Pal

ABES Engineering College, India

Pankaj Pathak

https://orcid.org/0000-0002-5875-0387

Symbiosis Institute of Digital and Telecom Management, Symbiosis International University, India

ABSTRACT

Quantum computation has the ability to revolutionize the treatment of patients. Quantum computing can help to detect diseases by identifying and forecasting malfunctions. But there's a threat associated here (i.e., healthcare data among the most popular cybercriminal targets, IoT devices notoriously lacking in effective safeguards, and quantum computers on the brink of an encryption/decryption breakthrough). Health agencies need a security prognosis and treatment plan as soon as possible. Healthcare companies recently worry more about the quantum security threats. The biggest threat of healthcare data breaches has come in the form of identity theft. There should be a strong mechanism to combat the security gaps in existing healthcare industry. If the healthcare data are available on the network, an attacker may try to modify, intercept, or even view this data stream. With the use of quantum security, the quantum state of these photons changes alert the security pros that someone is trying to breach the link.

DOI: 10.4018/978-1-7998-6677-0.ch008

Copyright © 2021, IGI Global. Copying or distributing in print or electronic forms without written permission of IGI Global is prohibited.

INTRODUCTION

The Internet of Things (IoT) is a communication system that defines a future in the day-to-day relation of physical objects to the Internet and the capacity to locate and interact locally or remotely (Coetzee, 2011). IoT grows rapidly and changes any technological area through the delivery of smart services, including healthcare. Such smart technologies to boost the standard of living and effectively drive healthcare sector development at the moment. These smart systems monitor numerous computer-based data and state-of-the-art IoT tools such as wearables, networks, etc. To answer the vast volume of knowledge gathered over the last two decades properly.

The concept of the Internet of Things (IoT) is clear: it requires the artifacts to create their own social networks and holds the two layers apart; it makes it possible for individuals to implement rules to preserve their privacy and to view only certain contact outcomes that take place on a social network (Atzori, Nitti, & Marche., 2016).The IoT has been a subject of global concern for a couple of decades. Nevertheless, the healthcare industry has just begun to understand the enormous potential and benefits offered by the implementation of new and more advanced healthcare equipment and services as well as links between several sectors of the industry. The Internet of Things has re-evaluated the healthsector with its numerous applications in the framework. IoT introduced health care to help doctors and nurses take improved medical decisions and reduce human contact by retrieving information from bedside devices to help them reduce error rates (Rao, 2019). The contribution of this chapter is as follows:

- For the healthcare environment, we offer a holistic perspective on IoT fundamentals. Various IoT views for the medical domain are outlined based on various types of relationships in an IoT to the healthcare system, and IoT's for the healthcare domain are discussed in detail.
- We addressed IoT healthcare architecture and technologies. We addressed in this article the 3-layer IoT structure consisting of the perception tier, network layer and application layer. We explained the idea and then demonstrated the way it operated.
- We also studied various research papers that provide approaches to various IoT healthcare problem areas. We evaluated the advantages and disadvantages of each research paper.
- This chapter sums up the importance of IoT in healthcare and offers a solution in Healthcare to design and implement IoT.

This is the rest of the book. Section 2 analyses similar IoT research in the healthcare sector, which increases healthcare productivity through healthcare alignment with other IoT fields. Remaining Sections discusses about Quantum Cryptography Fundamentals,, The Security of QKD, Secure Communications Using Quantum Key Distribution, Quantum Security, Post Quantum Cryptography, Asymmetric Versus Symmetric Encryption, Functions Quantum Cryptography, The Quantum Security for Remote Healthcare Data, IoT Application in Healthcare, Cost and Features of IoT Solutions for Healthcare. Finally conclusions are presented in section 8.

QUANTUM SECURITY FOR IOT

Security requirements of IoT devices can be very complex and it cannot be achieved by a single technology. There are many aspects of security in IoT devices has to be considered. For example secured software development, secure patch management, protection against various attack, and secure communication. Recently many companies started to implement chip-based quantum security mechanisms. In these mechanisms the applicability and practical implementation of quantum security cryptographic methods for embedded systems is the main concern. The quantum security cryptographic techniques ensures the confidentiality, authenticity, and integrity of the multiple data traveling in the IoT ecosystem, both the consumer and industrial one. If the cryptographic methods used in an IoT device can be broken by an attacker, this would expose it to a lot of vulnerabilities. With quantum-safe cryptography, provides security in the long term and against very powerful attackers. The development of post-quantum cryptography that should withstand quantum computing power. The defender could still be implementing cryptography on classical computers and machines, while the attacker may use a quantum computer in the near future. Current approaches for so-called quantum-key distribution [QKD], where quantum technology is used to achieve confidentiality, are currently too expensive or too constraining, whereas current assessments of post-quantum cryptography prove that it could be quantum-safe as well as affordable. Researchers have indicated that information protection will be particularly alarming, as modern quantum encryption techniques might be helpful, however quantum computing may be used to bust up traditional encryption systems and outdated certain established computer security protections.

We foresee other cyber security implications because of quantum computation. Current public key cryptography algorithms like Diffie-Hellman, RSS [Rivest-Shamir-Adleman] and elliptic curve cryptography rely on mathematical problems that are difficult for conventional computers to overcome. It is the basis of the protection of such algorithms. The problem is that a man named Peter Shor at MIT already showed that a quantum computer is able to deal with such mathematical problems within a reasonable period of time. It suggests that if we have a completely functional, realistic quantum machine now, it will be able to crack the RSA, the elliptical curve and the Diffie-Hellman in a fair period of time, not immediately, but in a reasonable amount of time. Each vpN will then be vulnerable, e-commerce, and more (Sharon Shea, 2020). Quantum cryptography is a methodology very relevant that utilizes quantum mechanics' principles in order to create a cryptosystem which is meant to be the securest. This can not be violated by anyone without the sender or receiver of the communication having heard. Quantum cryptography is focused around the usage of photons and their basic quantum properties in order to create an indestructible cryptosystem since the quantum state in every device can't be determined without informing the machine. The essence of quantum cryptography is the idea that it requires the smallest particles, i.e. photons, in existence. Such photons have a function that appears concurrently in more than one condition and that only affects their statuses as counted. It is the fundamental property of quantum cryptography algorithms. If a message travels from the sender to the receiver through a conduit and any hostile party wants to interrupt communications, the sender / receiver is automatically clear through the shift in state of the photon.

RELATED WORK

The IoT provides many opportunities for developing services and delivery of healthcare. IoT promotes a holistic commitment to health care by considering the population's health needs and not people, and promoting policies that minimize illness prevalence, impairment and accidental injury. The convergence of healthcare systems with other areas of IoT thus improves the efficacy of healthcare. The Internet of Things can change people's lifestyle (Rghioui & Oumnad, 2017).

Numerous independent studies have recently examined the potential to use IoT technology in healthcare. IoT may bring many advantages to improve the quality of life of people and provide safety advice on lifestyle. To clarify that the IoT refers to several good studies, each Healthcare protection display problem has been discussed recently. There are several papers publishing a study of different aspects of IoT innovation in health care. For example, the survey (Kwak, Kabir, Hossain, & Kwak, 2015) covers the core technology that allows wireless network and wireless network (WSN) components to be communicated. Jaime Lioret and her colleagues have proposed among these studies a smart communication system for Ambient Assisted Living (Lioret, Canovas, Sendra, & Parra, 2015). Inspired by (Ma, Wang, Yang, Miao, & Li, 2016), the big health model based on the Internet, the big data, was introduced in a recent study.

In elderly and disabled patients, several tools have been built to monitor human activity. This system's purpose is to continuously monitor physiological parameters (Khanna & Misra, 2013) (Riazul, Kwak, Humaun, Hossain, & Supkwak, 2015). The health monitoring system is largely dependent on the wireless sensor network and therefore benefits from lower energy consumption and increased coverage of communication (Singh, 2016). Themes such as less innovative technology, the low availability of smart devices and smart products that are highly required for intelligent healthcare must be addressed by developing countries (Mathew, Amreen, H.N & Verma, 2015) . IoT implementation in intelligent homes offers complex solution services and technology for customized healthcare (Yu & Lu, 2012). IoT is a smart healthcare architecture which uses sensors such as temperature sensors, barometric pressure and ECG sensors (Sreekanth & Nitha, 2016).

The state-of - the-art approaches for efficient and safe eHealth management is studied. They generally gave a detailed eHealth monitoring model by explaining the entire life cycle of monitoring in depth. The key service elements were also illustrated with a focus on data collection on the patient side. We have defined and analyzed the key issues to be resolved in order to develop an efficient and stable patient-centered monitoring system (Sawand, A., Djahel, S., Zhang, Z., & Abdesselam, 2015).

The paper then explains the security and privacy issues of the healthcare implementations of the Body Sensor Network (BSN). Earlier, they found that while the security issue was acknowledged in most popular BSN research projects, strong security services were not implemented which could protect the privacy of the patient. Eventually, BSN was introduced for a safety IoT-based system of healthcare that can efficiently satisfy various BSN healthcare safety requirements (Gope & Hwang, 2016).

To have end-to - end support for IoT applications from an IoT platform, there is a stable IoT program deployed. IoT's framework includes IoT applications, an IoT broker and IoT devices. Typically speaking, in real-time healthcare facilities intermediate protection concerns will be addressed as medical patient knowledge is one of the most important safety details. Growing IoT platform uses a specific identifier as one of its attributes. And if the IoT Broker is an intermediary node, it decrypts and shows data only if the conditions have been fulfilled. (Choi, In, Park, Seok, Seo, & Kim, 2016).

Patient information and health records have been provided with a Secure Patient Profiling System (Ko & Song, 2015). The patient and doctor exchange up-to-date data simultaneously. Data can be leaked while exchanging and transmitting. In order to resolve security problems, there should be established a safe communication network and a one-time key between a patient and a hospital and a dual hash should be used to generate an OTP output value. This work offers a dual-hash method for generating a one-time password that guarantees safe contact with a secure password.

FUNDAMENTAL OF QUANTUM CRYPTOGRAPHY

Quantum cryptography in the broadest context is a sub-set of quantum information processing, including quantum computing and quantum computation. The research for information retrieval functions that can be done utilizing quantum mechanical devices is quantum computation and quantum information. Quantum Mechanics is a conceptual framework or a set of theories for physical growth. Quantum mechanics have basic principles that remain counter-intuitive among scholars, and the early precedents of quantum physics and quantum knowledge can be found in physicists' lifelong need to grasp quantum mechanics more thoroughly. Perhaps the most important of these is a quantum quantum coherence analysis. Entanglement is a distinctly quantum mechanical phenomenon that plays a crucial role in many of the most significant applications of quantum computation and quantum information; entanglement is iron in the conventional bronze age of the world. A great deal of work has been made in recent years to further grasp the properties of entanglement called a fundamental property of Nature, of equal value to energy, information, entropy or some other fundamental tool.

Although there is no full quantum coherence theory yet, some progress has been made in the understanding of this unusual function of quantum mechanics. Most researchers expect that more study of the properties of the interference would include insights that will promote the creation of new technologies for quantum computation and quantum information.

It is important to remember, as we know, about a decade before a quantum computers were discovered to break public key cryptography, a workaround had already been created for that attack – QKD. QKD offers an unconditionally secure way of communicating random keys across insecure networks, focused on the fundamental principles of quantum mechanics. In addition, the protected key created by QKD may be used to improve information protection in the OTP scheme or other encryption algorithms. It chapter lays out the fundamental ideas behind the various QKD or QSS and discusses state-of-the-art techniques for quantum cryptography.

THE SECURITY OF QKD

The safety proof is essential because (a) it provides a QKD protection base, (b) it provides a specification for the QKD protocol 's key generation efficiency, and (c) the classic post-processing processing (for error correction and privacy amplification) protocol can also be built to help the ultimate key generation. A Real QKD system without any cryptographic evidence is incomplete because we will never learn how to build a valid key and how stable it is.

After a qubit and base reconciliation, sender and receiver each have a sifted key. Ideally, all keys are the same. But certain causes of error are still in actual life, so certain conventional information retrieval methods such as error correction so data filtering are introduced by the sender and receiver of their documents. To access the same keys, the first and second protocols are needed for a secret key. In essence, the problem with eavesdropping is finding protocols which can contain an authentically secured sender- and recipient key or stop the protocol as the sender and recipient can only measure the QBER and alert the users that it has failed in the key distribution. It is a complex issue at the crossroads between quantum mechanics and knowledge theory. It also entails several eavesdropping problems according to the exact procedure.

Many limited-generality eavesdrop strategies have been developed and evaluated in order to simplify the issue (Lütkenhaus 1996), (Biham, E & Mor, 1997). Especially important is Eve 's assumption to add individual samples to each song and test each sample one by one. We may be listed as:

Single attack: Eve independently launches an assault on a signal for a single attack. The intercept-resend assault is an illustration of a person's assault. Imagine a simple example of the intercept-resending attack by Eve, an eavesdropper who arbitrarily checks each photon and sends it back to Bob. Eve 's calculation will disrupt the photons Alice prepared on the diagonal bases and randomly respond, if for example Eve executes a clear measurement. E.g. When Eve sends straight images to Bob, when Bob makes a vertical calculation, he gets random replies. Since each group randomly selects such two bases, a bit error rate of $0.50.5 + 0.5 = 25$ percent is provided by such an intercept resending attack, which Alice and Bob readily detect. Strong QKD assaults are occurring. Thankfully, the health of QKD has now proved itself.

Collective attacks: A more general type of attacks is a cumulative attack where Eve separately couples it with an ancillary quantum device, usually referred to as ancilla, with each signal, and the combination signal / ancilla grows as a entity. She's going to send Bob the next signals, however she can catch all of the ancillas herself. In response to individual attacks, Eve is postponing her calculation decision. It is only after having a public debate between Alice and Bob that Eve decides what check to take on her ancilla to gather the final key information.

Joint attacks: The most frequent form of intrusion is mutual attack. Eve treats both signals as a specific quantum network during a joint assault instead of treating each signal separately. Then she enters the ancilla in the signal network and generates an interconnected signal and ancil frame unitarily. Before deciding the measure of her simple to behave, she watches the public conversation between Alice and Bob.

Of joint and community attacks Eve is typically just researching until any of the meetings on counseling, error fixing and privacy enhancement have been completed by Alice and Bob. Another assumes that Eve still exists as the grounds of the healing mechanism for public discussion within the more moral people attacks. This would therefore be fair to assume for modern technologies that Eve should quantify her analysis of person attacks before consolidating the base. (Malaney & Robert,2010).

SECURE COMMUNICATIONS USING QUANTUM KEY DISTRIBUTION

QKD does not necessarily encrypt user data, but encourages users to pass keys freely to each other, which can then be used for the resulting encrypted contact.

By using a security system, any sort of private information have to be held hidden almost always. Knowledge is shared in symmetric key systems in the form of a key but in asymmetric systems, each node has its own key when it exchsts the public key. In every instance, the mail is enabled with bugs. Symmetric key schemes often focus on physical key exchange – some financial firms with mobile storage mail – to bootstrap. They can share an encryption key for the further use on a secure connection via an asymmetrical system. One explanation for this is that asymmetric structures like Public Key do not allow secrets to be exchanged through the medium (in this case, private keys), whereas symmetrical structures are more powerful and therefore more stable, despite the large data volume after exchanging keys.

Quantum Key Distribution (QKD) is the most well-known and sophisticated method of quantum cryptography which require the use of quantum communication to define a shared key between two parties without third party information, however all communications between two parties may be refused by third parties. If third parties try to find out about the key, discrepancies will occur that will notice two parties. Once the key has been defined, it is typically used with traditional techniques for encrypted communication. The shared key for symmetrical encryption may be used, for example.

Unlike the classical key distribution, the security of the quantum key distribution may be proved mathematically without adding any constraint on the eavesdropper 's capability. It is generally defined as "unconditional protection," but a minimum of suppositories is needed, including the implementation of the laws of quantum mechanics and the identification of two parties, i.e. third parties would not be able to impersonate any side, or a man-in-the-middle attack could be feasible.

QKD is a modern tool in a cryptographer toolbox: it makes secure key agreements on an untrustworthy path, in which the output key is entirely different from all input values, an unrelated job. QKD does not eliminate the need to develop systems with state-of - art security elements such as authentication, but does QKD.

Figure 1. Diagram of the stages of a protocol of the quantum key distribution. Classically authenticated stage with dual lines.

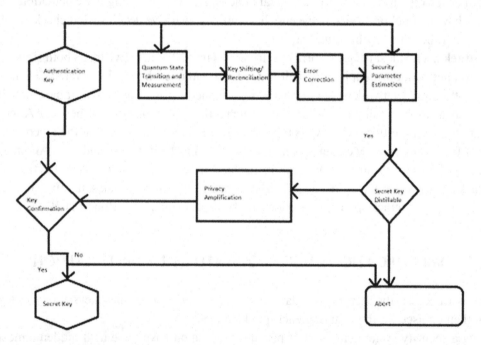

A secret-key agreement has been drawnup on a public channel for overcoming the noise and wire-tapping errors in the quantum channel, information reconciliation and confidentiality enhanced can be used to distribute the quantic key, or the cleanup of the quantum congestion should be used. The first general but very complex evidence of unconditional safety (Mayers, 2001), followed by several other evidence. (Mayers, 2006) In Mayers' proofs the BB84 scheme proposed by Bennett and Brassard proved to be safe. Lo and Chau suggested a conceptually simplified protection proof focused on the principle of quantum privacy enhancement (Lo & Chau,1999).

Two parties have these quantum states in QKD and check them. The research discusses to decide which findings may relate to hidden main bits. Others are tossed out as a sifting technique because of the incompatibility of the measuring settings. They fix the mistakes and then follow a security parameter that indicates how much the eavesdropper learns about the most critical information. If that is beyond a certain threshold, they must abort as they can no longer ensure any confidentiality. When the level is greater, secrecy will be improved to delete all residual information that the eavesdropper may potentially have and to insert a secret key. Each classic communications must be checked in order to avoid man-in-the-middle attacks.

Quantum Key Distribution (QKD) is a way to transmit encryption keystrokes which involve some very rare, technologically at least unhackable, subatomic particle behavior. QKD's land based variant is a network where photons are transmitted through a fiber optic cable one at a time. If someone is eavesdropping, then the polarization of the photons is influenced according to the rules of quantum physics, and the receiver may complain the message is not secure. (QuantumXchange, 2020)

Cryptography is the practice of encrypting messages, or translating plain text to encrypted text so that it can be interpreted only by anyone who has the correct "key." By contrast, quantum cryptography actually utilizes the concepts of quantum mechanics to encode and transfer data in a way that cannot be hacked out.

Although the concept sounds straightforward, the difficulty lies behind quantum cryptography in the concepts of quantic mechanics, such as:

- Particles which make up the universe are inherently uncertain and may exist in more than one place or more than one state of being at the same time.
- The photons are spontaneously produced in one of two quantum states.
- A quantum property can't be calculated without modifying or disrupting it.
- We can clone some of the particle's quantum properties but not the entire particle.

All these principles play a role in how quantum cryptography works.

POST-QUANTUM CRYPTOGRAPHY

Post-quantum cryptography is used for encryption algorithms (usually public key) defined as quantum computer-safe algorithms. These complicated mathematical calculations require months and even years for modern computers to break down. Quantum computers running the Shor algorithm separate mathematical programs at times.

In comparison to logical encryption, quantum cryptography utilizes the concepts of quantum mechanics to generate secure correspondence. Quantum computers become a technical reality; therefore, it is important to analyze the cryptographing schemes of opponents who have access to a quantum computer. The study of these structures is often referred to as post-quantum cryptography. The criteria for post-quantity cryptography are intended to bypass some traditional encrypting and signature systems (ECC and RSA-centered systems) by utilizing Shor 's algorithm to factor and measure distinctive logarithms on a quantum machine. McEliece and lattice-based systems as well as other symmetric keys are now recognizing the meanings of systems that have been defending against quantum adversaries.(Bernstein, 2009) Post-quantum cryptography surveys can be conducted. (Bernstein, 2009)

There is still some emphasis on improving existing techniques of cryptography to cope with quantum adversaries. For instance, different methods must be used to build zero-knowledge evidence systems which are safe from quantum adversaries. In a classical environment, a study of the zero-Knowledge-Bestoff method typically requires a rewinding, a procedure that allows the opponent's internal state to be replicated. Copying a state in a quantum setting is not always feasible (no-cloning theorem); the rewinding technique variant must be used (Watrous, 2009).

Post-quantum algorithms are often labeled "quantum resistant" because, unlike the spread of the quantum key, it is not understood or proven that any future quantum attacks against them do not occur. Though not susceptible to the Shor Algorithm, the NSA declares the decision to switch to quantum-resistant algorithms. The NINST appears to believe it is time for quantum-safe primitives. (CoinFabrik, 2017)

Post-quantum cryptography deals with cryptosystems that run on ordinary computers and that are free from attacks in quantum computation. This field was developed as most common public-key encryption schemes rely on the problem of integer factorization or a discrete logarithm which can be solved easily on large enough quantum computers using the Shor algorithm. While the latest publicly accessible computational theoretical computer program is about as effective as possible to target actual crypto schemes, other cryptographers are researching new techniques if quantum computation becomes a threat. Most symmetric encryptions (symmetric ciphers and hash functions) are by contrast secured against quantum computers. In this respect. The Quantum Grover algorithm speeds up attack on symmetrical ciphers, however, the key scale can be counteracted. Post-quantum cryptography also does not rely on symmetrical algorithms. Therefore, post-quantum encryption has no relation to quantum encryption and is connected to the usage of quantum effects of secretion. The cryptography post-quantum currently focuses mainly on four different methods:

Post-quantum cryptography is usually also another matter than quantum cryptography:

- As with most of the cryptography, post-quantum encryption covers a large range of protected mail functions, ranging from secret, public-key, and encryption to high-ranking activity like secure on-line voting. Quantum cryptography performs only one function: extending a brief common secret into a long shared secret.
- Like in other cryptographic approaches, post-quantum cryptography has some secure solutions but also has other, cost-effective methods. Quantum encryption prevents conjectural systems, initially asking how the key could be exchanged between Alice and Bob in a secure way.
- Post-quantum cryptography requires a range of techniques that can be used for a small fraction of today's Internet communication — the sender and receiver need to compute and relay certain data, but no additional hardware is required. The overwhelming majority of internet users at least currently do not need modern network devices for quantium cryptography.

Quantum encryption so far mainly deals with the development of quantum distribution protocols. Sadly symmetrical key-distributed cryptosystems for wide networks (many users) are unstable since many secret keys need to be configured and exploited in pairings (the so-called "key-management problem."). Nevertheless, this task alone does not tackle a variety of other cryptographic operations and roles that are important in everyday life. Kak 's three stage protocol has been suggested as a secure communication mechanism that is totally quantum unlike the quantum key distribution, which utilizes classic algorithms for cryptographic transformation (Thapliya.& Pathak,, 2018)

ASYMMETRIC SYMMETRIC ENCRYPTION

Binary digits (0s and 1s) are transferred regularly from one position to another, and decryted by means of a symmetrical (private)/asymmetrical (public) key. Encrypt runs on "normal" devices. The Advanced Encryption Standard (AES) symmetric key cipher uses the same key to encrypt a letter or the file and asymmetrical ciphers, such as RSA, use both private and public linked keys. The secret key for decrypting information is kept secure, while the public key is shared. (Maria & Doug, 2019)

The first objective of quantity machinery encryption is the weakest link in the ecosystem of cryptography: asymmetric cryptography. This is the RSA encryption standard PKI. The asymmetric encryption of emails, blogs, financing transfers and much more protects them. The typical explanation is that everyone may encrypt a message with the intended Public Key of the recipient but only the recipient may decode it with the corresponding private Key. This two-key approach is focused on the premise that it is far easier to do some kinds of mathematical operation than to reverse it. One could break a shell, but it's much harder to get it back together.

Longer keys are the first line of quantum encryption protection, and almost everyone is on board. In addition, NIST no longer considers the 1024-bit version of the RSA encryption standard safe, with a minimum of 2048 bits. Longer keys make for sluggish and more costly decoding, though, so the length of the key will greatly increase so that the quantum computers stay ahead. uMany authorities tend to research how different forms of encryption algorithms are being built that also involve public and private keys which work against quantum computers. For instance, adding two prime numbers together is easy, but it's very hard to break a large number back into its prime factors.

There is, however, no known quantum method to crack grid-based encryption that uses lattic-based cryptographic algorithms. A mixture of postquantum algorithms such as grid-based encryption, which safely exchange keys for initial communications and use symmetric encryption for large messages, may be the best option.

FUNCTIONS QUANTUM CRYPTOGRAPHY

Quantum cryptography (QKD) utilizes a series of photons (light particles) to pass data over a fiber optic wire, from one location to another. The two end points will decide what the secret is and if the usage is secure by measuring the measures of the characteristics of a fraction of such photons. Breaking the process down further helps to explain it better.

1. Sending the photons via a filter (or polarizer), which alertly provides them with one of the four possible polarizations or bit marks: Vertical (one bit), Horizontal (zero bit), 45 degree (one bit) or 45 degree (zero bit) on the left.
2. Photons are sent to a receiver, where the polarisation of each photon is "heard," utilizing two beam dividers (horizontal / vertical and diagonal). The receiver doesn't realize which beam splitter each photon will use and will infer which one to use.
3. When the photon stream was transmitted, the receiver told the recipient the splitter of the beam was included in the sequence of the photons, and the sender correlated the detail with the series of polarizers that the key was transmitted to. The images read using the incorrect beam fraction are discarded and the resultant fragment series is the key.

The condition of the photon will alter whether the photon is interpreted or replicated in some form by an eavesdropper. The transition is sensed via the endpoints. In other words, without being detected it is impossible to read and forward the photon or make a copy of it.

THE QUANTUM SECURITY FOR REMOTE HEALTH CARE DATA

Quantum computation is now a most common and important technology with large-scale players purchasing or developing their own quantum systems. In an almost different field: digital health care, a big investment in technology is also taking place. The healthcare sector for the Internet of Things (IoT) is rapidly growing and over the coming years, more businesses are aiming to have the technical data they need for the doctors and patients. But there's a threat associated here, i.e. health care data among the most popular cybercriminal targets, IoT devices notoriously lacking in effective safeguards and quantum computers on the brink of an encryption/decryption breakthrough, health agencies need a security prognosis and treatment plan as soon as possible. Health care companies recently more worry about the quantum security threats. Most of the health data breaches are due to criminal attacks. And these data breaches are high in terms of volume and frequency. The biggest threat of health care data breaches has come in the form of identity theft.

Despite the troubling track record of health care databases and networks, the industry is under pressure to increase availability of internet-based services. Few modern health care hospitals adopted 100 percent electronic health record (EHR) rate but these hospitals facing various difficulties to share this digital information with the agencies like laboratories or other health care facilities. IoT can provide a solution to this problem: By supplying doctors and nurses, locally and those in remote locations with mobile devices capable of connecting to hospital networks, it's possible to streamline communication and enhance collaboration. Patients outfitted with wearable devices, carrying easily accessible smartphones and tablets, create a massive pool of usable information for medical practitioners and the promise of better treatments directly informed by data. The problem of data security tends to be second (or third, or fourth) priority when designing IoT devices. When the IoT devices related to health care are hacked they may be life threatens devices. For example drug infusion pumps, if hacked it may change the delivered dosage. Increased efforts to mobilize health care may have the unintended consequence of ramping up security threats; not only is patient data up for grabs, but limited IT security could actually put lives at stake.

There should be a strong mechanism to combat the security gaps in existing health care industry. The health care data which is available on the network, an attacker may try to modify, intercept or even view this data stream. With the use of quantum security the quantum state of these photons changes alert the security pros that someone is trying to breach the link. It is very useful for the devices located at distance. If they're supported by a strong connection, key transmission and breach detection become almost instantaneous. Even if attackers are using traditional methods rather than quantum computers, their interference causes an observable state change that can be addressed immediately.

IOT APPLICATION IN HEALTHCARE

This section introduces a number of applications designed to help people and in particular the health sector:

IoT Applications

- Healthcare: Due to the availability of new technological technologies the idea of connected health care is increasing. Every day, a health application can be created to enable blood glucose levels to be monitored using IoT and new technologies, as well as automatically collecting patient data. The IoT device helps doctors to quickly respond to incidents and to track a patient's health in international hospitals. This enables the use of IoT equipment in the household, particularly for older persons with special needs, such as diabetes, congestive heart disease. The Medical RFID tag internet enables a smart individual to be easily and correctly identified, allowing fast and secure access to personal health information on the internet of things. (Domingo, 2012).

- People with Disability: People with hearing loss can receive (impairments in the ear) external or internal hearing aids for improved hearing. Cheap wirelesss, on the other side, help enhance the connectivity of the inexperienced and the deaf. It identifies and transforms hand gestures with a Java-enabled control station (Mobile Phone). The handle has bending controls on the finger side (passive resistors to sense twisting and stretching). It may also be utilized. The blind navigation helps them in seeking a place on the market. The shop's RFID system can use apps to direct shopping that is visually impaired. The market is divided in cells with a shelf, and RFID Tags for a cell pass are distributed on the whole. The monitoring station for mobile devices enables a person with visual impairments to inform the food company he or she wants to go. It allows the person to provide stronger confidentiality security by automatic classification of controls and changes to match individual preferences (Domingo, 2012).

- Tracking and Monitoring of objects and persons: Monitoring is an effort to detect an entity or a individual traveling (Kim, Seo, & Jeongwook,, 2016). Patient behaviour in the health system is controlled and recorded to increase patient efficiency and control mobility across choke points, for example access to specified areas. Most likely or not, follow up is performed to avoid operational problems, rather than constant maintaining supplies (e.g. maintenance, supply in instances of need and usage control) or material monitoring.

- Identification and Authentication: Patient detection is directed at preventing harmful patient incidents (for example, harmful medication / dose / time / procedure) and the complete and revised medical report defining, defining, and authenticating employees is used more commonly for obtaining entry and enhancing the ethics of workers focused on patient safety. (Anwar, Abdullah, Qureshi, & Majid, 2017).

- Transport and Data Collection: The wireless Bluetooth, Near Field Communication (NFC), ZigBee and Bluetooth Low Energy (BLE) systems now allow Personal Health applications to communicate information. Data delivery or automated compilation will reduce the preparation period, electronic diagnostics and the auditing and recording of medical procedures. This function refers to RFID integration technology.

- Clinical Care: The sensors are able to support hospitalized patients moving freely within the institution by committing to certain rooms. These are attached to other devices which avoid trouble going from pavilion to pavilion for measurement which review. This helps all healthcare providers perform their duties because it allows them to remotely monitor the condition of their patients and to work together to diagnose the condition of a patient across the various disciplines. It also saves doctors time between patients and their health. It saves them time. It will enable them respond to an incident faster and encourage them to work with local facilities and track the condition of a patient.

- Continuous Cardiac Monitoring: A continuous monitoring program is a healthcare device built for patients to be closely tracked. The growing security issue drives scientists and businesses to try the safest and fastest path to remote cardiac surveillance by leveraging global economic technologies to deliver in real time medical record alerts on the internet.

- A continuous monitoring system is a treatment device developed for patients to be treated safely and closely tracked. The emerging health crisis leads scientists and companies, using global economic solutions, to search for the best and quickest path to remote control, with on-line real-time medical record warning signs. (Santos, Macedo, Costa, & JoãoNicolau, 2014).

Figure 2. IoT Healthcare Monitoring System

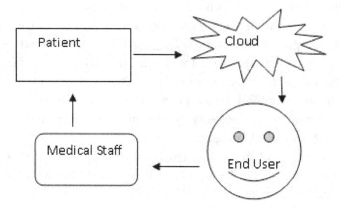

Examples of IoT in Healthcare

- Glucose-Level Monitoring: Most individuals have diabetes, so their glucose levels must be constantly tracked. The IoT device can continuously track glucose levels. Customizable sensors are used to evaluate health parameters and the captured data is distributed via an Internet Protocol (IPV6) network to major health care providers. The tracking device is fitted with a blood glucose monitor, a mobile phone and a diagnostic information screen based on IoT (Alqahtani, 2018). Monitoring of glucose levels involves specific trends of shifts in the glucose level which can be used to assess diet, physical activity, times etc.

- Electrocardiogram Monitoring: The device with the electrocardiogram (ECG) consists of a wireless transmitter and receiver. Automated use can detect a suspicious activity in the heart. The data is transmitted in real time via a network to remote and medical hospitals. The system manages HR and basic rhythm monitoring (Alqahtani, 2018).

- Blood Pressure Monitoring: The device consists of a BP unit with a network-based communication capability. Next, this machine records BP and then uploads the recorded data via the Wi-Fi network. It also has an LCD display of the recorded value of BP.

- Body Temperature Monitoring: The shifting temperature of the body is used to define homeostasis as a central aspect in healthcare. An embedded module for body temperature control is used in

TelosB mote in a clinical IoT device. The IoT Clinic gives the Jian and his partners (Jian, Zhanli and Zhuang, 2012) a body temperature regulation device with a home Server. For tracking the body's temperature, the home application uses infrared monitoring. The system mainly includes an RFID module which works with the body temperature monitoring unit.

- Wheelchair Management: Many studies to build electric wheelchairs for IoT users with disabilities have also been performed. For example (Yang, Ge, Li, Rao & Shen, 2014) an IoT health program supports disabled persons. The network uses wireless body area networks to monitor and coordinate various sensors through the WBAN technology. The machine monitors the movements of the wheelchair. This also monitors the individual with the wheelchair classification by tracking the person's sitting posture and gathering current environmental details.

COST AND FEATURES OF IOT SOLUTIONS FOR HEALTHCARE

IoT's currently happening all over the place. Companies have made significant investments in state-of - the-art technologies to streamline their business processes and cut costs. Consumers also buy smart home appliances and wearable devices to save time and change their own lifestyles. Everyone will need to know what it costs to build the IoT program if they are about to deploy their smart device or even imagine optimizing the company operation of their healthcare organization with any IoT solutions (Devtechnosys, 2018). Here's what the cost and features of IoT healthcare systems are. Components of Infrastructure of IoT and Additional Costs:

- Network: Despite low latency the IoT does not run without the provision of highly scalable or high-speed network infrastructure. Short-range wireless devices such as Wifi, Bluetooth and even cellular networks are often used to enable IoT connectivity. In this case, the IoT healthcare approach comprises of connected devices that communicate over a network, so it is appropriate to anticipate extra connectivity costs.
- Middleware: If someone is going to connect any third party device to their IoT ecosystem, then a software piece that is essentially used to interface between various IoT devices, known as middleware, will be required.
- Data Centre or Cloud-based infrastructure: There we find storage solutions as well as software that reduces to what is actually meaningful the enormous amount of raw data in gigabytes. IoT healthcare companies also make use of the application of small IoT healthcare devices and data analysis through various PaaS solutions.

Throughout the IoT-based healthcare system, as patient monitoring systems occur, there is a need for customer support staff along with electronic equipment and cellular network. This unit is helping people who have needed immediate assistance. In order to connect to the IoT healthcare solution, we must rely on cellular networks. There, there will be extra network expenses (Devtechnosys, 2018).

Cost of Healthcare IoT Application Development

Several factors that affect the development costs must be taken into account when developing IoT applications for health applications. They are (Devtechnosys, 2018):

- Total number of platforms endorsed.
- Full integration of different applications from third parties such as payment portals, healthcare APIs etc.
- Data source and requirements for data ingestion.
- Security standards.

If Bluetooth links the iOS and Android healthcare software to a variety of radiation monitoring devices, analyzes the readings of various sensors, produces medical reports, and also sends the results to any cloud-based server, then the total development hours will be around 2000. The estimated cost is around $70,000 for such a large-scale production of healthcare software. It takes nearly 6000 hours to build a multi-level IoT application with a web-based admin interface, with ERP / CRM applications and embedded software that operates on specialized medical devices and mobile applications. It could cost him approximately $200,000 to build an IoT framework (Devtechnosys, 2018).

Different factors decide the cost for IoT production of healthcare applications. The above cost of developing IoT applications in the medical industry is an estimation that offers an insight into the cost of developing IoT healthcare applications.

IoT Solutions to Health Providers

In delivering digital approaches to safety, we are heading into a whole new phase in medical treatment, clinical surveillance and management. Innovative healthcare innovations are now commonly implemented in medical institutions that enable healthcare facilities to hold costs down, optimize patients' safety and enhance workflows. Such strategies aim to alter the market significantly. Cell phones, mobile apps, bio-sensors, wearables, home virtual supports, blockchain-driven online surveillance networks, predictive analytics and automated data platforms represent a completely modern step of healthcare. In respect to the advantages of digital medicine, I would like, first of all, to mention the improved diagnosis procedure, the efficient handling of data and stronger customer support. In fact, organisations will benefit from automatic evaluations, continuous patient tracking and effective diagnosis through the use of advanced technological solutions. (Maltseva, 2018).

Sensors and Smart Devices

- Precise reading and evaluation of indicators for connecting sensors to mobile devices can help health centers substitute for large devices for smaller instruments. Sensor technology, such as smart monitors and apps, provides many benefits for health management.
- Intelligent devices such as sophisticated inhalers for bronchial asthma, syringe bolt monitoring diabetes mellitus, innovative smartphones and smart blisters have already been actively produced and introduced on the market. This intelligent technology render detection faster, treatment better and patient support more efficient, an significant move in the advancement of health care facilities. For example, the latest norm for medical care of bronchial asthma is smart inhalers. Many other significant smart technology uses, such as in real-time health services, sensors and automated health networks are available in the fields of healthcare (Maltseva, 2018).

Biosensors

- Biosensor is a key component of the physical safety movement. There are a number of biosensors that relay medical information through a wireless network to smartphones and web applications. Biosensors can support people throughout their lives, too, by gathering knowledge on both their daily life, sleep and general health care. Outside the hospital boundaries, the biosensors can monitor patient treatment. Biosensor systems, for example, can enable users to monitor insulin level, blood pressure, heart rhythm, oxygen content, pulse and blood alcohol levels. None of these methods are particularly sensitive and provide unique interventions that are especially valuable for managing the well-being of elderly patients with many chronic diseases.

- The capacity of biosensors to monitor patient medications in real time and provide physicians with all knowledge gathered, thus avoiding disease symptoms and improving diagnosis is essential. Because the data is read directly and is constantly monitored from the patient, the collected measurements are better than those submitted in patient visits and can give specialists a genuine clinical path in each individual case. (Maltseva, 2018).

Patient Health Portals

- Online information apps have already become a central feature of the healthcare industry. Improved client support and streamlined procedures, such as referrals for care and preparation, enhance physicians and patients' lives. Imagine, for example, a fitness network that helps patients to track tests and test information electronically with clinicians and experts, pay quickly and chat with patients to find nutritious food and suggestions and to have book meetings. IoT opportunities are not only restricted to medical professionals, but also patients and their relatives. The most impressive part of IoT is that global patient tracking is rendered better than ever because any medical clock from all around the planet is granted access to healthcare. Throughout the elderly region, IoT-enabled apps and tools are very useful (Maltseva, 2018).

Machine Learning Applications

- The healthcare sector, as with many other industries, gains from machine learning. Health organizations can enhance client satisfaction and derive value from a vast volume of knowledge, analyze health data correctly and optimize patients' care by machine learning technology. Health care and pharmaceutical firms utilize R&D analytics to develop their clinical trials and their decision-making processes for practical applications. When the judgments are drawn by specialists and other professionals, often it feels a bit confusing and complicated as a ton of knowledge can not be accessed quickly.

- There is also a high chance of human error. Intelligent data processing will make this possible by the integration of external data points from different outlets, the break down of information asymmetries and the implementation of sophisticated data mining algorithms. When types of evidence are increasingly diverse, innovative methods of knowledge gathering and interpretation may be found that enable researchers to assess increasingly easily and more comfortably.

- ML provides tremendous opportunities for innovation in clinical practice and enhancement in patient service, but the health industry currently lags behind software learner development deployments. (Maltseva, 2018).

Blockchain-Based Initiatives

- Blockchain technologies may be employed in numerous other areas, in addition to finance and funding. Although the system is identical, it has distinct uses and, in fact, healthcare professionals may profit tremendously from its use. The encrypted storing of data and protected processing are both benefits of Blockchain integrative Safe communication between healthcare institutions, unchanging data collection and open data transfer.
- Blockchain technology in the healthcare industry is becoming commonly used. For starters, the Estonian eHealth Fund and Guardtime cooperated in creating a Blockchain-based network that safeguards millions of medical documents. The healthcare industry is rapidly transforming by the development of revolutionary drugs and the implementation of emerging technology. They push into a whole new era of patient treatment and safety monitoring and automated diagnostic devices (Maltseva, 2018).

IMPACT OF QUANTUM COMPUTING IN HEALTHCARE

Quantum computers have profoundly groundbreaking consequences like medicine, pharms and health care – in many areas of our lives. (Shohini Gose, 2019)

Supersonic Drug Design

Pharmaceuticals are undoubtedly being produced through lengthy and expensive clinical trials: scientists and pharmaceutical firms began to experiment with alternative methods, for example through artificial intelligence, human chip organ or silicon trial, to speed up the process and improve the cost-effectiveness of the discovery and production of medicinal drugs.

Quantum computer searches may be carried out in the least time possible for any molecules at unprecedented pace, drug targeting experiments conducted on any cell model potential or in the human Silicon tissues and networks. This would open the doors to find the disease antidote we never thought of before.

Aging in Silicon Clinical Trials

For silicon clinical trials, there is no need for human or animal, or even a cell to test a new procedure, treatment choice or medication. It means a custom computer simulation used to create or control a medicinal drug, device or action.

The development of 'Virtual Human' and full simulations such as the HumMod which features more than 1,500 equations and 6,500 variables such as body fluid, breathing, electrolytes, hormones, metabolism and skin temperature will advance Quantum computing greatly. This also opened the door to "viving" clinical trials with the maximum number of simulated patients possible and tester loving components. The time needed for such trials, but also their quality and comprehensiveness, would be massively cut.

Sequencing and Evaluating the Maximum Pace of DNA

Quantum computation might provide an significant step into the area: it will require quicker sequencing and more detailed and quicker processing of the whole genome. For fact, forecasts would be more accurate because quantum computers will take far more knowledge into consideration than conventional computers, which may also apply a bit of genetic evidence to health records. Quantum computing could take the guesswork out of genomics and genetics to ensure better health for everyone.

Make Patients a Real Treatment Point

Quantum computation with measurements increases the prediction of lifestyle to a whole new level. While efforts are made to turn from preventive to predictive safety, these are intermittent and in their infancy. For instance, an ophthalmology app shows the patient how their vision would change with the cataract in five years. A detailed forecast of the potential wellbeing of a single entity can be achieved by the use of quantum computers supplied by a great deal of health parameters, genetic records, sensible details as well as other personal data. That is what we always should find safety predictive.

The Perfect Support System for Decision-Making

Quantum computing would make it entirely new and increase it even with special skills. They could skimp through all the studies, discover correlations and causes never found by the human eye, and stumble over diagnoses or treatment options the human physician would never find out. Quantums could develop an uplifted PubMed version in the endpoint of this development, with information not in the traditional written form, but in qubits of data, because nobody but the computer would 'read' the studies anymore.

Build the best Clinical Data Structures of all Time

The usage of quantum uncertainty as one of the most possible uses in quantum computation for encryption. It can be used to generate private keys to encrypt messages sent from one place to another – but hackers can't replicate the key exactly because of quantum uncertainty. To hack such keys, they must break the laws of quantum physics. Imagine that level of safety with respect to sensitive health information: electronic records of health, genetic and genomic data, or any personal information generated about our bodies by our health care system.

CONCLUSION

Worldwide academics have begun to uncover various technical approaches that strengthen healthcare through the application of IoT technology to expand current systems together. This chapter explores different aspects of the health system IoT and the structures of the numerous health networks that allow this IoT web integrated and enable patient data to be gathered and distributed. The chapter concluded with a study of the main problems that threaten consumer privacy in IoT's health care model.

Recent times have seen significant growth in the adoption of IoT. It is widely used in the healthcare industry for tracking progress and health status of patients. Hospitals and providers of health care can save the cost of operations, manage existing assets and spend more time enhancing overall performance of the system In the end, by increasing performance it saves their time. Overall efficiency of elderly care has improved in an IoT approach. This obviously has every benefit for the patients.

IoT is one of the world's most widely deployed development technologies in the health and medical industries. It is commonly used to build IoT healthcare applications with the help of sensors, biosensors and such other tools, to track patient processes, better management and advanced protection. The value of medical IoT is strengthened by the symbiosis of machine learning (ML) and artificial intelligence (AI). When large numbers of information are constantly being collected from sensor-aided systems, data analysis and ML, operational conclusions are drawn that help the therapeutic process much faster.

The potential of quantum computing in healthcare is to revolutionize patient care. Quantum computing can help to detect and detect diseases by identifying and forecasting malfunctions. Health researchers are currently working on how quantum computing-based cancer detection techniques can be used. Present technologies in cancer diagnosis require time, so it may be difficult to produce successful tests. More accurate, faster and more effective methods for optimizing the process are needed. In order to detect disease-specific clues and biomarkers, quantum data will look in greater depth at the data supplied for cancer testing. Quantum computing often theoretically enhances MRI technologies by incredibly accurate measurements that allow doctors to peer at tiny particles that could not be found in conventional computers any deeper (O'Dowd, 2017).

REFERENCES

Anwar, M., Abdullah, A. H., Altameem, A., Qureshi, K. N., Masud, F., Faheem, M., Cao, Y., & Kharel, R. (2018). Green communication for wireless body area networks: Energy aware link efficient routing approach. *Sensors (Basel)*, *18*(10), 3237. doi:10.339018103237 PMID:30261628

Bernstein, D. J. (2009). *Introduction to post-quantum cryptography*. Post-Quantum Cryptography. doi:10.1007/978-3-540-88702-7

Bernstein, D. J., Buchmann, J., & Dahmen, E. (Eds.). (2009). *Post-quantum cryptography*. Springer. doi:10.1007/978-3-540-88702-7

Bernstein. (2009). *Cost analysis of hash collisions: Will quantum computers make SHARCS obsolete?* (Report). Academic Press.

Biham, E., & Mor, T. (1997). Bounds on Information and the Security of Quantum Cryptography. *Physical Review Letters*, *79*(20), 4034–4037. doi:10.1103/PhysRevLett.79.4034

Biham, E., & Mor, T. (1997). Security of Quantum Cryptography against Collective Attacks. *Physical Review Letters*, *78*(11), 2256–2259. doi:10.1103/PhysRevLett.78.2256

Choi, J., In, Y., Park, C., Seok, S., Seo, H., & Kim, H. (2018). Secure IoT framework and 2D architecture for End-To-End security. *The Journal of Supercomputing*, *74*(8), 3521–3535. doi:10.100711227-016-1684-0

Devtechnosys. (2018). *Cost and Features of IoT Solutions for Healthcare*. https://devtechnosys.com/cost-and-features-of-iot-solutions-for-healthcare

Domingo, M. C. (2012). An overview of the Internet of Things for people with disabilities. *Journal of Network and Computer Applications, 35*(2), 584–596. doi:10.1016/j.jnca.2011.10.015

Gope, P., & Hwang, T. (2015). BSN-Care: A secure IoT-based modern healthcare system using body sensor network. *IEEE Sensors Journal, 16*(5), 1368–1376. doi:10.1109/JSEN.2015.2502401

Gose. (2019). https://medicalfuturist.com/quantum-computing-in-healthcare/

Islam, S. R., Kwak, D., Kabir, M. H., Hossain, M., & Kwak, K. S. (2015). The internet of things for health care: A comprehensive survey. *IEEE Access: Practical Innovations, Open Solutions, 3*, 678–708. doi:10.1109/ACCESS.2015.2437951

Johansson, M. (2019). *Synchronization of Acoustic Sensors in a Wireless Network.* Academic Press.

Ko, H., & Song, M. (2016). A study on the secure user profiling structure and procedure for home health-care systems. *Journal of Medical Systems, 40*(1), 1. doi:10.100710916-015-0365-5 PMID:26573639

Korolov & Drinkwater. (2019). https://www.csoonline.com/article/3235970/what-is-quantum-cryptog-raphy-it-s-no-silver-bullet-but-could-improve-security.html

Lloret, J., Canovas, A., Sendra, S., & Parra, L. (2015). A smart communication architecture for ambient assisted living. *IEEE Communications Magazine, 53*(1), 26–33. doi:10.1109/MCOM.2015.7010512

Lo, B. P., Ip, H., & Yang, G. Z. (2016). *Transforming health care: body sensor networks, wearables, and the internet of things.* Academic Press.

Lo, H. -K, & Chau, H. F. (1999). Unconditional Security of Quantum Key Distribution over Arbitrarily Long Distances. *Science, 283*(5410), 2050-2056.

Lütkenhaus, N. (n.d.). *Security against eavesdropping in quantum cryptography.* Physical.

Malaney, R. (2010). Location-dependent communications using quantum entanglement. *Physical Review A., 81*(4). Advance online publication. doi:10.1103/PhysRevA.81.042319

Maltseva, D. (2018). *IoT Solutions for Healthcare Providers.* https://www.iotforall.com/topdigital-health-solutions/

Mathew, A., Sa, F. A., Pooja, H. R., & Verma, A. (2015). Smart disease surveillance based on Internet of Things (IoT). *International Journal of Advanced Research in Computer and Communication Engineering, 4*(5), 180-183.

Mayers, D. (2001). Unconditional security in quantum cryptography. *Journal of the Association for Computing Machinery, 48*(3), 351–406. doi:10.1145/382780.382781

O'Dowd. (2017). https://hitinfrastructure.com/news/how-ibm-universal-quantum-computing-impacts-hit-infrastructure

Quantum Resistant Public Key Exchange: The Supersingular Isogenous Diffie-Hellman Protocol. (2016). CoinFabrik Blog.

Rao, S. (2019). *Evolution of IoT in Healthcare.* https://www.iotforall.com/evolution-iot-healthcare

Rghioui, A., & Oumnad, A. (2017). Internet of Things: Surveys for Measuring Human Activities from Everywhere. *International Journal of Electrical & Computer Engineering, 7*(5).

Rghioui, A., & Oumnad, A. (2018). Challenges and Opportunities of Internet of Things in Healthcare. *International Journal of Electrical & Computer Engineering, 8.*

Rghioui, A., Sendra, S., Lloret, J., & Oumnad, A. (2016). Internet of things for measuring human activities in ambient assisted living and e-health. *Network Protocols and Algorithms, 8*(3), 15–28. doi:10.5296/npa.v8i3.10146

Sawand, A., Djahel, S., Zhang, Z., & Nait-Abdesselam, F. (2015). Toward energy-efficient and trustworthy eHealth monitoring system. *China Communications, 12*(1), 46–65. doi:10.1109/CC.2015.7084383

SheaS. (2020). https://searchsecurity.techtarget.com/feature/Computer-Security-Fundamentals-Quantum-security-to-certifications

Singh, R. (2016). A proposal for mobile e-care health service system using IoT for Indian scenario. *Journal of Network Communications and Emerging Technologies, 6*(1).

Sreekanth, K. U., & Nitha, K. P. (2016). A study on health care in Internet of Things. *International Journal on Recent and Innovation Trends in Computing and Communication, 4*(2), 44–47.

Thapliyal, K., & Pathak, A. (2018). Kak's three-stage protocol of secure quantum communication revisited. *Quantum Information Processing, 17*(9). Advance online publication. doi:10.100711128-018-2001-z

Watrous, J. (2009). Zero-Knowledge against Quantum Attacks. *SIAM Journal on Computing, 39*(1), 25–58. doi:10.1137/060670997

Yu, L., Lu, Y., Tian, Y. M., & Zhu, X. L. (2012). Research on architecture and key technology of Internet of Things in hospital. *Transducer and Microsystem Technologies, 6*, 23.

Chapter 9
The Role of Quantum Computing in Software Forensics and Digital Evidence:
Issues and Challenges

Sandeep Kumar Sharma

(iD) https://orcid.org/0000-0002-2048-671X

Department of Computer Science and IT, Khwaja Moinuddin Chishti Language University, India

Mazhar Khaliq

Department of Computer Science and IT, Khwaja Moinuddin Chishti Language University, India

ABSTRACT

Quantum computing has immense computational advantages. It escorts today's world of computing towards qubits universe of computing by the logical superposition technique. Various new technologies will come to reality with replacement of existing problem-solving methodology. The development of quantum computing imposes significant impact on cyber security and digital forensics technologies. Cybercrimes may be dramatically increased and malicious code will get ability to harm speedily. The quantum computing in software forensics methodology needs to develop in order to counter the challenges such as traceability of malicious code automation, sources of malicious code generation, intellectual property right theft issues, source code validation, plagiarism, breach of copyright issues, and an acquisition of digital evidence with quality and quantity with the wings of quantum forensics. This chapter aims to concentrate on the key issues of quantum computing approach in the field of software forensics with ontological aspects.

DOI: 10.4018/978-1-7998-6677-0.ch009

Copyright © 2021, IGI Global. Copying or distributing in print or electronic forms without written permission of IGI Global is prohibited.

INTRODUCTION AND BACKGROUND STUDY

The advances in information technology have a large effect on our digital life and digital society. Quantum computing is an exciting technological development for a world of opportunities with safe environment and sustainable development and implementation. Amazon has launched its "quantum as a service" as Amazon Braket for scientists, researchers and developers to build, test and run quantum computing algorithms. Quantum computing would be accomplished in resolving extraordinarily complex problems within one decade with supercomputer competency. It would lead to revolutionize a variety of fields, including cryptography, cyber-security, digital forensics, medical computing, and many more. Quantum computing a single qubit can in general be an unequal linear superposition of the basis states zero and one:

$\Psi >= \alpha|1> + \beta|0>$, where $\alpha^2 + \beta^2 = 1$

From an n-particle quantum system an n-qubit register (qureg) may be constructed:

$\Psi >= > \otimes > \otimes \otimes >\equiv > n\ |1\ |1\ |1\ |11\ 1 \ldots \ldots$

"Applying a linear (n–1) number of operations to the qureg yields a register state which is a superposition of an exponential ($2n$) number of terms. This exponential performance is one crucial characteristic of the potential power of quantum computation." (Overill, 2012)

Quantum computing and the architecture of computation challenges to think differently in the world of computation. For quantum systems have to develop entirely new software coding languages, algorithms, measurement standards and a whole host of yet-to-be invented tools currently two technologies show great promise first superconducting qubits and second trapped ions.

The theory of quantum mechanics produces the fundamental principles of quantum computing. These fundamental concepts are superposition, entanglement and the uncertainty principle in quantum mechanical measurements. The theory of information that led to the development of quantum information theory, in which quantum computing originates alongside quantum communication and quantum sensing among many others. Any two (or more) quantum states can be added together ("superposed") and the result will be another valid quantum state; and conversely, that every quantum state can be represented as a sum of two or more other distinct states.

Quantum mechanics permits multiple register elements to collectively store superposition over multiple binary values. "This phenomenon, known as entanglement, is a form of information that cannot be reproduced by conventional bits. While the register elements remain independently addressable, the information they store can no longer be expressed piecewise. The principles of superposition and entanglement lead to an important conceptual difference about how to interpret the value of a register". Werner Heisenberg formulated the uncertainty principle at Niels Bohr's institute in Copenhagen, while working on the mathematical foundations of quantum mechanics. In quantum mechanics, the uncertainty principle is any of a variety of mathematical inequalities. (Sen, D., 2014)

"Asserting a fundamental limit to the precision with which the values for certain pairs of physical quantities of a particle, such as position, x, and momentum, p, can be predicted from initial conditions. The Heisenberg Uncertainty Principle states that the product of uncertainties in related physical quantities (e.g. position and momentum, energy and time, etc.) has a finite lower bound" (Bohr & Waldemar, 1958)

Humble elaborate "The blind quantum computing paradigm uses the principles of quantum mechanics to protect not only the input data but also the program delegated to the quantum processor. The methods make uses quantum error correction schemes mitigate against de-coherence as well as fault-tolerant protocols to extend operational sequences."

Overview of Quantum Data and Memory

Physicist Stephanie Simmons proposes a roundabout way of storing quantum data, first, convert data into binary data translating the numbers that describe quantum superposition into simple 1's and 0's. Then, you store that converted data in a classical storage format. (Hui, 2018)

"Quantum computers are powered by atomic-scale nodes called quantum bits, or "qubits." Quantum physicist Andrea Morello's team built a proof-of-concept quantum computer where the system's two qubits are the nucleus and a single orbiting electron of the phosphorus atom. In Quantum memory advancement the researchers published the first-ever demonstration of storing and retrieving quantum data from the nucleus of a solitary atom embedded in silicon". (Roos, 2017)

"Quantum memory stores a quantum state for later retrieval. These states hold useful computational information known as qubits. Quantum memory is essential for the development of many devices in quantum information processing, including a synchronization tool that can match the various processes in a quantum computer, a quantum gate that maintains the identity of any state, and a mechanism for converting predetermined photons into on-demand photons. Quantum memory can be used in many aspects, such as quantum computing and quantum communication. Continuous research and experiments have enabled quantum memory to realize the storage of qubits". (Tittel, et-al, 2009)

"Quantum memory is one such field, mapping the quantum state of light onto a group of atoms and then restoring it to its original shape. Quantum memory is a key element in information processing, such as optical quantum computing and quantum communication, while opening a new way for the foundation of light-atom interaction".

"Quantum information is stored in Fractals. DNA is such fractal that builds biosphere from information that it stores .As describe the situation in quantum computing it would have a chance, if we write software which runs in these very short times. After ending a result we could store it in classical way".

In quantum computer the information is stored in quantum mechanical systems. Accordingly, a quantum computer can make use of quantum mechanical properties, such as for example superposition or entanglement, to speed up computation and the execution of quantum algorithms. Quantum algorithms is Shor's algorithm other quantum algorithms allow the implementation of an oracle or fast searches in databases .Quantum simulation is quantum computers application. The idea is to use a well-controlled quantum mechanical system to simulate the behavior of another quantum mechanical system and gain insight into the behavior.

The quantum mechanical systems for information storage are subject to de-coherence, quantum error correction (QEC) has to be performed for fault-tolerant. "A quantum computer is a computer which executes sequences of instructions in a quantum mechanical system. Quantum algorithms exploit quantum mechanical properties like superposition and entanglement and can solve certain problems exponentially faster than classical computers. The quantum information in quantum computers is stored in quantum mechanical two-level systems which are called quantum bits, or short qubits. As with any quantum mechanical system, the qubits are subject to noise-induced de-coherence. Thus, quantum information cannot be stored infinitely long. A Quantum dot and other techniques used to capture electrons (since the information is stored in the respective spins of electron), A Quantum dot can be thought as a replacement of transistor". (Brandl, 2017)

"A variational quantum Eigen solver (VQE) simulation of two intermediate-scale chemistry problems performed by Google AI Quantum and collaborators. A series of quantum simulations of chemistry the largest of which involved a dozen qubits, 78 two-qubit gates, and 114 one-qubit gates. Generate highly entangled states over the computational basis, during establishing a foundation for scaling up more complex correlated quantum simulations of chemistry". (Rubin, 2020)

Quantum Cryptography Protocols

Quantum cryptographic protocols will be an essential part of cyberspace security issues for forthcoming perspective of Internet. As an important cryptographic basic protocol, the oblivious transfer protocol is one of the key technologies for privacy protection in cryptography. The concept of quantum oblivious transfer it was first put forward by Crépeau in 1994. In 1994, the the "oblivious transfer" security of against any individual measurement allowed by quantum mechanics was proved by Mayers and Salvail In 1998, the protocol was proposed, which proves the security of the QOT protocol under an eavesdropper. Quantum authentication (QA) protocol is also one of the quantum cryptographic protocols. It was proposed in 2001.

The quantum cryptography protocol has developed many branches now. In addition to the protocols as QKD protocol, QOT protocol, and QA protocol. Quantum cryptography protocols also include quantum bit commitment (QBC) protocols and quantum signature (QS) protocols. Quantum key distribution protocol takes the four-particle GHZ state as the quantum channel, chooses the specific measurement direction to express sensitive messages and takes the quantum blind signature as the basis to build a mobile quantum payment system.(Zhou,et-al,2018)

"Through Quantum cryptography techniques secure information exchange between legitimate users along communication lines. BB84 protocol was discussed in 1984, uses 4 quantum states that constitute 2 bases, BB84 which used coded qubits to most recently AK15, which uses decoy qubits to prevent data breach. State Protocol developed in 1992, according to that only 2 non-orthogonal quantum state suited without use of all the 4 states. EPR Protocol is also a variation to the BB84, and is based on the EPR Paradox in Quantum Mechanics that states that, the result of a measurement on one particle of an entangled quantum system can have an immediate effect on another particle, regardless of the distance of the two parts". (Murthy, 2019)

Quantum teleportation is an essential concept in many quantum information protocols and it is also considered as an important possible mechanism for building gates within quantum computers.

"According to Xu H., et.-al., mainly uses quantum cryptography within presented RFID middleware architecture to protect RFID systems from the clone attack, which is guaranteed by "no-cloning" properties of quantum mechanics. In this architecture, tags and readers are communicated through qubits, while the RFID middleware could prepare and measure qubits". (Xu,et-al, 2020)

In the year 1970, Quantum Cryptography was introduced by Stephen Wiesner and subsequently the concepts are modified and extended by Bennett in the year 1984. The entire process of Quantum Cryptography depends on the values of quantum mechanics. The basic level of matter is light weight particles known as photons. Quantum systems are constructed by considering the basic rules of quantum mechanics and depend upon the laws of classical physics.(Kaci,et-al, 2014),(Li,et-al,2015).

Quantum Cryptography can be defined as an integrated approach that combines the concepts of cryptography with laws of quantum physics. It can solve all issues of traditional cryptographic algorithms. It implements some mathematical methods to prevent and avoid attacks just like eavesdroppers. Quantum cryptography can be considered as an advanced and enhanced version of conventional cryptographic technique. MIT and IBM panel experts admitted that even after quantum computers become reality, the stability of qubits makes quantum machine learning feasible with various simulated tested algorithms.

Cyber Security, Cyber Crimes, Digital Forensics and Digital Evidence

Cyber terrorism is a kind of threat to government and general public to cause unpredictable violence and unexpected losses. If cyber security is weak, the country would not be strong at any point. Cyber security has many scopes. It is mainly focused on technical expertise, legal framework and security Infrastructure that can use the technology and the law towards achieving the objective of 'securing the information assets' of the country. Cyber security handle the protection of computer systems and networks from cyber-attacks but the new era of quantum computing cause both threats and technical enhancement in cyber security dimensions. Cyber criminals lead to quantum cyber criminals to breach system or network through quantum computing for illegal and harmful purpose. Nowadays cyber security is not only protection but innovation also for emerging areas. (Wallden & Kashefi, 2019)

The emergence of digital forensics is to prosecute cyber-crimes and criminals through efficient and updated versions of cyber law with respect to new technological growth. The impact of cyber-crimes on society is very dangerous and leads to mob lynching type of incidence nowadays in all over world as various examples in India. Cyber -crime is to crack personal confidentiality using fake information's and images/pictures through online activities use of internet to promote communal riots. In this era terrorists are incessantly using fake communal multimedia production over the internet using social networking apps .Therefore, it is necessary to identify the illegal elements to avoid the cyber- crimes. Digital forensics is the "process of identifying, preserving, analyzing and presenting digital evidence in a manner that is legally acceptable in any legal proceedings (i.e., a court of law).The methods that digital forensics uses to handle digital evidence are very much grounded in the field's roots in the scientific method of forensic science". (Mohay &et-al, 2003)

Digital forensics is the branch of forensic science in which we can able to restructure the precedent events by forensics tools for lawful proceedings in the court. The digital forensics challenges include many different types of hardware and mobile apps and huge number of mobile operating systems Social networking apps services used for a criminals to communicate and coordinate their criminal acts like defrauding, vishing, phishing, smishing, blue bugging violence dedicated viral messages etc. (Mahalik & Tamma 2014),

The advances in information technology have a large effect on our digital world. Cyber criminals are hazard to government and public to cause unpredictable violence and unexpected losses. Communication is the core weapon for terrorists and cyber criminals. Mobile Apps are mobile application services through Apple App Store, Google Play, Windows Phone Store, and BlackBerry App World. However there are independent app stores, such as Cydia, GetJar and open source apps.The digital evidence obtain from digital forensic is identical to any supplementary proof in the sense that it must be authentic, accurate, complete, convincing to jury, and in consistency with universal law and legislative policy. (Barmpatsalou, k & et-al, 2013), (Levinson, 2011).

Computer forensics tools assist forensics examiners by collecting information from a computer system making a true and permanent copy of that information so that it can be used in a legal proceeding and analyzing data to uncover information that may not be immediately obvious .Collected evidence is transferred from the collection tools directly to the files without human intervention. (Garfinkel, 2010) with the spreading of cyber-crime, internet forensics has emerged as a new discipline in the system security arena. (Karyda &etl, 2007) .Some work is being done towards the definition of methodologies for the collection of digital evidences from storage devices that can withstand legal analysis in court. On the contrary, the collection of network evidences that allows for a selection of the traffic and guarantees legal admissibility is still an open field. Trusted Internet forensics is a network appliance that collects data from the network for forensics purposes. Such an appliance relies on a trusted computing platform in order to allow for the verification of the computational chain so that the data collected could be used as evidence in court. (Bruschi & et.-al, 2005)

IT forensics tools are forensics imaging tool safe back, Helix, Niksun net detector, safe suite decision, List open files (LISOF), DDutility, FIND Tool,, XRY, Oxygen Forensics etc.(John S&etl.,2018) Software Forensics is the area of Software Science aimed at authorship analysis of computer source code. Authorship analysis of any kind, whether it be applied upon source code or written word, is based upon the premise that authors develop a style and approach that is identifiable. The first reference to Software Forensics its base has been in computer security. When a security breach has been detected, often the only evidence other than the damage is the occasional code fragment. The concept of authorship analysis for software source code has been briefly introduced, and a subset of the field has been identified that is called software forensics. (Sallis & et.-al., 1996)

Quantum Cyber Security

"Quantum cyber security is the field that studies all aspects affecting the security and privacy of communications and computations caused by the development of quantum technologies". (Wallden & Kashefi, 2019).The development of large quantum computers it will bring consequences for cyber security. For example, it is known that important problems such as factoring and the discrete log, problems whose presumed hardness ensures the security of many widely used protocols (for example, RSA, DSA, ECDSA), can be solved efficiently. (William & Alan, 2017), (Vernacchia, 2019).

Quantum Computing and Security Algorithms

Quantum computing is still in extravagant, quantum forensics has gotten negligible from research communities .Even research completed so far there are theories of potential impact in capability of live forensics on quantum system with minimal digital evidence artifacts recoverable. (Sachowski, 2018) Quantum bits are represented by qubits. The representing information is 0 or 1 and combination of both at the same time that is superposition. The qubit's superposition can provide more computing power in the same space. "Quantum states are fragile and quantum errors are notoriously difficult to measure". (Bridgwater, 2017), (Ludlow, 2019). "Shor's algorithm is a polynomial-time quantum computer algorithm for integer factorization. Informally, it solves the given an integer, find its prime factors and Public key cryptography system can be compromised by shor's algorithms". (Shor, 1994)

The purpose of Grover's algorithm is usually described as "searching a database". It may be more accurate to describe it as "inverting a function". In fact since the oracle for an unstructured database requires at least linear complexity, the algorithm cannot be used for actual databases. (Grover, 1996). Quantum Approximate Optimization Algorithm (QAOA): Approximate optimization is a way of finding an approximate solution to an optimization problem, Quantum semi definite programming, and Quantum data fitting. Harrow Hassidim Lloyd (HHL) algorithm, the algorithm is one of the main fundamental algorithms expected to provide a speedup over their classical counterparts, along with Shor's factoring algorithm, Grover's search algorithm and quantum simulation. Provided the linear system is sparse. (Wikipedia)

New Wings of Digital Quantum Forensics

Computational quantum theory has high-performance computing, it includes many aspects of cyber security including fraud detection, information warfare, cybercrime and digital forensics. (Woodward, 2012). The quantum computing implementation in ontology aspect of Digital Forensics gives new wing of digital quantum forensics (Overill, 2012). Ontology based discipline of Digital Forensics explored in study include Computer forensics, Software forensics, Data forensics, Network forensics, Mobile forensics and Satellite forensics with cyber law perspective (Konstadopoulou, 2006). Computer forensics is divided into Desktop, Server, Laptop, Digital Camera, CCTV, Memory (Hard-Disk, RAM etc.) and Electronics Components & Device Forensics.

Software Forensics focuses on operating system forensics (open source and proprietary), application software forensics, and forensic tools analysis which also include IPR, Software Patents, Copyrights open source and proprietary) Web forensics, Web Browser, Mobile apps Forensics, E-commerce services E-Banking & payment, Malicious Source code or Binary Code. (Barmpatsalou&etl., 2013), Data Forensics include Data base Log files DBMS Statistics,Meta data Financial Medical data Multimedia Data(Images, Video, Audio etc.) and Stochastic Forensics (Insider Data Theft) .Network Forensics concentrates on Wired & Wireless(Wi-Fi, 4G,5G, VOIP,LTE, Bluetooth) Net Camera, Cloud, IOT, Internet Forensics, Firewall, Router, Networking Tools & Peripheral Devices Forensics. Mobile forensics focuses on Mobile Phones, PDA, Tab, Smart Watch, Small Scale Portable Devices, Digital jewelry, SIM Card Forensics. Satellite Forensics involves Satellite Navigation System Device Forensics, Satellite Phone Forensics, Global Positioning System (GPS) Forensics and Google Earth Forensics. (Karie & Venter, 2014), (Sharma & Khaliq, 2020).

Figure 1. Ontology based discipline of Digital Forensics &Cyber Law, source: own

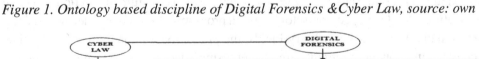

Figure 2. Levels of Quantum Languages , Source: permitted by author, http://quantumwa.org/

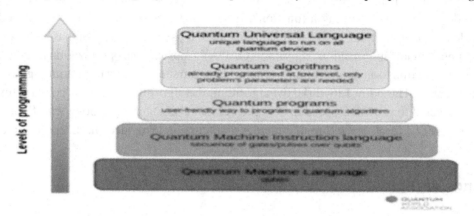

QUANTUM COMPUTING AND SOFTWARE FORENSICS

Quantum computing has immense potential as a force for good but it also poses an extensive risk in the wrong hands. In progress it is necessary to prevent future disasters, criminals and cyber-terrorists with access to equivalent facilities and skills could use the technology to instigate security crises, generate fear and frustrate positive progress. (Vernacchia, 2019) All security concepts, such as authentication, encryption but also more involved concepts as computation on encrypted data and secure multiparty computation, would need to be modified to apply to *quantum* information and *quantum* computation., (Konstadopoulou, 2006), (Woodward, 2012)

2.1 Quantum Software Application Development Window

According to Microsoft, programming language Q # (Q sharp) collaborates with Visual Studio. It is tools simulation of quantum algorithms. It will evolve software bridge between classical and quantum computing. In 2018, D-wave developed LEAP. It is Real-Time Quantum Application Environment (QAE) and cloud-based QAE. To fill the gap in D-wave system, Los Alamos National Laboratory has developed a quantum macro-assembler language called QMASM .In January 2019; IBM is offering an integrated commercial use quantum computing system IBM Q. Using their Q Network and Q Quantum Computational Center, developers can easily submit quantum programs with Quantum Information Software Kit (Qiskit).It translates quantum programs into a lower level language called quantum instruction language (QASM).Rigetti Computing have developed Forest for quantum programs. AI group has developed Cirq, a quantum language. Xanadu developed Strawberry Fields, the photon-based quantum computer they are designing and constructing. Quantum circuits are written using Blackbird quantum programming language Qilimanjaro has launched the alpha version of Qibo, the language that will be used to program its quantum annealer. ProjectQ, may be to program IBM devices and Google devices.XACC, which is a full-stack library to program IBM, Rigetti and D-Wave quantum computers (wikipedia).

Figure 3. Quantum Computing Programming Languages, Source: permitted by author (Alba Cervera –lierta, 2018) for quantum world association http://quantumwa.org/

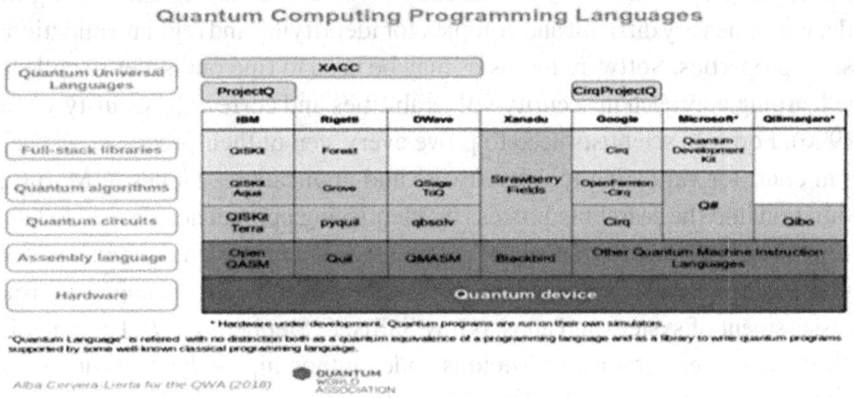

Quantum Computing Programming Languages

	XACC						
Quantum Universal Languages	ProjectQ				CirqProjectQ		
	IBM	Rigetti	DWave	Xanadu	Google	Microsoft*	QISmanjaro*
Full-stack libraries	QISKit	Forest			Cirq	Quantum Development Kit	
Quantum algorithms	QISKit Aqua	Grove	QSage TsQ	Strawberry Fields	OpenFermion -Cirq	Q#	
Quantum circuits	QISKit Terra	pyquil	qbsolv		Cirq		Qibo
Assembly language	Open QASM	Quil	QMASM	Blackbird	Other Quantum Machine Instruction Languages		
Hardware	Quantum device						

* Hardware under development. Quantum programs are run on their own simulators.

"Quantum Language" is referred with no distinction both as a quantum equivalence of a programming language and as a library to write quantum programs supported by some well known classical programming language.

Alba Cervera-Lierta for the QWA (2018)   QUANTUM WORLD ASSOCIATION

ONTOLOGY OF SOFTWARE FORENSICS WITH REFERENCE TO QUANTUM COMPUTING

Ontological approach may leads to develop digital quantum forensic theory and methodologies to proper handle Software Forensics. (Overill, 2012) "It is the science of analyzing software source code or binary code to determine whether intellectual property infringement or theft occurred. It is the centerpiece of lawsuits, trials, and settlements when companies are in dispute over issues involving software patents, copyrights, and trade secrets. Software forensics tools can compare code to determine correlation, a measure that can be used to guide a software forensics expert." (Sallis & et-al, 1996; Garfinkel, 2010). Through quantum computing algorithms realization, software forensics wings like operating system forensics, application software forensics, forensics tools, infringements of copy right, malicious code classification, attribution of intellectual property, web forensics, mobile applications, play stores validation and patent related crimes can be retaliate with digital evidence and quantum cyber law enforcement. But there is much lack of intension for digital quantum forensics technology contrary to cryptography system. It may be issues due to basics of digital forensics if any types of quantum crimes have been occurred then system have to learn the investigation procedures and approaches for quantum digital evidence with development of best practices for quantum crimes.

The Quantum Communication and Networks Project develop quantum devices and study them for use in quantum communications and networking applications. It focuses on research on the creation, transmission, transduction/interfacing, storage, processing and measurement of optical qubits .The quantum states of single photons. They proposed build and study quantum devices detectors, optical quantum memory and quantum transduction/interfaces. A long-term goal is to apply these devices into quantum systems such as a quantum repeater. They are working towards to implement a quantum network testbed in which the suitability and performance of new and existing quantum devices and systems can be studied in a real-life network environment. The test bed will lead to the development of best-practices and protocols for quantum networks. (Slattery, 2020)

Software forensic is used for analysing computer source, binary code for investigation, analysis, or prevention purposes. Malicious code is unethical intentions. It may be seem inoffensive, the code created to harm purposely. Software forensic is usually involve in detecting and finding the perpetrator of unethical code. It may be very difficult and complex for identifying and regular validation and verification regarding testing properties. Software forensics may be used to find out issues to collect artefact pattern with machine learning approach in security vulnerabilities and correcting security vulnerabilities. (Sallis & et.al., 1996). Forensic scientists need to prove every step of their processes, especially if they plan on testifying in court for validating tools, software and applications. (Jones & Maria, 2017). It should focus on automation into the searching process by identifying approaches s can also fall under the scope of software forensics. Software fault analysis as evidence leads implementations of software forensics system to automate digital evidence acquisition. So there should be mechanisms to trace the criminals and security assessment of system and apps. (Gray,Sallis, & Stephen, 1997).The role of Software forensics is to track message perpetrator of malicious code, authorship analysis of mobiles source and apps store, binary code and tracing the root culprit. The software forensics tools categories as recompilation, reverse engineering desquirr, dcc boomerang, plagiarism,jplag, yap, The Sleuth Kit (Autopsy), authorship analyzer. It should be trend with quantum computing. (Zeidman, 2011)

Figure 4. Ontology based Ontology of Software Forensics Source: Own.

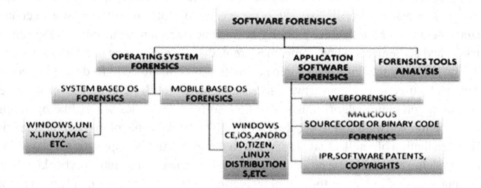

Quantum Computing and Forensics Software Engineering Approach

It is very difficult to find traceability of software reliability breach causes. It may be code errors, architectural, testing errors, less fault tolerance capability and get infected malicious code change their actual behavior and leads to failures. By this incidence, system may escorts to major accidents. So there is actual need of techniques to promote forensics software engineering .Through this approach we can list the root causes and profiling investigation with digital evidence but it is not possible to code tracing and evidence collection such type of environment. Nowadays Software complexity and reasons of accidents cannot be exposing by software development techniques. There are challenges as architectural variation, configuration specifications, testing validation and verification approach, poor communication development team, safety critical applications, stopping rules, investigation of faulty code, proper error handling and quality training (Johnson, 2013).

There is some hope from quantum computing and its algorithms which can be used as digital quantum forensics. Quantum computing and machine learning algorithms can be classified malicious codes. Grover's algorithm is used for searching .Researchers of University of Maryland have been using a D-Wave machine to classify malware. "Quantum computing will definitely be applied anywhere where we are using machine learning, cloud computing, data analysis. In security the focus on intrusion detection, looking for patterns in the data and more sophisticated forms of parallel computing" (Curran, 2017).

Lockheed Martin and University of Southern California (USC) researchers have developed an algorithm that allows D-Wave computers to tell whether a piece of software code is bug-free .The USC's Information Sciences Institute website3 states that Source Code Validation Research is being conducted. However, it has not yet released any practical findings (Jones, 2013).

Quantum Forensics Accounting

There is lack of technological guidelines from financial service provider of countries to handle quantum cyber security threats that is futuristic risk of quantum computer implementation in real world scenario. Cyber criminals have more intension for financial gain .Cyber criminals break the security algorithms and gain control over financial driven system to financial loss. So there is need for quantum algorithms in financial services technology with quantum cyber security approach. (Oyedokun, 2015).It may also include quantum forensics accounting to gather digital evidence as forensic investigation, forensic audit & audit reporting from such type criminal activities. It includes clarifications and verification of financial transactions and each and every event. "Once considered too futuristic to pose a real risk, quantum computers will soon become a reality and financial institutions (FI) are not yet prepared to deal with potential threats to cyber security". (Olsson, 2019)

QUANTUM EVIDENCE APPROACH

Digital Evidence is any probative information stored or transmitted in digital form that a party to a court case may uses at trial. Traceability and legality of digital forensics evidence might be having serious concern. The digital evidence obtained from cyber forensic evidence is just like any other evidence in the sense that it must be: authentic, accurate, complete, convincing to juries, and in conformity with common law. (Mali, 2015) .According to Wikipedia "Digital evidence or electronic evidence is any probative information stored or transmitted in digital form that a party to a court case may use at trial".

"In order to understand the possibilities for digital forensic examination and analysis of quantum computers, it is convenient to employ the conventional division into in live forensics and post mortem forensics. From what has already been said above it will be clear that it is not possible to perform live system forensics on a quantum computer". (Overill, 2012)

In digital forensics the main focus is to identify, collect, analysis, preserve and reporting evidence from source like systems, server, cell phones and networks etc. Advanced gadgets has quickly become a standard practice in law enforcement investigation .The collection of advanced proof from the Web or internet has become very tedious, crime scene investigation that manages the making sure about of information as proof from the internet source or web source. Following fig. shows digital evidence process framework. (Shipley, 2007)

Figure 5. Digital Evidence processes , source: (Shipley, 2007)

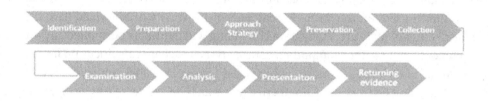

"According to Overill after the termination of a quantum algorithm and the recovery of an output state by controlled de-coherence. It will not be possible to reconstruct a timeline for the evolution of the quantum computation. This restriction places quite severe limitations on both the quantity and the quality of the evidential traces that may ultimately be recoverable". (Overill, 2012). The complexity collecting evidence as time limitation. "Photon pair polarization and linearity of quantum mechanics forbids such replication for all quantum systems so photons could not be cloned as state of quantum state" (Wootters & et.-el, 1982). According Reyes substantial evidence will be followed in quantum digital evidence. Because "Transistor" has technological baseon zero or one but "Quantum Energy State" has uncertain value of one or zero or both. If a quantum cryptanalysis generate fraudulent out through manipulating quantum process .it is not very easy to trace manipulation of data and their timeline for quantum digital evidence. (Reyes, 2019)

EMERGENCE OF QUANTUM CYBER LAW

Cyber legal implication of quantum computing may cause of emergence of quantum cyber law with worldwide collaboration need for future growth because cyber -crime has no boundary. It may futuristic need of world quantum cyber court as the international quantum court with technically enabled for real time justice for quantum cyber -crimes. According to Overill, there is lack of supplementary digital evidence for live digital forensics prosecution of quantum cyber- crime that deviate from law enforcement significance path and focuses the need of mitigating new technological crimes perspective. "A road-map for future digital forensic investigations of quantum cyber-crimes .The lack of ancillary evidence will prove to be a significant barrier to mounting successful judicial prosecutions in cases of serious quantum cyber-crime." (Overill, 2012).

It is challenging to establish cyber legal framework for illegal activities through quantum computing. To mitigate international cyber warfare there should be existence of uniform policies and legal framework on common platform. According to Dominic Rota it should have more attention towards development of quantum-resistant algorithms and technologies. (Rota, 2018).Quantum computing has very powerful data analysis capability that poses legal issues and risk for users .New technologies may create new legal issues, consequences may be arises for "quantum lawyer" as future perspective also . It should be procedure for liability of data loss due to errors generated by quantum computers. (Schrijver, 2019)

According to vijashakar, Quantum Computing has significance between two classical computing scenarios. Data captured by a classical computing system and it is part of Big Data technologies also. Data is processed by a Quantum Computing. For electronic evidence binary representation of '1'and'0' leads to qubits representation of data .there is limitation of classical cyber law section Sec 65B which has based on zero and one bit presentation certifier views it and converts it into a Computer output. The reliability of an electronic document certified under the Section 65B and Forensic witnesses under Section 79A may be verified by court of cyber law in India. There are many implications of Cyber Law in India and world also. It poses revise or change impact due to emerging technologies like Quantum Computing with new focus term the quantum cyber law. (Na, 2018)

Table 1. Key paper of Quantum forensics approach

S.No.	Name of the Author	Research Paper Title and Publication year	Key issues of the Paper
1.	Richard E. Overill	*"Digital quantum forensics: future challenges and prospects,* Int. J. Information Technology, Communications and Convergence, Vol. 2, No. 3, pp.205–211, 2012."	**a.** Quantum computing enabled gadgets become commonly accessible they will without a doubt be utilized by digital crooks to perform beast power decoding undertakings that were beforehand infeasible. **b.** This paper tends to the central points of interest of the quality and the amount of advanced legal evidence from quantum computing gadgets through the digital forensic point of view. **c.** On the basis of any perception or estimation made on a developing superposed state will make it breakdown to a solitary haphazardly chose segment presumably that is the reason it is preposterous to expect to perform live framework of crime scene through digital forensic investigation on a quantum computer. **d.** It won't be likely to reproduce a time schedule outline proofing for the advancement of the quantum computing. **e.** The absence of this subordinate proof will end up being a critical hindrance to mounting fruitful judicial charges in instances of genuine quantum digital cyber-crime. **f.** The potential impacts of quantum mechanical spillage of electronic charge on the probative estimation of advanced legal proof mended or recovered for digital forensic evidence.
2-	Richard E Overill, Jantje A M Silomon, K P Chow	"A Complexity Based Model for Quantifying Forensic Evidential Probabilities, International Conference on Availability, Reliability and Security, 2010."	**a.** Operational complexity model **b.** The complexity of formation of a set of traces by which route can be determined.
3-	A.Konstadopoulou,	*"From quantum security to quantum forensics', Proc. 1st* Conference on Advances in Computer Security and Forensics (ACSF), Liverpool, UK, July, pp.105–111. 2006"	Quantum forensics has acknowledged so far virtually no contemplation from researchers.
4-	W. K. Wootters &W. H. Zurek	*"A single quantum cannot be cloned', Nature, Vol. 299, No. 5889, pp.802–803, 1982"*	This paper focuses on photon pair polarization and linearity of quantum mechanics forbids such replication for all quantum systems so photons could not be cloned as state of quantum state.

LIMITATIONS

1. Quantum information cannot be stored infinitely long so evidence collection is possibly very complex towards perspective of quantum forensic scheme.
2. It won't be likely to reproduce a time schedule outline proofing for the advancement of the quantum computing.
3. It is difficult to measure error in the states of quantum due its fragile nature.

4. Effective design of a fault-tolerant scalable qubits. (Mosca, 2018)
5. Realization of crime reconstruction process that includes criminal activities.
6. Automatic detection methodology of post-attack analysis through quantum computing to gather digital evidence.
7. There is lack of standards to ensure the quality, quantity and interoperability.
8. There should be existence of quantum cyber security standard in quantum driven world.
9. There is no quantum cyber legal framework for futuristic quantum techno-legal perspective.
10. Less attention towards quantum-resistant algorithms and technologies
11. There is no proper guideline and quantum software exists for digital quantum forensics and evidence traditional to quantum era.
12. Have to develop plans and guide lines migrate to quantum safe algorithms.
13. The de-coherence problem in quantum technology.

CONCLUSION

Quantum computing crypt analysis will become a reality in near future so valid steps must be taken towards to hostage such threats for breaching data within encrypted communications. Quantum information cannot be stored infinitely long so evidence collection is possibly very complex towards views of forensic scheme. Quantum computing would be used to support in find out malware in the upcoming decades. Konstadopoulou and Overill initiated the term digital quantum forensics and quantum evidence and discussed complexity futuristic view for qubit forensic approach. The malwares are an existential threats to intellectual property so consideration of software forensics approach applied for investigation of root cause. This chapter aim to extract current issues and challenges to tackle software forensics classical to quantum computing means and acquisition of quality and quantity quantum evidence with digital forensics ontological based quantum forensics. This chapter focuses on limitations which are extracted by theory building such as issues and challenges of cyber-crime, cyber security, digital forensics and digital evidence in the new form of digital quantum forensics. Software forensics as a new realm for quantum computing based development of quantum application, forensics tools and draw researcher attention towards development of standards, guidelines, techno-legal framework for quantum cyber security and digital quantum forensics with quantum cyber law.

REFERENCES

Alex, L. (2011). Third Party Application Forensics on Apple Mobile Devices. *Proceedings of the 44th Hawaii International Conference on System Sciences.*

Anglano, C. (2014). Forensic Analysis of WhatsApp Messenger on Android Smartphones. *The Digital Investigation Journal., 11*(3), 201–213. doi:10.1016/j.diin.2014.04.003

Atkinson, Mitchell, Rio, & Matich. (2018). *WiFi is leaking: What do your mobile apps gossip about you?* Academic Press.

Barmpatsalou, Damopoulos, Kambourakis, & Katos. (2013). A critical review of 7 years of Mobile Device Forensics. *D.I.,* (4), 323–349.

Bohr, N., & Noll, W. (1958). Atomic Physics and Human Knowledge. American Journal of Physics, 26(8), 38. doi:10.1119/1.1934707

Boneh, D., & Zhandry, M. (2013). Secure signatures and chosen ciphertext security in a quantum computing world. Advances in Cryptology–CRYPTO 2013, 361–379.

Brandl, F. M. (2017). *A Quantum von Neumann Architecture for Large-Scale Quantum Computing.* Institut f'ur Experimentalphysik, Universit'at Innsbruck.

Brassard, G., Lütkenhaus, N., Mor, T., & Sanders, B. C. (2000). Limitations on practical quantum cryptography. *Physical Review Letters, 85*(6), 6. doi:10.1103/PhysRevLett.85.1330 PMID:10991544

Bridgwater, A. (2017). *Five Ways Quantum Computing Will Change Cybersecurity Forever.* https://www.raconteur.net/risk-management/five-ways-quantum-computing-will-change-cybersecurity-forever

Brunty, J. (2016). *Mobile device forensics: threats, challenges, and future trends. Marshall* University.

Bruschi, Monga, & Rosti. (2005). Trusted Internet forensics: design of a network forensics appliance. In Security and Privacy for Emerging Areas in Communication Networks. IEEE.

Buchanan & Woodward. (2017). Will quantum computers be the end of public key encryption? *Journal of Cyber Security Technology, 1*(1), 1-22. Doi:10.1080/23742917.2016.1226650

Caloyannides, M. A. (2004). *Privacy Protection and Computer Forensics.* Artech House. www.artech-house.com

Chanajitt, Wantanee & Choo. (2016). Forensic analysis and security assessment of Android m-banking apps. Academic Press.

Dargahi, T., Dehghantanha, A., & Conti, M. (2017). *Forensics Analysis of Android Mobile VoIP Apps.* University of Padua Padua. doi:10.1016/B978-0-12-805303-4.00002-2

Garfinkel, S. L. (2010). *Digital forensics Research: The next ten years.* Elsevier.

Gray, A., & Sallis, P. (1997). Software Forensics: Extending Authorship Analysis, Techniques to Computer Programs. *The Information Science Discussion.*

Grover, L. K. (1996). A fast quantum mechanical algorithm for database search. *Proceedings, 28th Annual ACM Symposium on the Theory of Computing,* 212. 10.1145/237814.237866

Harrow, Aram, Hassidim, & Lloyd. (2008). Quantum algorithm for solving linear systems of equations. *Physical Review Letters, 103.* ArXiv: 0811.3171.

Johnson, C. (2013). *Forensic Software Engineering: Are Software Failures Symptomatic of Systemic Problems?* Department of Computing Science, University of Glasgow. http://www.dcs.gla.ac.uk/~johnson

Jones, G. M. (2017). Forensics Analysis on Smart Phones Using Mobile Forensics Tools. *IJIR,* (8), 1859.

Kaci, A., & Bouabana-Tebibel, T. (2014). Access Control Reinforcement over Searchable Encryption. *IEEE IRI 2014*, 130-137.

Karie, N. M., & Venter, H. S. (2014). *Towards a General Ontology for Digital Forensic Disciplines.* Department of Computer Science, University of Pretoria. https://onlinelibrary.wiley.com/doi/abs/10.1111/1556-4029.12511

Karyda, M., & Mitrou, L. (2007). *Internet Forensics: Legal and Technical Issues.* IEEE.

Konstadopoulou, A. (2006). From Quantum Security to Quantum Forensics. *Proc. 1st Conference on Advances in Computer Security and Forensics (ACSF).*

Li, J., Shi, Y., Zhang, Y. (2015). Searchable ciphertext-policy attribute-based encryption with revocation in cloud storage. *International Journal of Communication Systems International Journal of Communication System.*

Lin, Chen, Zhu, Yang, & Fengguo. (2018). Automated forensic analysis of mobile applications on Android devices. *Science Direct Digital Investigation Journal.*

Mahalik, H., & Tamma, R. (2014). *Practical Mobile Forensics* (2nd ed.). https://hub.packtpub.com/mobile-forensics-and-its-challanges/

Mohay, G. M., Anderson, A. A., Collie, B., McKemmish, R. D., & de Vel, O. (2003). *Computer and Intrusion Forensics.* Artech House.

Mosca, M. (2018). Cybersecurity in an era with quantum computers: will we be ready? Institute for Quantum Computing and Department of Combinatorics and Optimization. University of Waterloo. doi:10.1109/MSP.2018.3761723

Murthy. (2019). *Novel Chaotic Quantum Based Homomorphic CPABE Authentication Protocol against Malicious Attack in Wireless Communication Networks.* Doi:10.6025/Jisr/2019/10/1/1-17

Nolan, R. (2005). First Responders Guide to Computer Forensics. Academic Press.

Overill, R. E. (2012). *Digital quantum forensics: future challenges and prospects.* Department of Informatics, King's College London.

Overill, R.E., & Silomon, J.A.M. (2010). Digital Meta-Forensics: Quantifying the Investigation. *Proc. 4th International Conference on Cybercrime Forensics Education and Training (CFET 2010).*

Parvez, S., Dehghantanha, A., & Broujerdi, H. G. (2011). *Framework of digital forensics for the Samsung Star Series phone. ICECT'11.*

Rubin, N. (2020). *Quantum Physics, "Hartree-Fock on a superconducting qubit quantum computer".* https://arxiv.org/abs/2004.04174

Sachowski, J. (2018). *Digital Forensics and Investigations: People, Process, and Technologies.* CRC Press.

Sallis, Asbjorn, & MacDonell. (1996). Software Forensics: old methods for a new science. IEEE.

Sen, D. (2014). The Uncertainty relations in quantum mechanics. *Current Science, 107*(2), 203–218.

Sharma & Khaliq. (2020). *A review on software forensics and software quality approach.* Department of Computer Science & IT, Khwaja Moinuddin Chishti Urdu, Arabi-Farsi University.

Shor, P.W. (1994). Algorithms for quantum computation: discrete logarithms and factoring. *Proceedings 35th Annual Symposium on Foundations of Computer Science.* Doi:10.1109fcs.1994.365700

Slattery, O. T. (2020). *Quantum Communications and Networks.* https://www.nist.gov/people/oliver-t-slattery

Tittel, W., Sanders, B. C., & Lvovsky, A. I. (2009). Optical quantum memory. *Nature Photonics, 3*(12).

Vernacchia, S. (2019). *The darker side of quantum computing: risks and challenges.* Partner, Digital, Cyber Security, Resilience and Infrastructure. worldgovernmentsummit.org

Wallden, P., & Kashefi, E. (2019, April). *Cyber Security in the Quantum Era. Communications of the ACM, 62*(4), 120. doi:10.1145/3241037

Xu, H., Chen, X., Li, P., Ding, J., & Eghan, C. (2019). A Novel RFID Data Management Model Based on Quantum Cryptography. In *Third International Congress on Information and Communication Technology. Advances in Intelligent Systems and Computing, vol 797.* Springer. 10.1007/978-981-13-1165-9_41

Zeidman, B. (2011). *The Software IP Detective's Handbook, Software forensics for embedded systems developers.* https://www.embedded.com/software-forensics-for-embedded-systems-developers/

Zhou, Shen, Li, Wang, & Shen. (2018). Quantum Cryptography for the Future Internet and the Security Analysis. *Security and Communication Networks.* https://doi.org/ doi:10.1155/2018/8214619

Chapter 10
Image Processing Using Quantum Computing:
Trends and Challenges

Bably Dolly
Babasaheb Bhimrao Ambedkar University, Lucknow, India

Deepa Raj
Babasaheb Bhimrao Ambedkar University, Lucknow, India

ABSTRACT

Image processing via the quantum platform is an emerging area for researchers. Researchers are more interested to move on towards quantum image processing instead of classical image processing. This chapter starts with the review of different quantum image computing-based research papers with a brief idea of the ethics which inspire quantum computing in the background and focus on the current scenario of recent trends of quantum image representation, pitfalls, and summarization of the pros and cons of it, with the limitations of the technologies used and focus on the recent work to be going on and application of it in a different field. In the next, it will focus on the different methods used by the researcher in the previous papers. The next section discussed the different methods based on quantum image representation used. Some different techniques of image storage, retrieval, and representation in a quantum system are discussed. Also, this chapter briefs the pros and cons of using different techniques in quantum systems in comparison to classical systems.

INTRODUCTION

Recently some years ago, there were two concepts like the field of computer science and biological science. 'Emergent Computing', 'Complexity Theory', and 'Evolutionary Computing' have emerged as a new field in the era. Further, later on, challenging the classical explanations in quantum physics. (Batouche et al., 2009) Quantum mechanics is one main interesting branch of quantum physics, further subdividing quantum mechanics; we get an interesting branch called quantum computing. The main

DOI: 10.4018/978-1-7998-6677-0.ch010

Copyright © 2021, IGI Global. Copying or distributing in print or electronic forms without written permission of IGI Global is prohibited.

function of quantum physics is based on the elementary atomic structure. By achieving the desired manipulation of quantum physics computing speed and performance can be significantly improved. Digital image processing with the effect of growing technology its continuously upgrading itself by the effect from in volume and relevancy, with the continuous demands of storing data, information, transmission, and power to process. The improvement is done in the standard image processing by the utilization of quantum computing in the form of encoding the given information of an image to the quantum mechanical systems and also replacing the classical information processing into the quantum information processing. By the analysis of different work based on this, in this research, try to chase the issues and challenges found within it and further what will be the future scope of it in the coming generations. As the quantum image processing is the point of attraction in the field of digital image processing and gains more consideration in modern years with respect to quantum image representation, operation, and encryption. With the development of revolutionary technology, information hiding in the form of image scrambling and digital watermarking is the crucial state in this scenario. These were the issues that are considered to be forward in this research paper.

Quantum Computing

Quantum computing is significantly new technology. As per Moore's law, computer supremacy doubles itself approximately in two years. The concept of quantum computing will help us in building or electronic devices that will perform the calculation much faster and in a robust manner after the principle of quantum physics, the quantum machine is several times faster than a conventional machine. Quantum computing is still an experimental phase but experiments are being carried out on a smaller scale with the desired result. There are several private and government organization which are developing a quantum computer. Quantum computers can be used in a number of fields such as information technology, research, and development, health care finance education, etc. Al detailed diagram below...shows the working of a quantum computer.

One of the major uses of quantum computing is in the field of image processing. The image processing algorithm can be significantly improved in terms of accuracy and speed with the use of quantum computers. This paper mainly focuses on the use of quantum computing in image processing. Other areas of concerns will be processing compression, enhancement, storing and retrieval and restoring, 2D image data and visual information.

Quantum Image Processing

In today's world, most of the data is in the form of images. These include the images that are transmitted and stored in a digital environment. The major use of images is in health care, social media, satellite communication, and another day to day life. The image can be processed by a digital computer which is also called digital image processing also the image can be processed by the quantum computer; this process is called quantum image processing. Quantum image processing is a branch of quantum information processing. Quantum image processing implies the use of cohesion, entanglement, superposition, and parallelism. So we can sum up quantum image processing as a method that uses a quantum method to speed up image processing, making it more efficient and quick. As shown in fig1. Several image processing techniques such as retrieval representation, noise filtration, processing, and storage can be made more efficient as compared to classical computing by using quantum image processing (Chakraborty et al., 2018)

Figure 1.

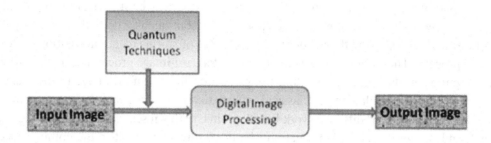

Analysis of Classical Image Processing and Quantum Image Processing

In Quantum Computing the actual color value is calculated with reference to its respective frequency Image information is stored with the help of qubit which is continuous in nature. In classical system problems such as white noise is present also there is a lack of reaching an exclusive level of control relegation. The algorithm used in Image Processing using Quantum Computing used parameters such as quantum-based for computing the complexity whereas in classical computer complexity is calculated by running time. While designing quantum hardware, the designer must calculate the ratio of classical and quantum resources to implement the Quantum Computing Image Processing protocol. The imp point to keep in mind is in an image compression based quantum neural network approach. Quant noise restoration image and video processing application and automatic object extraction. Image noise is color information and variation of brightness which is random in nature. Image noise is useless information that may add false information.(Chakraborty et al., 2018)

PREVIOUS WORK

According to the M. Batouche et.al(Batouche et al., 2009), focus on the reverse emergence and quantum computing, proposed a new approach in which there is a quantum-inspired algorithm to shake of searching technique. And give the concept of a quantum evolutionary algorithm to rain the cellular automatically in the image processing job and the author tries to work towards minimizing the hurdles of reverse emergence. In the research paper(Chakraborty & Mandal, 2017), the author suggests two approaches to help in the representation of color images two-approach based on the modified method of FRQI model, in a ternary quantum system. And the normalized amplitude based concept of quantum representation model. But the have several complications and disadvantages. And 3 level quantum system is presented to deal with a set of quantum states of different color levels and for different l position coordinates. Author(Venegas-Andraca & Ball, 2009) introduces a new technique for storing and retrieving binary geometric shapes in quantum computing which allows reconstructing shapes because of the employment of quantum entanglement. At the end of the most of the work to be done in the area of quantum computing, there is still the need of the security in all over the work carried out in past present and future, in this regards the many authors have been working on in which is shown by fig 2 (Yan, 2017) and according to the author (Iliyasu, 2013) in the previous work have been tried to focus on the secure and efficient image and video processing system applications using quantum computing.

Figure 2.

COMPARATIVE STUDY OF QUANTUM IMAGE REPRESENTATION APPROACHES

There are various approaches already being done in previous work for which some sort of techniques and approaches have been analyzed and the comparative study is shown by the below (fig 3):

In FRQI (Flexible Representation of Quantum Images) Approach (Le & Iliyasu, 2011; Le et al., 2011)

The essentiality to programme the location information of a pixel in an image of 2nx2n is being carried out by the original state of 2n qubit sequence and the so forth information of color is being encoded for the one qubit state with respect to a probability amplitudes. The possibility amplitudes of a quantum status cannot be defined exactly as per regards of a fixed number of capacity. As per the usability of the single-qubit state, operations of only simple color pixels are being feasible. There is a requirement for the implementation of this approach is a complex quantum circuit. It is hard to recognize to which point of view(with respect to angle) represent the color because of values of angle parameter are not quantified. At the side of this, practically there is a limitation to physical representation for an angle parameter of a qubit.

Normalized Amplitude Based Approach (Srivastava et al., 2013)

In the duration of storing an image, the quantity of qubit keeps on growing with respect to the image dimension. There is the requirement of one additional fractional bit for the representation of row position vector or column position vector. It is less complex as per the comparison of FRQI (Flexible Representation of Quantum Images) approach. Here is no concept for the angle parameter. This is well-founded for whichever color channel of any color space for an image either partially of full.

Figure 3.

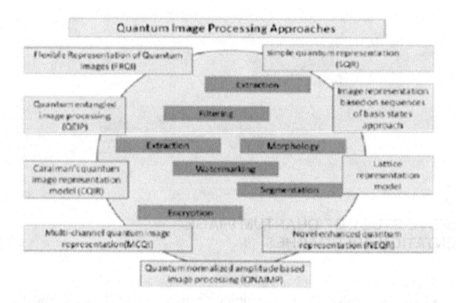

Lattice Representation Model (Yuan et al., 2014)

In this approach value of radiation power of every pixel is being stored in terms of probability of projection extent, instead of using the FRQI model where there is storing the parameter of the angle of a color qubit. Hence it has less complexity in comparison to the FRQI approach and to build the circuit, simple quantum is being utilized. As it is much better than the FRQI with respect to achieving a speedup in preparation of quantum image but there is still some limitation as quantification-problem of angle-parameter. This model gets more flexible and clear with respect to quantified to the relationship between the values of radiation energy and projection measurement-probabilities on qubits. This approach is applicable for the infrared image operations.

Image Representation in the Entangled Quantum System ()

In this approach, as the use of tremendous entangled qubits, hence there is a lesser amount of storage space is necessary by which it possible to reconstruct images or shapes in spite of using any of additional information. It is basically deployed for binary images and the concept of quantum entanglement is being used by the whole course of action. There is no theory for angle parameters. The application of this approach is being used in Image Segmentation and compression.

Image Representation Based on Sequences of Basis States Approach (Caraiman & Manta, 2012; Le & Iliyasu, 2011; Zhang et al., 2013)

This approach engages additional memory to represent color values of a particular image whereas the FRQI approach used only one qubit. So this approach requires m qubits to represent L=2m color values. Instead of using one qubit state to represent an image, it uses m qubit states. It requires a lesser amount of quantum gates as compared to the Lattice representation approach. Here is no dependency on the physical representation of angle parameters for color representation and location of an image. Either to date, this approach has been tested on greyscale images only. It may be used in Image segmentation, filtering, or other complex image processing areas too.

Novel Enhanced Quantum Representation (NEQR) (Zhang et al., 2013)

By this approach, the original image can be retrieved exactly via quantum measurement in spite of utilizing probability in comparison with FRQI. In this representation, many qubits are required to encode a quantum image likewise, q_2n qubits are to be required to construct a model of quantum image for a 2nx2n with a grey range of 2q where q qubits are required to encode color information while 1 qubit is required for FRQI representation. It is not as much complex as the FRQI approach. In this, there is no space for the concept for angle parameters. In this image compression ratio is one and half times greater than the FRQI model.

Quantum Normalized Amplitude Based Image Processing (QNAIMP) (Chakraborty et al., 2018):

This approach emphasizes two characters of images, the image signal - amplitude and its corresponding pixels position on the image space. To reduce the values of normalized amplitudes to quantum states, this approach used to represent multiple qubits quantum states so that the storing and transmission get easy in a quantum environment. In this approach, with respect to all the amplitudes present in the image, storing and transmission are carried out for all the pixel positions that have similar amplitude values, instead of the image signal. The aim of this is to keep visual information in a 3D set of qubit lattices, every layer of 3D used to keep a copy of the image.

Quantum Entangled Image Processing (QEIP) (Latorre, 2005; Venegas-Andraca & Ball, 2004; Venegas-Andraca & Ball, 2010)

This approach is a new method that emphasizes on to keep an image within the quantum system by utilizing the entanglement concept of quantum which a type of correlation used to keep binary images. In this move towards, an array of N qubits (each qubit have two parameters say a and b which symbolize grid points of some 2D images to be in together) is stored within a memory register.

Quantum Inspired Shape Representation for Content-Based Image Retrieval (Jobay & Sleit, 2014)

Content-Based Image Retrieval CBIR, a well-known technique in image processing, is one of the image retrieval methods, where the images are being indexed on the basis of their visual information and hence the retrieval process of images can be done on this indexed images. Here in this, the features are divided mainly in two: one is local features and other is global features, basically local features such as color, shape, and color of an image are considered whereas in global the location of the image is also considered in the image retrieval process. In this approach (Jobay & Sleit, 2014), By using Quantum supervision (with the basis of distance histogram), This model initiates a representation of a novel simple shape for the CBIR method. The boundary of the overall shape of the image is carried out by taking the numeric values of image content. By using the shape signature this technique known as a contour-based shape representation method. In this, the Euclidian distance is calculated for both the images for similarity checking based on shape features. The centroid distance is taken between the shape boundaries of an image, these distance having the information about the queried image for which distance histogram has been taken.(Jobay & Sleit, 2014)

In Table 1 the analysis of different methods to secure data using image-based quantum cryptography have been summerisedthat are shown below:

Table 1. Analysis Of Different Methods To Secure Data Using Image-Based Quantum Cryptography

Sn.	Year	Author	Title	Security technique for data	Advantages
1.	2019	Jian Wang, Ya-Cong Geng, et.al(Wang et al., 2019).	Quantum Image Encryption Algorithm Based on Quantum Key Image	Quantum Key Images based security	Efficiencient and have large key space and lower computational complexity.
2.	2014	Xian-Hua Song, Shen Wang et.al. (Song et al., 2014)	Quantum image encryption based on restricted geometric and color-transformations	A novel encryption-scheme for quantum-images based on restricted geometric and color-transformations is proposed	e better performance and higher security is in favor of the proposed quantum image encryption strategy than the other scheme only based on geometric transformations
3.	2015	• Mohammed Misbahuddin, C. S. Sreeja(Misbahuddin & Sreeja, 2015)	A Secure Image-Based Authentication Scheme Employing DNA Crypto and Steganography	two-way secure authentication scheme using DNA cryptography and steganography	to secure pharmaceutical-research data where data-security and information-privacy are major concerns
4.	2019	• Majid Khan1 & Iqtadar Hussain et.al.(Khan & Hussain, 2019)	A Privacy Scheme for Digital Images Based on Quantum Particles	Secure data by quantum particles and utilized the notions of quantum-spinning	suitable for real time applications because of small processing time and better ability to hostile the assaults and appropriate execution than other encryption frameworks.
5.	2016	• Nishat I Mowla • , Inshil Doh, et.al. (Mowla et al., 2016)	Securing information flow in content delivery networks with visual and quantum cryptography	Steganography combine with the unique key distribution mechanism of Quantum Cryptography with some other additional security features	free from eavesdropping or any other third party intrusion in the key distribution system.
6.	2016	Ru-Chao Tan, Tong Lei, et.al.(Tan et al., 2016) •	Quantum Color Image Encryption Algorithm Based on A Hyper-Chaotic System and Quantum Fourier Transform	By a Hyper-Chaotic System and Quantum Fourier Transform	possesses large key space to resist illegal attacks
7.	2015	Nan Run Zhou et.al,(Zhou et al., 2015)	Quantum image encryption based on generalized Arnold transform and double random-phase encoding	generalized Arnold transform and double random-phase encoding	good feasibility and effectiveness has lower computational complexity than its classical counterpart

4. DISCUSSION

As per previous study and analysis of different research papers and articles over the quantum image processing and classical image processing, here seen a number of approaches in the form of models proposed and work had been carried out and give the tremendous different result in a positive way and also opens the different number of open questions to the coming research in this area has been mentioned. There is a number of new results to be opened by using image searching and image similarity matching over the dataset of images in a state of FRQI.(Chakraborty et al., 2018) To address the high real-time computational requirements with respect to classical image processing, the combination of quantum computing with image processing is effective and important for today's research in this regard.

4.1 Importance

The very first usable quantum computer are in the race to be build, because of it, there are number of organizations and governments under the quantum arms race. The technology assure to build a number of computing problems a lot, at large easier to resolve better than today's classical computers.

One of individuals problems is breach certain types of encryption, mainly the techniques used in today's public key infrastructure (PKI), which lies behind practically all of today's online communications. "I'm certainly scared of what can be the result of quantum computing," says Michael Morris, CEO at Topcoder, a global network of 1.4 million developers.

"Instead of solving one problem at a time, with quantum computing we can solve thousands of problems at the same processing speed, with the same processing power," Morris says. "Things that would take hundreds of days today could take just hours on a quantum computer."

The commercial quantum computers available today are still far from being able to do that. "The theories have advanced farther than the hardware," says William Hurley, IEEE senior member.

Who knows what kind of technology isn't available on the public market, or is operated in secret by foreign governments? "My fear is that we won't know that the quantum computer capable of doing this even exists until it's done," says Topcoder's Morris.

Though complex, Quantum Computers have a lot of advantages which make it a need for thefuture. Its powerful processor is a major breakthrough in the field of science. Some of itsadvantages are:

- It can process massive amount of complex data.
- It has the ability to solve scientific and commercial problems.
- Its powerful processor can process data in a much faster speed.
- It has the capability to convey more accurate answers.

TOP APPLICATIONS OF QUANTUM COMPUTING

Logistics Optimization

Improved information investigation and powerful displaying will without a doubt empower a wide scope of businesses to advance their coordinations and planning work processes related with their gracefully chain the board. The working models need to persistently compute and recalculate ideal courses of traffic the board, armada activities, airport regulation, cargo and circulation, and that could severy affect applications. Ordinarily, to manage these responsibilities, ordinary figuring is utilized; nonetheless, some of them could transform into more perplexing for an ideal processing arrangement, though a quantum approach might have the option to do it. Two normal quantum moves toward that can be utilized to take care of such issues are — quantum toughening and general quantum PCs. Quantum strengthening is a serious streamlining method that is required to outperform conventional PCs. Interestingly, general quantum PCs are fit for tackling a wide range of computational issues, not yet economically accessible.

Computerized Reasoning and Machine Learning

Computerized reasoning and AI are a portion of the unmistakable zones at the present time, as arising advances have entered pretty much every part of people's lives. A portion of the far-reaching applications we see each day are in voice, picture, and penmanship acknowledgment. Be that as it may, as the number of uses expanded, it turns into a difficult undertaking for conventional PCs, to coordinate the exactness and speed. Also, that is the place where quantum registering can help in preparing through complex issues in exceptionally less time, which would have taken conventional PCs thousand of years.

Computational Chemistry

IBM, when stated, one of the most encouraging quantum registering applications will be in the field of computational science. It is accepted that the quantity of quantum states, even in a smallest of a particle, is incredibly tremendous, and in this way hard for customary registering memory to handle that. The capacity for quantum PCs to zero in on the presence of both 1 and 0 at the same time could give the huge capacity to the machine to effectively plan the particles which, thus, conceivably opens open doors for drug research. A portion of the basic issues that could be explained through quantum figuring are — improving the nitrogen-obsession measure for making smelling salts based compost; making a room-temperature superconductor; eliminating carbon dioxide for a superior atmosphere, and making strong state batteries.

Medication Design and Development

Planning and building up medication is the most testing issue in quantum figuring. Generally, drugs are being created by means of the experimentation technique, which isn't truth be told, extravagant yet in addition a dangerous and moving assignment to finish. Analysts accept quantum registering can be a successful method of understanding the medications and their responses to people which, thus, can set aside a huge load of cash and time for drug organizations. These headways in processing could improve proficiency significantly, by permitting organizations to complete more medication revelations to uncover new clinical medicines for the better drug industry.

Cryptography and Cyber-Security

The online security space at present has been beautiful in peril in view of the developing measure of digital assaults happening everywhere on the world, on a day premise. despite the fact that associations are setting up the necessary security system in their associations, the strategy ends up being frightening and illogical for traditional computerized PCs. Likewise, along these lines, network assurance has continued being a major concern the world over. Through our creating dependence on digitization, we are getting essentially more vulnerable against these risks. Quantum preparing with the help of AI can help in making various techniques to fight these organization wellbeing perils. In addition, quantum figuring can help in creation encryption systems, in any case called, quantum cryptography.

Financial Modeling

For an account industry to locate the correct blend for productive speculations dependent on anticipated returns, the danger related, and different variables are imperative to get by on the lookout. To accomplish that, the procedure of 'Monte Carlo' recreations are constantly being run on ordinary PCs, which, thusly, devour a gigantic measure of PC time. Notwithstanding, by applying quantum innovation to play out these enormous and complex computations, organizations can improve the nature of the arrangements as well as decrease an opportunity to create them. Since monetary pioneers are occupied with taking care of billions of dollars, even a little improvement in the normal return can be worth very much for them. Algorithmic exchanging is another potential application where the machine utilizes complex calculations to consequently trigger offer dealings dissecting the market factors, which is a preferred position, particularly for high-volume exchanges.

Protein Folding

Reproducing the collapsing of proteins could prompt an extreme change of our comprehension of complex organic frameworks and our capacity to plan incredible new medications. This application investigates how to utilize the quantum PC to investigate the conceivable collapsing setups of these fascinating particles. With a galactic number of conceivable primary game plans, protein collapsing is an immensely unpredictable computational issue. Logical examination shows that nature upgrades the amino corrosive arrangements to make the most steady protein - which relates well to the quest for the least energy arrangements. With analysts at Harvard, we planned a framework for foreseeing the collapsing designs for grid protein collapsing models and effectively ran little protein collapsing issues in equipment.

Climate Forecasting

Presently, the way toward breaking down climate conditions by customary PCs can in some cases take longer than the climate itself does to change. Be that as it may, a quantum PC's capacity to crunch immense measures of information, in a brief period, could to be sure prompt improving climate framework demonstrating permitting researchers to anticipate the changing climate designs instantly and with fantastic exactness — something which can be fundamental for the flow time when the world is going under an environmental change.

Climate determining incorporates a few factors to consider, for example, pneumatic stress, temperature and air thickness, which makes it hard for it to be anticipated precisely. Utilization of quantum AI can help in improving example acknowledgment, which, thus, will make it simpler for researchers to anticipate outrageous climate occasions and conceivably spare large number of lives a year. With quantum PCs, meteorologists will likewise have the option to produce and break down more definite atmosphere models, which will give more noteworthy understanding into environmental change and approaches to relieve it.Image

Optimization

Envision you are constructing a house, and have a neglected of things you need to have in your home, however you can't bear the cost of the whole lot on your rundown because you are obliged by a spending plan. What you really require to work out is the couple of things that gives you the best incentive for your money. This is an illustration of an advancement issue, where you are trying to locate the best couple of things given a some limitations. Regularly, these are difficult issues to comprehend as a result of the gigantic number of potential mixes. With only 270 on/off switches, there are added potential blends than iotas known to mankind! These kinds of enhancement issues exist in a wide range of areas - frameworks plan, mission arranging, carrier planning, monetary investigation, web search, malignant growth radiotherapy, and a number of more. They are the absolute generally complex issues on the planet, with possibly tremendous advantages to organizations, individuals, and science if ideal arrangements can be promptly registered. "improved issues are the absolute most complex issues to understand."

Radiotherapy Optimization

There are numer of instances of issues where, a quantum PC can supplement a HPC (elite processing) framework. While the quantum PC is suitable to discrete advancement, the HPC framework is greatly improved everywhere scale mathematical recreations. Issues like streamlining malignant growth radiotherapy, where a patient is treated by infusing a few radiation radiates into the patient converging at the tumor, outlines how the two frameworks can cooperate. The objective when concocting a radiation plan is to limit the inadvertent blow-back to the encompassing tissue and body parts – a confounded enhancement issue with a great many factors. To show up at the ideal radiation plan requires numerous reenactments until an ideal arrangement is resolved. With a quantum PC, the skyline of potential outcomes that can be well thought-out between every rebuilding is a lot more extensive. In any case, HPC is as yet the more impressive calculation device for running reproductions. Utilizing the quantum PC with a HPC framework will permit quicker union on an ideal plan than is achievable by utilizing HPC alone.

Machine Learning

At the point when you take a gander at a photo it is exceptionally simple for you to choose the various items in the picture: Trees, Mountains, Velociraptors, and so forth This assignment is practically easy for people yet is indeed a gigantically troublesome undertaking for PCs to accomplish. This is on the grounds that developers don't have the foggiest idea how to characterize the quintessence of a 'Tree' in PC code. AI is the best way to deal with tackling this issue, by which software engineers compose calculations that consequently figure out how to perceive the 'characters' of items by distinguishing repeating designs in colossal measures of information. In light of the measure of information engaged with this cycle, and the tremendous number of possible mixes of information components, this is a computationally costly advancement issue. Similarly as with other improvement issues, these can be planned to the local capacity of the D-Waveprocessor. "Machines figure out how to perceive objects by distinguishing repeating designs."

Item Detection

Quantum equipment, prepared to utilize a double order calculation, can recognize whether a picture contains a vehicle. Along with specialists at Google, we fabricated programming for deciding if there is a vehicle in a picture utilizing a paired characterization calculation run in equipment. More than 500,000 discrete advancement issues were explained during the learning stage, with Google designers getting to the D-Wave framework distantly.

Naming News Stories

We constructed programming for naturally applying class marks to reports and pictures. We found that our methodology gave preferable marking precision over a best in class regular methodology. The naming of reports can be hard for PCs as should be obvious the catchphrases however don't comprehend the importance of the words when consolidated. For marking news, stories the corpus we utilized for preparing and testing execution was the REUTERS corpus, a notable informational index for testing different name task calculations. We adopted a comparative strategy to name pictures and utilized the SCENE corpus for preparing and testing execution, a notable informational index for testing various mark task calculations. We found that our methodology functioned admirably on these issues, exhibiting the quantum PC's capacity to do different mark task and to name pictures.

Video Compression

Utilizing unaided AI draws near, one can computerize the revelation of an exceptionally meager approach to speak to objects. This method can be utilized for unbelievably effective pressure.

Monte Carlo Simulation

Numerous things on the planet are questionable, and administered by the standards of likelihood. We have, in our minds, a model of how things will turn out later on, and the better our model is, the better we are at foreseeing what's to come. We can likewise fabricate PC models to attempt to catch the measurements of the real world. These will in general be extremely confounded, including a enormous number of factors. To verify whether a PC's factual model speaks to the real world, we should be ready to draw tests from it and watch that the insights of our model match the measurements of genuine information. Monte Carlo reproduction, which depends on rehashed arbitrary examining to rough the likelihood of specific results, is a methodology utilized in numerous businesses, for example, money, energy, producing, designing oil and gas, and the climate. For a perplexing model, with various factors, this is a troublesome errand to do rapidly.

QUANTUM COMPUTING IN CLOUD

Aliyun

1. Chinese internet business goliath Alibaba, in association with the Chinese Academy of Sciences, has added quantum registering to its cloud administration.
2. Alibaba Cloud presently has a superconducting cloud PC offering 11quantum bit(qubit) speed, making it the second-quickest on the planet behind IBM 20-qubit cloud PC.
3. Alibaba Cloud clients would now be able to get to the quantum PC to run code and direct trials with quantum applications in a genuine climate to more readily comprehend the property and execution of the equipment, just as driving the path in creating quantum instruments and programming universally

IBM Q Experience

1. The IBM Q Experience is an online stage that gives clients in the overall population admittance to a bunch of IBM's model quantum processors by means of the Cloud, an online web gathering for examining quantum registering pertinent subjects, a bunch of instructional exercises on the best way to program the IBM Q gadgets, and other instructive material about quantum figuring.
2. As of May 2018, there are three processors on the IBM Q Experience: two5-qubit processors and a 16-qubit processor. This administration can be utilized to run calculations and tries, and investigate instructional exercises and reenactments around what may be conceivable with quantum registering.
3. Users cooperate with a quantum processor through the quantum circuit model of calculation, applying quantum doors on the qubits utilizing a GUI called the quantum author, composing quantum low-level computing construct code or through QISKit.

Benefits of Quantum Computer Cloud Service

1. Quantum PCs invigorate the comprehension of nuclear and subatomic movement, particularly when making new medications. The roundabout advantages that individuals can appreciate are high caliber and low rates.
2. These PCs can likewise help interpretation programming or other little, however for gainful employment.
3. It has a perpetual capability of taking care of various responsibilities from account to energy to financial aspects and so on.
4. Most of the researchers accept that its applications are practically unending, from improving crafted by sun based boards, making medications, composts.
5. It is the framework that will give you quicker speed, lower value rate, and other various applications.
6. Through this trend-setting innovation, individuals will have the option to sort out some way to utilize the test plan.
7. It can without much of a stretch discover answers to the arrangement of complex issues with fewer deterrents. Quantum PCs will permit calculations to finish their undertaking of examination quickly. Quantum PCs are rapidly dispensing with the hole among machine and human reasoning.

Advantages and Disadvantages

The experts are restricted somewhat of the flawlessness in giving out and in the purpose of capacity with fundamental assets. As the publically inaccessibility of a quantum PC, there is an ascent in the number of situations where they could utilize them, it is possible that it is public or private substances. Here we can take the model, for example, CCTV in the United Kingdom which has the limit of day in and day out catching 30 edges for each second and give bring about 725,760 x edges in 7 days for each which are in the middle of 4 and 5.9 million cameras. The necessity for a speedier and extra added effective method of getting and putting away pictures may profoundly valuable frameworks like this and for this, quantum picture handling is exceptionally popular. Numerous issues identified with the information base of the given arrangement of information can be taken care of and safer through picture-based quantum cryptography. It tends to be additionally used in picture acknowledgment which is these days more regular as the dataset is progressively developing step by step. Numerous organizations attempt to create novel methodologies in the field of AI, profound learning, and so on the moreover procedures are zeroing in on the malware identification of information, and so on

Other than over the are heaps of issues which arrangements are not actualized, they are simply hypothetical and even less application continued. As utilization of AI is progressively is in utilized for quantum picture preparing and quantum learning. It should be considered on application and commonsense drew nearer. Quantum PCs are far off to the public in view of its excessively costly. So normally there exist restrictions in the region of examination and to novel methodologies, since the majority of the specialists are deprived to get to them Hence before quantum PCs can be promptly accessible, frameworks that can incorporate the quantum actual layer with conventional programming and equipment are necessary. (http://mtrteamanalysis.blogspot.com/ 2017/01/accelerating-pace-of-quantum-software.html)

FUTURE DIRECTIONS

In the addition of above pertinent techniques and solutions, there exists still the scope of improvement and innovations towards the quantum computing with respect to the image processing to give solutions to the problems related to the science and engineering such as computer vision, pattern recognition, medicine and most of the others field. Furthermore when we focus on practical manner research related to quantum sensor, quantum nanoscale materials, the quantum radar should be focused more with respect to research.

REFERENCES

Batouche, M., Meshoul, S., & Al Hussaini, A. (2009). *Image processing using quantum computing and reverse emergence. Int. J. Nano and Biomaterials.*

Caraiman, S., & Manta, V. (2012). Image processing using quantum computing. In *System theory, control and computing.* ICSTCC.

Chakraborty, S., & Mandal, S. B. (2017). *Ternary Quantum Circuit for Color Image Representation. In Computing and Systems for Security.* Advances in Intelligent Systems and Computing.

Chakraborty, S., Mandal, S. B., & Shaikh, S. H. (2018). *Quantum image processing: challenges and future research issues. Int. J. Inf. Tecnol.*

Iliyasu, A. M. (2013). Towards Realising Secure and Efficient Image and Video Processing Applications on Quantum Computers. *Entropy (Basel, Switzerland)*, *15*(12), 2874–2974. doi:10.3390/e15082874

Jobay, R., & Sleit, A. (2014). Quantum inspired shape representation for content based image retrieval. *J Signal Inf Process*.

Khan & Hussain. (2019). A Privacy Scheme for Digital Images Based on Quantum. *International Journal of Theoretical Physics*. doi:10.100710773-019-04301-6

Latorre, J. (2005). Image compression and entanglement. arXiv:quant-ph/0510031

Le, P., & Iliyasu, A. (2011). *A flexible representation and invertible transformations for images on quantum computer, New advances in intelligent signal processing of studies in computational intelligence*. Springer.

Le, P. Q., Dong, F., & Hirota, K. (2011). A flexible representation of quantum images for polynomial preparation, image compression, and processing operations. *Quantum Information Processing*, *10*(1), 63–84. doi:10.100711128-010-0177-y

Misbahuddin, M., & Sreeja, C. S. (2015). A Secure Image-Based Authentication Scheme Employing DNA Crypto and Steganography. *Proceedings of the Third International Symposium on Women in Computing and Informatics - WCI '15*. 10.1145/2791405.2791503

Mowla, N. I., Doh, I., & Chae, K. (2016). Securing information flow in content delivery networks with visual and quantum cryptography. *2016 International Conference on Information Networking (ICOIN)*, 463-468. 10.1109/ICOIN.2016.7427160

Song, Wang, El-Latif, & Niu. (2014). Quantum image encryption based on restricted geometric and color transformations. *Quantum Inf Process*. doi:10.100711128-014-0768-0

Srivastava, M., Moulick, S. R., & Panigrahi, P. K. (2013). *Quantum image representation through two-dimensional quantum states and normalized amplitude*. arXiv:1305.2251

Tan, R., Lei, T., Zhao, Q., Gong, L.-H., & Zhou, Z.-H. (2016). Quantum Color Image Encryption Algorithm Based on A Hyper-Chaotic System and Quantum Fourier Transform. *International Journal of Theoretical Physics*, *55*(12), 5368–5384. doi:10.100710773-016-3157-x

Venegas-Andraca, S. E., & Ball, J. L. (2004). *Storing images in entangled quantum systems*. Report number: arXiv:quant-ph/0402085

Venegas-Andraca & Ball. (2009). *Processing images in entangled quantum systems, Quantum Inf Process*. Springer Science+Business Media, LLC.

Venegas-Andraca, S. E., & Ball, J. L. (2010). Processing images in entangled quantum systems. *Quantum Information Processing*, *9*(1), 1–11. doi:10.100711128-009-0123-z

Wang, J., Geng, Y., Han, L., & Liu, J.-Q. (2019). Quantum Image Encryption Algorithm Based on Quantum Key Image. *International Journal of Theoretical Physics*, *58*(1), 308–322. doi:10.100710773-018-3932-y

Yan, F. (2017). Quantum image processing: A review of advances in its security technologies. International Journal of Quantum Information, 15(3).

Yuan, S., Mao, X., Xue, Y., Chen, L., Xiong, Q., & Compare, A. (2014). SQR: A simple quantum representation of infrared images. *Quantum Information Processing, 13*(6), 1353–1379. doi:10.100711128-014-0733-y

Zhang, Y., Lu, K., Gao, Y., & Wang, M. (2013). NEQR: A novel enhanced quantum representation of digital images. *Quantum Information Processing, 12*(8), 2833–2860. doi:10.100711128-013-0567-z

Zhou, N. R., Hua, T. X., Gong, L. H., Pei, D. J., & Liao, Q. H. (2015). Quantum image encryption based on generalized Arnold transform and double random-phase encoding. *Quantum Information Processing, 14*(4), 1193–1213. doi:10.100711128-015-0926-z

Chapter 11
Data Hiding in Color Image Using Steganography and Cryptography to Support Message Privacy

Sabyasachi Pramanik
https://orcid.org/0000-0002-9431-8751
Haldia Institute of Technology, India

Ramkrishna Ghosh
Haldia Institute of Technology, India

Digvijay Pandey
https://orcid.org/0000-0003-0353-174X
Department of Technical Education, India & Institution of Engineering and Technology, India

Mangesh M. Ghonge
https://orcid.org/0000-0003-0140-4827
Sandip Institute of Technology and Research Centre, India

ABSTRACT

The immense measure of classified information has been moved on the internet. Information security turns out to be progressively significant for some applications, for instance, private transmission, video observation, military, and clinical applications. Lately, there has been a great deal of enthusiasm for steganography and steganalysis. Steganography is the specialty of covering up and transmitting information through clearly harmless transporters with an end goal to disguise the presence of information. The advanced picture information, for example, BMP, JPEG, and GIF, are generally utilized as a transporter for steganography. Here the mystery message is implanted into a picture (or any media) called spread picture and afterward sent to the beneficiary who extricates the mystery message from the spread message. This picture ought not to be discernible from the spread picture, with the goal that the aggressor can't find any implanted message. The authors have proposed three approaches of steganography that can easily support message privacy.

DOI: 10.4018/978-1-7998-6677-0.ch011

Copyright © 2021, IGI Global. Copying or distributing in print or electronic forms without written permission of IGI Global is prohibited.

INTRODUCTION

The security of the difference in disguised data can be gotten by two unique ways: encryption (Lorente, A. S. and Berres, S., 2017) what's more, steganography (Pramanik, S. also, Raja, S. S., 2019). A blend of the two procedures can be used to grow the data security. In encryption, the message is changed in such a path thusly that no data can be disclosed if it is gotten by an aggressor. While in steganography, the riddle message is embedded into an image often called spread picture, and subsequently sent to the gatherer who isolates the secret message from the spread message. Exactly when the secret message is embedded into spread picture then it is known as a stego-picture. The deceivability of this image should not to be detectable from the spread picture, with the objective that it almost gets shocking for the attacker to discover any introduced message. Three unique methodologies for concealing information are proposed:

1. Approach based on steganography through LSB Modification for both Sender & Receiver for sending & extracting data respectively.

   Receiver compatible data hiding in color image based on the needed LSB modification

2. Approach based on the symmetric cryptography (Pramanik, S., Bandyopadhyay, S. K., & Ghosh, R., 2020) blending with steganography with concise storage
3. Data Hiding (Kim, P. H et. al., 2019) in Color Image using Steganography blending with Cryptography to support message privacy.

   Motivation:

- Steganography shrouds the presence of records.
- Provides high security (Pramanik, S., Bandyopadhyay, S. K., 2014) for information transmission.
- No one can foresee that the records even exist.

FIRST APPROACH: BASED ON STEGANOGRAPHY THROUGH LSB MODIFICATION

This is an approach based on LSB Modification (Swain, G., 2019) for both Sender and Receiver for sending and extracting data respectively. The content of the information file is converted to equivalent binary value and embedded into cover image and extracted from stego image. Some Tables are shown below that is describing the ASCII (Pramanik, S. et. al., 2019) value of the characters and also the equivalent binary value.

In simple LSB modification, bits from data that has to be hidden are put at the LSB of the cover image. Digitized images are made of pixels in which each pixel can use three bytes i.e. 24 bits. Here, three bytes are the representation of red, green and blue colors respectively. In the LSB method the least significant bit of each byte is set to zero. Now, according to the bits 0 or 1 in data, the LSB is being changed. If data bit is 0, then LSB remains same and if the data bit is 1 then the LSB is changed to 1. For doing this modification, the image becomes a little bit lighter than the original one. Nowadays, more sophisticated approach is used for hiding data. The most widely used technique to hide data is the usage of the LSB.

In spite of the fact that there are a few drawbacks to this methodology, the general ease to execute it, makes it a well known technique. To conceal a mystery message inside a picture, a legitimate spread picture is required. Since this strategy utilizes pieces of every pixel in the picture, it is important to utilize a lossless pressure design, in any case the shrouded data will lose all sense of direction in the changes of a lossy pressure (Bao, Z. et. al., 2018) calculation. When utilizing a 24-digit shading picture, a touch of every one of the red, green and blue shading parts can be utilized, so an aggregate of 3 pieces can be put away in every pixel. While utilizing a 24 cycle picture gives a moderately huge measure of room to shroud messages, it is likewise conceivable to utilize a 8 bit picture as a spread source.

In light of the littler space and various properties, 8 cycle pictures require a more cautious methodology. Though 24 bit pictures utilize three bytes to speak to a pixel, a 8-cycle picture utilizes just one. Changing the LSB of that byte will bring about a noticeable difference in shading, as another shading in the accessible palette will be shown. In this way, the spread picture should be chosen all the more cautiously and ideally be in grayscale (Joshi, K. et. al. 2018), as the natural eye won't distinguish the distinction between various dim qualities as simple similarly as with various hues. Detriments of utilizing LSB modification are chiefly in the way that it requires a genuinely enormous spread picture to make a usable measure of concealing space.

The size of a picture record, accordingly, is legitimately identified with the quantity of pixels and the granularity of the shading definition. A normal 640 x 480 pixel picture utilizing a palette of 256 hues would require a record around 307 KB in size (640 x 480 bytes), though a 1024 x 768 pix high-goal 24-cycle shading picture would bring about a 2.36 MB document (1024 x 768 x 3 bytes).

The most straightforward way to deal with concealing information inside a picture record is called least huge piece (LSB) inclusion. In this strategy, we can take the twofold portrayal of the shrouded information and overwrite the LSB of every byte inside the spread picture. On the off chance that we are utilizing 24-bit shading, the measure of progress will be negligible and indistinguishable to the natural eye. For instance, assume that we have three contiguous pixels (nine bytes) with the accompanying RGB (Prasad, S., and Pal, A. K. 2017) encoding:

```
10010101   00001101   11001001
10010110   00001111   11001010
10011111   00010000   11001011
```

Presently assume we need to "cover up" the accompanying 9 pieces of information (the shrouded information is generally compacted preceding being covered up): 101101101. In the event that we overlay these 9 pieces over the LSB of the 9 bytes above, we get the accompanying (where bits in strong have been changed):

```
10010101   00001100   11001001
10010111   00001110   11001011
10011111   00010000   11001011
```

Note that we have successfully hidden 9 bits but at a cost of only changing 4, or roughly 50%, of the LSBs.

This depiction is implied uniquely as an elevated level review. Comparable strategies can be applied to 8-bit shading however the changes, as the peruser may envision, are more sensational. Dark scale pictures, as well, are exceptionally valuable for steganographic purposes. One possible issue with any of these techniques is that they can be found by a foe that is looking. Likewise, there are different strategies other than LSB addition used to embed concealed data.

Without really expounding, it merits referencing steganalysis (Attaby, A. A. et. al. 2017)) is the specialty of recognizing and breaking steganography. One type of this investigation is to look at the shading palette of a graphical picture. In many pictures, there will be a special twofold encoding of every individual shading. On the off chance that the picture contains shrouded information, in any case, numerous hues in the palette will have copy parallel encodings since, for every single pragmatic reason, the LSBs can't be checked. In the event that the investigation of the shading palette (Margalikas, E., Ramanauskaitė, S., 2019) of a given record yields numerous copies, at that point it tends to be reasoned that the document has shrouded data.

Table 1. Decimal-Hex-Octal-Character List

Dec	Hx	Oct	Char	Dec	Hx	Oct	Html	Chr	Dec	Hx	Oct	Html	Chr	Dec	Hx	Oct	Html	Chr
0	0	000	NUL (null)	32	20	040	&#32;	Space	64	40	100	&#64;	@	96	60	140	&#96;	`
1	1	001	SOH (start of heading)	33	21	041	&#33;	!	65	41	101	&#65;	A	97	61	141	&#97;	a
2	2	002	STX (start of text)	34	22	042	&#34;	"	66	42	102	&#66;	B	98	62	142	&#98;	b
3	3	003	ETX (end of text)	35	23	043	&#35;	#	67	43	103	&#67;	C	99	63	143	&#99;	c
4	4	004	EOT (end of transmission)	36	24	044	&#36;	$	68	44	104	&#68;	D	100	64	144	&#100;	d
5	5	005	ENQ (enquiry)	37	25	045	&#37;	%	69	45	105	&#69;	E	101	65	145	&#101;	e
6	6	006	ACK (acknowledge)	38	26	046	&#38;	&	70	46	106	&#70;	F	102	66	146	&#102;	f
7	7	007	BEL (bell)	39	27	047	&#39;	'	71	47	107	&#71;	G	103	67	147	&#103;	g
8	8	010	BS (backspace)	40	28	050	&#40;	(	72	48	110	&#72;	H	104	68	150	&#104;	h
9	9	011	TAB (horizontal tab)	41	29	051	&#41;	)	73	49	111	&#73;	I	105	69	151	&#105;	i
10	A	012	LF (NL line feed, new line)	42	2A	052	&#42;	*	74	4A	112	&#74;	J	106	6A	152	&#106;	j
11	B	013	VT (vertical tab)	43	2B	053	&#43;	+	75	4B	113	&#75;	K	107	6B	153	&#107;	k
12	C	014	FF (NP form feed, new page)	44	2C	054	&#44;	,	76	4C	114	&#76;	L	108	6C	154	&#108;	l
13	D	015	CR (carriage return)	45	2D	055	&#45;	-	77	4D	115	&#77;	M	109	6D	155	&#109;	m
14	E	016	SO (shift out)	46	2E	056	&#46;	.	78	4E	116	&#78;	N	110	6E	156	&#110;	n
15	F	017	SI (shift in)	47	2F	057	&#47;	/	79	4F	117	&#79;	O	111	6F	157	&#111;	o
16	10	020	DLE (data link escape)	48	30	060	&#48;	0	80	50	120	&#80;	P	112	70	160	&#112;	p
17	11	021	DC1 (device control 1)	49	31	061	&#49;	1	81	51	121	&#81;	Q	113	71	161	&#113;	q
18	12	022	DC2 (device control 2)	50	32	062	&#50;	2	82	52	122	&#82;	R	114	72	162	&#114;	r
19	13	023	DC3 (device control 3)	51	33	063	&#51;	3	83	53	123	&#83;	S	115	73	163	&#115;	s
20	14	024	DC4 (device control 4)	52	34	064	&#52;	4	84	54	124	&#84;	T	116	74	164	&#116;	t
21	15	025	NAK (negative acknowledge)	53	35	065	&#53;	5	85	55	125	&#85;	U	117	75	165	&#117;	u
22	16	026	SYN (synchronous idle)	54	36	066	&#54;	6	86	56	126	&#86;	V	118	76	166	&#118;	v
23	17	027	ETB (end of trans. block)	55	37	067	&#55;	7	87	57	127	&#87;	W	119	77	167	&#119;	w
24	18	030	CAN (cancel)	56	38	070	&#56;	8	88	58	130	&#88;	X	120	78	170	&#120;	x
25	19	031	EM (end of medium)	57	39	071	&#57;	9	89	59	131	&#89;	Y	121	79	171	&#121;	y
26	1A	032	SUB (substitute)	58	3A	072	&#58;	:	90	5A	132	&#90;	Z	122	7A	172	&#122;	z
27	1B	033	ESC (escape)	59	3B	073	&#59;	;	91	5B	133	&#91;	[	123	7B	173	&#123;	{
28	1C	034	FS (file separator)	60	3C	074	&#60;	<	92	5C	134	&#92;	\	124	7C	174	&#124;	|
29	1D	035	GS (group separator)	61	3D	075	&#61;	=	93	5D	135	&#93;	]	125	7D	175	&#125;	}
30	1E	036	RS (record separator)	62	3E	076	&#62;	>	94	5E	136	&#94;	^	126	7E	176	&#126;	~
31	1F	037	US (unit separator)	63	3F	077	&#63;	?	95	5F	137	&#95;	_	127	7F	177	&#127;	DEL

Source: www.LookupTables.com

SOME CONSIDERATIONS

- Here the data is inserted in the Least Significant Bit of the Blue shade of every pixel of spread picture.
- Size limitation for Text File: To store 1 byte data (8 pieces) in any event 8 pixels are required i.e., Cover Image File ought to be at any rate multiple times greater (regarding pixels) than the Text File.

- In the current work, .bmp document with RGB shading design gave by Microsoft is utilized as spread picture. Every pixel is spoken to by the hues Red, Green and Blue that takes 1 byte space to store every one of the hues.
- Text File's Format is kept up so that the content must be ended by a . (Dot). It might be some other arranged character/image.

Table 2. Non-Printable Character List

128	Ç	144	É	161	í	177	▒	193	⊥	209	╤	225	ß	241	±
129	ü	145	æ	162	ó	178	▓	194	┬	210	╥	226	Γ	242	≥
130	é	146	Æ	163	ú	179	│	195	├	211	╙	227	π	243	≤
131	â	147	ô	164	ñ	180	┤	196	─	212	╘	228	Σ	244	⌠
132	ä	148	ö	165	Ñ	181	╡	197	┼	213	╒	229	σ	245	⌡
133	à	149	ò	166	ª	182	╢	198	╞	214	╓	230	µ	246	÷
134	å	150	û	167	º	183	╖	199	╟	215	╫	231	τ	247	≈
135	ç	151	ù	168	¿	184	╕	200	╚	216	╪	232	Φ	248	°
136	ê	152	ÿ	169	⌐	185	╣	201	╔	217	┘	233	Θ	249	·
137	ë	153	Ö	170	¬	186	║	202	╩	218	┌	234	Ω	250	·
138	è	154	Ü	171	½	187	╗	203	╦	219	█	235	δ	251	√
139	ï	156	£	172	¼	188	╝	204	╠	220	▄	236	∞	252	ⁿ
140	î	157	¥	173	¡	189	╜	205	═	221	▌	237	φ	253	²
141	ì	158	₧	174	«	190	╛	206	╬	222	▐	238	ε	254	■
142	Ä	159	ƒ	175	»	191	┐	207	╧	223	▀	239	∩	255	
143	Å	160	á	176	░	192	└	208	╨	224	α	240	≡		

Source: www.LookupTables.com

Inserting Algorithm

1. Calculate the quantity of bytes in information document that should hold a book of the sequential key of any product that is being sent through web to the collector. The outcome is put away in a whole number variable size_of_data.
2. A spread picture record is opened in read mode.
3. another stego picture record is opened in compose mode.
4. The header data from spread picture record is perused.
5. This header data is composed to stego picture record.
6. The data record is opened.
7. One character from information record is perused and the ASCII estimation of the character is changed over into proportional twofold incentive into a 8 cycle cluster, assume An, in such a way, so that from MSB to LSB it will be put away like A[7] to A[0].
8. From the spread picture document, the RGB shade of every pixel is perused. The last piece of every pixel is perused i.e., from RGB (8+8+8) bits – blue shading's eighth piece i.e., 24th piece.
9. Information is inserted at LSB of the blue shading
10. The above pixel is composed to stego picture document.

11. Steps (7 to 10) are rehashed until all the pieces of information document are installed in pixels of stego picture and after consummation of implanting of the information record, the remainder of the pixels in spread picture document is composed to stego picture record all things considered.
12. The stego picture record is picked
13. The spread picture record is shut
14. The data record is shut
15. End.

Extraction Algorithm

1. The stego image file is opened in read mode
2. An array A is initialized
3. The LSB of blue color of the stego image file is read.
4. That LSB is put in the array and it is done for 8 consecutive pixels to find the binary of each of the ASCII characters of text file.
5. The 8 bit binary value is converted to decimal value which is the ASCII value of the character.
6. The character is printed
7. Step 3 to Step 6 is repeated until terminating character is found.
8. The stego image file is closed
9. End.

The above algorithm has following advantages:

1. Minimal change is allowed in Stego (Pramanik, S., Singh, R. P., Ghosh, R. and Bandyopadhyay, S. K, 2020) Image and typical individuals' eyes can't get any distinction.
2. This new calculation needn't bother with any mystery key (Rehman, A. et. al., 2019).

The creators can infer that the appropriateness of steganography as an instrument to hide profoundly delicate data has been talked about by utilizing another philosophy. This proposes a picture containing concealed information can be communicated to anyone anyplace on the planet in a made sure about structure. Downloading such picture and utilizing it for some, multiple times won't grant any unapproved individual to share the shrouded data. Consequently, this procedure has been utilized to conceal information in a double picture. The pre-owned calculation is secure and the concealed data is very undetectable.

RECEIVER COMPATIBLE DATA HIDING IN COLOR IMAGE

Approach based on relative change needed to embed 0 or 1 from data file to cover image's LSB position. Here also algorithm has been discussed for both Sender & Receiver for sending & extracting data respectively.

Here, objective is to hide any information written in a text file within the suitable image file that is used as cover image with minimal change on pixels' color information.

Table 3. ASCII Alphabet Character List

ASCII Alphabet Characters

Symbol	Decimal	Binary	Symbol	Decimal	Binary
A	65	01000001	a	97	01100001
B	66	01000010	b	98	01100010
C	67	01000011	c	99	01100011
D	68	01000100	d	100	01100100
E	69	01000101	e	101	01100101
F	70	01000110	f	102	01100110
G	71	01000111	g	103	01100111
H	72	01001000	h	104	01101000
I	73	01001001	i	105	01101001
J	74	01001010	j	106	01101010
K	75	01001011	k	107	01101011
L	76	01001100	l	108	01101100
M	77	01001101	m	109	01101101
N	78	01001110	n	110	01101110
O	79	01001111	o	111	01101111
P	80	01010000	p	112	01110000
Q	81	01010001	q	113	01110001
R	82	01010010	r	114	01110010
S	83	01010011	s	115	01110011
T	84	01010100	t	116	01110100
U	85	01010101	u	117	01110101
V	86	01010110	v	118	01110110
W	87	01010111	w	119	01110111
X	88	01011000	x	120	01111000
Y	89	01011001	y	121	01111001
Z	90	01011010	z	122	01111010

Table 4. Pixel Information Analysis of Cover Image and Stego Image for First Approach

Table 4. Continued

window	cover	stego	(mean-stego)*(mean-stego)
1	255	254	0.49
2	255	255	2.89
3	255	255	2.89
4	255	254	0.49
5	255	254	0.49
6	255	254	0.49
7	255	254	0.49
8	255	255	2.89
9	255	254	0.49
10	255	254	0.49
11	255	255	2.89
12	255	254	0.49
13	255	254	0.49
14	255	254	0.49
15	255	254	0.49
16	255	254	0.49
17	255	254	0.49
18	255	254	0.49
19	255	255	2.89
20	255	255	2.89
21	255	254	0.49
22	255	255	2.89
23	255	254	0.49
24	255	254	0.49
25	255	254	0.49
26	255	254	0.49
27	255	255	2.89
28	255	254	0.49
29	255	254	0.49
30	255	254	0.49
31	255	254	0.49
32	255	254	0.49
33	255	254	0.49
34	255	255	2.89
35	255	255	2.89
36	255	254	0.49
37	255	254	0.49

continues in next column

window	cover	stego	(mean-stego)*(mean-stego)
38	255	254	0.49
39	255	254	0.49
40	255	255	2.89
41	255	254	0.49
42	255	255	2.89
43	255	255	2.89
44	255	255	2.89
45	255	254	0.49
46	255	254	0.49
47	255	254	0.49
48	255	254	0.49
49	255	254	0.49
50	255	255	2.89
51	255	255	2.89
52	255	255	2.89
53	255	254	0.49
54	255	254	0.49
55	255	254	0.49
56	255	254	0.49
57	255	254	0.49
58	255	255	2.89
59	255	255	2.89
60	255	254	0.49
61	255	255	2.89
62	255	255	2.89
63	255	254	0.49
64	255	254	0.49
65	255	254	0.49
66	255	255	2.89
67	255	255	2.89
68	255	254	0.49
69	255	254	0.49
70	255	255	2.89
71	255	254	0.49
72	255	255	2.89
73	255	254	0.49
74	255	254	0.49

continues on following page

Table 4. Continued

Table 4. Continued

window	cover	stego	(mean-stego)*(mean-stego)
75	255	254	0.49
76	255	254	0.49
77	255	255	2.89
78	255	255	2.89
79	255	254	0.49
80	255	255	2.89
81	255	254	0.49
82	255	254	0.49
83	255	254	0.49
84	255	254	0.49
85	255	255	2.89
86	255	254	0.49
87	85	85	28324.89
88	255	254	0.49
89	255	254	0.49
90	255	255	2.89
91	255	255	2.89
92	255	254	0.49
93	255	254	0.49
94	255	254	0.49
95	255	255	2.89
96	255	254	0.49
97	255	254	0.49
98	255	254	0.49
99	255	255	2.89
100	255	254	0.49
101	255	254	0.49
102	255	254	0.49
103	255	254	0.49
104	255	254	0.49
105	255	254	0.49
106	255	254	0.49
107	255	255	2.89
108	255	255	2.89
109	255	254	0.49
110	255	255	2.89
111	255	254	0.49

continues in next column

window	cover	stego	(mean-stego)*(mean-stego)
112	255	254	0.49
113	255	254	0.49
114	255	254	0.49
115	255	255	2.89
116	255	254	0.49
117	255	254	0.49
118	255	254	0.49
119	255	254	0.49
120	255	254	0.49
121	255	254	0.49
122	255	255	2.89
123	255	255	2.89
124	255	254	0.49
125	255	254	0.49
126	255	254	0.49
127	255	255	2.89
128	255	254	0.49
129	255	254	0.49
130	255	255	2.89
131	255	255	2.89
132	255	254	0.49
133	255	254	0.49
134	255	254	0.49
135	255	254	0.49
136	255	255	2.89
137	255	254	0.49
138	255	255	2.89
139	255	255	2.89
140	255	255	2.89
141	255	254	0.49
142	255	255	2.89
143	255	254	0.49
144	255	254	0.49
145	255	254	0.49
146	255	254	0.49
147	255	254	0.49
148	255	254	0.49

continues on following page

Table 4 Continued

Table 4. Continued

window	cover	stego	(mean-stego)*(mean-stego)
149	255	255	2.89
150	255	255	2.89
151	255	254	0.49
152	255	255	2.89
153	255	254	0.49
154	255	254	0.49
155	255	254	0.49
156	255	254	0.49
157	255	255	2.89
158	255	254	0.49
159	255	255	2.89
160	255	254	0.49
161	255	254	0.49
162	255	255	2.89
163	255	255	2.89
164	255	254	0.49
165	255	254	0.49
166	255	254	0.49
167	255	255	2.89
168	255	255	2.89
169	255	254	0.49
170	255	254	0.49
171	255	255	2.89
172	255	254	0.49
173	170	170	6938.89
174	170	169	7106.49
175	255	254	0.49

continues in next column

window	cover	stego	(mean-stego)*(mean-stego)
176	255	254	0.49
177	255	254	0.49
178	255	254	0.49
179	255	255	2.89
180	255	255	2.89
181	255	254	0.49
182	255	255	2.89
183	255	254	0.49
184	255	254	0.49
185	255	254	0.49
186	255	254	0.49
187	255	255	2.89
188	255	254	0.49
189	255	254	0.49
190	255	254	0.49
191	255	254	0.49
192	255	254	0.49
193	255	254	0.49
194	255	255	2.89
195	255	255	2.89
196	255	254	0.49
197	255	254	0.49
198	255	254	0.49
199	255	255	2.89
200	255	255	2.89
mean=>	253.3		213.114

Standard Deviation 14.59842457

Text File's Format is maintained in such a way so that the text must be terminated by any character chosen by sender with the negotiation with receiver and it should be chosen in such a way so that chosen character will not be part of info. File.

The authors consider an algorithm that would change the visual effect of the image so little that it is almost impossible to notice any change in image by human being's eye interpretation.

Here we take an image file where each pixel is represented by red green & blue color through three bytes i.e. 24 bits. Only the LSB of the color red, green or blue i.e. the either 8th/16th/24th bit of the pixel is used to hide the data bits.

Figure 1. Pixel Information Chart of First Approach

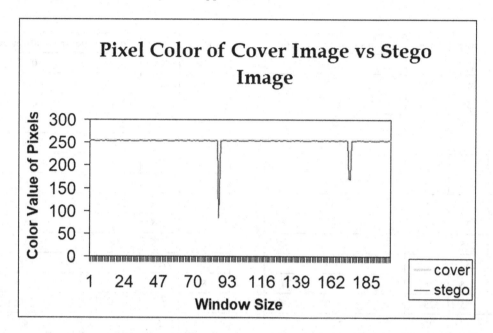

It will be calculated how many times a 0 is converted to 1 in cover image to embed the data of info. File & vice versa.

Now this change of LSB bit of either red or green or blue at image File has been calculated by tallying bit by bit data from Cover image's bit of each pixel. It may also consider 8th, 16th & 24th bit all of each pixel depending on the volume of data of information file that is to be embedded.

Suppose change at LSB calculated and it is greater than the no of bits needed any change. Now if we store the cumulative sum of change and no change at integer variable change & no_change and if total number of LSB needed to embed data is calculated in another integer variable as total_lsb_needed then percentage of need of modification at most can calculate as (Change/total_lsb_needed)*100.

Now Picture should be cleverly chosen so that the percentage of change is high so that data of Info File has been inverted to bring minimal effect on cover image & a indicator bit of say the middle one pixel's 7th bit will hold 1 that will assure data has been inverted otherwise if its value is 0 that will be the indicator of probation of simple LSB implementation which is not at all desirable.

Embedding Algorithm

1) Calculate the quantity of bytes in information record that is putting away a classified content and being sent through web to the recipient. Store the outcome in an Integer variable data_size.

2) Read character from information document and convert the ASCII estimation of the character into equal parallel an incentive into a number cluster guess An in such a manner so capacity begins from MSB and closures to LSB.

3) Repeat Step 1 to Step 2 until a terminating character is found. Sender can explicitly choose this Character. It may be or any negotiated character present in keyboard and absence in data file because this character cannot be a part of data file.

4) Open a Cover Image file in read mode.

5) From the Cover Image file, Read the LSB of each pixel i.e. from RGB (8+8+8) bits – read the red/green/blue color's LSB i.e. the 8th/16th/24th bit of the pixel's color. Selection will be serially and repeatedly i.e. 1st pixel's 8th bit, 2nd pixel's 16th bit & 3rd pixel's 24th bit is selected then 4th pixel's 8th bit 5th pixel's 16th bit & 6th pixel's 24th bit has been chosen. Thus selection will be carried out in this sequence serially & repeatedly.

6) Store 8th or 16th or 24th bit of each pixel at repetitive sequence in an integer array B

7) Repeat this Step 5 to Step 6 for 8 x data_size times. This is the number of pixels actually needed to be read to hide all bits of data file.

8) Read the bit stream of data file from array A one by one & Tally the data bit from array A with array B

9) Calculate cumulative sum of change or no_change based on the needed modification at LSB from 0 to 1 or 1 to 0 to embed data of Info File.

10) Repeat step 8 to 10 until all the bits are tallied

11) Choose picture such that where value of change is much greater than value of no_change.

12) Now invert the value of info file & set the flag=1.If direct LSB is implemented then flag=0

13) Now write the value of flag i.e. 1 or 0 which is put just at the left position of the last bit of red color of the first pixel's information of the Stego Image file that is started to use to store the data.

14) Open a Cover Image file in read mode.

15) Open a new Stego Image file in write mode.

16) Read the header information from Cover Image File.

17) Write this header information to Stego Image File.

18) Write the inverted data of Info File at LSB of RGB color of each pixel in the same fashion as indicated in step 5.

19) Repeat the Step 18 all the bits of data file would be embedded in Pixels of Stego Image and after completion of embedding of data file write the rest pixel in Cover Image File to Stego Image File as it is.

20) End.

Extraction Algorithm

1. Open the Stego picture File in read mode

2. Read the seventh piece not long before the last piece of shading red of first pixel's shading data in Stego Image File. In view of its Value set whole number variable marker 0 or 1

3. Read every pixel of the Stego Image document.

4. If marker is 0 at that point read the comparing piece of every pixel and put it legitimately in an Array in any case take the modify estimation of that bit and put it on Array

5. Read the every one of 8 Pixels' red, green, blue hues' LSB sequentially and consistently thusly and then substance of the cluster changes over into decimal worth that is really ASCII estimation of shrouded character.

6. If ending character's ASCII discovered print nothing in any case print the comparing character of the determined ASCII esteem.

7. Repeat Step 3 to Step 6 until decimal benefit of ending character's ASCII is found End.

8. End

SECOND APPROACH: BASED ON THE SYMMETRIC CRYPTOGRAPHY BLENDING WITH STEGANOGRAPHY WITH CONCISE STORAGE

In symmetric key cryptography, a similar key is utilized by sender (for encryption) and the recipient (for decoding), the key is shared. Here Cover Image (Bhardwaj, R. & Sharma, V., 2016) is used as symmetric key for both sender & receiver. LSB modification technique sequentially for the needed pixels in cover image resulting stego image is very common technique. Rather than that technique, in Stego Image, data is being stored with concise storage approach of sparse matrix and thus a much lesser modification is needed to store data through LSB. At receiver, Stego image (Pramanik, S., Singh, R. P. & Ghosh, R., 2020) is tallied with Cover Image i.e. working here as symmetric key to retrieve the embedded data. Symmetric encryption is utilized to scramble communicated information, utilizing a one time or transient meeting key. The meeting key can be disseminated by a believed key circulation place. This approach retain data confidentiality & also use of steganography approach helps to pretend an illusion that a simple picture is being sent whereas this image is nothing but the carrier of confidential data.

Figure 2. Result of the symmetric cryptography blending with steganography with concise storage

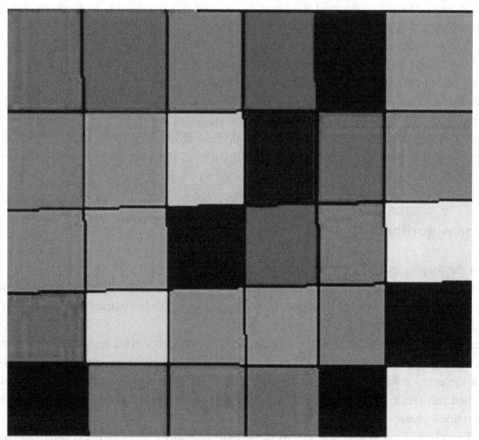

Embedding Algorithm

1) Open the spread picture record in read mode, stego picture document in compose Mode.
    1. Open text file.
    2. Count the number of characters, decide number of columns and count number of non zero elements based on the binary representation of the characters in text file.
    3. Embed number of characters, number of column, number of non zero elements in the stego image using LSB modification in the blue color of the pixels.
    4. Read each character from the text file & report from the step 6 to 7 until all the character is being processed.
    5. Convert the ASCII estimation of the character to 8 digit parallel proportionate.
    6. Invert the LSB of red color of the pixel for all 1s in the binary representation of the ASCII value of the character and for 0s, the original values of the pixels are retained same.
    7. Close all the files.

Extraction Algorithm

1. Open the stego & cover image in read mode & output text file at write Mode.
2. Extract the bits for number of characters from the blue colors LSB of first 16 pixels & convert each 16 bit into corresponding decimal value.
3. Extract the bits for number of columns from the blue colors LSB of next 16 pixels & convert each 16 bit into corresponding decimal value.
4. Extract the bits for number of non zero elements from the blue colors LSB of next 16 pixels & convert each 16 bit into corresponding decimal value.
5. Initialize counter by 0
6. Read pixels (started from 49th pixel) from both cover & stego image. Here cover image is being used as symmetric key.
7. Compare the LSB of red color of these two corresponding pixels through XOR operation.
8. If LSB of the red color of these pixels are equal then the retrieved value is determined as 0 otherwise 1
9. Repeat step 6 to 8 and increment counter by 1 for each 8 pixels and convert the retrieved bits into the equivalent decimal value which is the ASCII value of the character and write the character into the output text file until counter reaches the value of number of characters.
10. Close all files.

N.B In stego image, occurrence of number of non zero elements can be also counted and tallied with retrieved value for number of non zero values for cross checking.

Figure 3. Pixel Information Chart of Second Approach

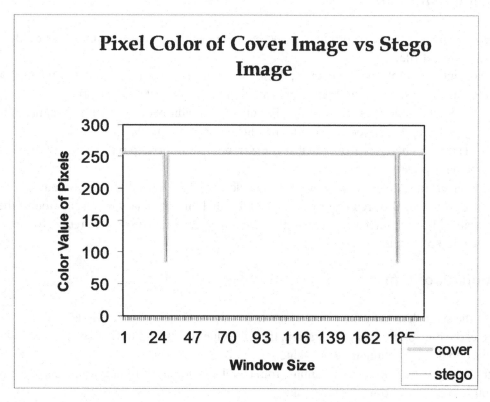

Table 5. Comparative Study of Cover Image vs Stego Image for Second Approach

Table 5. Continued

window	cover	Stego	(mean-stego)*(mean-stego)
1	255	254.667	1.868689
2	255	254.667	1.868689
3	255	254.667	1.868689
4	255	254.667	1.868689
5	255	254.667	1.868689
6	255	254.667	1.868689
7	255	254.667	1.868689
8	255	254.667	1.868689
9	255	254.667	1.868689
10	255	254.667	1.868689
11	255	254.667	1.868689
12	255	254.667	1.868689
13	255	254.667	1.868689
14	255	254.667	1.868689
15	255	254.667	1.868689

continues in next column

window	cover	Stego	(mean-stego)*(mean-stego)
16	255	254.667	1.868689
17	255	254.667	1.868689
18	255	254.667	1.868689
19	255	254.667	1.868689
20	255	254.667	1.868689
21	255	254.667	1.868689
22	255	254.667	1.868689
23	255	254.667	1.868689
24	255	254.667	1.868689
25	255	254.667	1.868689
26	255	254.667	1.868689
27	255	254.667	1.868689
28	255	254.667	1.868689
29	255	254.667	1.868689
30	85	85.3333	28212.81231

continues on following page

Table 5. Continued

window	cover	Stego	(mean-stego)*(mean-stego)
31	255	254.667	1.868689
32	255	254.667	1.868689
33	255	254.667	1.868689
34	255	254.667	1.868689
35	255	254.667	1.868689
36	255	254.667	1.868689
37	255	254.667	1.868689
38	255	254.667	1.868689
39	255	254.667	1.868689
40	255	254.667	1.868689
41	255	254.667	1.868689
42	255	254.667	1.868689
43	255	254.667	1.868689
44	255	254.667	1.868689
45	255	254.667	1.868689
46	255	254.667	1.868689
47	255	254.667	1.868689
48	255	254.667	1.868689
49	255	254.667	1.868689
50	255	254.667	1.868689
51	255	254.667	1.868689
52	255	254.667	1.868689
53	255	254.667	1.868689
54	255	254.667	1.868689
55	255	254.667	1.868689
56	255	254.667	1.868689
57	255	254.667	1.868689
58	255	254.667	1.868689
59	255	254.667	1.868689
60	255	254.667	1.868689
61	255	254.667	1.868689
62	255	254.667	1.868689
63	255	254.667	1.868689
64	255	254.667	1.868689
65	255	254.667	1.868689
66	255	254.667	1.868689

continues in next column

Table 5. Continued

window	cover	Stego	(mean-stego)*(mean-stego)
67	255	254.667	1.868689
68	255	254.667	1.868689
69	255	254.667	1.868689
70	255	254.667	1.868689
71	255	254.667	1.868689
72	255	254.667	1.868689
73	255	254.667	1.868689
74	255	254.667	1.868689
75	255	254.667	1.868689
76	255	254.667	1.868689
77	255	254.667	1.868689
78	255	254.667	1.868689
79	255	254.667	1.868689
80	255	254.667	1.868689
81	255	254.667	1.868689
82	255	254.667	1.868689
83	255	254.667	1.868689
84	255	254.667	1.868689
85	255	254.667	1.868689
86	255	254.667	1.868689
87	255	254.667	1.868689
88	255	254.667	1.868689
89	255	254.667	1.868689
90	255	254.667	1.868689
91	255	254.667	1.868689
92	255	254.667	1.868689
93	255	254.667	1.868689
94	255	254.667	1.868689
95	255	254.667	1.868689
96	255	254.667	1.868689
97	255	254.667	1.868689
98	255	254.667	1.868689
99	255	254.667	1.868689
100	255	254.667	1.868689
101	255	254.667	1.868689
102	255	254.667	1.868689

continues on following page

Table 5. Continued

window	cover	Stego	(mean-stego)*(mean-stego)
103	255	254.667	1.868689
104	255	254.667	1.868689
105	255	254.667	1.868689
106	255	254.667	1.868689
107	255	254.667	1.868689
108	255	254.667	1.868689
109	255	254.667	1.868689
110	255	254.667	1.868689
111	255	254.667	1.868689
112	255	254.667	1.868689
113	255	254.667	1.868689
114	255	254.667	1.868689
115	255	254.667	1.868689
116	255	254.667	1.868689
117	255	254.667	1.868689
118	255	254.667	1.868689
119	255	254.667	1.868689
120	255	254.667	1.868689
121	255	254.667	1.868689
122	255	254.667	1.868689
123	255	254.667	1.868689
124	255	254.667	1.868689
125	255	254.667	1.868689
126	255	254.667	1.868689
127	255	254.667	1.868689
128	255	254.667	1.868689
129	255	254.667	1.868689
130	255	254.667	1.868689
131	255	254.667	1.868689
132	255	254.667	1.868689
133	255	254.667	1.868689
134	255	254.667	1.868689
135	255	254.667	1.868689
136	255	254.667	1.868689
137	255	254.667	1.868689
138	255	254.667	1.868689

continues in next column

Table 5. Continued

window	cover	Stego	(mean-stego)*(mean-stego)
139	255	254.667	1.868689
140	255	254.667	1.868689
141	255	254.667	1.868689
142	255	254.667	1.868689
143	255	254.667	1.868689
144	255	254.667	1.868689
145	255	254.667	1.868689
146	255	254.667	1.868689
147	255	254.667	1.868689
148	255	254.667	1.868689
149	255	254.667	1.868689
150	255	254.667	1.868689
151	255	254.667	1.868689
152	255	254.667	1.868689
153	255	254.667	1.868689
154	255	254.667	1.868689
155	255	254.667	1.868689
156	255	254.667	1.868689
157	255	254.667	1.868689
158	255	254.667	1.868689
159	255	254.667	1.868689
160	255	254.667	1.868689
161	255	254.667	1.868689
162	255	254.667	1.868689
163	255	254.667	1.868689
164	255	254.667	1.868689
165	255	254.667	1.868689
166	255	254.667	1.868689
167	255	254.667	1.868689
168	255	254.667	1.868689
169	255	254.667	1.868689
170	255	254.667	1.868689
171	255	254.667	1.868689
172	255	254.667	1.868689
173	255	254.667	1.868689
174	255	254.667	1.868689

continues on following page

Table 5. Continued

Table 5. Continued

window	cover	Stego	(mean-stego)*(mean-stego)
175	255	254.667	1.868689
176	255	254.667	1.868689
177	255	254.667	1.868689
178	255	254.667	1.868689
179	255	254.667	1.868689
180	255	254.667	1.868689
181	255	254.667	1.868689
182	255	254.667	1.868689
183	85	85.3333	28212.81231
184	255	254.667	1.868689
185	255	254.667	1.868689
186	255	254.667	1.868689
187	255	254.667	1.868689
188	255	254.667	1.868689

continues in next column

window	cover	Stego	(mean-stego)*(mean-stego)
189	255	254.667	1.868689
190	255	254.667	1.868689
191	255	254.667	1.868689
192	255	254.667	1.868689
193	255	254.667	1.868689
194	255	254.667	1.868689
195	255	254.667	1.868689
196	255	254.667	1.868689
197	255	254.667	1.868689
198	255	254.667	1.868689
199	255	254.667	1.868689
200	255	254.667	1.868689
mean=>	253.3		283.9781252

Standard Deviation 16.85165052

THIRD APPROACH: DATA PRIVACY IN COLOR IMAGE WITH STEGANOGRAPHY AND ASYMMETRIC CRYPTOGRAPHY

Here, at sender's end, original data file is taken & using RSA (Jain, M. et. al., 2016) algorithm each character of data file is being encrypted using encryption key (Pramanik, S. & Bandyopadhyay, S. 2013) set & then the encrypted file is being embedded into the LSB of blue color of the Cover Image file resulting in a Stego Image file. At Receiver's end, from the Stego image, the encrypted data is being extracted & that encrypted data is finally decrypted using decryption key set.

Step 1: Take the Information file as input
Step 2: Generate Public & Private key pair using RSA key Generation algorithm
Step 3: Encrypt Information file using public key.
Step 4: Take this Cover image file as INPUT
Step 5: Insert the scrambled data document into the spread picture and now, the Stego Image is recovered
Step 6: Extract the encrypted information from the Stego Image File.
Step 7: Using the Decryption key the actual information is being retrieved.

RESULT OF DATA PRIVACY IN COLOR IMAGE USING STEGANOGRAPHY AND ASYMMETRIC CRYPTOGRAPHY

Step 1: The Information File's Content is as follows

Music is an art form whose medium is sound, Common elements of music are pitch (which governs melody and harmony), rhythm (and its associated concepts tempo, meter, and articulation), dynamics, and the sonic qualities of timbre and texture.

Step 2: Generated Public & Private key pair using RSA key Generation algorithm

Generation of Two Random Prime Numbers p=131 q=157

```
***** Encrypted Key pair ******
20567
 7
***** Decrypted Key pair *****
20567
17383
```

Step 3: Encryption is taken place as follows-

OUTPUT

18910 6126 3849 9948 6924 14560 9948 3849 14560 15176 15001 14560 15176 8609 18990 14560 3392 14493 8609 17697 14560 18438 8718 14493 3849 8137 14560 17697 8137 13225 9948 6126 17697 14560 9948 3849 14560 3849 14493 6126 15001 13225 167 14560 12502 14493 17697 17697 14493 15001 14560 8137 4592 8137 17697 8137 15001 18990 3849 14560 14493 3392 14560 17697 6126 3849 9948 6924 14560 15176 8609 8137 14560 473 9948 18990 6924 8718 19167 4438 7847 18438 8718 9948 6924 8718 14560 6774 14493 614 8137 8609 15001 3849 14560 17697 8137 4592 14493 13225 8924 14560 15176 15001 13225 14560 8718 15176 8609 17697 14493 15001 8924 3461 167 14560 8609 8718 8924 18990 8718 17697 14560 7847 15176 15001 13225 14560 9948 18990 3849 14560 15176 3849 3849 14493 6924 9948 15176 18990 8137 13225 14560 6924 14493 15001 6924 8137 473 18990 3849 14560 18990 8137 17697 473 14493 167 14560 17697 8137 18990 8137 8609 167 14560 15176 15001 13225 14560 15176 8609 18990 9948 6924 6126 4592 15176 18990 9948 14493 15001 3461 167 14560 19167 4438 13225 8924 15001 15176 17697 9948 6924 3849 167 14560 15176 15001 13225 14560 18990 8718 8137 14560 3849 14493 15001 9948 6924 14560 8468 6126 15176 4592 9948 18990 9948 8137 3849 14560 14493 3392 14560 18990 9948 17697 2387 8609 8137 14560 15176 15001 13225 14560 18990 8137 8511 18990 6126 8609 8137 6702 32767

Step 4: Cover image file as INPUT

Step 5: Stego Image File as OUTPUT

Step 6: The extracted content from stego image file is as follows-

OUTPUT

18910 6126 3849 9948 6924 14560 9948 3849 14560 15176 15001 14560 15176 8609 18990 14560 3392 14493 8609 17697 14560 18438 8718 14493 3849 8137 14560 17697 8137 13225 9948 6126 17697 14560 9948 3849 14560 3849 14493 6126 15001 13225 167 14560 12502 14493 17697 17697 14493 15001 14560 8137 4592 8137 17697 8137 15001 18990 3849 14560 14493 3392 14560 17697 6126 3849 9948 6924 14560 15176 8609 8137 14560 473 9948 18990 6924

8718 19167 4438 7847 18438 8718 9948 6924 8718 14560 6774 14493 614 8137 8609 15001 3849 14560 17697 8137 4592 14493 13225 8924 14560 15176 15001 13225 14560 8718 15176 8609 17697 14493 15001 8924 3461 167 14560 8609 8718 8924 18990 8718 17697 14560 7847 15176 15001 13225 14560 9948 18990 3849 14560 15176 3849 3849 14493 6924 9948 15176 18990 8137 13225 14560 6924 14493 15001 6924 8137 473 18990 3849 14560 18990 8137 17697 473 14493 167 14560 17697 8137 18990 8137 8609 167 14560 15176 15001 13225 14560 15176 8609 18990 9948 6924 6126 4592 15176 18990 9948 14493 15001 3461 167 14560 19167 4438 13225 8924 15001 15176 17697 9948 6924 3849 167 14560 15176 15001 13225 14560 18990 8718 8137 14560 3849 14493 15001 9948 6924 14560 8468 6126 15176 4592 9948 18990 9948 8137 3849 14560 14493 3392 14560 18990 9948 17697 2387 8609 8137 14560 15176 15001 13225 14560 18990 8137 8511 18990 6126 8609 8137 6702

Step 7: Plain Text is retrieved using Decryption Key as follows

OUTPUT

Music is an art form whose medium is sound, Common elements of music are pitch (which governs melody and harmony), rhythm (and its associated concepts tempo, meter, and articulation), dynamics, and the sonic qualities of timbre and texture.

Comparative Study of Cover Image vs Stego Image for the Approaches:

The first approach is an existing one. It has an importance in this respect that this is the mostly used technique and has been used to hide data. Least Significant Bit of the pixel is used as because it will hamper the picture intensity least.

In Second approach, Steganography & Cryptography is blended together to enhance the security. In this approach, Steganography hides the data at LSB of the cover image but this data is not the original one rather the encrypted data & encryption is made using encryption key set. From the Stego image the data is received at receiving end but the the data is in encrypted form. Even if the data is hacked by LSB attack, it would be a meaningless one because the decryption key is not available to the attacker. Only the original receiver would know the decryption key and hence can retrieve the original data.

Having gone through the above two approaches it can be said that second one is a better approach than the first one as because it provides more security to protect data. Here two existing approaches cryptography & steganography are mixed & thus we can have the advantages of both of them together & consequently a better security for the message transmission can be achieved successfully.

In second approach, each of 16 pixels' blue color is being affected, we can plot a curve based on the average blue color's information for each group of 16 successive pixels.

This will be carried out upto those numbers of pixels, used to embed data. For stego-image, we also plot another curve based on the average blue color's information for each group of changed 16 pixels.

Now we calculate the mean of the cover image's blue colors that will be used to measure the deviation of the blue color data of the stego-image.

Figure 4. Pixel Information Chart of Third Approach

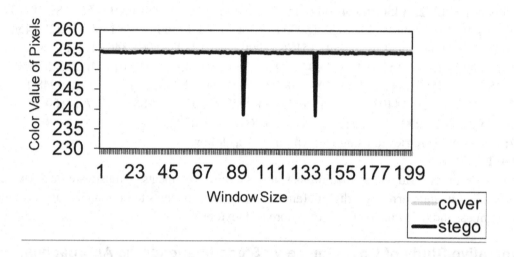

Table 6. Pixel Information Analyses of Cover Image and Stego Image on Third Approach

Table 6. Continued

window	cover	Stego	(mean-stego)*(mean-stego)
1	255	254.563	0.077353516
2	255	254.625	0.046494141
3	255	254.375	0.216806641
4	255	254.5	0.116025391
5	255	254.375	0.216806641
6	255	254.375	0.216806641
7	255	254.5	0.116025391
8	255	254.375	0.216806641
9	255	254.375	0.216806641
10	255	254.438	0.162509766
11	255	254.5	0.116025391
12	255	254.375	0.216806641
13	255	254.438	0.162509766
14	255	254.313	0.278916016
15	255	254.438	0.162509766
16	255	254.375	0.216806641
17	255	254.25	0.348837891
18	255	254.5	0.116025391
19	255	254.313	0.278916016

continues in next column

window	cover	Stego	(mean-stego)*(mean-stego)
20	255	254.313	0.278916016
21	255	254.375	0.216806641
22	255	254.25	0.348837891
23	255	254.313	0.278916016
24	255	254.5	0.116025391
25	255	254.375	0.216806641
26	255	254.563	0.077353516
27	255	254.375	0.216806641
28	255	254.313	0.278916016
29	255	254.563	0.077353516
30	255	254.5	0.116025391
31	255	254.5	0.116025391
32	255	254.625	0.046494141
33	255	254.313	0.278916016
34	255	254.375	0.216806641
35	255	254.5	0.116025391
36	255	254.375	0.216806641
37	255	254.375	0.216806641
38	255	254.375	0.216806641

continues on following page

Table 6. Continued

Table 6. Continued

window	cover	Stego	(mean-stego)*(mean-stego)
39	255	254.5	0.116025391
40	255	254.625	0.046494141
41	255	254.5	0.116025391
42	255	254.5	0.116025391
43	255	254.313	0.278916016
44	255	254.375	0.216806641
45	255	254.438	0.162509766
46	255	254.5	0.116025391
47	255	254.313	0.278916016
48	255	254.313	0.278916016
49	255	254.5	0.116025391
50	255	254.5	0.116025391
51	255	254.375	0.216806641
52	255	254.563	0.077353516
53	255	254.375	0.216806641
54	255	254.563	0.077353516
55	255	254.313	0.278916016
56	255	254.563	0.077353516
57	255	254.5	0.116025391
58	255	254.438	0.162509766
59	255	254.375	0.216806641
60	255	254.375	0.216806641
61	255	254.5	0.116025391
62	255	254.25	0.348837891
63	255	254.375	0.216806641
64	255	254.313	0.278916016
65	255	254.625	0.046494141
66	255	254.375	0.216806641
67	255	254.5	0.116025391
68	255	254.375	0.216806641
69	255	254.375	0.216806641
70	255	254.438	0.162509766
71	255	254.313	0.278916016
72	255	254.563	0.077353516
73	255	254.375	0.216806641
74	255	254.375	0.216806641

continues in next column

window	cover	Stego	(mean-stego)*(mean-stego)
75	255	254.5	0.116025391
76	255	254.438	0.162509766
77	255	254.375	0.216806641
78	255	254.313	0.278916016
79	255	254.625	0.046494141
80	255	254.375	0.216806641
81	255	254.563	0.077353516
82	255	254.25	0.348837891
83	255	254.313	0.278916016
84	255	254.5	0.116025391
85	255	254.375	0.216806641
86	255	254.313	0.278916016
87	255	254.375	0.216806641
88	255	254.5	0.116025391
89	255	254.5	0.116025391
90	255	254.313	0.278916016
91	255	254.563	0.077353516
92	255	254.313	0.278916016
93	239.06	238.625	262.9464941
94	255	254.375	0.216806641
95	255	254.375	0.216806641
96	255	254.313	0.278916016
97	255	254.563	0.077353516
98	255	254.375	0.216806641
99	255	254.5	0.116025391
100	255	254.5	0.116025391
101	255	254.438	0.162509766
102	255	254.375	0.216806641
103	255	254.438	0.162509766
104	255	254.5	0.116025391
105	255	254.5	0.116025391
106	255	254.375	0.216806641
107	255	254.313	0.278916016
108	255	254.438	0.162509766
109	255	254.313	0.278916016
110	255	254.313	0.278916016

continues on following page

Table 6. Continued

window	cover	Stego	(mean-stego)*(mean-stego)
111	255	254.5	0.116025391
112	255	254.5	0.116025391
113	255	254.438	0.162509766
114	255	254.375	0.216806641
115	255	254.313	0.278916016
116	255	254.375	0.216806641
117	255	254.313	0.278916016
118	255	254.313	0.278916016
119	255	254.438	0.162509766
120	255	254.438	0.162509766
121	255	254.313	0.278916016
122	255	254.313	0.278916016
123	255	254.375	0.216806641
124	255	254.563	0.077353516
125	255	254.438	0.162509766
126	255	254.5	0.116025391
127	255	254.5	0.116025391
128	255	254.375	0.216806641
129	255	254.5	0.116025391
130	255	254.438	0.162509766
131	255	254.375	0.216806641
132	255	254.375	0.216806641
133	255	254.438	0.162509766
134	255	254.375	0.216806641
135	255	254.375	0.216806641
136	255	254.5	0.116025391
137	255	254.375	0.216806641
138	255	254.5	0.116025391
139	239.06	238.563	264.9773535
140	255	254.438	0.162509766
141	255	254.563	0.077353516
142	255	254.5	0.116025391
143	255	254.375	0.216806641
144	255	254.375	0.216806641
145	255	254.5	0.116025391
146	255	254.5	0.116025391

continues in next column

Table 6. Continued

window	cover	Stego	(mean-stego)*(mean-stego)
147	255	254.375	0.216806641
148	255	254.563	0.077353516
149	255	254.375	0.216806641
150	255	254.438	0.162509766
151	255	254.375	0.216806641
152	255	254.375	0.216806641
153	255	254.438	0.162509766
154	255	254.563	0.077353516
155	255	254.313	0.278916016
156	255	254.375	0.216806641
157	255	254.5	0.116025391
158	255	254.313	0.278916016
159	255	254.375	0.216806641
160	255	254.313	0.278916016
161	255	254.563	0.077353516
162	255	254.438	0.162509766
163	255	254.563	0.077353516
164	255	254.313	0.278916016
165	255	254.313	0.278916016
166	255	254.375	0.216806641
167	255	254.438	0.162509766
168	255	254.5	0.116025391
169	255	254.5	0.116025391
170	255	254.375	0.216806641
171	255	254.438	0.162509766
172	255	254.313	0.278916016
173	255	254.438	0.162509766
174	255	254.5	0.116025391
175	255	254.375	0.216806641
176	255	254.625	0.046494141
177	255	254.375	0.216806641
178	255	254.438	0.162509766
179	255	254.438	0.162509766
180	255	254.5	0.116025391
181	255	254.5	0.116025391
182	255	254.5	0.116025391

continues on following page

Table 6. Continued

Table 6. Continued

window	cover	Stego	(mean-stego)*(mean-stego)
183	255	254.375	0.216806641
184	255	254.313	0.278916016
185	255	254.375	0.216806641
186	255	254.625	0.046494141
187	255	254.375	0.216806641
188	255	254.5	0.116025391
189	255	254.438	0.162509766
190	255	254.5	0.116025391
191	255	254.438	0.162509766
192	255	254.313	0.278916016

continues in next column

window	cover	Stego	(mean-stego)*(mean-stego)
193	255	254.5	0.116025391
194	255	254.375	0.216806641
195	255	254.375	0.216806641
196	255	254.313	0.278916016
197	255	254.375	0.216806641
198	255	254.438	0.162509766
199	255	254.5	0.116025391
200	255	254.5	0.116025391
mean=>	254.841		2.819365234

Standard Deviation 1.679096553

ANALYSIS OF RESULTS

As stated in first case, bmp file is taken as cover image and text file's content is embedded into the LSB of cover image resulting stego image. At receiver, this stego image is retrieved and from this image, information is being extracted.

In another technique used for the same case, Receiver compatible data hiding in color image, compatibility between information and cover image is established. This is done based on needed relative changes at LSB, therefore information is being changed to maintain least distortion on image after embedding of information & setting the flag to indicate the changes. This technique contributes an improved security (Jassim, K. N. et al., 2019) support rather using simple LSB modification technique.

In the second case, text file's content is converted into binary values and then this value is represented into m X n matrix. From this matrix, the sparse representation is done and that concise information is embedded into cover image resulting stego image, here cover image is used as symmetric key for both sender and receiver. At receiver, stego image & cover image that is working as symmetric key is being tallied and sparse storage information is retrieved and from this information, original matrix is obtained that is nothing but the original information. Thus Steganography is blended with symmetric cryptography to provide privacy & security in message transmission.

In the third case, text file's content is encrypted by encryption key and then this encrypted information is being embedded into cover image resulting in stego image. At receiver, from this stego image, information is being extracted and receiver uses his/her decryption key to get back the original information. In this way, Steganography is blended with asymmetric cryptography to enhance confidentiality in digital transmission.

ADVANTAGES AND TARGETED APPLICATIONS

In the first approach Steganography is implemented through LSB modification technique. This is providing the privacy during message transmission; here even the existence of the message is concealed.

In the second approach information is being represented in concise way and then it is being hidden into the cover object, using the symmetric key Concise information is being retrieved as original information at receiver after extraction of concise information from stego object, blending of cryptography and steganography provide a better support for message privacy through cryptography and also a secured transmission approach through steganography that is used to conceal that information even exists.

In case of third approach asymmetric key is used by sender and receiver, sender encrypts the message by his/her encryption key and then that encrypted information is being embedded into cover object. Receiver extract information from stego object and from that extracted information, original is retrieved using receiver's decryption key which is not known to sender. Here blending of steganography and asymmetric cryptography supports for the hidden approach for encrypted information transmission and message confidentiality, transmission privacy and therefore security in data transmission is being enhanced.

Real Life Application of Steganographic Framework:

Computerized picture steganography has been proposed as a technique to upgrade clinical information security, privacy and respectability. A considerable lot of the investigation frameworks utilized for clinical determination depend on the clinical examination pictures. Clinical picture steganography requires outrageous consideration while installing extra information inside the clinical pictures in light of the fact that the extra data must not influence the picture quality. Clinical pictures are put away for various purposes, for example, conclusion, long time stockpiling and research. In the clinical field, the significance of clinical information security has been stressed, particularly as for the data alluding to the patients (individual information, studies and finding). On one hand, the measure of advanced clinical pictures transmitted over the web has expanded quickly; then again the need for quick and secure finding is significant in the clinical field, for example, telemedicine, making steganography the response to progressively make sure about picture transmission. For applications that manage pictures, the steganography point is to insert an undetectable message in a picture.

The development in the clinical field has prompted the progression of the paper information to the advanced information. As the clinical field is moving towards the computerized world the security has become a significant issue. To make the treatment quick and precise the computerized pictures are being presented. Information is installed in the clinically examined pictures utilizing the consolidated methodology of cryptography and steganography. The calculation keeps the conclusion and the patient data assists with making the patient treatment precise and quick. The medical clinics are changing from papers to the computerized pictures. The patient data is being put away on the computerized pictures. The treatment of the patients is done through these computerized pictures. The conclusion by the specialist is based on these clinical advanced pictures. On the off chance that the clinical checked pictures are altered, the specialist analyzes can be reflected and bring about poor treatment. In clinics, the treatment of the patients is postponed as the patient information is dispersed to different offices in the emergency clinics. So the issue details, by which a framework is to be made utilizing both cryptography and steganography approaches on a solitary stage. This procedure will make sure about the patient's data and specialists analyze which brings about the correct treatment of the patients. By utilizing this methodology both the patient's very own data and the specialists analyze a solitary stage.

Research Technique

The methodology is partitioned into two modules: implanting information and extraction of information from the patient filtered x-beam. The primary module contains two fundamental procedures: cryptography and steganography. In this, the patient rather than any paper report can be furnished with the x-beam computerized picture containing the patient's history and conclusion. The subsequent module contains the stego extraction, unscrambling calculation and one included method by which the specialists analyze and understanding history both is put away in the database for future reference. The proposed of Z Shrewd LSB Approach is roused from the keen LSB approach. The analysts utilized a java based application and gave another plan to the clinical stream. In this situation, the patient data and the X-ray of the patient are being examined by the specialist and on this examination, the specialist analyzes the patient. After that the specialist analysis comes into the java application made in this exploration and the determination by a specialist is being encoded and the information after encryption process with the new Zigzag based steganography procedure and the information are implanted into the picture and the stego picture is produced. Along these lines, the patient X-ray contains the analysis of the specialist in a mysterious way. Next time when the patient goes to the specialist, the specialist simply utilized the computerized X-ray of the patient into the picture and the patient past history appears to the specialist:

Device Utilized

The device utilized in this exploration is Z Brilliant LSB device. The Z Keen LSB apparatus is utilized to give the general public another method of seeing the clinical reports of the patients. This apparatus is utilized to shroud the finding of the specialist into the advanced X-ray pictures. The Z Savvy LSB instrument has different utilizations and they are:

- Z Savvy LSB instrument is utilized to conceal information into the X-beam pictures.
- Z Brilliant LSB instrument utilizes the new methodology utilizing Crisscross, for example, LSB.
- By the Z SMart LSB device we can perform multiway stego for example at the point when we shroud information in the record; we can again conceal information in that document.
- Z SMart LSB apparatus is essentially the improvement to the fundamental LSB.

The Z SMart LSB apparatus utilizes four fundamentals procedure to perform and they are as per the following:

Process 1: Encryption: In this activity, the Z SMart LSB instrument previously read the mystery message and encodes the mystery message.

Process 2: Encoding: After the encryption of the mystery message, the scrambled message is added something extra to a parallel structure. Then again, the X-beam picture is added something extra to the decimal structure. At that point, the bits are changed over into a solitary 1-D exhibit and install into the picture pixels utilizing the LSB procedure. Finally, the picture is made utilizing the estimation of the new pixel containing the scrambled content inserts into it.

Process 3: Decoding: After the encoding procedure, the deciphering procedure begins. In this procedure, the Stego record is added something extra to the pixels esteems and the length of the encoded mystery is brought from the initial four pixels.

Process 4: Decryption: The decryption is the last procedure that acts in the Z Smart LSB apparatus. In this procedure, the scrambled mystery content is decoded utilizing the AES unscrambling strategy.

RESULTS AND DISCUSSIONS

The proposed approach is an improvement in the clinical field. The examination is on making persistent data increasingly secure and specialists analyze progressively precisely. The exploration worry with utilizing the two significant calculations, cryptography and steganography on a solitary stage to make the patient's data progressively secure with the emergency clinic. The methodology is partitioned into two modules: implanting information and extraction of information from the patient checked x-beam. The patient rather than any paper report is given the x-beam examined containing the patient history and specialists analyze. The subsequent module contains the stego extraction, decoding calculation, and one included strategy by which the specialists analyze and understanding history both is put away in the database for future reference. As the medical clinics are getting digitized, all the information of the emergency clinic is put away in the advanced pictures like CT-SCAN and X-beams.

Quantum Cryptography

Quantum steganography is a novel and rising idea in a field of data security because of the benefits of quantum mechanics. As of late, numerous calculations have been proposed based on quantum data preparing, for example, picture handling and changes, quantum streamlining and so on. Numerous quantum picture steganography has been gotten ready for the need of putting away picture data in quantum states, i.e., Qu-bit Lattice, and Flexible Representation of Quantum Images (FRQI). Data covering inserts the extra mystery data into media, for example, a condition where the transporter experiences minimal changed. Numerous data disguising strategies for the traditional picture steganography have been created. The traditional LSB data disguising calculation just substitutes the least noteworthy piece of spread picture utilizing the mystery data. LSB assumes a critical job in picture data disguising since numerous data covering calculations depend on the LSB calculation. Presently the investigation of quantum picture LSB data hiding calculation is still in its underlying stage. While talking about LSB data covering calculations for quantum pictures, the shading encoding ought to be as the twofold Qu-square. At this stage, LSQu-square dependent on twofold Qublock is a perfect portrayal of the quantum picture. Attributable to the way that shading data and position data are snared together in the Novel Enhanced Quantum Representation (NEQR), so in the system of LSQu-square calculation, the researchers structure the unitary change following up on the quantum picture state. By means of the one activity, one can understand the reason for inserting the mystery message into a quantum spread picture.

Limitations of Quantum Cryptography

Following are the drawbacks or shortcomings of Quantum Cryptography:

- The by and large use of this can take up stores of occupations and hereafter joblessness will increase.
- While adhering to the procedure (for instance optical fiber or air), there is an opportunity of a modification in the polarization of photons in view of various causes.
- Quantum cryptography needs various essential features, for instance, mechanized mark, guaranteed mail, etc.
- The prerequisite for a submitted channel is a flat out need among sources and objectives which derives a critical cost. It is hard to send keys to in any event two remarkable regions using a quantum channel as multiplexing is in opposition to quantum's principles. This solicitations separate channels among sources and various objectives. This is a critical obstacle to quantum correspondence through optical channels.
- The greatest detachment maintained by Quantum Key Distribution (QKD) is around 250 KM at a speed of 16 bps through a guided medium.

Effect for future utilizations of quantum cryptography

Quantum Cryptography for Future Internet Security for the web later on the Internet should be guaranteed as it is the combination of all information systems and the information condition for human perseverance. For the creating security issue on the web, quantum cryptography transforms into the essential idea.

Unequivocal Security

Connection and light are the essential carriers of the current Internet correspondence. Alice and Bob are credible customers in the structure while Eve is an eavesdropper. To ensure security, they scramble messages and subsequently send them on the open channel. The old-style cryptosystem is commonly isolated into two sorts, which are symmetric-key cryptosystems and topsy-turvy key cryptosystems. For these two cryptosystems, their security is generally subject to the multifaceted idea of the preparing. Furthermore, the fast headway of quantum figuring has moreover made various inconvenient issues in old-style science have sensibility in the field of quantum material science. Shannon, the creator of the information theory, made a leading examination of boundless security during the 50s of the main outstanding century. In particular, instead of the pseudo-self-assertive number, the encryption/unscrambling key are amazingly sporadic. Besides, this key is used only a solitary time. Furthermore, the key length is comparable to the plaintext and plays out the select or action with the plaintext by bit.

Sniffing Detection

Alice and Bob exchange information the open channels. To ensure security, their information is encoded, yet they can't shield an attacker from listening subtly on the channel. What's more, because of the characteristics of the device itself, the busybody can't be perceived whether it is in interface exchanges or in optical fiber correspondences. In interface correspondences, the crowd can use a multimeter or oscilloscope to screen. In optical fiber trades, the eavesdropper can get information from a bit of the light sign. In quantum correspondence, the busybody makes sure to be distinguished inferable from the quantum no-cloning speculation. For the quantum information of n-bit, the probability of the covert agent being recognized is $1 - (1/2)n$.

CONCLUSION AND FUTURE SCOPE

The motivation behind this exploration is to give a down to earth review of both the standards and practice of steganography with the assistance of cryptography for better help of organization security. In future, we can utilize more mind boggling calculation that may acquire lesser change stego object that would offer more made sure about information transmission. Likewise we may improve our undertaking by offering the help for blunder location and in this manner mistake amendment. The specialists have an arrangement to offer a proceeding with help that can improve the capacity of better message verification, protection, security and uprightness for the correspondence of e-world. While there have been liberal degrees of progress in the field of quantum cryptography in the latest decade, there are still troubles ahead before quantum cryptography can transform into a for the most part passed on key assignment structure for governments, associations, what're more, solitary inhabitants. In particular, these challenges join developing additionally created hardware to engage higher bore and longer transmission partitions for quantum key exchange. Nevertheless, the advances in PC taking care of intensity and the risk of outdated quality for the current cryptography systems will remain a central purpose in the continued with creative work of quantum cryptography. Honestly, it is typical that nearly $50 million of both open and private accounts will be placed assets into quantum cryptography advancement all through the accompanying three years. Quantum cryptography is still in its beginning phases so far looks extremely encouraging. This advancement can make a huge responsibility to web business and business security, singular security, and security among government affiliations. If quantum cryptography goes out to over the long haul meet even a portion of its wants; it will have a critical and reformist effect on the whole of our lives.

REFERENCES

Attaby, A. A., Mursi Ahmed, M. F. M., & Alsammak, A. K. (2017). Data hiding inside JPEG images with high resistance to steganalysis using a novel technique: DCT-M3. *Ain Shams Engineering Journal.* Advance online publication. doi:10.1016/j.asej.2017.02.003

Bao, Z., Luo, X., Zhang, Y., Yang C. & Liu, F. (2018). A Robust Image Steganography on Resisting JPEG Compression with No Side Information. *IETE Technical Review*, *35*(S1), 4-13. doi:10.1080/025 64602.2018.1476192

Bhardwaj, R., & Sharma, V. (2016). Image Steganography based on Completed Message and Inverted bit LSB Substitution. *Procedia Computer Science*, *93*, 832–838. doi:10.1016/j.procs.2016.07.245

Jain, M., Lenka, S. K., & Vasistha, S. K. (2016). Adaptive Circular Queue Image Steganography with RSA Cryptosystem. *Perspectives in Science*, *8*, 417–420. doi:10.1016/j.pisc.2016.04.093

Jassim, K. N. (2019). Hybrid Cryptography and Steganography method to Embed Encrypted Text Message with Image. *Journal of Physics: Conference Series*, 1339, 26–27.

Joshi, K., Swati Gill, S., & Yadav, R. (2018). A New Method of Image Steganography using 7th bit of a Pixel as Indicator by Introducing the Successive Temporary Pixel in the Grayscale Image. *Journal of Computer Networks and Communication*. doi:10.1155/2018/9475142

Kim, P. H., Yoon, E. J., Ryu, K. W., & Jung, K. H. (2019). Data-Hiding Scheme Using Multidirectional Pixel-Value Differencing on Color Images. *Security and Communication Networks*, *2019*, 1–11. Advance online publication. doi:10.1155/2019/9038650

Lorente, A. S., & Berres, S. (2017). A Secure Steganographic Algorithm Based on Frequency Domain for the Transmission of Hidden Information. *Security and Communication Networks*, *2017*, 1–14. Advance online publication. doi:10.1155/2017/5397082

Margalikas, E., & Ramanauskaitė, S. (2019). Image steganography based on color palette transformation in color space. *J Image Video Proc.*, *82*(1), 82. Advance online publication. doi:10.118613640-019-0484-x

Pramanik, S., & Bandyopadhyay, S. (2013). Application of Steganography in Symmetric Key Cryptography with Genetic Algorithm. *International Journal of Computers and Technology*, *10*(7), 1791–1799. doi:10.24297/ijct.v10i7.7027

Pramanik, S., & Bandyopadhyay, S. K. (2014). An Innovative Approach in Steganography. *Scholar Journal of Engineering and Technology*, *2*(2B), 276–280.

Pramanik, S., Bandyopadhyay, S. K., & Ghosh, R. (2020). Signature Image Hiding in Color Image using Steganography and Cryptography based on Digital Signature Concepts. *2020 2nd International Conference on Innovative Mechanisms for Industry Applications (ICIMIA)*, 665-669. 10.1109/ICIMIA48430.2020.9074957

Pramanik, S., & Raja, S. S. (2019). Analytical Study on Security Issues in Steganography. *Think India Journal*, *22*(3), 106–114.

Pramanik, S., Singh, R. P., & Ghosh, R. (2019). A New Encrypted Method in Image Steganography. *Indonesian Journal of Electrical Engineering and Computer Science*, *14*(3), 1412–1419. doi:10.11591/ijeecs.v14.i3.pp1412-1419

Pramanik, S., Singh, R. P., & Ghosh, R. (2020). *Application of bi-orthogonal wavelet transform and genetic algorithm in image steganography. Multimed Tools Appl.* doi:10.100711042-020-08676-1

Pramanik, S., Singh, R. P., Ghosh, R., & Bandyopadhyay, S. K. (2020). A Unique Way to Generate Password at Random Basis and Sending it Using a New Steganography Technique. *Indonesian Journal of Electrical Engineering and Informatics*, *8*(3). Advance online publication. doi:10.11591/ijeei.v8i3.831

Prasad, S., & Pal, A. K. (2017). An RGB colour image steganography scheme using overlapping block-based pixel-value differencing. *Royal Society Open Science*, *4*(4), 161066. doi:10.1098/rsos.161066 PMID:28484623

Rehman, A., Saba, T., Mahmood, T., Mehmood, Z., Shah, M., & Anjum, A. (2019). Data hiding technique in steganography for information security using number theory. *Journal of Information Science*, *45*(6), 767–778. doi:10.1177/0165551518816303

Swain, G. (2019). Very High Capacity Image Steganography Technique Using Quotient Value Differencing and LSB Substitution. *Arabian Journal for Science and Engineering*, *44*(4), 2995–3004. doi:10.100713369-018-3372-2

Chapter 12
Recent Progress in Quantum Machine Learning

Amandeep Singh Bhatia

Chitkara University Institute of Engineering and Technology, Chitkara University, Patiala, India

Renata Wong

ⓘD https://orcid.org/0000-0001-5468-0716

Nanjing University, China

ABSTRACT

Quantum computing is a new exciting field which can be exploited to great speed and innovation in machine learning and artificial intelligence. Quantum machine learning at crossroads explores the interaction between quantum computing and machine learning, supplementing each other to create models and also to accelerate existing machine learning models predicting better and accurate classifications. The main purpose is to explore methods, concepts, theories, and algorithms that focus and utilize quantum computing features such as superposition and entanglement to enhance the abilities of machine learning computations enormously faster. It is a natural goal to study the present and future quantum technologies with machine learning that can enhance the existing classical algorithms. The objective of this chapter is to facilitate the reader to grasp the key components involved in the field to be able to understand the essentialities of the subject and thus can compare computations of quantum computing with its counterpart classical machine learning algorithms.

INTRODUCTION

In computer science, the machine learning and artificial intelligence are problem solving methods in several research and academic communities. Machine learning spans a wide range of algorithms which are used to uncover the unknown patterns from data. The machine learning algorithms can learn by an interaction and learn from data (Alpaydin, 2020, Marsland, 2015). There are mainly three sub-categories of learning i.e. supervised (task-driven), unsupervised (data-driven) and reinforcement learning (learn from mistakes) (Ayodele, 2010). The applications of machine learning are fraud detection, products

DOI: 10.4018/978-1-7998-6677-0.ch012

Copyright © 2021, IGI Global. Copying or distributing in print or electronic forms without written permission of IGI Global is prohibited.

recommendation systems, risk assessment in financial sector, spam mail filter, traffic alerts, image recognition, sentiment analysis, social media, customer supports, robot control, weather prediction, medical diagnosis and many more (Jordan et al, 2015). These applications involve an enormous amount of formerly collected data in an input-output pairs so called big data. Hence, machine learning methods need to be highly efficient and effective in order to process the data. Nowadays, it is achievable task due to increase in computational power of systems.

Quantum computing is a compelling research area, that is blend of computer science, physics and mathematics. It has the capability to revolutionize the different scientific fields due to its massive computational power, enabled by entanglement and superposition principle. Quantum computers are known to solve problems which cannot be solved using a classical computer (Gruska, 1999). Quantum computers have shown remarkable improvements in the field of optimization and simulation (Biamonte et al. 2017). It includes computing the properties of partition functions, performing approximate optimization and simulating different quantum systems. Recently, machine learning techniques have been introduced to deal with several quantum information processing (QIP) tasks that consist the exploitation of quantum states (Nielsen and Chuang, 2002). QIP utilizes the concept of superposition principle of states for expedite processing of classical data and its amenable simulation on quantum computers (Ladd et al., 2010). The quantum machine learning techniques provide great potential, better flexibility and efficient performance analogous to classical machine learning techniques.

The rapid development in quantum computing reflects the advancement build in artificial intelligence and machine learning. The HHL algorithm is at center of quantum machine learning, proposed by Harrow, Hassidim, Lloyd in 2009. It is used to solve the linear equations and considered as the most crucial asset in quantum machine learning algorithms. Since the HHL algorithm introduced, the quantum versions of machine learning algorithms have been proposed and witnessed the exponential speed-up over the existing classical machine learning algorithms (Schuld, 2015). The principles of quantum computing can be applied to basic algorithms such as k-nearest neighbour algorithm, support vector machine, principal component analysis, classification and many more.

Table 1. Summary of quantum machine learning theories, algorithms and concepts

Quantum machine learning algorithms	Proposed by	Grover's algorithm	Speedup	Quantum data
Quantum k-nearest neighbor method	Wiebe et al., 2015	Yes	Quadratic	No
Quantum principal component analysis	Lloyd et al., 2013	No	Exponential	Yes
Quantum support vector machine	Auguita et al., 2003	Yes	Quadratic	No
	Rebentrost et al., 2014	No	Exponential	Yes
Quantum reinforcement learning	Dong et al., 2008	Yes	-	Yes
Quantum Boltzmann machines	Amin et al., 2018	No	Exponential	No
Quantum neural network	Narayanan & Meneer, 2000	Yes	Numerical	No
Quantum clustering	Aimeur et al, 2007	Yes	Quadratic	No

In this advanced outline, the current implementation results of quantum machine learning algorithms have shown that quantum computers could be effective in dealing problems in the area of artificial intelligence efficiently as compared to classical variants (Schuld et al. 2014, Biamonte et al., 2017, Schuld and Petruccione 2018, Dunjko and Briegel 2018). In last few years, data scientists investigate the intersection of machine learning and quantum computing. Table 1 shows the summary of proposed quantum machine learning algorithms. In this chapter, the brief description of emerging field of quantum machine learning with focus on algorithms is given. Firstly, the concept of classical machine learning and quantum computing is discussed. Further, the aforementioned quantum machine learning algorithms are explored.

CLASSICAL MACHINE LEARNING

Classical machine learning is subclass of artificial intelligence. Formally, it is defined as the science of providing systems to learn a task without being programmed explicitly. In recent decades, it has been making enormous progress in various research directions. The recently developed methods (like deep learning) have made the algorithms highly capable of generalized and flexible learning (Ciliberto et al., 2018). Figure 1 shows the three sub-categories of machine learning.

Figure 1. Classification of machine learning

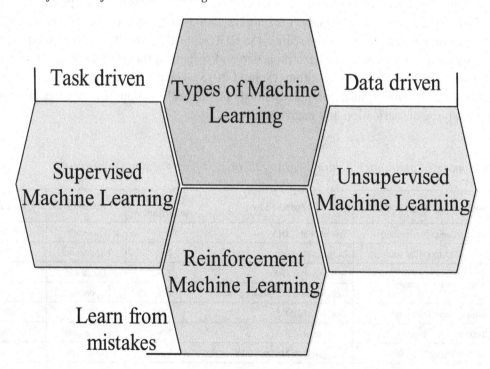

Supervised Machine Learning

In supervised machine learning, the model is trained under some supervision. The model is trained on some labelled dataset, which consists input variable (x) as well as output variable (y). Thus, the model is used is learn the mapping function ($f(x)$) that maps the input to the output (Kotsiantis, 2007). The data is split into two parts: training and testing datasets. The mode is trained with training dataset and tested on unseen data to determine the accuracy of our model.

$$y = f(x)$$

The main objective is to predict the function, when the trained model is tested on new input data to predict the output variables. The model accomplishes the task efficiently because the model can be trained in less time due to desired results are present in dataset. Random forest, linear regression, support vector machine are algorithms of supervised machine learning.

Unsupervised Machine Learning

In unsupervised learning, the input variables are given without corresponding output variables. In other words, the dataset used to train the model is neither labelled nor classified. Therefore, the information used to train is neither classified nor labelled in the dataset. It shows that how the system can deduce a mapping function to represent an unseen pattern from unlabelled data (Ayodele, 2010). It is mainly used to determine the patterns in the data. K-means algorithm, principal component analysis algorithm, singular-value decomposition algorithm are algorithms of unsupervised machine learning. The main objective is to model the unseen pattern or dispensation in the data to learn regarding the data.

Reinforcement Learning

Reinforcement learning (RL) is the most active research areas in the field of machine learning (i.e. it enables the agent to learn and interact with the environment to achieve reward), artificial intelligence, robotics and many more. It uses mapping between input and output, where feedback is given to an agent based on its own experiences and actions. It is different in terms of objectives as compared to unsupervised learning. RL is a computational method for automating and compassionating decision making and purposive behavior learning. The main purpose is to find an action that can enhance the total cumulative reward of an agent. Model-free (uses model and planning) and model-based (that uses explicitly trail-and-error learners) are two categories of RL algorithms (Song and Sun, 2019). It is applicable for the problems where the long-term objective is achieved with step-wise decision making process, such as robotics, game playing, logistics or resource management (Littman, 1996).

3. QUANTUM STATES AND SUPERPOSITION

Over the past few years, the field of quantum computing has got remarkable response among academic and research communities. A qubit is the quantum concept of a bit. A bit of data is represented by single atom that is in one of two quantum states denoted by $|0\rangle$ and $|1\rangle$. The quantum states grow as 2^N, where

N is the number of qubits. Consider a quantum state, $|\varphi\rangle = \alpha|0\rangle + \beta|1\rangle$, where α, β are complex amplitudes and $|0\rangle, |1\rangle$ stored in very long range vector in memory. It can be seen as linear combination of other distinct quantum states separated by amplitudes (Nielsen and Chuang, 2002). The absolute squares of the complex probability amplitudes should be equal to 1, i.e. measure the probability of qubit to be in 0 or 1 state. Thus, the evolution between the quantum states must satisfy the unitary property. The state $|\varphi\rangle$ is in superposition state makes a new valid quantum state.

Figure 2. Representation of unitary quantum gates

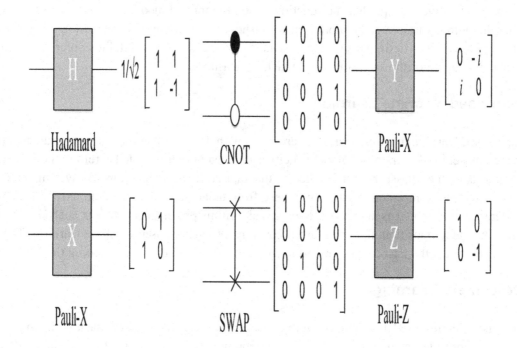

For the last few years, the major information technology companies are racing to build the quantum computer. It works like Single Instruction, multiple data (SIMD), where the single instruction can be executed multiple qubits simultaneously (Fu et al., 2019). It is based on the entanglement and superposition principle of quantum mechanics. The quantum state of the system cannot be described independently. The quantum computer is more powerful than classical one due to superimposed state and qubits are entangled with each other. Therefore, several number of NP-hard combinatorial problems can be solved on quantum computers (such as database search, travelling salesman problem and many more), which are untraceable on classical computers (Aaronson, 2008).

Quantum gates are described by unitary matrices. The quantum gates are performed on 2^N-dimensional vectors, where *n* is the number of qubits (De Wolf, 2019). The frequently used quantum gates and their matrices representations are shown in Figure 2. Hadamard gate (H) is performed on single qubit to make superimposed state with an equal probability. The controlled NOT gate (CNOT) is executed on two qubits, where first qubit is used a control qubit and other as target. The flip operation is performed over the target qubit if the control qubit is 1. The flip gate (X) is called as quantum NOT gate, i.e. used to change the phase of the qubit $|0\rangle$ to $|1\rangle$ and vice versa (Bhatia and Saggi, 2018). The Pauli (Y) and (Z) are equivalent to rotation around Y-axis and Z-axis by π–radians respectively. The swap gate is performed on two qubits to swap their states using CNOT gate.

QUANTUM MACHINE LEARNING

The problems of machine learning are solved by quantum machine learning algorithms using the effectiveness of quantum computing. The main objective is to determine how quantum computers can learn and predict the patterns in data efficiently than classical ones. It is expected that quantum computers can process the huge amount of global data quickly (Liu and Rebentrost, 2018) Thus, quantum computers can recognize the paradoxical patterns in data, which cannot be recognized by classical computers (Wittek, 2014, Schuld et al., 2014). Before describing the quantum machine learning algorithms, the basic question is that how quantum computers can represent the classical information. Commonly, the method is to represent the information as binary input strings, that can be transcribed into quantum states easily and get the output after the measurement.

Figure 3. The quantum circuit of HHL algorithm to compute linear systems of equations

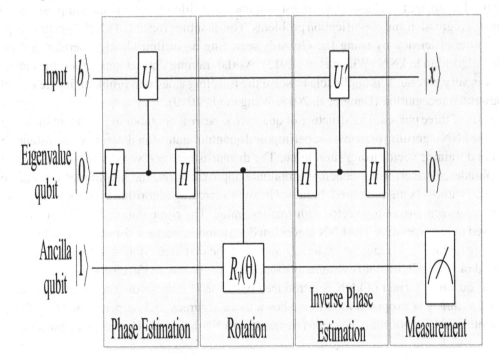

Harrow-Hassidim-Lloyd (HHL) quantum algorithm to compute linear equations is recognized as a heart of several quantum machine learning algorithms. It solves the linear systems of equations exponentially faster than the classical variants (Harrow et al., 2009). The problem is to find $\vec{x}$ in system $A\vec{x} = \vec{b}$, where the vector $\vec{b}$ and matrix A are given. It consists of four steps to determine the $\vec{x}$ vector, the phase estimation, controlled rotation and reverse phase estimation and measurement. The three set of qubits are required, memory to store the vector $\vec{b}$ at starting and vector $\vec{x}$ later, a register to store the eigenvalues of matrix A and an ancilla qubit.

The first step is to initialize the vector $\vec{b}$ to quantum state $|b\rangle$ and estimate the eigenvalues of A using an phase estimation algorithm. Second step is to perform controlled rotation according to approximated eigenvalues of A. Next, perform the reverse of first step. Finally, measure the ancilla qubit if the result is $|1\rangle$ and the corresponding quantum state $|b\rangle = |x\rangle$. Figure 3 shows the schematic quantum circuit of HHL algorithm to compute the linear systems of equations. HHL algorithm shown significant impact on quantum algorithms for solving high-order differential equation and quantum machine learning algorithms (Biamonte et al., 2017). It is considered as an important tool for computing optimization problems.

Quantum *k*-Nearest Neighbor Algorithm

In supervised learning, the classical *k*-nearest neighbor algorithm (kNN) is the simplest and essential algorithm for regression and classification problems. The quantum variant of kNN algorithm is proposed to enhance the efficiency by using the Grover's searching algorithm Oracle operator and the phase estimation algorithm in kNN (Wiebe et al., 2015). As the training dataset gets larger, the classification with kNN is very precise. It is applicable to solve the traveling salesman problem, image classification and handwritten recognition (Dang et al, 2018, Wang et al., 2019).

It consists of three phases. The structure of quantum k-nearest neighbor algorithm is shown in Figure 4. Firstly, the kNN algorithm prepares a superimposed quantum state after determine the distance between the input and training vector using subroutine. The distances between vectors are encoded in quantum state amplitudes. Further, using coherent amplitude approximation, the amplitudes are transferred to ancilla qubit, without being measured. Finally, Grover's searching algorithm is employed to observe the closest training vector to testing vector with smallest value. The computational power of Grover's algorithm is used to gain speedup. The kNN algorithm determines a vector x for each set called as centroid, computed by taking the average of vectors U and V. If the distance computed by subroutine is less to the centroid of vector U, then it is written as $|x–mean(U)| \leq |x–mean(V)|$, else V.

Another quantum variant of kNN is introduced based on Hamming distance metric by (Ruan et al., 2017). The accuracy of proposed algorithm shown more accuracy and outperformed the (Wiebe et al., 2015) quantum kNN algorithm. The steps of quantum kNN based on Hamming distance are given in Table 2.

Figure 4. The structure of quantum k-nearest neighbor algorithm

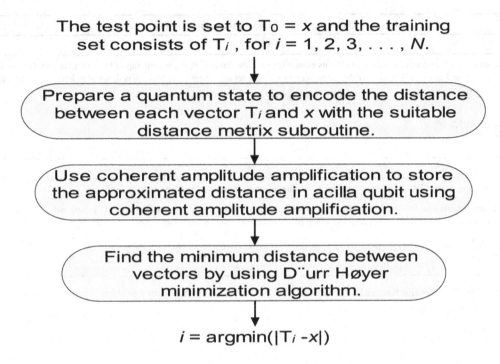

Quantum Principal Component Analysis

The classical principal component analysis (PCA) is a crucial method to reduce the dimension of data. The quantum variant of principal component analysis (QPCA) using phase estimation and Hamiltonian simulation is presented by (Lloyd et al., 2014). The proposed QPCA is exponentially superior than classical PCA. Consider the classical data consisting n-dimensional vector space v_s. A quantum random access memory (qRAM) is utilized to map the randomly chosen data vector v_s to quantum state such that $v_s \rightarrow |v_s$. It outlines the vector with $\log n$ qubits and qRAM needs $O(n)$ operations in parallel over $O(\log d)$ steps. It can efficiently produce the exponent of any random density matrix ρ (Ostaszewski et al., 2015). The density matrix of randomly selected quantum state from N-dimensional vectors is determined as

$$\rho = \frac{1}{N} \sum_{s}^{N} |v_s v_s|$$

It has been determined that the calculated density matrix for QPCA is covariance matrix on comparison with the covariance matrix C of classical PCA indeed. Using quantum phase estimation algorithm with density matrix exponentiation, it is easy to decompose the quantum variant of any classical data vector v_s into principal components $|pc_i$ and calculating the eigenvalues of covariance matrix C simultaneously as

$$|v_s = \sum_{i}^{N} v_i |pc_i| \tilde{e}_i$$

Table 2. Steps of quantum K-neighbors nearest algorithms based on Hamming distance

QkNN algorithm based on Hamming distance
Initialization:
Store the features as bit vectors of training set after its extraction from the dataset. Perform mapping of bit vectors to quantum ground state such as $1\rightarrow|1$ and as $0\rightarrow|0$. The class of N feature vectors training set $|v^q$, where $q=1, 2, ..., N$ is denoted as $|c^q\in\{1,2,...,x\}$ such that $\left|v_1^q,...v_n^q,c^q\in\mathbb{H}_2^{\otimes n}\otimes\mathbb{H}_x\right.$. Prepare a superposition training set $$\left|T_s=\frac{1}{\sqrt{N}}\sum_q^x\right|v_1^q,...v_n^q,c^q$$
Transformation:
Transform the input sample into a quantum state $|p$ i.e. a n-dimensional normalized feature vector $|p_1,p_2,...,p_n$.
Construct a quantum state as follows: n-dimensional normalized feature vector $|p_1,p_2,...,p_n$. in first register, superposition training set $|T_s$ in second register and ancilla qubit in last register, which is initialized to zero. The resultant state is $$\left|\psi_0=\frac{1}{\sqrt{N}}\sum_q^x\right|p_1,p_2,...,p_n;v_1^q,...v_n^q,c^q;0$$
Perform the subtraction operation between $|p_1,p_2,...,p_n$. and $\left|v_1^q,...v_n^q\right.$ and store it in first register as $\left|k_1^q,...k_n^q\right.$ as reverse. The resultant state after performing operation is as $$\left|\psi_1=\frac{1}{\sqrt{N}}\sum_q^x\right|k_1^q,...k_n^q;v_1^q,...v_n^q,c^q;0$$
The Hamming distance is computed in $\left|k_1^q,...k_n^q\right.$ and change the ancilla qubit as $|0\rightarrow|1$. n based on threshold value t of distance. It can be performed by applying unitary operator (U) as $$\left|\psi_2=U\right|\psi_1=\frac{1}{\sqrt{N}}\left(\sum_{q\in\gamma}^x\left|k_1^q,...k_n^q;v_1^q,...v_n^q,c^q;1+\sum_{q\notin\gamma}^x\right|k_1^q,...k_n^q;v_1^q,...v_n^q,c^q;1\right)$$ where γ consists index values q to show the Hamming distance.
Measurement:
Perform a projection operator $\mathcal{P}=1\otimes\|11\|$ on $|\psi_2$. The resultant state after renormalization is as: $$\left|\psi_3=\mathcal{P}\right|\psi_2=\alpha\sum_{q\in\gamma}^x\left|k_1^q,...k_n^q;v_1^q,...v_n^q,c^q;1\right.$$ where α denotes the renormalized amplitude such that $\Sigma|\alpha|2=^1$. The quantum state $|\psi_3$ consists a vector $|vq$ whose Hamming distance is less than to the testing set $|p$.
Perform measurement on c^q alone and we get the class to which $|p$ belongs.

The main purpose is to produce a quantum state which can obtain information of the eigenvalues and eigenvectors of the state. The query and computational complexity of quantum variant of PCA is $O[(\log N)]^2$. The properties of principal components of classical covariance matrix C can be investigated by carrying out measurement on its quantum eigenvectors. QPCA is most effective algorithm when state consists large eigenvalues and it can be shown well by its $|pc_i$. The QPCA algorithm has some limitations that should be considered before applying in scenario of machine learning. Some of eigenvalues require to be large enough to increase speedup of QPCA. Otherwise, it shows no improvement as compared to classical PCA if the eigenvalues are equal. The scaling of QPCA with error ε and need of QRAM should be considered. It needs a considerable number of quantum gates and qubits (LaRose et al., 2019). Thus, it is hard to execute in near term, in spite of promise for future. The description of QPCA is shown in Table 3.

Quantum Support Vector Machine

The classical support vector machine is popular and simplest algorithm in supervised machine learning. It is used for binary classification problems. It seeks to find a hyperplane separating two classes of data, in which training set of class lies on one side of hyperplane with high probability. The classical SVM is also called as maximum margin classifiers because it helps to locate the maximum margin between the closed data points and the hyperplane. The generalization of SVM to nonlinear hyperplanes has found significant interest among research communities due to its success in biological science and image segmentation by using kernel functions. The first quantum variant of classical SVM is proposed using Grover's searching algorithm to minimize functions. It solves the non-convex optimization problem.

Another variant of QSVM is based on the least-squares approximation of classical SVM (Anguita et al., 2003). QSVM shows an exponential speedup over classical SVM, i.e., $O(\log(NM))$ where M and N are number of features and training data points, respectively (Rebentrost et al., 2014). Figure 5 shows the support vector machine for separating two dimensional classes.

Table 3. Steps of quantum principle component analysis algorithm

QPCA Algorithm
Encoding:
Encode the classical date into quantum states after normalization. Consider a N-dimensional vectors v^j, where $j=1, 2, ...Z$. The mean ($\bar{v}$) is subtracted as $v^j = v^j - \bar{v}, \frac{1}{Z}\sum_{j=1}^{Z} v^j$ Normalize the vectors as $v^j = \frac{v^j}{|v^j|}, |v^j| = \sqrt{\sum_{j=1}^{N} v^{j2}}$ Encode the classical data to quantum state as $v = |v = \sum_{j=1}^{N} v^j |j$
Determine the density matrix:
The density matrix of randomly selected quantum state from N-dimensional vectors is determined as $\rho = \frac{1}{Z}\sum_{j}^{Z} |v^j v^j|$
Apply quantum phase estimation. The unitary operator ($U = e^{-i\rho t}$) is performed on density matrix ρ, instead of eigenvector $\tilde{e}_i$. The resultant state is as $\sum_{k=1}^{M} \tilde{e}_i |\tilde{e}_i \tilde{e}_i| \otimes |v^j v^j|$
Finally, the sampling is performed to attain eigenvectors features.

Figure 5. Linearly separating two-dimensional classes with hyperplane

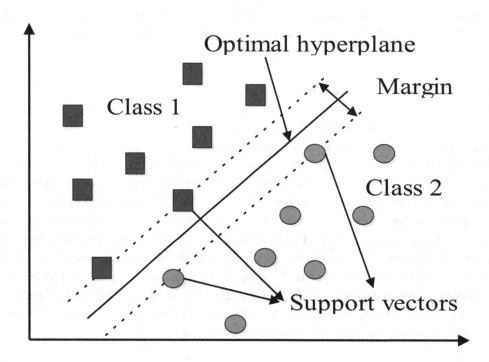

In classical SVM, the hyperplane is equivalent to $\vec{w}.\vec{x} + b = 0$ where b is offset constant and $\vec{w}$ defines the normal vector. The minimization of normal vector leads to maximization of margin between two classes, $\underset{\vec{w},b}{max}\dfrac{2}{|\vec{w}|}$ such that $\vec{y_i}\left(\vec{w}.\vec{x_i} + b\right) \geq 1$ where $\vec{x_i}$ is the ith training positive class. After estimating the parameters $\vec{w}$ and b, the new vector $\vec{x_0}$ is calculated as

$$y\left(\vec{x_0}\right) = sgn\left(\vec{w}.\vec{x_0} + b\right).$$

In QSVM, the normal vector $\vec{w}$ is represented as $\vec{w} = \sum\limits_{i=1}^{N}\alpha_i\vec{x_i}$ where αI signifies the weight. The steps of QSVM algorithm is described in Table 4.

The kernel is compressed exponentially, but the model trained is not sparse to perform classification. The performance will be poor, if the learned model overfits the data massively. In future, it is good to see how QSVM performs on real-world data sets.

Quantum Boltzmann Machine

Boltzmann machine is a kind of recurrent neural network, in which neurons like units make stochastic decisions whether true or false. The main idea of Boltzmann machine is to learn the behavior of visible neurons and discover interesting properties. It is used to optimize the solution of a problem. Inspired by the efficiency of classical Boltzmann machine, the quantum variant is proposed by Amin et al., 2018. Figure 6 shows the instance of quantum Boltzmann machine with visible layer (green) and hidden layer (red).

The training phase of model in quantum Boltzmann machine (QBM) is non-trivial because of non-commutative behavior of quantum mechanics. QBM produces an output quantum state unlike the classical Boltzmann machine. Therefore, the quantum states representing significant number of systems can be produced by deep quantum networks, which is not present in classical one. Hence, QBM provides rich models for classical data beyond classifying quantum states (Kulchytskyy et al., 2016). Instead of energy function in classical Boltzmann machine, the Hamiltonian is considered as

$$H = -\sum_a b_a \sigma_a^z - \sum_{a,b} w_{ab} \sigma_a^z \sigma_b^z .$$

Table 4. Summary of quantum support vector machine algorithm

QSVM Algorithm
Encoding: Perform the training-data oracle to encode the classical dataset as $\left\|\vec{x_i}\right. = \dfrac{1}{\left\|\vec{x_i}\right\|} \sum_{i=1}^{M} \left(\vec{x_i}\right)_j \left\|j\right.$ Prepare the quantum state with an initial state $\dfrac{1}{\sqrt{M}} \sum_{i=1}^{M} \left\|i\right.$ as $\left\|z\right. = \dfrac{1}{\sqrt{N}} \sum_{i=1}^{M} \left\|\vec{x_i}\right\| \left\|i\right. \left\|\vec{x_i}\right.$
Determine hyperplane parameters:
Perform matrix inversion of $F\begin{pmatrix} b \\ \vec{\alpha} \end{pmatrix} = \begin{pmatrix} 0 & 1 \\ I & K + \gamma^{-1} IN \end{pmatrix}\begin{pmatrix} b \\ \vec{\alpha} \end{pmatrix} = \begin{pmatrix} 0 \\ \vec{y} \end{pmatrix}$ $\left(b, \vec{a}^T\right)^T = F^{-1}\left(0, \vec{y}^T\right)^T$ The quantum register is declared as $\left\|0, y\right. = \dfrac{1}{\sqrt{N_{0,y}}}\left(\left\|0\right. + \sum_{j=1}^{M} y_j \left\|j\right.\right)$ The resultant quantum state becomes $\left\|b, a\right. = \dfrac{1}{\sqrt{N_{b,a}}}\left(b\left\|0\right. + \sum_{j=1}^{M} a_j \left\|j\right.\right)$
Measurement:
After optimizing the hyperplane parameters, the classification result is measured as $y\left(\vec{x_0}\right) = \mathrm{sgn}\left(\sum_{j=1}^{M} a_j \left(\vec{x_j}.\vec{x_0}\right) + b\right)$

Figure 6. Representation of quantum Boltzmann machine

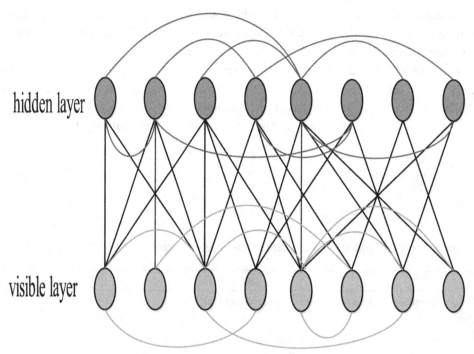

It is constricted with its diagonal elements as energy values. The eigenstates are represented as $|v,h$ where v denotes visible and h hidden variables. The density matrix is determined as $\rho = \dfrac{e^{-H}}{Z}$ where e^{-H} is a diagonal matrix of Hamiltonian and Z is a partition function calculated as $Z=\mathrm{Tr}[e^{-H}]$. The marginal Boltzmann probability of a quantum state $|v$ for visible variables is $P_v = Tr[\Lambda,\rho]$ where Λv restricts the trace to diagonal elements only (Wiebe et al., 2015). When the visible variables are in $|v$ then diagonal elements of Λv are 1, else zero, such that

$$\Lambda_{v=} |v\,v| \otimes I_h$$

where I_h denotes the identity matrix performed on hidden variables. On training QBM, the probability distributions P_d is close to P_v where P_d is used for an input data. It can be attained by minimize the log-likelihood as

$$L = -\sum_v P_d \log \frac{Tr\left[\Lambda_v e^{-H}\right]}{Tr\left[e^{-H}\right]}.$$

Quantum Neural Network

A neural network is the most promising and popular machine learning algorithm that models itself after the human brain. The main idea is to simulate several interconnected cells of brain to classify, recognize the complex patterns and make appropriate decisions (Beale et al., 1996). It learns by itself i.e. explicitly. The several analogies have been established to show the connection between classical neural networks and quantum mechanics. Table 5 shows the connection between classical neural network and its quantum variant. The concept of quantum neural network (QNN) combines the properties of quantum computing and neural computing (Schuld et al., 2014 and Altaisky et al., 2001). It has got significant response in the last decades. It is proposed by combining neural network and quantum computation, which is more powerful than the classical one.

Table 5. The analogies used between classical neural network and quantum version.

Neural network	Quantum neural network
Superposition principle	Interconnections
Entanglement	Learning rule
Wave function	Neuron
Unitary evolution	Gain function
Measurement	Network attractors

Several types of quantum version of neural networks have been proposed till date namely quantum associate neural network, quantum inspired neural network, qubit neural network, quantum M-P neural network, quantum dot neural network, quantum competitive neural network and quantum cellular neural network. The applications of quantum neural network are across several domains such as pattern recognition, image compression, classification, breast cancer prediction, fault diagnosis, time series prediction, forecasting series, curve fitting, handwritten numerals recognition and many more. Figure 7 shows the three layer quantum neural network.

Since the Kak introduced the concept of quantum neural computation, researchers proposed quantum neural network models based on different dynamics (Kak, 1995). The concept of quantum associative memory proposed by Ventura and Martinez in 2000. Later, it was associated with distributed queries by Ezhov and Ventura, 2000) Subsequently, the quantum associative memory models have been proposed (Loo et al., 2004, Rigatos and Tzafestasin, 2006). The fuzzy neural network associated with non-linear quantum learning and classical neural network with quantum learning and architecture is proposed (Panella and Martinelli, 2008). Afterwards, quantum competitive neural network model is presented based on quantum characteristics by Zhou, 2010. Most of the models skipped the problem of training quantum neural networks. The training method of quantum neural network shown by Ricks and Ventura in 2004.

Figure 7. Representation of three-layer quantum neural network

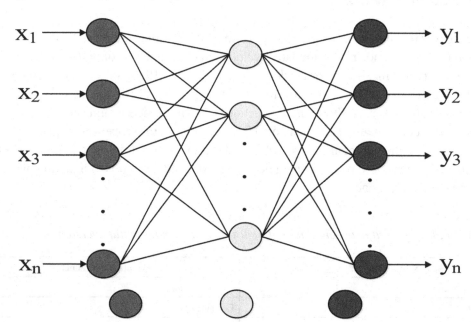

Input layer Hidden layer Output layer

Figure 8. Quantum neural network to determine XOR function

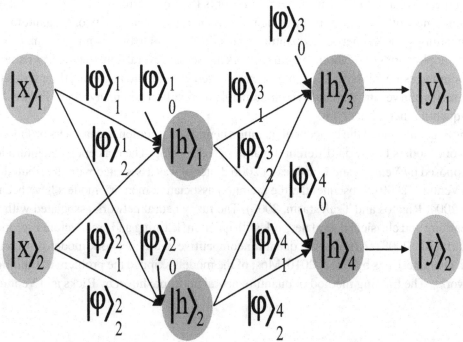

A QNN works much like classical neural network. It consists various perceptron layers: an input, hidden and the output layer. Every layer is completely connected to the preceding layer and hidden layer calculates a weighted sum of an output from the input layer. The whole network determines a function by looking for the high output bit. It allows the model to learn the input data, which have binary outputs or one high output exactly (Ricks and Ventura, 2004). Figure 8 represents the QNN to determine the to compute the XOR function, where $|x_i$ denotes input node, $|h_i$ represent the internal calculations and hidden units determine the weighted sum of inputs $|\varphi_{i1}$ .and $|\varphi_{i2}$ and compare it with the threshold. The output layer compares the calculated weighted sum with a threshold. The target values are kept in registers $|y_1$ and $|y_2$.

The quantum associative neural network has got overwhelming response, introduced by Ventura and Martinez, 2000. The working of quantum associative neural network for pattern recognition is divided into two components, storing and recall of patterns from memory (Zhou et al, 2012).

Storing Patterns

The concept of a quantum binary decision tree is used for storing the patterns. It is based on the quantum superposition principle of states. Figure 9 shows the binary decision tree, where *a, b, c, d, e, f, g, h, I, j, k, l* are used for quantum gates, $|\phi^a \rangle ... |\phi^l \rangle$ are quantum states, $z_a, z_b, z_c, ..., z_l$ are used for nodes and z_a denotes the root node.

Figure 9. Quantum binary decision tree

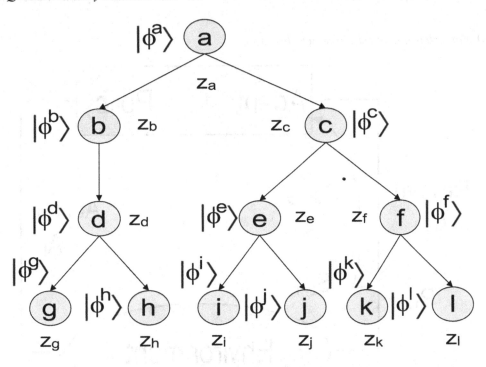

Recall Patterns

The procedure of recalling the patterns is similar to classical variant. The quantum associative neural network is an efficient algorithm in pattern storing. It avoids the extra quantum states and operators. The time complexity of algorithm is $O\left(log_2^{2^{n-t}}\right) = (n-t)$, i.e. linear, where n denotes the number of quantum bit (Singh et al, 2012). The probability of recalling the patterns can be increased by revising the non-linear searching algorithm in this algorithm.

Quantum Reinforcement Learning

The area of reinforcement learning (RL) is the most active research field for academic and research communities. It is sub field of machine learning, where agent learns to interact with an environment. It has been extensively studied in control theory, operations research, game theory, multi-agent systems and swarm intelligence. Figure 10 shows the four elements of RL.

The four elements of RL are policy, reward, value and model. The policy is main component of RL to define the mapping between states and actions to be occur. The function of reward is to map the states of an environment to a number. It is unchanged by an agent and given by the environment directly. The main aim of estimating the values to obtain more reward. Model is the optional element to mimic the functioning of an external condition. QRL algorithm is described in Table 6. A novel quantum reinforcement learning (QRL) algorithm is an introduced by Dong et al. in 2008. It is a combination of classical reinforcement learning and quantum computing. Just like the classical reinforcement learning, it consists four components as representation, policy, quantum parallelism and probability amplitude updating.

Figure 10. Four elements of reinforcement learning

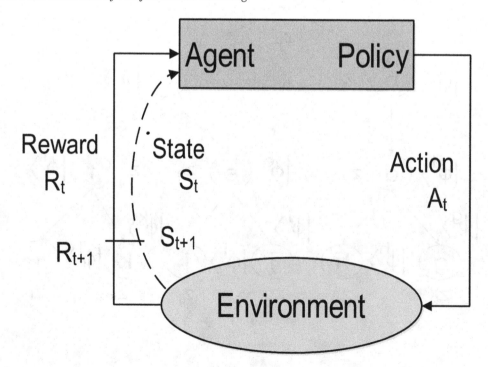

Table 6. Quantum reinforcement learning algorithm

Quantum reinforcement learning algorithm
Initialization:
Initialize the eigen state and eigen action $\left|q_s^n = \sum\limits_{s=00\ldots0}^{n=11\ldots1} \alpha_s \right|s, f(s) = \left|q_a^m = \sum\limits_{a=00\ldots0}^{m=11\ldots1} \beta_a \right|a$
Repeat for all states ιs in $\left|q_s^n = \sum\limits_{s=00\ldots0}^{n=11\ldots1} \alpha_s \right|s$
• Examine $f(s) = \left|q_a^m\right.$ and obtain ιa
• Perform the action ιa to examine the next state $\left|s'\right.$ and reward r,
– Update the value of state as $V(s) \leftarrow V(s) + \mu\left(r + \gamma V(s') - V(s)\right)$ – Update the probability amplitudes, Repeat unitary Grover operation U_G for L times $U_G\left|q_a^m = U_{a_0 m} U_a \right|q_a^m$
Until for all states satisfy $\|\Delta V(s)\| \leq \epsilon$

Representation

The state (action) of classical reinforcement learning are represented by eigen state (eigen action) in quantum RL. It can be represented as linear combination of states (action) ιφn as

$$\left|\phi = \sum_n \alpha_n \right|\phi_n.$$

The quantum state for state ιq_s (or action ιq_a are represented as an orthogonal set of eigen states ιS_i (or eigen actions ιa_i, respectively.

$$\left|q_s = \sum_n \alpha_n \right|s_n, \left|q_a = \sum_n \beta_n \right|s_n.$$

Suppose, Z_s and Z_a are number of states and actions, n and m are used to represent the eigen state and eigen action, respectively.

$$\left|q_s^n = \sum_{s=00\ldots0}^{n=11\ldots1} \alpha_s \right|s, \left|q_a^m = \sum_{a=00\ldots0}^{m=11\ldots1} \beta_a \right|a.$$

The states (or actions) are represented as superposition of eigen states (or eigen actions) in QRL, where $\alpha s_, \beta a_a$ re the complex amplitudes.

Policy

In QRL algorithm, the policy of action selection is based on mapping from states to actions. The agent is to learn a policy π: S→A. It will enhance the sum of reward of each state.

$$f(s) = \left| q_a^m = \sum_{a=00\ldots0}^{m=11\ldots1} {}^2{}_a \right| a .$$

In QRL, the probability amplification of the action is performed based on corresponding rewards.

Quantum Parallelism

A unitary evolution U is performed on qubits according to quantum parallelism. Consider an operation that process 2^n states with the temporal difference (TD) rule as

$$V(s) \leftarrow V(s) + \mu\left(r + \gamma V(s') - V(s)\right).$$

where r is reward and μ defines the learning rate. It gives an exponential speedup in n-qubit linear physical space (Chen et al., 2006)

Updating probability Amplitude

$$H^{\Delta m}\left|00\ldots0 = \frac{1}{\sqrt{2^m}} \sum_{a=00\ldots0}^{m=11\ldots1} \left| a \right. .$$

In QRL, the action selection is implemented by observing action $\left| q_a^m \right.$ corresponding to some state $|s$ and it will collapse to probability of occurrence $|\beta_a|^2$. Thus, the action is in superposition state of eigen actions, determining $|s$ is usually interacting with updating the probability amplitude (Dong et al., 2008). The changing of probability amplitude is according to Grover's iteration. The updating of probability amplitude is based on the Grover iteration. It is performed by applying Hadamard gates to m qubits independently.

Quantum Clustering Algorithm

Finding the clusters with common features present in the data is an unsupervised learning task. The main objective of clustering algorithm is make group of data points in same cluster sharing similar features while dissimilar in other clusters. The important applications of clustering are genomic data, determine sociological groups, clustering stars, grouping of molecules and gathering news. The quantum clustering algorithms are proposed by Aimeur in 2008. The quantum subroutines based on Grover's searching algorithm are used to speedup quantum clustering algorithm (Yao et al., 2008). The quantum clustering algorithm is introduced to enhance the accuracy using the quantum mechanics principles and quantization of classical clustering algorithm. The quantum variant uses time independent Schrodinger equation. The state of quantum system is represented as function $\varphi(x)$. where m is the number of particles, x indicates the coordinates of particle and σ is a scale parameter.

$$\varphi(x) = \sum_{i=1}^{m} e^{\frac{-(x-x_i)^2}{2\sigma^2}} .$$

Table 7. The steps of quantum k-median clustering algorithm

Quantum k-median clustering algorithm: k-median(P, k)
Initialization: Select *k*-points randomly at the initial centres of each cluster.
Repeat
for each datapoint in *P* do
link it to its closest centre
End for
for each cluster *C* do
Determine the median of each cluster and set its new centre
End for
Until (quasi-)stabilization of *C*
Return the centres of found clusters

Quantum k-Medians Clustering Algorithm

Initially, each datapoint is set to its closet centre of cluster. In second step, update the centre of each cluster by selecting the point that is its median among all the points. The process continues until the clusters centre have stabilized (Aïmeur et al., 2013). Table 7 shows the steps of quantum *k*-median clustering algorithm. In *k*-median (*P*, *k*) algorithm, the *k*-points are randomly selected as starting centres. It is used for the number of clusters. It is noted that the median of a cluster can be determined in $\Theta\left(\frac{n}{k}\sqrt{\frac{n}{k}}\right)$ using quantum subroutine based on Grover's algorithm. It produces $\Theta\left(\frac{1}{\sqrt{k}} n^{3/2}\right)$ tunning time of single iteration, which is faster than classical version $\sqrt{n/k}$ times. The quantum subroutine is used to determine the median of a set $P_n = \{p_1, p_2, \ldots, p_n\}$ of n points in $\Theta\left(\sqrt{n}\right)$ shown by Nayak and Wu, 1999.

Other Algorithms

The quantum algorithm for linear regression using the least-squares method is presented by Wang in 2017. It encodes the optimal parameters to form quantum state and produces output state in classical form. Thus, it examines the fitted model to make predictions about dataset. The proposed algorithm runs in a polynomial time $\log_2 n$, $1/\epsilon$, d, k, where ϵ is the expected precision in an output, k denotes the condition number of design matrix, d is the adjustable parameters and n denotes the size of dataset. The quantum linear regression algorithm can approximate the norm of projection after applying the pseudo inverse of dense rectangular matrix to vector.

A low-depth variational quantum circuit for classification is proposed by Schuld et al., 2018. The input feature vectors are encoded into probability amplitudes and quantum circuit with a qubit measurement is used to classify the input state. In circuit centric quantum classifier, a unitary circuit is a main building block of a model with few parameters for training and uses entanglement property to represent the correlations in data. The proposed circuit centric model guarantees the parameters learnt are poly-logarithmic to size of an input dataset. The concept of quantum ensembles of quantum classifiers has been proposed by Schuld et al., 2018. It has demonstrated the exponentially large ensemble, that is weighted based on its accuracy of the input dataset. The quantum circuit architecture is constructed for quantum ensemble of quantum classifier. The decision is made in parallel and the measurement is performed from a single qubit.

The quantum circuit with hierarchical structures such as tree tensor network (TTN) and multi-scale entanglement renormalization ansatz (MERA) for binary classification have been proposed by Grant et al., 2018. It has been investigated that the proposed quantum circuit architectures attain better accuracy and shown great ability to classify the entangled quantum states. The matrix product state to classify the classical data encoded in quantum states has been proposed by Bhatia et al., 2019. It has shown great learning ability to classify Iris dataset and evapotranspiration (ETo) for the Patiala meteorological station.

Quantum-inspired machine learning algorithms provide new ways to train the model and evaluate for quantum information processing community. The quantum machine learning algorithms based on quantum generative models have been introduced and shows strong ability to represent the probability distributions by Gao et al., 2018. A special purpose quantum simulators and quantum computers shown encouraging applications is machine learning and data analytics. (Brunner et al, 2013, Cai et al., 2015, Neven et al., 2009, O'Gorman et al, 2015, Grant et al., 2018, Bhatia et al, 2019, Dridi et al, 2015, Schuld et al., 2018).

CONCLUSION

In this chapter, the recent breakthroughs and progress in the emerging area of quantum machine learning have been described. The quantum machine learning explores the intersection between classical machine learning techniques and quantum computing principles. The quantum machine learning algorithms are mostly based on Grover's searching algorithm or quantum phase estimation and represent the classical data exponentially with probabilistic quantum systems. The scientific and academic communities have shown strong interest in the area of machine learning and quantum computing. This emerging field is still finding the complete recognition and its right position. It will grow and crystallize as the quantum machine learning algorithms get implement, practical and quantum technologies become mature.

REFERENCES

Aaronson, S. (2008). The limits of quantum. *Scientific American, 298*(3), 62–69.

Aïmeur, E., Brassard, G., & Gambs, S. (2007, June). Quantum clustering algorithms. In *Proceedings of the 24th international conference on machine learning* (pp. 1-8). Academic Press.

Aïmeur, E., Brassard, G., & Gambs, S. (2013). Quantum speed-up for unsupervised learning. *Machine Learning, 90*(2), 261–287.

Alpaydin, E. (2020). *Introduction to machine learning*. MIT Press.

Altaisky, M. V. (2001). *Quantum neural network*. arXiv preprint quant-ph/0107012.

Amin, M. H., Andriyash, E., Rolfe, J., Kulchytskyy, B., & Melko, R. (2018). Quantum boltzmann machine. *Physical Review X, 8*(2), 021050. doi:10.1103/PhysRevX.8.021050

Anguita, D., Ridella, S., Rivieccio, F., & Zunino, R. (2003). Quantum optimization for training support vector machines. *Neural Networks, 16*(5-6), 763–770. doi:10.1016/S0893-6080(03)00087-X PMID:12850032

Ayodele, T. O. (2010). Types of machine learning algorithms. *New Advances in Machine Learning*, 19-48.

Ayodele, T. O. (2010). Types of machine learning algorithms. *New advances in machine learning*, 19-48.

Beale, H. D., Demuth, H. B., & Hagan, M. T. (1996). Neural network design. Pws.

Behrman, E. C., Nash, L. R., Steck, J. E., Chandrashekar, V. G., & Skinner, S. R. (2000). Simulations of quantum neural networks. *Information Sciences, 128*(3-4), 257–269.

Bhatia, A. S., & Saggi, M. K. (2018). *Implementing Entangled States on a Quantum Computer*. arXiv preprint:1811.09833.

Bhatia, A. S., Saggi, M. K., Kumar, A., & Jain, S. (2019). Matrix Product State–Based Quantum Classifier. *Neural Computation, 31*(7), 1499–1517.

Biamonte, J., Wittek, P., Pancotti, N., Rebentrost, P., Wiebe, N., & Lloyd, S. (2017). Quantum machine learning. *Nature, 549*(7671), 195–202. doi:10.1038/nature23474 PMID:28905917

Brunner, D., Soriano, M. C., Mirasso, C. R., & Fischer, I. (2013). Parallel photonic information processing at gigabyte per second data rates using transient states. *Nature Communications, 4*(1), 1–7.

Cai, X. D., Wu, D., Su, Z. E., Chen, M. C., Wang, X. L., Li, L., ... Pan, J. W. (2015). Entanglement-based machine learning on a quantum computer. *Physical Review Letters, 114*(11), 110504.

Chen, C. L., Dong, D. Y., & Chen, Z. H. (2006). Quantum computation for action selection using reinforcement learning. *International Journal of Quantum Information, 4*(06), 1071–1083.

Ciliberto, C., Herbster, M., Ialongo, A. D., Pontil, M., Rocchetto, A., Severini, S., & Wossnig, L. (2018). Quantum machine learning: A classical perspective. *Proceedings - Royal Society. Mathematical, Physical and Engineering Sciences, 474*(2209), 20170551. doi:10.1098/rspa.2017.0551 PMID:29434508

Dang, Y., Jiang, N., Hu, H., Ji, Z., & Zhang, W. (2018). Image classification based on quantum K-Nearest-Neighbor algorithm. *Quantum Information Processing*, *17*(9), 239.

De Wolf, R. (2019). *Quantum computing: Lecture notes.* arXiv preprint arXiv:1907.09415.

Dong, D., Chen, C., Li, H., & Tarn, T. J. (2008). Quantum reinforcement learning. *IEEE Transactions on Systems, Man, and Cybernetics. Part B, Cybernetics*, *38*(5), 1207–1220. doi:10.1109/TSMCB.2008.925743 PMID:18784007

Dong, D., Chen, C., Tarn, T. J., Pechen, A., & Rabitz, H. (2008). Incoherent control of quantum systems with wavefunction-controllable subspaces via quantum reinforcement learning. *IEEE Transactions on Systems, Man, and Cybernetics. Part B, Cybernetics*, *38*(4), 957–962.

Dridi, R., & Alghassi, H. (2015). *Homology computation of large point clouds using quantum annealing.* arXiv preprint:1512.09328.

Dunjko, V., Taylor, J. M., & Briegel, H. J. (2016). Quantum-enhanced machine learning. *Physical Review Letters*, *117*(13), 130501. doi:10.1103/PhysRevLett.117.130501 PMID:27715099

Ezhov, A. A., & Ventura, D. (2000). Quantum neural networks. In *Future directions for intelligent systems and information sciences* (pp. 213–235). Physica.

Fu, X., Riesebos, L., Rol, M. A., van Straten, J., van Someren, J., Khammassi, N., ... de Sterke, J. C. (2019). eQASM: An executable quantum instruction set architecture. In *2019 IEEE International Symposium on High Performance Computer Architecture (HPCA)* (pp. 224-237). IEEE.

Gao, X., Zhang, Z. Y., & Duan, L. M. (2018). A quantum machine learning algorithm based on generative models. *Science Advances*, *4*(12), eaat9004.

Grant, E., Benedetti, M., Cao, S., Hallam, A., Lockhart, J., Stojevic, V., ... & Severini, S. (2018). Hierarchical quantum classifiers. *NPJ Quantum Information, 4*(1), 1-8.

Gruska, J. (1999). *Quantum computing* (Vol. 2005). McGraw-Hill.

Harrow, A. W., Hassidim, A., & Lloyd, S. (2009). Quantum algorithm for linear systems of equations. *Physical Review Letters*, *103*(15), 150502. doi:10.1103/PhysRevLett.103.150502 PMID:19905613

Jordan, M. I., & Mitchell, T. M. (2015). Machine learning: Trends, perspectives, and prospects. *Science*, *349*(6245), 255–260. doi:10.1126cience.aaa8415 PMID:26185243

Kak, S. C. (1995). Quantum neural computing. *Advances in Imaging and Electron Physics*, *94*, 259–313.

Kotsiantis, S. B., Zaharakis, I., & Pintelas, P. (2007). Supervised machine learning: A review of classification techniques. *Emerging Artificial Intelligence Applications in Computer Engineering, 160*, 3-24.

Kulchytskyy, B., Andriyash, E., Amin, M., & Melko, R. (2016). Quantum boltzmann machine. In *APS Meeting Abstracts*. Academic Press.

Ladd, T. D., Jelezko, F., Laflamme, R., Nakamura, Y., Monroe, C., & O'Brien, J. L. (2010). Quantum computers. *Nature*, *464*(7285), 45–53. doi:10.1038/nature08812 PMID:20203602

LaRose, R., Tikku, A., O'Neel-Judy, É., Cincio, L., & Coles, P. J. (2019). Variational quantum state diagonalization. *NPJ Quantum Information, 5*(1), 1-10.

Littman, M. L., & Szepesvári, C. (1996). A generalized reinforcement-learning model: Convergence and applications. In ICML (Vol. 96, pp. 310-318). Academic Press.

Liu, N., & Rebentrost, P. (2018). Quantum machine learning for quantum anomaly detection. Physical Review A, 97(4).

Lloyd, S., Mohseni, M., & Rebentrost, P. (2014). Quantum principal component analysis. *Nature Physics, 10*(9), 631–633. doi:10.1038/nphys3029

Loo, C. K., Peruš, M., & Bischof, H. (2004). Associative memory based image and object recognition by quantum holography. *Open Systems & Information Dynamics, 11*(03), 277–289.

Marsland, S. (2015). *Machine learning: an algorithmic perspective*. CRC Press.

Narayanan, A., & Menneer, T. (2000). Quantum artificial neural network architectures and components. *Information Sciences, 128*(3-4), 231–255. doi:10.1016/S0020-0255(00)00055-4

Nayak, A., & Wu, F. (1999, May). The quantum query complexity of approximating the median and related statistics. In *Proceedings of the thirty-first annual ACM symposium on Theory of computing* (pp. 384-393). ACM.

Neven, H., Denchev, V. S., Drew-Brook, M., Zhang, J., Macready, W. G., & Rose, G. (2009). Binary classification using hardware implementation of quantum annealing Demonstrations at NIPS-09. In *24th Annual Conf. on Neural Information Processing Systems* (pp. 1-17). Academic Press.

Nielsen, M. A., & Chuang, I. (2002). *Quantum computation and quantum information*. Academic Press.

O'Gorman, B., Babbush, R., Perdomo-Ortiz, A., Aspuru-Guzik, A., & Smelyanskiy, V. (2015). Bayesian network structure learning using quantum annealing. *The European Physical Journal. Special Topics, 224*(1), 163–188.

Ostaszewski, M., Sadowski, P., & Gawron, P. (2015). *Quantum image classification using principal component analysis*. arXiv preprint arXiv:1504.00580.

Panella, M., & Martinelli, G. (2008). Neurofuzzy networks with nonlinear quantum learning. *IEEE Transactions on Fuzzy Systems, 17*(3), 698–710.

Rebentrost, P., Mohseni, M., & Lloyd, S. (2014). Quantum support vector machine for big data classification. *Physical Review Letters, 113*(13), 130503. doi:10.1103/PhysRevLett.113.130503 PMID:25302877

Ricks, B., & Ventura, D. (2004). Training a quantum neural network. In Advances in neural information processing systems (pp. 1019-1026). Academic Press.

Rigatos, G. G., & Tzafestas, S. G. (2006). Quantum learning for neural associative memories. *Fuzzy Sets and Systems, 157*(13), 1797–1813.

Ruan, Y., Xue, X., Liu, H., Tan, J., & Li, X. (2017). Quantum algorithm for k-nearest neighbors classification based on the metric of hamming distance. *International Journal of Theoretical Physics*, *56*(11), 3496–3507.

Schuld, M., Bocharov, A., Svore, K. M., & Wiebe, N. (2020). Circuit-centric quantum classifiers. *Physical Review. A*, *101*(3), 032308.

Schuld, M., & Petruccione, F. (2018). Quantum ensembles of quantum classifiers. *Scientific Reports*, *8*(1), 1–12.

Schuld, M., Sinayskiy, I., & Petruccione, F. (2014). The quest for a quantum neural network. *Quantum Information Processing*, *13*(11), 2567–2586.

Schuld, M., Sinayskiy, I., & Petruccione, F. (2015). An introduction to quantum machine learning. *Contemporary Physics*, *56*(2), 172–185. doi:10.1080/00107514.2014.964942

Singh, M. P., & Rajput, B. S. (2016). Applications of Singh-Rajput MES in recall operations of quantum associative memory for a two-qubit system. *International Journal of Theoretical Physics*, *55*(3), 1753–1770.

Song, Z., & Sun, W. (2019). *Efficient model-free reinforcement learning in metric spaces*. arXiv preprint: 1905.00475.

Ventura, D., & Martinez, T. (2000). Quantum associative memory. *Information Sciences*, *124*(1-4), 273–296.

Wang, G. (2017). Quantum algorithm for linear regression. *Physical Review. A*, *96*(1), 012335.

Wang, Y., Wang, R., Li, D., Adu-Gyamfi, D., Tian, K., & Zhu, Y. (2019). Improved Handwritten Digit Recognition using Quantum K-Nearest Neighbor Algorithm. *International Journal of Theoretical Physics*, *58*(7), 2331–2340.

Wiebe, N., Kapoor, A., Granade, C., & Svore, K. M. (2015). *Quantum inspired training for Boltzmann machines*. arXiv preprint arXiv:1507.02642.

Wiebe, N., Kapoor, A., & Svore, K. M. (2015). Quantum algorithms for nearest-neighbor methods for supervised and unsupervised learning. *Quantum Information & Computation*, *15*(3-4), 316–356.

Wittek, P. (2014). *Quantum machine learning: what quantum computing means to data mining*. Academic Press.

Yao, Z., Peng, W., Gao-yun, C., Dong-Dong, C., Rui, D., & Yan, Z. (2008). *Quantum clustering algorithm based on exponent measuring distance. In 2008 IEEE international symposium on knowledge acquisition and modeling workshop*. IEEE.

Zhou, R. (2010). Quantum competitive neural network. *International Journal of Theoretical Physics*, *49*(1), 110.

Zhou, R., Wang, H., Wu, Q., & Shi, Y. (2012). Quantum associative neural network with nonlinear search algorithm. *International Journal of Theoretical Physics*, *51*(3), 705–723.

Chapter 13
Advances of Quantum Machine Learning

Bhanu Chander

https://orcid.org/0000-0003-0057-7662

Pondicherry University, India

ABSTRACT

The basic idea of artificial intelligence and machine learning is that machines have the talent to learn from data, previous experience, and perform the work in future consequences. In the era of the digitalized world which holds big data has long-established machine learning methods consistently with requisite high-quality computational resources in numerous useful and realistic tasks. At the same time, quantum machine learning methods work exponentially faster than their counterparts by making use of quantum mechanics. Through taking advantage of quantum effects such as interference or entanglement, quantum computers can proficiently explain selected issues that are supposed to be tough for traditional machines. Quantum computing is unexpectedly related to that of kernel methods in machine learning. Hence, this chapter provides quantum computation, advance of QML techniques, QML kernel space and optimization, and future work of QML.

INTRODUCTION

From the past decades, owing to the increased technical fields like computer networks, embedded systems, micro-electro-mechanical systems the quantity of information or records created in our society is estimated to rise faster than the development. However, there is a huge lack in our computational capabilities; so there is an essential requirement of more powerful ways of processing information are desired (Carlo et al., 2018; Jun et al., 2018). In recent times, increased computational power, an enormous amount of data accessibility and algorithmic progressions directed Machine Learning (ML) models achieved tremendous, remarkable outcomes in data generation, classification as well as clustering, from computer vision to playing composite games and reinforcement learning tasks. Nonetheless, the success of these revolution results faces new challenges, the physical restrictions of chip production along with the growing size of datasets constantly rising and soon it will reach Moore's law someplace we may arrive at a point

DOI: 10.4018/978-1-7998-6677-0.ch013

Copyright © 2021, IGI Global. Copying or distributing in print or electronic forms without written permission of IGI Global is prohibited.

where existing computational apparatus will no longer be adequate. These above-mentioned disputes encouraging research commonalities to discover the potentials of exploiting the influence of quantum computation to accelerate conventional ML algorithms (Nana et al., 2018; Vedran et al., 2016). Even though personalized hardware structural designs graphics processing units (GPUs) and Tensor processing units (TPUs) be capable of developing production, but they may not proffer a structural clarification to the dilemma. Quantum estimation is like computational exemplar, which designed on rules of quantum technicalities. If researches going well on careful utilization of quantum effects like interfering or else entanglement, then quantum computers can resourcefully resolve special troubles that are assumed to be tough for standard machinery. The word QML bring in to symbolize a special demo of research like using ML practices to explore the productivity of quantum procedures or else the proposal of standard ML models enthused through quantum formations (Ewin 2019; Carlo et al., 2018; Blum et al., 1994).

In detail, quantum computation is attractive research filed where the interaction taking place on computer science, engineering and laws of physics. It attracts both industrial as well as academic by a hopeful riot in computing performance. At present research attention of quantum computing is on a quantum benefit or else quantum predominance where the construction quantum models presenting a principal accelerate in-contrast toward the most excellent feasible model on a standard computer to impel the progression of new-fangled infringes in dissimilar appliances like medicine, security, chemistry, and financial services.

Quantum computations re-labeling the ways of classical computers generate and exploit information with the help of basic principles of quantum physics. Here the principles of quantum computation use Q-bits instead of bits, classical bits play an important role in traditional computing machines. Q-bits enhance the stability of quantum models faster than the traditional models. As mentioned above there are lots of schemes for QML models that probable to proffer great speed-ups over the consequent standard models, either exponential or large polynomials. However, the transformation from hypothetical conse-quences into real-time appliances there is a need for highly developed quantum hardware's, moreover, it is necessary to know the association among traditional as well as QML areas which will help where, when and how QML models utilized as a commanding authority in ML outline. In QML, Quantum communications like quantum secure direct communication, quantum key distributions (QKD) shown extreme performance in secure communications. Most of ML algorithms outperform the best-known classical counterparts; a bit of them are Shor's models for integer factorization, Optimal Long's models for unsorted database search (Iordano et al., 2019; Carlo et al., 2018; Patrick et al., 2014).

Artificial intelligence (AI) produces results based on learning rules and reasoning, which makes tremen-dous modifications in the digital-world. Machine learning (ML) is sub-part of AI, gains knowledge from earlier practice to optimize performance, which is extensively employed in computer sciences, industrial business, health management, robotics, space crafts, bioinformatics, and financial transactions, etc. On the next side, ML operates as a modern procedure for making predictions through mining information from huge data sources. But when it comes to QML, the question arises on how to implement original ideas to related technologies in ML to quantum information or vice-versa and expand progression in both fields. Research community proposes numerous directions in both fields, especially ML principally enhances quantum entanglement, and quantum-based support vector machine and principal component analysis are some of the examples. Moreover, some special ML algorithms can be applied to special quantum tasks, like the classification of quantum states and employing new models. Results of the above-mentioned methods hint the ML of Quantum states stands for an innovative stage for solving troubles in quantum information discipline (Romero et a., 2017; Maria et al., 2018; Jun et al., 2018; Carlo et al., 2018).

The research of QML is most considerable since the quantum computing is no longer imaginary because at present most of the quantum computers able to access and designed from end-to-end an internet correlation, anyone has the right to access through internet connection and at their hand re-programmed for appropriate implementation, Shor's and Grover's algorithms completely re-programmed for new quantum models. The principal interest in applying machine learning to quantum computing is suitable for the exceptional boost in the number of magnitudes it can perform concerning standard ML methods. For example, a standard ML algorithm can procedure an input of N dimension, a quantum algorithm be capable of practice 2N dimensions, which shows the speedup of both training and classification procedures. More importantly, the up-to-date development in numerous standard existed ML algorithms employed to implement, design, and discovery of quantum devices, materials, circuits, and models. As a result, the scientific society consent that AI may a groundbreaking appliance for approaching generation of computational campaigns supports quantum facts. The well-built concentration in the integration of quantum computing and AI is extra attested by the rising number of conferences and workshops that, from 2014, take place each year on this topic.

IMPACT OF QUANTUM CALCULATION

Quantum computing guarantees to accelerate more than traditional computing for certain troubles like unstructured data, factoring and searching. These things depend on procedures like quantum time inference, amplitude amplification, and quantum matrix inversion, etc. Quantum computing mainly spotlights on learning the difficulty of the store, processing plus transmit information prearranged in quantum structures which called Quantum information. In quantum theory, physical statuses are scientifically stood-for compactness of possibility distributions. The consistent circumstances utilize in quantum replicas, next acknowledged by physical circumstances of quantum design that outfit them. A computation is accomplished reversibly through concern a series of unitary molds to an initialized condition. A probabilistic production achieved according to the distribution encoded as a result of the last density matrix (Ewin et al., 2019; Patrick et al., 2014; Carlo et al., 2018).

The basic part of quantum computing is the circumstances of any quantum format with two degrees of choice distinct through spectator, which they agree with the common reasonable assessments 0 and 1, this is entitled as Q-bit. Classical information symbolizes in standard bits as 0 and 1 and typically employ in conventional crypto-system. Q-bits: quantum cryptography system facility with quantum bits also acknowledged as Q-bits. Q-bits are dissimilar from traditional bits normally receive superposition standards stuck among zero and one, they can not be duplicated. When the term Q-bits employed it refer to be error-free and idealize. In observing quantum status tremendously weak as well as force wide-ranging error adjustments from the special things of noise. But if the physical faults are beneath an assured threshold, it's feasible to accurate the system proficiently. Many researchers stated that computational task requires most resources for complexity studies; one major advantage from quantum computation is it divides problems depend on their time complication, that generally matches to the number of uncomplicated steps essential to resolve the problems as a task with the equal mass of the input (Patrick et al., 2014; Carlo et al., 2018; Sheng et al., 2017; Jun et al., 2018).

The field ML mainly discusses on a mixture of statistical processes to evaluate datasets. Here the major intention headed for conclude future behavior of an unidentified, non-deterministic process. From the last few years, ML had grown excitedly produce great reviews about the most famous thoughts and frameworks. In the process of learning theory, mathematical foundations place the main role which helps problems to learn from data. While learning any theory some typical questions will raise like how many computational assets requisite to train assignment, how many samples needed to learn a specific task, how many assumptions needed to access the representation. In most of the ML models training datasets supposed to pinch from an anonymous possibility distribution along with prediction hardened on points drained from the related distribution. Statistical learning assumption represents the effectiveness of an estimator comes with test, time complication. Here the sample or model difficulty related with the lowest quantity of instances requisite to discover a task equal to a few guesstimated constraints as well as it is openly associated with the capability of the hypothesis space plus reliability of the data allotment. Time complexity keeps in touch with the runtime of the, for the most part, excellent learning model. A learning theory said well-organized if its runtime is polynomial in the portion of elements of the field, principles and converse polynomial in the error constraints (Carlo et al., 2018; Sheng et al., 2017; Vedran et al., 2016; Maria et al., 2018).

COMPARISON OF CLASSICAL AND QUANTUM MACHINE LEARNING

Most classical machine learning algorithms employed to categories data instances into classes which could either abuser define or originate from the inherent configuration of data. For example consider data set X = {x1, x2,....xn} here every xi is a data feature which is itself define by the amount of parameters xi = (x1i, x2i,.....xmi). If the presented dataset may have a group of images, where each image definite via parameters like many pixels, the color substance across a certain state. Categorization of this kind of data may sort among images that hold cars, those do not and it was part of ML models to obtain the classification tenet. ML algorithms classified as supervised, unsupervised and reinforcement learning. In supervised learning: there are predefined training data set which is also known as a labeled dataset (Xt). The labeled dataset encloses data features that have previously properly classify to construct a group of classifications Y = {y1, y2,.....yn}, at this point yi is the categorization of data feature xi. Proposed ML takes Y and Xt then try to optimize the internal parameters until the best taxonomy of the training set for Y has been achieved. Once the machine has sound learned it is then fed with fresh, unlabelled information X which it classifies but does not learn from it. In unsupervised learning: there is no pre-modeled dataset, models learn from the data up to some learning level, and compare it with the new dataset. (Carlo et al., 2018; Long et al., 2010; Iordanis et al., 2019). Coming to reinforcement learning, it does not contain any training set. As a substitute, the abuser enthusiastically inputs the outcome of ML or reward on the unstructured dataset as right or false. It was much like a response or feed-back right through the model also results in a learning procedure. Here the classifications labels are not mentioned before which similar to unsupervised learning because most of the real-time datasets are outsized or composite.

At first, researchers put the classical machine learning into the group-1, where a classical machine learns from the classical data. Some of the specified ML algorithms performed on a standard machine that comes from the quantum method. QML models added into group-2; however, the learning procedure runs with classical calculation, though only part of the protocol requiring access to a quantum workstation. Means acceleration gain by quantum computing approach straightforwardly from a part of the method. In some cases, standard data feed into the model created as of in cooperation of standard as well as quantum structure. Researchers denoted that while just a little element of model wants a quantum computer, the overall course experience no negative aspect from computing completely on a quantum mechanism, as traditional computation can be executed proficiently on the quantum mainframe (Carlo et al., 2018; Long et al., 2010; Nana et al., 2018).

Comparison

To know the probable profits of QML, it should be potential to create similarities flanked by standard and QML method, in provisions of momentum and classifier performance. To evaluate algorithms, researchers, academicians, and computer-scientists think about two distinctive resources: Space complexity and Time complexity. Officially, the space needed for any machine and is calculated as the amount of computational complexity desired to run the model. In quantum theory, space indication for the number of Q-bits requisite. For the S amount of Q-bits, the dimension of related Hilbert space is 2S. It was very essential to differentiate these two measures because there was no exponential aspect among them. In time complexity, the time in use to guide moreover categorize within a specific fault. Time refers to several processes requisite and, in the quantum structure; be able to be demonstrated as the number of successive entries functional to the Q–bits. Both of these complexities have good relation with the amount of training data (n) – the amount of data instances in training set forward to method, The amount of the dataset (N) - amount of data instances to be classify during proposed method, dimension of data-points (m) – in ML every data instance considered in a vector formation, where the numeric assessment related with every feature symbolize like element of vector, fault – refers to the small part of erroneous non-training categorization formulated in method. For instance, unsupervised knowledge doesn't hold on (n), because there is no training record present (Carlo et al., 2018; Jun et al., 2018; Vedran et al., 2016).

QUANTUM MACHINE LEARNING ALGORITHMS

Quantum Neural Networks

Artificial Neural Networks working system the same as the human brain. It stands for a complete variety of methods that have been broadly useful in compression, statistical methods, taxonomy, natural language processing, and regression. Their major characteristics are the modification of linear operations with nonlinear transformation and mostly preselected. It was a very well known truth that neural networks have shown booming in lots of applications, a few basic questions concerning their success remain largely unanswered (Carlo et al., 2018; Wiebe et al., 2014).

From the most recent years, neural networks have demonstrated success in countless appliances, basic questions relating to their accomplishment mostly remained as unrequited. Are there any official promises regarding their optimization as well as the forecast they return? How do they accomplish high-quality simplification illustrations even with the ability to entirely over-fit the training records? In recent years ANN's tremendously applied in QML literature. The foremost work on Quantum Neural-Networks (QNN) materializes in the 1990s as well as a high quantity of research articles followed afterward. On the other hand, it is important to discern that the QNN field has not achieved heights of technical expansion similar to other regions of QML. Probable causes for the complicatedness encounter in building growth in this area can be traced to the intrinsic variations flanked by the linearity of quantum mechanics as well as the major task play by non-linear essentials of ANNs (Amin et al., 2016; Long et al., 2010; Romero et al., 2017).

RBMs (Smolensky et al., 1986) are generative forms those principally measured from quantum insight owing to their well-built associations with the learning replica. It has been exposed that calculating the log-possibility as well as sampling from an RBM is computationally tough (Long et al., 2010). (Wiebe et al., 2014) constructed pair of models for proficiently instruct an RBM based on amplitude magnification (Brassard et al., 2002) along with quantum Gibbs samples. These all attain a quadratic enhancement in the numeral of example that essential to educate RBM, however the balancing the model is quadratically inferior in a number of boundaries than in contrastive deviation (Hinton et al., 2002). Proposed work (Wiebe et al., 2014) also helped to train full Boltzman machines. In full Boltzman machine, neurons communicate to all nodes of a diagram and it has a superior amount of parameters compared through regular RBMs. However, they are not participating in observation owing to high computational rate of exercise. A hybrid method among training ANNs along with complete QNN is the quantum Boltzmann mechanism projected in (Amin et al., 2016). In this method, normal RBM energy task expands merely a quantum phrase that, allocate a richer class of troubles to be modeled. Whether these models can grant any benefit for traditional tasks is unidentified. Even though there was no approval on the significant properties of a QNN, the most recent decades have seen a mixture of mechanisms those endeavor to construct systems whose fundamentals as well as update regulations are standing exclusively on the rules of quantum technicalities. In recent times, (Wan et al., 2016; Romero et al., 2018) works conquer the trouble of modeling nonlinearities through dimensions as well as establish many over-head q-bits in input/output of every node of arrangement. Nonetheless, these representations still not have a few vital characteristics of a complete QNN. For illustration, model constraints continue established, moreover it is not sufficient to verify that the models capable to meet a polynomial amount of iterations. In present time researchers identify that the most possible appliances of these models emerge to learn quantum objects moderately than improving the learning of conventional data. In conclusion, the authors recognized that, to date, there are no stabs to structure non-linearities directly on the data-size.

Quantum Bayesian Network (QBN)

Classical Bayesian networks are an acyclic probabilistic graphical representation of random variables and their dependencies on one another. Classical BN showed improved results in various fields, it applies to determine the likelihood of a new-fangled piece of data being sorted into an offered class through similarity with training records, with the great results BN made it own mark in ML. there is one drawback in BN's, they are intelligent to flexible data representations, building every piece of record utilizable for training. At present Hidden Markov Model (HMM) is the special case in BN with dynamic data instances, where outputs can able to be seen as well as states are hidden. These kinds of models are gaining interest in speech and handwritten recognition fields, as they productively estimate what chain of words are mostly regular. From the last 10 years, QBN and Hidden Quantum Markov Models (HQMM) explained in various ways however there are no tentative results shown to the date (Iordanis et al., 2018; Sheng et al., 2017; Patrick et al., 2014; Carlo et al., 2018).

Quantum Principle Component Analysis (QPCA)

With the result of technology development, the amount of data growing higher range. The data which was employed in ML generally high dimensional, include redundant or inappropriate information. As a consequence ML profit from pre-processing records via statistical measures like Principle Component

Analysis (PCA). PCA shrinks the aspects via converting data to original sets of unpredictable variables, where first few maintain the majority of disparity that existing in original dataset. The typical mode to analyze principal components heat downward to discover Eigen standards of a data matrix (Maria et al., 2018; Nana et al., 2018; Jun et al 2018; Ewin et al., 2019; Vedran et al., 2016).

Recent work from Rebentrost, Lloyd, and Mohseni recommended a new quantum class of PCA (QPCA). The volume of the model can produce an exemplar of a random density matrix ρ resourceful. However, QPCA has numerous cautions which must be solved before it applied to ML scenarios. One of them is, to expand a speedup; a little number of Eigenvalues of p must be big. For the scenario where every eigenvalue is equivalent along with size O (1/d), the algorithm decreases to stability in time O (d) that offers no progress higher than normal algorithms (Ewin et al., 2019; Maria et al., 2018; Jun et al 2018; Nana et al., 2018; Vedran et al., 2016).

Quantum K-means Algorithm

In ML, the clustering algorithm divides the unstructured, unlabelled dataset into k modules. It is an unsupervised, NP-hard problem. Comparing the distance measurements of new data vectors by the centroids vector of every class is a well-liked technique for categorizing the input data, although reducing standard case difficulty is an open research. The class which has direct detachment to corresponding vector is the one classified from additional vectors; this kind of taxonomy is sub-routine for the k-means clusters algorithm.

Quantum k-Nearest Neighbor

K-Nearest Neighbor (K-NN) comes under supervised ML models where data instances evaluate with labeled training data instances. The categorization of test vector carries out by considering greater part votes of class for the K-Nearest training vector. K-NN algorithm has a rich interest in handwritten character recognition, marketing, regression appliances, and traveling salesman problem, etc. Notably, there two major principles in K-NN: first one – the distance among every data vector along with each training data have to be determined for every categorization, which is resource exhaustive. Second – a particular dataset holds the majority of training values along with the bias value. Which needs the weight of each classification computation with the distance of a test vector from the training vector. An extension for K-NN discovered by the (wiebe et al., 2014) where algorithm set-up a superposition of Q-bit states with the distance among every training/input vector, with an appropriate quantum sub-routine that encode distance in Q-bit amplitude. Instead of calculating the states, the values transmit on an ancilla record via reliable amplitude inference. Grover's search utilize to discover the minimum valued record, For that reason, the complete classification take place inside the quantum workstation, then it sorts out into quantum k-NN as an L2 algorithm (Jun et al 2018; Maria et al., 2018; Nana et al., 2018; Vedran et al., 2016; Ewin et al., 2019).

Quantum k-NN model is not a universal remedy; here noticeable states of affairs on use of Quantum k-NN, however, like addiction on sparsity records. The taxonomy determined via best part law amid no-weighting, it is inappropriate on behalf of predisposed datasets. Additional study would grasp discovering sensible datasets as well as the amount of q-bits requisite for the proof term.

Quantum Reinforcement Learning (QRL)

Reinforcement learning is special kind of learning procedure compare other ML procedures; it spent more time to build the interior ML model. It shows great results in AlphaGo and AlphaGo Zero. Combination of AlphaGo and Reinforcement made AlphaGo productively defeated human expert in Go. After that AlphaGo Zero beat AlphaGo. In the development of QML, quantum reinforcement learning captures its own place in present research topics (Lucas Lamata 2020). In (Dunjko and Taylor et al., 2016) authors briefly explain how dissimilar quantum reinforcement learning among other kind of procedures of QML. Moreover they applied quantum agent and oracular environment to show the quadratic progression in learning competence along with exponential computation performances in limited resource. In (Albarr and Retamal et al., 2018) authors move forwards by considering numerous copies of environmental states where agents can benefit more. Coming to [Albarr and Retamal et al., 2020] authors proposed novel technique which analyzes unknown operations. Proposed technique allocates to establish an unidentified quantum operation or consistently, its eigen-vectors plus eigen-values via QRL (Lucas Lamata 2020).

Quantum Auto-Encoder

The concept of auto-encoder is different, it holds kind of neural networks which help for data compressing. It follows a style where the network holds an input layer (encoder) with n number of neurons. It contains one or additional inner layers (the number of layers depends on application) with n number of neurons n. At last, connects with output layer (decoder) which contains n neurons. The procedure works on intention of toning output signal of the set-up with input signal (Lucas Lamata 2020). If the procedure is exultant, one may reject the decoder moreover maintain just the input layer, the encoder, as a result compress the data. In recent time's experiments on quantum encoders has growing interest in academic as well as industrial fields. In (Romero and Olson et al., 2017; Wan and Dahlsten et al., 2017) authors designed a set of states, in Hilbert space to grasp all the data in a smaller section that is to say, to someway condense the quantum records onto a slighter quantity of quantum bits or q-bits. For this author employed traditional auto-encoders with quantum circuit collected of an input series of q-bits through a parameterized unitary operation. If training is thriving, and then one could abandon the last unitary gate equal to decoder, plus remain the primary one. So dipping the quantity of quantum information desired for realistic appliances. In (Li and Alvarez et al., 2017), authors designed an optimization of estimated address base on genetic methods. And in (Ding and Lamata et al., 2019) the proposed work of (Li and Alvarez et al., 2017) executed in Rigetti cloud quantum computer for showing its possibility.

Quantum Biometric Learning (QBL)

Quantum biometric is the new emerging filed that connects two eminent research technologies like quantum technologies and biological systems [Logton 1997; Gardner 1970]. QBL associates both QML with quantum neural networks which has good usage in biometric systems. Quantum artificial life and Quantum biomimetics are the two inside techniques plays crucial role in QBL. Quantum artificial life is an essential in the interior region in QBL, quantum biomimetics and its main purpose was to propose quantum individualities that will self-replicate in quantum mode, that too in a well-suited approach with no-cloning principle. Coming to Quantum memristors which inspired from traditional memristir, this was also known as fourth component in addition to resistor, inductor and capacitor. In (Feiffer and

Egusquiza et al., 2017) authors implied a quantum edition of a memristor, model consists with two stage quantum scheme encodes quantum data, in addition includes with fragile size to accumulate information moreover depend outcome stores feedback also. It was verified that this machine possesses hysteresis. Next, two schemes for execution of quantum memristors in dissimilar quantum stands were put ahead; those are superconducting tracks (Salmilehto and Deppe et al., 2017).

Quantum Machine Learning for Knowledge Graphs

Basically knowledge graphs are utilizes huge amount triple-oriented records for knowledge Graph (KG) and reasoning. If the dimensions of knowledge graphs keep on producing, traditional modeling turns into increasingly computational resource exhaustive (Yunpu and Yuyi et al., 2018). Semantic Knowledge Graphs base on graph-structured databases consist of subject, predict and object. Here both object and subject are nodes within the graph, and predicate is the lable of a directed link among object and subject. Google knowledge vault is the largest knowledge graph representation and it controls above 100 billion particulars along with hundreds millions of noticeable units. The large number of facts and entity units formulates it as tough to balance learning and inference methods to execute complete knowledge graph. Popular learning-base KGs methods are stand on a factorization of adjacency tensor (Jacob and peter et al., 2017; Siddartha and George et al., 2018).

Quantum Tensor Singular Value Decomposition

Quantum singular value decomposition works on theory that novel semantic tensor (χ) molds the complete knowledge graph has a low-rank orthogonal guess, designate (C_r) .with diminutive rank r. Here low-rank hypothesis is imaginable if the KG encloses global as well as precise relational outlines. A 3-dimensional semantic tensor illustrated as $\chi \hat{I} \{0,1\}^{d1 \times d2 \times d3}$. χ could be thereof restructured something like from $\chi^{\wedge}$ by tensor SVD. From description in (Petros and Iordanis et al., 2002) remember that the preference matrix of a reference structure usually includes numerous nonzero accesses in a specified user-row; items suggestions are prepared according to non-zero accesses in user-row via presumptuous that the abuser is 'typical'. But KG has solitary non-zero admission in the row (s, p, ?). For that reason, (Yunpu and Yuyi et al., 2018), advise presumption on a KG quantum models require to sample triples with the prearranged theme along with post-select on predicate p. The most complicated methodological confronts of QML loads standard data as quantum states and evaluate the sates because analysis or else writing high-dimensional facts from quantum states may eliminate the quantum speeding-up. Thus the procedure (Vittori and Seti et al., 2008) quantum Random Access Memory (qRAM) was designed, which load standard data into quantum states by exponential acceleration.

QUANTUM BASED LEARNING WITH NOISE

In any learning, theory noise plays special and possible beneficial functions. In particular, noise can alleviate local optima and generalization which are the most common model-fitting issues. Some changes in gradients could help in local optima but input-output can steps forward the results. The opportunity of exploiting favorably the special consequences of noise is principally motivating in the circumstance of quantum computation. At the starting stage quantum computers contains very few Q-bits, those used to execute complete error-correction, so the research society enthusiastically stares for solutions where noise does not demolish the computation instead it can take part in a positive job. The analyses of noisy learning subjects from a quantum point of view turn out to be the most vital part of selected appliances. Additional research in this course may afford innovative situations of a partition among the traditional as well as a quantum in noise based learning. If the noise added directly to the training inputs, outputs, weights and weight updates of NN moreover examined that input noise in some situations advances the generalization performance. In recent times research community finds that Gaussian noise to the gradients exposed to assist in optimizing the composite neural-network model. Besides, noise en-route for an update of the model parameter was also executed; at each echo, parameter modernizes is disturbed by Gaussian noise. It allows enumerate model insecurity and evade over-fitting at no-extra computational rate (Carlo et al., 2018; Ewin et al., 2019; Iordais et al., 2019).

To address the issues which occur while learning quantum theory with noise, it is compulsory to confer what kind of noise influences quantum computation. Bit-flips and phase-flips are the two-weight base quantum errors those take place of noise insertion. Both of them simplified with forecast more composite errors. Specified a quantum status $\psi = \alpha 0e0 + \alpha 1e1$, a bit-flip error spins the status into $\psi^{\sim} = \alpha 0e1 + \alpha 1e0$. Likewise, a phase-flip error transforms the comparative phase of a quantum status, i.e. the resultant status is $\psi^{\sim} = \alpha 0e0 - \alpha 1e1$. More composite, as well as rational forms of errors contain amplitude damping; seep-out to superior stages along with loss. Several authors have revised how noise influences learning capacity tasks in quantum theory. (Bshouty et al., 1998) demonstrated that DNF principles could powerfully educate beneath the standardized distribution with a quantum exemplar prediction. This distinguishes among standard problems where (Blum et al., 1994) illustrated that DNFs are not learnable in noise with revere to standardized distribution. The exited work on accelerating the training of NN by quantum assets has essentially focus on Restricted Boltzmann machines (RBMs) (Carlo et al., 2018; Ewin et al., 2019; Iordais et al., 2019).

Statistical Learning for Fast QML

Recently numerous authors designed quantum techniques for learning issues toward development fast quantum linear algebraic models for the accomplishment of runtimes which naturally quicker than their traditional foils like Quantum Support Vector Machines, Quantum Linear Regression and Quantum Least Squares (Carlo and Andrea et al., 2020; Aronson 2015). Complete scrutiny of mentioned models acknowledged numeral limitations that edge respected realistic applicability's like requirement of tough structure of quantum admission to the input data, limitations on structural possessions of data matrix along with modes of access to the output. Statistical learning statement computes the statistical resources that requisite to resolve a supervised learning difficulty. Here the target is to discover a representation that fits sound for set of training instances however notably, promises good forecast concert on novel observations (Carlo and Andrea et al., 2020; Celiberto 2019).

Wide variety of methodologies has been proposed and some of them openly imposed limitations on the hypotheses category of applicant predictor are regularization. A number of regularization models lead to trendy ML advances which widely utilized in observations like logistic regression, Regularized Least Squares, Support Vector Machines and Gaussian Process Regression. Most of these methodologies employed with kernel methods, to search a possible consequence for learning trouble via optimizing constraint intention, which normally consists of a series of typical linear algebra actions like matrix multiplication plus inversion. Higher quantity of long-established ML approaches has O(N3) computational cost. This is related to the time for capsize a square matrix that have magnitude equivalent to the number (N) instances in training set (Rebentrost and Mohseni et al 2014; Bishop 2006; Schuld and Sinayskiy et al., 2016).

Instead of employing optimization techniques some other techniques also got their attention in research field those like performing limited amount of steps to avoid overfitting the training data, applying generalization techniques and early stopping advances. Divide and conquer, random sub-sampling is some other well-known techniques. The main point of statistical dialogue is standard error putrefaction which briefly discussed in (Carlo and Andrea et al., 2020).

Quantum Embedding

Quantum taxonomies contain quantum circuits which trained with machine learning models. Primary component of quantum circuits holds a feature map which encodes standard inputs into quantum states, inserts data inside high-dimensional Hilbert space; the secondary component of the circuit performs a quantum magnitude construe the output of representation. Generally, the depth is skilled to discriminate quantum-embedded information.

Kernel models applied for learning operation with inserted data points x as vectors ~x $\hat{I}$ H within a Hilbert space H, a vector space by an interior invention. Then after data records explored through performing linear algebra on the embedded vectors. The objective of the embedding method is to discover a sign of data like recognized metric of Hilbert space authentically mimic unidentified metric of unique data. If one capable locates an authentic embedding, the calculations mandatory to evaluate data vectors moreover allot them for clusters capable of present by ordinary linear algebraic methods.

Quantum advances in reinforcement learning transport new research scheme for progress RL agents. For instance, prearranged standard environment (E) next explain fair unitary oracular equivalent (Eq). Here, (Eq) should not afford additional information than E below traditional admission, which was assured, when Eq feasible from a reversible adaptation of E. Next, admission to every quantum environment (Eq) cannot usually accelerate every portions of an interface. After that, build an enhanced agent to exploits the assets from the prior points.

Anomaly Detection in Quantum Machine Learning

Anomaly detection techniques identify Outlier/Anomaly data through compare the standard data with some predictable data patterns. Important resources for generating outliers in captured data are faulty systems, naturally occurring novel phenomena that rarely occurs and malicious intrusion into a system. This is also linked to the change-point exposure problem. Supervised, unsupervised, and semi-supervised are the three wide-ranging modules of anomaly-detection. Supervised anomaly exposure presumes labeled training sets in support of standard as well as abnormal data. In unsupervised learning method neither standard nor abnormal data labeled, although imagine that standard cases arise more recurrently than abnormal ones. Coming to semi-supervised methods standard data can be eagerly recognized and congregated, however abnormal data might be excessively inadequate to structure a training set. Contextual anomalies are individual data instance which are abnormal in deference to a particular situation, which frequent in time-series data. Coming to collective anomalies are groups of data instances that are abnormal with deference to entire data set.

Authors (Nanu and Patrick et al., 2018) provide report about existing QML methods for anomaly detection to identify outliers form both pure as well as mixed quantum states. Authors mentioned that anomaly resources as well as pure states accomplish with logarithmic in the measurement of quantum states. In this model, hadamard product of two matrices given as quantum states. (Li 2015) develops QNN model anomaly exposure which is incorporated by quantum computing; explain the difficulty of data overlap of two tentative natures of services on pattern classification. (Hoque and Bhattacharyya et al., 2014) designed a wavelet scrutiny base WNN (Wavelet Neural Network) model to fundamentally evade the local optimum in system training that tremendously improvise the convergence speed. Authors of (Wanwei Huang, Jianwei et al., 2017) designed novel anomaly detection with Normalized Mutual Information Feature Selection (NMIFS) which elects best feature mixture from the high-dimensional datasets. After that Quantum-Wavelet-Neural-Network (QWNN) utilize the best data features for training and learning. At the detection stage, the data is fed into the detection model and ultimately generates accurate detection results. Simulation results of NMIFS-QWNN shows high range anomaly detection. There is a wide range of anomaly-detection techniques base on ML which can be unmitigated to the quantum sphere moreover remain yet new and unexplored.

QUANTUM KERNEL FEATURE

The theme behind the working procedure of Quantum Learning (QL) is similar to kernel space in machine learning, where the computation of data instances happened at high dimensional space. In detail, the objective of quantum models is to achieve systemized computation in the Hilbert gap which expands in haste by the range of the quantum structure (Maria et al., 2018; Ewin et al., 2019). The quantity of procedures useful to the system rises to a high polynomial with the system dimension. In the ML model, kernel methods fixed in the right manner with an astonishingly related logic. The scheme of kernel officially implants data-instances into a higher-dimensional feature space, where it modifies to trouble-free for evaluating. SVMs is the best paradigm for kernel methods where the so-called decision limit among two classes of data points through plot the data toward a feature space where it turns into linearly distinguishable. Here the stratagem is model never clearly achieves computations with vectors in feature space, although utilizing a self-styled kernel task that describe on the realm of novel input data. Just like quantum computing, the kernel technique performs embedded computations in a conceivably, inflexibly big Hilbert space for the proficient exploitation of data vectors (Maria et al., 2018; Ewin et al., 2019; Nana et al., 2018; Wanwei et al., 2017).

Quantum kernels interrupt the procedure of encoding traditional data-instances into a quantum status like feature mapping that transforms data-inputs into Hilbert-space of quantum-system. This entire process consists of two stages of quantum algorithm preparations. In the first stage of the quantum design process, it estimates the internal creation of quantum states, moreover supply the estimations as a "quantum kernel" headed for standard kernel model. Coming to the second stage, data can be directly evaluated in the "feature Hilbert space" of quantum shapes, where effortless classifiers like linear forms expand massive influence. Both tactics presents an augment in characteristically obdurate mixture QML techniques with imminent quantum knowledge (Maria et al., 2018; Ewin et al., 2019; Nana et al., 2018; Wanwei et al., 2017).

In ML, inputs of the given dataset represented as D = { X1....Xm) from particular input X as well as recognize patterns to estimate previously unseen data. The kernel measurement among any two input values x and x' defined as K (x, x') which detain the features of data distribution. In other words, kernels defined as the interior results of data in a feature-space, wherever the data-point planned in the direction of feature space through a feature-map. As mentioned in the above discussion feature space a lot like superior to the original space. In case a feature map is non-linear task, it transforms comparative position among data points, and a dataset can turn into an easier to categorize in feature space. Assume $\phi:X\circledR F$ be a feature map. The internal calculation of any two input values mapped to feature space explained via kernel k (x, x') = F(ϕ (x), ϕ(x), where F (., .) is the interior creation definite on F. The correlation among feature maps as well as kernels shows that each feature map equal to a distance measure in input-space. While a given kernel can be associated with numerous dissimilar feature spaces, kernel assumption also label an exceptional Hilbert space-related with each kernel, the reproducing kernel Hilbert space (RKHS). While a feature map grants amplify to kernel and kernel augment to a repeated kernel Hilbert space, then it's simple to create an exclusive reproducing kernel Hilbert space for every specified feature map (Maria et al., 2018; Ewin et al., 2019; Nana et al., 2018; Wanwei et al., 2017). Quantum feature maps input x in the input set X into a quantum status defined as a vector I ϕ (x)> which places on the Hilbert space (F). This kind of input encoding completes the explanation of Quantum feature map ϕ: X ® F. F (x, w) = (w I ϕ (x) >. Here <.I.> indication of calculation of inner product in Quantum Hilbert space. As of sideline of quantum computation, a quantum feature-map x -> IQ (x)>correspond to a status training track U ϕ (x) behave as a ground implanting path I0.....0> of a Hilbert space F as U ϕ (x) I0....0> = I ϕ (x). There are two dissimilar strategies to build QML models with the mixture of quantum computing along with kernel assumption which is an implicit strategy and explicit strategy.

Coming to implicit strategy, we can utilize the quantum mainframe to study the internal product of K (x, x') = ϕ (x) I ϕ (x'). In this quantum computer could do two things, put into practice U ϕ (x) for any x Î X as well as calculates inner products among quantum states. Both the computation of model with kernel and training models are done through classical devices. Here we make use of kernel capably compute and exercise it as a traditional kernel in SVM. These kinds of models effortlessly discover the decision boundary of small two-dimensional standard data-set. In explicit strategy: we able to evade the learning theorem and truthfully execute the categorization in feature Hilbert space of quantum scheme. Variation circuit W (θ) builds on top of the feature map track to fabricate an aggregate classifier. For two-dimensional datasets, two vacuity forms I0> Ä I0>. In order to categorize a data instance x Î R2, foremost step is to map input to quantum state, Ic, x> = Ic, x> Ä Ic, x2> through squeezing process on every mode. After that relate variation circuit W (θ) to IC, X>. Repetitive photon number dimensions prepare us to guess probability p (n1, n2) by measuring the aggregate states In1, n2>.(Maria et al., 2018; Ewin et al., 2019; Nana et al., 2018; Wanwei et al., 2017).

Probabilistic Quantum Memory

Probabilistic Quantum Memory (PQM) is information/data-records development to calculate the distance from a binary input to every binary pattern accumulated in superposition on memory. This accumulated data structure allocate expansion of heuristics to increase speed of ANN structural design range (Rodrigo and Sousa et al., 2020)

Authors of (Ventura, T. Martinez et al., 2000) implemented the first version of Quantum Associative Memory (QAM) with variations in Grovers model. The foremost plan of QAM is accumulate patterns in superposition, agree to accumulate 2n patterns with n q-bits. The exploit of Grover's model searches for accurate patterns and not related patterns. Quantum associative memories have been utilized to execute taxonomy tasks in numerous works (Singh and Radhey et al., 2017; De paula and Silva et al., 2019). In (Singh and Radhey et al., 2017) Grover's model along with quantum associative memory are utilized to perform taxonomy responsibilities with toy dataset representing orange and apples with 3-qubit patterns (Rodrigo and Sousa et al., 2020; Zhou 2010).

Probabilistic Quantum Memories

The Probabilistic quantum memory representation utilized to construct a weightless network classifier, which is like a content-addressable quantum memory. Possible outputs of a given input prototype stored in the memory with hamming distance among input pattern and the entire the patterns accumulated in memory. It is a probabilistic representation considered to identify imperfect, noisy records (Rodrigo and Sousa et al., 2020).

The Quantum Weightless Classifier

Quantum Weightless Neural Network Classifier (Silva and De et al., 2010) (QWNNC) is assemble of Probabilistic Quantum memoirs substitute as system neurons. Here representation is formulated in array of PQM examples proficient of distance-based categorization. Every PQM illustration, by itself, efforts as a solitary classifier, accountable for categorization of at least one of the classes in dataset. The representation does not persist some training inside logic where neurons do not iteratively adapted to discover from the training patterns.

QUANTUM OPTIMIZATION

The optimization technique is the essential building block of various ML algorithms. An optimization technique is a route that is accomplished iteratively through evaluating various results until a most favorable or acceptable result found. With the huge development of computer hardware, optimization has turned out to be a part of computer-aided intends activities. Quantum computing solves well-known optimization troubles like semi-definite programming (SDP), constraint satisfaction. In SDP, the main intention to reduce a linear function of an N*N optimistic semi distinct matrix X above an affine space illustrates by a set of m restraints. O(m(m2 + nω + mns)logO(1)(mnR/)) is the best run time for standard SDP where parameter approximation ω Î [2, 2.373), s is a sparsity of A, R is a bound on an outline of most favorable or finest X. Coming to quantum algorithms for constraint satisfaction problems (CSP), there will be a set of variables, a collection of limitations and a list of feasible work to every variable. The intent here is to find the values of the variables that suit each constraint. The quantum approximate optimization algorithms (QAOA), as well as the Quantum adiabatic algorithm (QAA), are the two famous algorithms for CSPs. In QAOA, the method holds on integer parameter p ³ 1 along with estimation advances as p enlarge. For miniature values of p, the QAOA might accomplish on a one-dimensional circuit. Coming to QAA, it could be a reflection of the quantum analog of simulated annealing. The model encodes the answer to computational trouble in unidentified low status of the quantum scheme. Both QAA and QAOA spot the dissimilarities among the computational model and the method (Carlo et al., 2018; Maria et al., 2018; Patrick et al., 2014; Iordanis et al., 2019).

CHALLENGES

1. Due to the result of various technologies, the field of Quantum computing has made great progress. However, error-corrected quantum workstation with carrying a great number of Q-bits is still unknown. Moreover, the disputes incurred in large-scale quantum computers need more investigation.
2. None of the Q-bit implementations solves Q-bit error rates and error correction, scalable error correction along with resourceful multiplicative extensions in system size.
3. The problems arise while developing quantum computer and quantum algorithm design are not fully answered. Like Arbitrary state building with the number, Q-bits is exponentially hard, preparing bound on various working states of designed model, running complexity of an algorithm.
4. As stated from various pieces of literature, the course of encoding traditional data to quantum status is a crucial ingredient in every quantum model. In provisions of state preparation, information is characteristically encoded in state amplitudes. Q-RAM allocates quantum shapes and allows queries to prepare in super-position. In recent times, there has been a focal point on the effectiveness of the mentioned implementations in the existence of errors. Embedding QRAM in QML designs has many troubles in theoretical as well as in the experimental view.
5. Implementation of learn hidden Markov representations is familiarly interrelated to unsupervised learning, which could be efficiently applied in classification. Furthermore their correlation with ML is pretty noticeable as they are unique cases of Bayesian systems. Applying hidden quantum Markov representations into QML will improve the model performance; hence researchers must look into it.
6. Quantum Natural Language Processing: Learn the meaning from elements is another milestone and it acknowledged as Natural language processing. Quantum logicians tremendously employed in investing the suitability of non-commutative construction of quantum theory to model characteristics of natural languages. Word Vectors and Quantum Logic: Experiments with negation and disjunction, Quantum Algorithms for Compositional Natural Language Processing and Quantum Language Processing. These progressions will no doubt power thoughts in quantum related AI, ML domains.

CONCLUSION

Applying Quantum physics to Machine learning open a fresh door for exploring various technological and engineering fields. Machine learning as well as Quantum Computing methods are the two great methodological areas both be studied well ahead of their intersection discoveries. From the past two decades, the best part of QML research draw closer from either one of these two areas, moreover, this kind of research is extremely supportive. In particular, polynomial levels in the amount of data points might not be sufficient in the age of big size ML. Quantum algorithms offered here diminish the complication of a few ML with some advanced regularization techniques. In this chapter, we discussed various advanced Quantum Machine Learning (QML) techniques and their importance in ML, then we explore Optimization techniques, Quantum Memory, Quantum Embedding and importance statistical learning models for fast QML. And finally we discussed QML kernel tricks and Challenges.

REFERENCES

Aaronson, S. (2015). Read the fine print. *Nature Physics*, *11*(4), 291–293. doi:10.1038/nphys3272

Albarr'an-Arriagada, F., Retamal, J. C., Solano, E., & Lamata, L. (2018). Measurement-based adaptation protocol with quantum reinforcement learning. *Physical Review Letters*, *98*, 042315.

Albarr'an-Arriagada, F., Retamal, J. C., Solano, E., & Lamata, L. (2020). Reinforcement learning for semi-autonomous approximate quantum eigen solver. *Machine Learning: Science and Technology*, *1*, 015002.

Amin, M. H., Andriyash, E., Rolfe, J., Kulchytskyy, B., & Melko, R. (2016). Quantum Boltzmann machine. https://arxiv.org/abs/1601.02036

Biamonte, J., Wittek, P., Pancotti, N., Rebentrost, P., Wiebe, N., & Lloyd, S. (2017). Quantum machine learning. *Nature*, *549*(7671), 195–202. doi:10.1038/nature23474 PubMed

Bishop, C. M. (2006). *Pattern recognition and machine learning*. Springer.

Blum, A., Furst, M., Jackson, J., Kearns, M., Mansour, Y., & Rudich, S. (1994). Weakly learning DNF and characterizing statistical query learning using Fourier analysis. In *Proc. of the 26th Annu. ACM Symp. on Theory of Computing* (pp. 253–262). ACM., doi:10.1145/195058.195147.

Brassard, G., Hoyer, P., Mosca, M., & Tapp, A. (2002). Quantum amplitude amplification and estimation. *Contemporary Mathematics*, *305*, 53–74. doi:10.1090/conm/305/05215

Ciliberto, R. Rudi, & Wossnig. (2020). Fast Quantum learning with statistical gurantees. Academic Press.

Ciliberto, C., Herbster, M., Ialongo, A. D., Massimiliano, P. A. R., Severini, S., & Wossnig, L. (2018). Quantum machine learning: A classical perspective. *Proc. R. Soc. A*, *474*(2209), 20170551. doi:10.1098/rspa.2017.0551 PubMed

Ciliberto, C., Herbster, M., Ialongo, A. D., Pontil, M., Rocchetto, A., Severini, S., & Wossnig, L. (2018). Quantum machine learning: A classical perspective. *Proceedings - Royal Society. Mathematical, Physical and Engineering Sciences*, *474*(2209), 20170551. doi:10.1098/rspa.2017.0551 PubMed

Das, S., Siopsis, G., & Weedbrook, C. (2018). Continuous-variable quantum gaussian process regression and quantum singular value decomposition of nonsparse low-rank matrices. *Physical Review Letters*, *97*(2), 022315.

de Paula Neto, F. M., da Silva, A. J., de Oliveira, W. R., & Ludermir, T. B. (2019). Quantum probabilistic associative memory architecture. *Neurocomputing*, *351*, 101–110. doi:10.1016/j.neucom.2019.03.078

Di Ventra, M., Pershin, Y. V., & Chua, L. O. (2009). Circuit elements with memory: Memristors, memcapacitors, and meminductors. *Proceedings of the IEEE*, *97*(10), 1717–1724. doi:10.1109/JPROC.2009.2021077

Ding, Y., Lamata, L., Sanz, M., Chen, X., & Solano, E. (2019). Experimental Implementation of a Quantum Autoencoder via Quantum Adders Adv. Quantum Technology, 2(7-8), 1800065. doi:10.1002/qute.201800065

Dong, D., Chen, C., Li, H., & Tarn, T. J. (2008). Quantum reinforcement learning. IEEE Trans. Syst, 38, 1207. PubMed

Drineas, P., Kerenidis, I., & Raghavan, P. (2002). Competitive recommendation systems. In *Proceedings of the thiry-fourth annual ACM symposium on Theory of computing* (pp. 82–90). ACM., doi:10.1145/509907.509922.

Dunjko, V., Taylor, J. M., & Briegel, H. J. (2016). Quantum-Enhanced Machine Learning. *Physical Review Letters*, *117*(13), 130501. doi:10.1103/PhysRevLett.117.130501 PubMed

Dunjko, V., Taylor, J. M., & Briegel, H. J. (2016). Quantum Enhenced Machine Learning. *Physical Review Letters*, *117*(13), 130501. doi:10.1103/PhysRevLett.117.130501 PubMed

Gao, J., Qiao, L.-F., Jiao, Z.-Q., Ma, Y.-C., Hu, C.-Q., Ren, R.-J., Yang, A.-L., Tang, H., Yung, M.-H., & Jin, X.-M. (2018). Experimental Machine Learning of Quantum States. *Physical Review Letters*, *120*(24), 240501. doi:10.1103/PhysRevLett.120.240501 PubMed

Gardner, M. (1970). The fantastic combinations of John Conway's new solitaire game life. *Scientific American*, *223*, 120. doi:10.1038/scientificamerican1070-120

Giovannetti, V., Lloyd, S., & Maccone, L. (2008). Quantum random access memory. *Physical Review Letters*, *100*(16), 160501. doi:10.1103/PhysRevLett.100.160501 PubMed

Hinton, G. E. (2002). Training products of experts by minimizing contrastive divergence. *Neural Computation*, *14*(8), 1771–1800. doi:10.1162/089976602760128018 PubMed

Hoque, N., Bhattacharyya, D. K., & Kalita, J. K. (2014). MIFS-ND: A mutual information-based feature selection method. *Expert Systems with Applications*, *41*(14), 6371–6385. doi:10.1016/j.eswa.2014.04.019

Huang, W., Zhang, J., Haiyan, S. H. M., & Cai, Z. (2017). An Anomaly Detection Method Based on Normalized Mutual Information Feature Selection and Quantum Wavelet Neural Network. In *Wireless Press Communication*. Springer.

Huang, W., Zhang, J., Sun, H., Ma, H., & Cai, Z. (2017). An Anomaly Detection Method Based on Normalized Mutual Information Feature Selection and Quantum Wavelet Neural Network. In *Wireless Personal Communications*. Springer.

Kerenidis, I., Landman, J., & Luongo, A. (2019). q-means: A quantum algorithm for unsupervised machine learning. *33rd Conference on Neural Information Processing Systems (NeurIPS 2019)*.

Lamata. (2020). Quantum machine learning and quantum biomimetics: A perspective. Machine Learning: Science and Technology 2020.

Langton, C. G. (1997). *Artificial Life: An overview*. MIT Press.

Li, J. (2015). Quantum-inspired neural networks with application. *Ozean Journal of Applied Sciences*, *5*(06), 233.

Li, R., Alvarez-Rodriguez, U., Lamata, L., & Solano, E. (2017). Approximate Quantum Adders with Genetic Algorithms: An IBM Quantum Experience. Quantum Measurements and Quantum Metrology, 4(1), 1–7. doi:10.1515/qmetro-2017-0001

Li, Z., Liu, X., Xu, N., & Du, J. (2015). Experimental Realization of a Quantum Support Vector Machine. *Physical Review Letters*, *114*(14), 140504. doi:10.1103/PhysRevLett.114.140504 PubMed

Liu, N., & Rebentrost, P. (2018). Quantum machine learning for quantum anomaly detection. *Physical Review Letters*, *97*, 042315.

Lloyd, S., Mohseni, M., & Rebentrost, P. (2013). Quantum algorithms for supervised and unsupervised machine learning. *Nature*.

Long, P. M., & Servedio, R. (2010). Restricted Boltzmann machines are hard to approximately evaluate or simulate. In *Proc. of the 27th Int. Conf. on Machine Learning (ICML-10)*, (pp. 703–710). Brookline, MA: Microtome Publishing.

Ma, W. (2018). *Tresp*. Quantum Machine Learning Algorithm for Knowledge Graphs., doi:10.1145/1122445.1122456

Pfeiffer, P., Egusquiza, I. L., Di Ventra, M., Sanz, M., & Solano, E. (2016). Quantum Memristors. *Scientific Reports*, *6*(1), 29507. doi:10.1038/srep29507 PubMed

Rebentrost, P., Mohseni, M., & Lloyd, S. (2014). Quantum Support Vector Machine for Big Data Classification. *Physical Review Letters*, *113*(13), 130503. doi:10.1103/PhysRevLett.113.130503 PubMed

Rebentrost, P., Mohseni, M., & Lloyd, S. (2014). Quantum support vector machine for big data classification. *Physical Review Letters*, *113*(13), 130503. doi:10.1103/PhysRevLett.113.130503 PubMed

Romero, J., Olson, J., & Aspuru-Guzik, A. (2017). Quantum auto encoders for efficient compression of quantum data. Quantum Science and Technology, 2(4), 045001. doi:10.1088/2058-9565/aa8072

Romero, J., Olson, J. P., & Aspuru-Guzik, A. (2017). Quantum auto-encoders for efficient compression of quantum data. Quantum Science and Technology, 2(4), 045001. doi:10.1088/2058-9565/aa8072

Salmilehto, J., Deppe, F., Di Ventra, M., Sanz, M., & Solano, E. (2017). Quantum Memristors with Superconducting Circuits. *Scientific Reports*, *7*(1), 42044. doi:10.1038/srep42044 PubMed

Schuld, M., & Killoran, N. (2018). Quantum Machine Learning in Feature Hilbert Spaces. *Physical Review Letters*, *122*(4), 040504. doi:10.1103/PhysRevLett.122.040504 PubMed

Schuld, M., Sinayskiy, I., & Petruccione, F. (2016). Prediction by linear regression on a quantum computer. *Physical Review Letters*, *94*(2), 022342.

Sheng, Y.-B., & Zhou, L. (2017). distributed secure quantum machine learning. Science Bulletin, 62(14), 1025–1029. Advance online publication. doi:10.1016/j.scib.2017.06.007

Shouty, N. H., & Jackson, J. C. (1998). Learning DNF over the uniform distribution using a quantum example oracle. *SIAM Journal on Computing*, *28*, 1136–1153. doi:10.1137/S0097539795293123

Silva, A., de Oliveira, W., & Ludermir, T. (2010). A weightless neural node based on a probabilistic quantum memory. 2010 Eleventh Brazilian Symposium on Neural Networks, 259–264. doi:10.1109/SBRN.2010.52

Singh, M. P., Radhey, K., Saraswat, V., & Kumar, S. (2017). Classification of patterns representing apples and oranges in three-qubit system. *Quantum Information Processing*, *16*(1), 16. doi:10.1007/s11128-016-1472-z

Smolensky, P. (1986). Information processing in dynamical systems: foundations of harmony theory. Technical Report no. CU-CS-321-86. University of Colorado Boulder, Department of Computer Science.

Sousa, R. S., dos Santos, P. G. M., Verasa, T. M. L., de Oliveirac, W. R., & da Silva, A. J. (2020). Parametric probabilistic Quantum memory. *Neurocomputing*, *416*, 360–369. doi:10.1016/j.neucom.2020.01.116

Tang, E. (2019). Quantum-inspired classical algorithms for principal component analysis and supervised clustering, University of Washington. *Nature*.

Ventura, D., & Martinez, T. (2000). Quantum associative memory. *Information Sciences*, *124*(1-4), 273–296. doi:10.1016/S0020-0255(99)00101-2

Wan, K. H., Dahlsten, O., Kristjánsson, H., Gardner, R., & Kim, M. (2016). Quantum generalisation of feedforward neural networks. https://arxiv.org/abs/1612.01045

Wan, K. H., Dahlsten, O., Kristj'ansson, H., Gardner, R., & Kim, M. S. (2017). Quantum generalization of feed-forward neural networks npj. *Quantum Information*, *3*, 36.

Wiebe, N., Kapoor, A., & Svore, K. M. (2014). Quantum deep learning. https://arxiv.org/abs/1412.3489

Wittek, P. (2014). *Quantum Machine Learning: What Quantum Computing Means to Data Mining*. Academic Press.

Zhou, R. (2010). Quantum competitive neural network. *International Journal of Theoretical Physics*, *49*(1), 110–119. doi:10.1007/s10773-009-0183-y

Compilation of References

Aaronson, S. (2008). The limits of quantum. *Scientific American*, *298*(3), 62–69.

Aaronson, S. (2015). Read the fine print. *Nature Physics*, *11*(4), 291–293. doi:10.1038/nphys3272

Aaronson, S., & Arkhipov, A. (2013). The computational complexity of linear optics. *Theory of Computing.*, *9*(1), 143–252. doi:10.4086/toc.2013.v009a004

Aditya & Rao. (2005). Quantum cryptography. *Proceedings of Computer Society of India.*

Aïmeur, E., Brassard, G., & Gambs, S. (2007, June). Quantum clustering algorithms. In *Proceedings of the 24th international conference on machine learning* (pp. 1-8). Academic Press.

Aïmeur, E., Brassard, G., & Gambs, S. (2013). Quantum speed-up for unsupervised learning. *Machine Learning*, *90*(2), 261–287.

Ajtai, M. (1998). The Shortest Vector Problem in L2 is NP-hard for Randomized Reductions. *Proc. thirtieth Annual ACM Symposium on Theory of Computing -STOC*, 10–19 10.1145/276698.276705

Ajtai, M. (1998).The shortest vector problem in L2 is NP-hard for randomized reductions. *Proceedings of the Thirtieth Annual ACM Symposium on Theory of Computing*, 1-10.

Ajtai, M., & Dwork, C. (1997). A public-key cryptosystem with worst-case/average-case equivalence. *Proceedings of the Twenty-Ninth Annual ACM Symposium on Theory of Computing*, 284-293. 10.1145/258533.258604

Albarr'an-Arriagada, F., Retamal, J. C., Solano, E., & Lamata, L. (2018). Measurement-based adaptation protocol with quantum reinforcement learning. *Physical Review Letters*, *98*, 042315.

Albarr'an-Arriagada, F., Retamal, J. C., Solano, E., & Lamata, L. (2020). Reinforcement learning for semi-autonomous approximate quantum eigen solver. *Machine Learning: Science and Technology*, *1*, 015002.

Alex, L. (2011). Third Party Application Forensics on Apple Mobile Devices. *Proceedings of the 44th Hawaii International Conference on System Sciences.*

Alpaydin, E. (2020). *Introduction to machine learning*. MIT Press.

Altaisky, M. V. (2001). *Quantum neural network.* arXiv preprint quant-ph/0107012.

Amin, M. H., Andriyash, E., Rolfe, J., Kulchytskyy, B., & Melko, R. (2016). Quantum Boltzmann machine. https://arxiv.org/abs/1601.02036

Amin, M. H., Andriyash, E., Rolfe, J., Kulchytskyy, B., & Melko, R. (2018). Quantum boltzmann machine. *Physical Review X*, *8*(2), 021050. doi:10.1103/PhysRevX.8.021050

Amit, Y., Hay, R., Saltzman, R., & Sharabani, A. (2013). *Pinpointing security vulnerabilities in computer software applications.* US Patent 8,510,842.

Ananthaswamy, A. (2019). *Scientific American, The Quantum Internet Is Emerging, One Experiment at a Time.* https://www.scientificamerican.com/article/the-quantum-internet-is-emerging-one-experiment-at-a-time/

Anglano, C. (2014). Forensic Analysis of WhatsApp Messenger on Android Smartphones. *The Digital Investigation Journal., 11*(3), 201–213. doi:10.1016/j.diin.2014.04.003

Anguita, D., Ridella, S., Rivieccio, F., & Zunino, R. (2003). Quantum optimization for training support vector machines. *Neural Networks, 16*(5-6), 763–770. doi:10.1016/S0893-6080(03)00087-X PMID:12850032

Anwar, M., Abdullah, A. H., Altameem, A., Qureshi, K. N., Masud, F., Faheem, M., Cao, Y., & Kharel, R. (2018). Green communication for wireless body area networks: Energy aware link efficient routing approach. *Sensors (Basel), 18*(10), 3237. doi:10.339018103237 PMID:30261628

Ardehali, M., Chau, H. F., & Lo, H.-K. (1998). *Efficient Quantum Key Distribution.* quant-ph/9803007.

Arute, F., Arya, K., Babbush, R., Bacon, D., Bardin, J. C., Barends, R., Biswas, R., Boixo, S., Brandao, F. G. S. L., Buell, D. A., Burkett, B., Chen, Y., Chen, Z., Chiaro, B., Collins, R., Courtney, W., Dunsworth, A., Farhi, E., Foxen, B., ... Martinis, J. M. (2019). Quantum supremacy using programmable superconducting processor. *Nature, 574*(7779), 505–510. doi:10.103841586-019-1666-5 PMID:31645734

Aspect, A., Dalibard, J., & Roger, G. (1982). Experimental Test of Bell's Inequalities Using Time-Varying Analyzers. *Physical Review Letters, 49*(25), 1804–1807. doi:10.1103/PhysRevLett.49.1804

Atkinson, Mitchell, Rio, & Matich. (2018). *WiFi is leaking: What do your mobile apps gossip about you?* Academic Press.

Attaby, A. A., Mursi Ahmed, M. F. M., & Alsammak, A. K. (2017). Data hiding inside JPEG images with high resistance to steganalysis using a novel technique: DCT-M3. *Ain Shams Engineering Journal.* Advance online publication. doi:10.1016/j.asej.2017.02.003

Ayodele, T. O. (2010). Types of machine learning algorithms. *New advances in machine learning*, 19-48.

Ayodele, T. O. (2010). Types of machine learning algorithms. *New Advances in Machine Learning*, 19-48.

Babai, L. (1986). On Lovaśz lattice reduction and the nearest lattice point problem. *Combinatorica, 6*(1), 1–13. doi:10.1007/BF02579403

Babai, L. (2016). Graph isomorphism in quasipolynomial time. In *Proceedings of the 48th ACM STOC* (pp. 684-697). ACM.

Bacon, D. (2019, February 25). *Applied Science: Quantum: Google Research.* Retrieved from Google Research: https://youtu.be/16ZfkPRVf2w

Banerjee, C. (2020). *The Times of India, Indian-led research team brings quantum internet closer to reality.* https://timesofindia.indiatimes.com/india/indian-led-research-team-brings-quantum-internet-closer-to-reality/articleshow/79470191.cms

Bao, Z., Luo, X., Zhang, Y., Yang C. & Liu, F. (2018). A Robust Image Steganography on Resisting JPEG Compression with No Side Information. *IETE Technical Review, 35*(S1), 4-13. doi:10.1080/02564602.2018.1476192

Barmpatsalou, Damopoulos, Kambourakis, & Katos. (2013). A critical review of 7 years of Mobile Device Forensics. *D.I., (4)*, 323–349.

Batouche, M., Meshoul, S., & Al Hussaini, A. (2009). *Image processing using quantum computing and reverse emergence. Int. J. Nano and Biomaterials.*

Beale, H. D., Demuth, H. B., & Hagan, M. T. (1996). Neural network design. Pws.

Beals, R., Buhrman, H., Cleve, R., Mosca, M., & de Wolf, R. (2001). Quantum lower bounds by polynomials. *Journal of the Association for Computing Machinery*, *48*(4), 778–797. doi:10.1145/502090.502097

Bechmann-Pasquinucci, H., & Gisin, N. (1999). Incoherent and Coherent Eavesdropping in the 6-state Protocol of Quantum Cryptography. *Physical Review A*, *59*(6), 4238–4248. doi:10.1103/PhysRevA.59.4238

Bechmann-Pasquinucci, H., & Peres, A. (2000). Quantum cryptography with 3-state systems. *Physical Review Letters*, *85*(15), 3313–3316. doi:10.1103/PhysRevLett.85.3313 PMID:11019329

Bechmann-Pasquinucci, H., & Tittel, W. (2000). Quantum cryptography using larger alphabets. *Physical Review A*, *61*(6), 062308–1. doi:10.1103/PhysRevA.61.062308

Behrman, E. C., Nash, L. R., Steck, J. E., Chandrashekar, V. G., & Skinner, S. R. (2000). Simulations of quantum neural networks. *Information Sciences*, *128*(3-4), 257–269.

Bell, J. S. (1964). On the problem of hidden variables in quantum mechanics. Review of Modern Phys., 38, 447-452.

Bennett, C. H., & Brassard, G. (1984). Quantum cryptography: public key distribution and coin tossing. *Int. Conf. Computers, Systems & Signal Processing*, 175-179. doi:10.1103/PhysRevLett.68.3121

Bennett, C. H. (1992). Quantum cryptography using any two nonorthogonal states. *Physical Review Letters*, *68*, 3121–3124.

Bennett, C. H., Bernstein, E., Brassard, G., & Vazirani, U. (1997). Strengths and weaknesses of quantum computing. *SIAM Journal on Computing*, *26*(5), 1510–1523. doi:10.1137/S0097539796300933

Bennett, C. H., & Brassard, G. (1984). *Quantum cryptography: Public key distribution and coin tossing. IEEE Intl. Conf. Computers, Systems and Signal Processing*.

Bennett, C. H., & Brassard, G. (1985). Quantum public key distribution system. *IBM Technical Disclosure Bulletin*, *28*, 3153–3163.

Bernstein. (2009). *Cost analysis of hash collisions: Will quantum computers make SHARCS obsolete?* (Report). Academic Press.

Bernstein, D. J., Buchmann, J., & Dahmen, E. (2009). *Post-Quantum Cryptography*. Springer. doi:10.1007/978-3-540-88702-7

Bernstein, D. J., Heninger, N., Lou, P., & Valenta, L. (2017). Post-quantum RSA. In *Proceedings of the International Workshop on Post-Quantum Cryptography* (pp. 311-329). 10.1007/978-3-319-59879-6_18

Bhardwaj, R., & Sharma, V. (2016). Image Steganography based on Completed Message and Inverted bit LSB Substitution. *Procedia Computer Science*, *93*, 832–838. doi:10.1016/j.procs.2016.07.245

Bhatia & Sumbaly. (2014). *Framework For Wireless Network Security Using Quantum Cryptography*. Academic Press.

Bhatia, A. S., & Kumar, A. (2018). *McEliece Cryptosystem Based On Extended Golay Code*. arXiv preprint: 1811.06246.

Bhatia, A. S., & Kumar, A. (2019). Post-Quantum Cryptography. *Emerging Security Algorithms and Techniques*, 139.

Bhatia, A. S., & Saggi, M. K. (2018). *Implementing Entangled States on a Quantum Computer*. arXiv preprint: 1811.09833.

Bhatia, A. S., Saggi, M. K., Kumar, A., & Jain, S. (2019). Matrix Product State–Based Quantum Classifier. *Neural Computation*, *31*(7), 1499–1517.

Bhatia, A. S., & Zheng, S. (2020). Post-Quantum Cryptography and Quantum Cloning. In *Quantum Cryptography and the Future of Cyber Security* (pp. 1–28). IGI Global.

Bhatt, A. P., Babuta, T., & Sharma, A. (2018, February). Quantum information processing and communication: Asian perspective. *Intl. Journal of Computer and Mathematical Sciences*, *7*(2), 616–621.

Bhatt, A. P., & Sharma, A. (2019). Quantum Cryptography for Internet of Things Security. *Journal of Electronic Science and Technology*, *17*(3), 213–220.

Biamonte, J., Wittek, P., Pancotti, N., Rebentrost, P., Wiebe, N., & Lloyd, S. (2017). Quantum machine learning. *Nature*, *549*(7671), 195–202. doi:10.1038/nature23474 PMID:28905917

Biham, E., & Mor, T. (1997). Bounds on Information and the Security of Quantum Cryptography. *Physical Review Letters*, *79*(20), 4034–4037. doi:10.1103/PhysRevLett.79.4034

Biham, E., & Mor, T. (1997). Security of Quantum Cryptography against Collective Attacks. *Physical Review Letters*, *78*(11), 2256–2259. doi:10.1103/PhysRevLett.78.2256

Bishop, C. M. (2006). *Pattern recognition and machine learning*. Springer.

Blum, A., Furst, M., Jackson, J., Kearns, M., Mansour, Y., & Rudich, S. (1994). Weakly learning DNF and characterizing statistical query learning using Fourier analysis. In *Proc. of the 26th Annu. ACM Symp. on Theory of Computing* (pp. 253–262). ACM., doi:10.1145/195058.195147.

Bohr, N., & Noll, W. (1958). Atomic Physics and Human Knowledge. American Journal of Physics, 26(8), 38. doi:10.1119/1.1934707

Boixo, S. (2019, March 4). *Applied Science: Quantum: Google Research*. Retrieved from Google Research: https://youtu.be/gylmjTOUfCQ

Boneh, D., & Zhandry, M. (2013). Secure signatures and chosen ciphertext security in a quantum computing world. Advances in Cryptology–CRYPTO 2013, 361–379.

Brandl, F. M. (2017). *A Quantum von Neumann Architecture for Large-Scale Quantum Computing*. Institut f¨ur Experimentalphysik, Universit¨at Innsbruck.

Brassard, G. (1984). Quantum Cryptography: Public Key Distribution & Coin Tossing. *IEEE Conference on Computer, Systems, and Signal Processing*.

Brassard, G. (2000). Security aspects of practical quantum cryptography. In *International conference on the theory and applications of cryptographic techniques*. Springer. 10.1109/IQEC.2000.907967

Brassard, G. (1997). Searching a quantum phone book. *Science*, *275*(5300), 627–628. doi:10.1126cience.275.5300.627

Brassard, G., & Høyer, P. (1997). An exact quantum polynomial-time algorithm for Simon's problem. In *Proceedings of Fifth Israeli Symposium on Theory of Computing and Systems* (pp. 12-23). IEEE Computer Society Press. 10.1109/ISTCS.1997.595153

Brassard, G., Hoyer, P., Mosca, M., & Tapp, A. (2002). Quantum amplitude amplification and estimation. *Contemporary Mathematics*, *305*, 53–74. doi:10.1090/conm/305/05215

Brassard, G., Høyer, P., & Tapp, A. (1998). Quantum counting. In K. G. Larsen, S. Skyum, & G. Winskel (Eds.), *Automata, Languages and Programming* (pp. 820–831). Springer. doi:10.1007/BFb0055105

Brassard, G., Lütkenhaus, N., Mor, T., & Sanders, B. C. (2000). Limitations on practical quantum cryptography. *Physical Review Letters*, *85*(6), 6. doi:10.1103/PhysRevLett.85.1330 PMID:10991544

Bridgwater, A. (2017). *Five Ways Quantum Computing Will Change Cybersecurity Forever.* https://www.raconteur.net/risk-management/five-ways-quantum-computing-will-change-cybersecurity-forever

Brunner, D., Soriano, M. C., Mirasso, C. R., & Fischer, I. (2013). Parallel photonic information processing at gigabyte per second data rates using transient states. *Nature Communications*, *4*(1), 1–7.

Brunty, J. (2016). *Mobile device forensics: threats, challenges, and future trends. Marshall* University.

Bruschi, Monga, & Rosti. (2005). Trusted Internet forensics: design of a network forensics appliance. In Security and Privacy for Emerging Areas in Communication Networks. IEEE.

Buchanan & Woodward. (2017). Will quantum computers be the end of public key encryption? *Journal of Cyber Security Technology, 1*(1), 1-22. Doi:10.1080/23742917.2016.1226650

Buchmann, J. A., & Williams, H. C. (1989). A key exchange system based on real quadratic fields. In G. Brassard (Ed.), Advances in Cryptology—CRYPTO '89. Academic Press.

Bui, N., & Zorzi, M. (2011). Health care applications: a solution based on the internet of things. In *Proceedings of the 4th International Symposium on Applied Sciences in Biomedical and Communication Technologies (ISABEL '11)*. ACM. 10.1145/2093698.2093829

Cai, X. D., Wu, D., Su, Z. E., Chen, M. C., Wang, X. L., Li, L., ... Pan, J. W. (2015). Entanglement-based machine learning on a quantum computer. *Physical Review Letters*, *114*(11), 110504.

Caloyannides, M. A. (2004). *Privacy Protection and Computer Forensics*. Artech House. www.artechhouse.com

Campagna & Chen. (2015). *Quantum Safe Cryptography and Security: An introduction, benefits, enablers and challenges*. ETSI White Paper No. 8.

Caraiman, S., & Manta, V. (2012). Image processing using quantum computing. In *System theory, control and computing*. ICSTCC.

Chakraborty, S., & Mandal, S. B. (2017). *Ternary Quantum Circuit for Color Image Representation. In Computing and Systems for Security*. Advances in Intelligent Systems and Computing.

Chakraborty, S., Mandal, S. B., & Shaikh, S. H. (2018). *Quantum image processing: challenges and future research issues. Int. J. Inf. Tecnol.*

Chanajitt, Wantanee & Choo. (2016). Forensic analysis and security assessment of Android m-banking apps. Academic Press.

Chaqfeh, M. A., & Mohamed, N. (2012). Challenges in middleware solutions for the internet of things. *Proceedings of the 13th International Conference on Collaboration Technologies and Systems (CTS '12)*, 21–26. 10.1109/CTS.2012.6261022

Chen, C. L., Dong, D. Y., & Chen, Z. H. (2006). Quantum computation for action selection using reinforcement learning. *International Journal of Quantum Information*, *4*(06), 1071–1083.

Chen, C. Y., Zeng, G.-J., Lin, F. J., Chou, Y. H., & Chao, H.-C. (2015, October). Quantum Cryptography and Its Applications over the Internet. *IEEE Network*, *29*(5), 64–69. doi:10.1109/MNET.2015.7293307

Chen, S., Xu, H., Liu, D., Hu, B., & Wang, H. (2014, April). A Vision of IoT: Applications, Challenges, and Opportunities with China Perspective. *IEEE Internet of Things Journal*, *1*(4), 349–359. doi:10.1109/JIOT.2014.2337336

Choi, J., In, Y., Park, C., Seok, S., Seo, H., & Kim, H. (2018). Secure IoT framework and 2D architecture for End-To-End security. *The Journal of Supercomputing, 74*(8), 3521–3535. doi:10.100711227-016-1684-0

Ciliberto, R. Rudi, & Wossnig. (2020). Fast Quantum learning with statistical gurantees. Academic Press.

Ciliberto, C., Herbster, M., Ialongo, A. D., Massimiliano, P. A. R., Severini, S., & Wossnig, L. (2018). Quantum machine learning: A classical perspective. *Proc. R. Soc. A, 474*(2209), 20170551. doi:10.1098/rspa.2017.0551 PubMed

Ciliberto, C., Herbster, M., Ialongo, A. D., Pontil, M., Rocchetto, A., Severini, S., & Wossnig, L. (2018). Quantum machine learning: A classical perspective. *Proceedings - Royal Society. Mathematical, Physical and Engineering Sciences, 474*(2209), 20170551. doi:10.1098/rspa.2017.0551 PMID:29434508

Crane, L. (2020). *New Scientist, Record-breaking quantum memory brings quantum internet one step closer.* https://www.newscientist.com/article/2233317-record-breaking-quantum-memory-brings-quantum-internet-one-step-closer/

Dang, Y., Jiang, N., Hu, H., Ji, Z., & Zhang, W. (2018). Image classification based on quantum K-Nearest-Neighbor algorithm. *Quantum Information Processing, 17*(9), 239.

Daniels, K., & Marcellino, C. (n.d.). *Security of Quantum Cryptography using Photon for Quantum Key Distribution.* Physics C191C.

Dargahi, T., Dehghantanha, A., & Conti, M. (2017). *Forensics Analysis of Android Mobile VoIP Apps.* University of Padua Padua. doi:10.1016/B978-0-12-805303-4.00002-2

Dasgupta, S., Papadimitriou, C. H., & Vazirani, U. (2011). *Algorithms.* McGraw-Hill.

Das, S., Siopsis, G., & Weedbrook, C. (2018). Continuous-variable quantum gaussian process regression and quantum singular value decomposition of nonsparse low-rank matrices. *Physical Review Letters, 97*(2), 022315.

de Paula Neto, F. M., da Silva, A. J., de Oliveira, W. R., & Ludermir, T. B. (2019). Quantum probabilistic associative memory architecture. *Neurocomputing, 351*, 101–110. doi:10.1016/j.neucom.2019.03.078

De Wolf, R. (2019). *Quantum computing: Lecture notes.* arXiv preprint arXiv:1907.09415.

Devtechnosys. (2018). *Cost and Features of IoT Solutions for Healthcare.* https://devtechnosys.com/cost-and-features-of-iot-solutions-for-healthcare

Di Ventra, M., Pershin, Y. V., & Chua, L. O. (2009). Circuit elements with memory: Memristors, memcapacitors, and meminductors. *Proceedings of the IEEE, 97*(10), 1717–1724. doi:10.1109/JPROC.2009.2021077

Diffie, W., & Hellman, M. E. (1976). New directions in cryptography. *IEEE Transactions on Information Technology, 22*(6), 644–654. doi:10.1109/TIT.1976.1055638

Ding, Y., Lamata, L., Sanz, M., Chen, X., & Solano, E. (2019). Experimental Implementation of a Quantum Autoencoder via Quantum Adders Adv. Quantum Technology, 2(7-8), 1800065. doi:10.1002/qute.201800065

Domingo, M. C. (2012). An overview of the Internet of Things for people with disabilities. *Journal of Network and Computer Applications, 35*(2), 584–596. doi:10.1016/j.jnca.2011.10.015

Dong, D., Chen, C., Li, H., & Tarn, T. J. (2008). Quantum reinforcement learning. IEEE Trans. Syst, 38, 1207. PubMed

Dong, D., Chen, C., Li, H., & Tarn, T. J. (2008). Quantum reinforcement learning. *IEEE Transactions on Systems, Man, and Cybernetics. Part B, Cybernetics, 38*(5), 1207–1220. doi:10.1109/TSMCB.2008.925743 PMID:18784007

Dong, D., Chen, C., Tarn, T. J., Pechen, A., & Rabitz, H. (2008). Incoherent control of quantum systems with wavefunction-controllable subspaces via quantum reinforcement learning. *IEEE Transactions on Systems, Man, and Cybernetics. Part B, Cybernetics*, *38*(4), 957–962.

Dridi, R., & Alghassi, H. (2015). *Homology computation of large point clouds using quantum annealing.* arXiv preprint:1512.09328.

Drineas, P., Kerenidis, I., & Raghavan, P. (2002). Competitive recommendation systems. In *Proceedings of the thiry-fourth annual ACM symposium on Theory of computing* (pp. 82–90). ACM., doi:10.1145/509907.509922.

Dunjko, V., Taylor, J. M., & Briegel, H. J. (2016). Quantum Enhanced Machine Learning. *Physical Review Letters*, *117*(13), 130501. doi:10.1103/PhysRevLett.117.130501 PubMed

Dunjko, V., Taylor, J. M., & Briegel, H. J. (2016). Quantum-enhanced machine learning. *Physical Review Letters*, *117*(13), 130501. doi:10.1103/PhysRevLett.117.130501 PMID:27715099

Dunjko, V., Taylor, J. M., & Briegel, H. J. (2016). Quantum-Enhanced Machine Learning. *Physical Review Letters*, *117*(13), 130501. doi:10.1103/PhysRevLett.117.130501 PubMed

Dzau, V. J. (2019). *Quantum Computing: Progress and Prospects*. The National Academics Press.

Elliott, C. (2002, July). *New Journal of Physics: Building the Quantum Network*. BBN Technologies.

Ettinger, M., & Høyer, P. (1999). On quantum algorithms for noncommutative hidden subgroups. In *Annual Symposium on Theoretical Aspects of Computer Science* (pp. 478-487). 10.1007/3-540-49116-3_45

Ezhov, A. A., & Ventura, D. (2000). Quantum neural networks. In *Future directions for intelligent systems and information sciences* (pp. 213–235). Physica.

Fedorov, A. K. (2018). Educational potential of quantum cryptography and its experimental modular realization. In *Proceedings of the Scientific-Practical Conference" Research and Development-2016*. Springer. 10.1007/978-3-319-62870-7_9

Fernholz, T. (2016, Aug. 20). *China's new Quantum Satellite will try to teleport data outside the bounds of space and time*. Quantum Supremacy.

Ferreira, P., Martinho, R., & Domingos, D. (2010). Iot-aware business processes for logistics: limitations of current approaches. *Proceedings of the Inforum Conference*, *3*, 612–613.

Flaherty, N. (2020). *eeNews Europe, Quantum network for Amsterdam*. https://www.eenewseurope.com/news/quantum-network-amsterdam

Fowler, A. G., Mariantoni, M., Martinis, J. M., & Cleland, A. N. (2012). Surface codes: Towards practical large-scale quantum computation. *Physical Review A*, *86*(3), 032324. doi:10.1103/PhysRevA.86.032324

Fu, X., Riesebos, L., Rol, M. A., van Straten, J., van Someren, J., Khammassi, N., ... de Sterke, J. C. (2019). eQASM: An executable quantum instruction set architecture. In *2019 IEEE International Symposium on High Performance Computer Architecture (HPCA)* (pp. 224-237). IEEE.

Gao, J., Qiao, L.-F., Jiao, Z.-Q., Ma, Y.-C., Hu, C.-Q., Ren, R.-J., Yang, A.-L., Tang, H., Yung, M.-H., & Jin, X.-M. (2018). Experimental Machine Learning of Quantum States. *Physical Review Letters*, *120*(24), 240501. doi:10.1103/PhysRevLett.120.240501 PubMed

Gao, X., Zhang, Z. Y., & Duan, L. M. (2018). A quantum machine learning algorithm based on generative models. *Science Advances*, *4*(12), eaat9004.

Gardner, M. (1970). The fantastic combinations of John Conway's new solitaire game life. *Scientific American, 223*, 120. doi:10.1038/scientificamerican1070-120

Garfinkel, S. L. (2010). *Digital forensics Research: The next ten years*. Elsevier.

Giovannetti, V., Lloyd, S., & Maccone, L. (2008). Quantum random access memory. *Physical Review Letters, 100*(16), 160501. doi:10.1103/PhysRevLett.100.160501 PubMed

Giustina, M. (2018, December 10). *Google Research*. Retrieved from https://research.google.com: https://youtu.be/k-21vRCC0RM

Goel, R., Garuba, M., & Girma, A. (2007). Research Directions in Quantum Cryptography. *International Conference on Information Technology (ITNG'07)*, 1-6.

Goldreich, O., Goldwasser, S., & Halevi, S. (1997). Public-key Cryptosystems from Lattice Reduction Problems. In *Proc. 17th Annual International Cryptology Conference on Advances in Cryptology (CRYPTO '97)*. Springer-Verlag.

Goldreich, O., Goldwasser, S., & Halevi. (1997). Eliminating decryption errors in the Ajtai-Dwork cryptosystem. *Lecture Notes in Computer Science, 1294*, 105–111.

Gope, P., & Hwang, T. (2015). BSN-Care: A secure IoT-based modern healthcare system using body sensor network. *IEEE Sensors Journal, 16*(5), 1368–1376. doi:10.1109/JSEN.2015.2502401

Gordon, D. M. (1993). Discrete logarithms in GF(p) using the number field sieve. *SIAM Journal on Discrete Mathematics, 6*(1), 124–139. doi:10.1137/0406010

Gose. (2019). https://medicalfuturist.com/quantum-computing-in-healthcare/

Goyal, A., Aggarwal, S., & Jain, A. (2011). Quantum Cryptography & its Comparison with Classical Cryptography: A Review Paper. *5th IEEE International Conference on Advanced Computing & Communication Technologies*, 428-432.

Goyal, A., Aggarwal, S., & Jain, A. (n.d.). Quantum Cryptography and its Comparison with Classical Cryptography: A Review Paper. *5th IEEE Conference on Advanced Computing and Communication Technology*.

Grant, E., Benedetti, M., Cao, S., Hallam, A., Lockhart, J., Stojevic, V., ... & Severini, S. (2018). Hierarchical quantum classifiers. *NPJ Quantum Information, 4*(1), 1-8.

Gray, A., & Sallis, P. (1997). Software Forensics: Extending Authorship Analysis, Techniques to Computer Programs. *The Information Science Discussion*.

Grover, L. K. (1996). A fast quantum mechanical algorithm for database search. In *Proceedings of the 28th Annual ACM symposium on Theory of computing* (pp. 212–219). ACM. 10.1145/237814.237866

Grover, L. K. (1998). Quantum computers can search rapidly by using almost any transformation. *Physical Review Letters, 80*(19), 4329–4332. doi:10.1103/PhysRevLett.80.4329

Gruska, J. (1999). *Quantum computing* (Vol. 2005). McGraw-Hill.

Gruzelier, J. H. (2014). EEG-neurofeedback for optimising performance. I: A review of cognitive and affective outcome in healthy participants. *Neuroscience and Biobehavioral Reviews, 44*, 124–141. doi:10.1016/j.neubiorev.2013.09.015 PMID:24125857

Guo, B., Zhang, D., Wang, Z., Yu, Z., & Zhou, X. (2013). Opportunistic IoT: Exploring the harmonious interaction between human and the internet of things. *Journal of Network and Computer Applications, 36*(6), 1531–1539. doi:10.1016/j.jnca.2012.12.028

Guo, B., Zhang, D., Yu, Z., Liang, Y., Wang, Z., & Zhou, X. (2013). From the internet of things to embedded intelligence. *World Wide Web (Bussum)*, *16*(4), 399–420. doi:10.100711280-012-0188-y

Hallgren, S. (2002). Polynomial-time quantum algorithms for Pell's equation and the principal ideal problem. *Symposium on the Theory of Computation STOC*. 10.1145/509907.510001

Hallgren, S., Russell, A., & Ta-Shma, A. (2003). The hidden subgroup problem and quantum computation using group representations. *SIAM Journal on Computing*, *32*(4), 916–934. doi:10.1137/S009753970139450X

Hariharan, P., & Sanders, B. C. (1996). Quantum phenomena in optical interferometry. *Progress in Optics*, *36*, 49–128. doi:10.1016/S0079-6638(08)70313-5

Harrow, Aram, Hassidim, & Lloyd. (2008). Quantum algorithm for solving linear systems of equations. *Physical Review Letters, 103*. ArXiv: 0811.3171.

Harrow, A. W., Hassidim, A., & Lloyd, S. (2009). Quantum algorithm for linear systems of equations. *Physical Review Letters*, *103*(15), 150502. doi:10.1103/PhysRevLett.103.150502 PMID:19905613

Hensley, B., & Terhorst, J. (2016, Sept. 13). *Heisenberg Uncertainty Principle*. Chemistry 2, Period 8.

Hinton, G. E. (2002). Training products of experts by minimizing contrastive divergence. *Neural Computation*, *14*(8), 1771–1800. doi:10.1162/089976602760128018 PubMed

Hooshmand, R. (2015). *Improving GGH Public Key Scheme Using Low Density Lattice Codes*. Available: https://eprint.iacr.org/2015/229

Hoque, N., Bhattacharyya, D. K., & Kalita, J. K. (2014). MIFS-ND: A mutual information-based feature selection method. *Expert Systems with Applications*, *41*(14), 6371–6385. doi:10.1016/j.eswa.2014.04.019

Hsu, J. (2015). *Google Tests First Error Correction in Quantum Computing*. IEEE Spectrum, (March), 4.

Huang, W., Zhang, J., Haiyan, S. H. M., & Cai, Z. (2017). An Anomaly Detection Method Based on Normalized Mutual Information Feature Selection and Quantum Wavelet Neural Network. In *Wireless Press Communication*. Springer.

Huang, W., Zhang, J., Sun, H., Ma, H., & Cai, Z. (2017). An Anomaly Detection Method Based on Normalized Mutual Information Feature Selection and Quantum Wavelet Neural Network. In *Wireless Personal Communications*. Springer.

Hughes, R. J., Alde, D. M., Dyer, P., Luther, G. G., Morgan, G. L., & Schauer, M. (1995). Quantum cryptography. *Contemporary Physics*, *36*(3), 149–163. doi:10.1080/00107519508222149

Hutchinson, A. (2008). *Popular Mechanics, Lasers Could Send World's Most Secure Messages Through Space*. https://www.popularmechanics.com/space/satellites/a3597/4279669/

Huttner, B., Imoto, N., Gisin, N., & Mor, T. (1995, March). Quantum cryptography with coherent states. *Physical Review A*, *51*(3), 1863–1869. doi:10.1103/PhysRevA.51.1863 PMID:9911795

Iliyasu, A. M. (2013). Towards Realising Secure and Efficient Image and Video Processing Applications on Quantum Computers. *Entropy (Basel, Switzerland)*, *15*(12), 2874–2974. doi:10.3390/e15082874

Islam, S. R., Kwak, D., Kabir, M. H., Hossain, M., & Kwak, K. S. (2015). The internet of things for health care: A comprehensive survey. *IEEE Access: Practical Innovations, Open Solutions*, *3*, 678–708. doi:10.1109/ACCESS.2015.2437951

Ivanyos, G., Sanselme, L., & Santha, M. (2007). An efficient quantum algorithm for the hidden subgroup problem in nil-2 groups. *Algorithmica*, *62*(1-2), 480–498. doi:10.100700453-010-9467-0

Jain, M., Lenka, S. K., & Vasistha, S. K. (2016). Adaptive Circular Queue Image Steganography with RSA Cryptosystem. *Perspectives in Science, 8*, 417–420. doi:10.1016/j.pisc.2016.04.093

Jassim, K. N. (2019). Hybrid Cryptography and Steganography method to Embed Encrypted Text Message with Image. *Journal of Physics: Conference Series, 1339*, 26–27.

Jaynes, E. T., & Cummings, F. W. (1963). Comparison of quantum and semiclassical radiation theories with application to the beam maser. *Proceedings of the IEEE, 51*(1), 89–109. doi:10.1109/PROC.1963.1664

Jobay, R., & Sleit, A. (2014). Quantum inspired shape representation for content based image retrieval. *J Signal Inf Process.*

Johansson, M. (2019). *Synchronization of Acoustic Sensors in a Wireless Network.* Academic Press.

Johnson, C. (2013). *Forensic Software Engineering: Are Software Failures Symptomatic of Systemic Problems?* Department of Computing Science, University of Glasgow. http://www.dcs.gla.ac.uk/~johnson

Jones, A. Z. (2016). *What is Quantum Entanglement.* Thought Co.

Jones, G. M. (2017). Forensics Analysis on Smart Phones Using Mobile Forensics Tools. *IJIR,* (8), 1859.

Jordan, S. (n.d.). *The Quantum Algorithm Zoo.* Retrieved March 10, 2020, from https://quantumalgorithmzoo.org

Jordan, M. I., & Mitchell, T. M. (2015). Machine learning: Trends, perspectives, and prospects. *Science, 349*(6245), 255–260. doi:10.1126cience.aaa8415 PMID:26185243

Joshi, K., Swati Gill, S., & Yadav, R. (2018). A New Method of Image Steganography using 7th bit of a Pixel as Indicator by Introducing the Successive Temporary Pixel in the Grayscale Image. *Journal of Computer Networks and Communication.* doi:10.1155/2018/9475142

Jozsa, R. (2003). *Notes on Hallgren's efficient quantum algorithm for solving Pell's equation.* Technical report, quant-ph/0302134.

Jozsa, R. (2001). Quantum factoring, discrete logarithms and the hidden subgroup problem. *Computing in Science & Engineering, 3*(2), 34–43. doi:10.1109/5992.909000

Kaci, A., & Bouabana-Tebibel, T. (2014). Access Control Reinforcement over Searchable Encryption. *IEEE IRI 2014,* 130-137.

Kak, S. C. (1995). Quantum neural computing. *Advances in Imaging and Electron Physics, 94*, 259–313.

Kamm'uller, F., Kerber, M., & Probst, C. W. (2017). Insider threats and auctions: Formalization, mechanized proof, and code generation. *Journal of Wireless Mobile Networks, Ubiquitous Computing and Dependable Applications, 8*(1), 44–78.

Karie, N. M., & Venter, H. S. (2014). *Towards a General Ontology for Digital Forensic Disciplines.* Department of Computer Science, University of Pretoria. https://onlinelibrary.wiley.com/doi/abs/10.1111/1556-4029.12511

Karyda, M., & Mitrou, L. (2007). *Internet Forensics: Legal and Technical Issues.* IEEE.

Kerenidis, I., Landman, J., & Luongo, A. (2019). q-means: A quantum algorithm for unsupervised machine learning. *33rd Conference on Neural Information Processing Systems (NeurIPS 2019).*

Khan & Hussain. (2019). A Privacy Scheme for Digital Images Based on Quantum. *International Journal of Theoretical Physics.* doi:10.100710773-019-04301-6

Khan, S., Abdullah, J., Khan, N., Julahi, A. A., & Tarmizi, S. (2017). *Quantum-Elliptic curve Cryptography for Multihop Communication in 5G Networks.* IJCSNS International Journal of Computer Science and Network Security.

Kim, J., Benson, O., Kan, H., & Yamamoto, Y. (1999). A single-photon turnstile device. *Nature, 397*(6719), 500–503. doi:10.1038/17295

Kim, P. H., Yoon, E. J., Ryu, K. W., & Jung, K. H. (2019). Data-Hiding Scheme Using Multidirectional Pixel-Value Differencing on Color Images. *Security and Communication Networks, 2019*, 1–11. Advance online publication. doi:10.1155/2019/9038650

Kitaev, A. Y. (1995). *Quantum measurements and the Abelian stabilizer problem.* Retrieved March 15, 2020 from arxiv.org, quant-ph/9511026

Kleinjung, T. (2010). Factorization of a 768-Bit RSA Modulus. *Advances in Cryptology – CRYPTO 2010. LNCS, 6223*, 333–350.

Knapp, A. (2013). *Los Alamos, Scientists Build a prototype Quantum Network.* www.forbes.com

Knuth, D. E. (1981). The Art of Computer Programming, Vol. 2: Seminumerical Algorithms. Addison-Wesley.

Ko, H., & Song, M. (2016). A study on the secure user profiling structure and procedure for home healthcare systems. *Journal of Medical Systems, 40*(1), 1. doi:10.100710916-015-0365-5 PMID:26573639

Konstadopoulou, A. (2006). From Quantum Security to Quantum Forensics. *Proc. 1st Conference on Advances in Computer Security and Forensics (ACSF).*

Korolov & Drinkwater. (2019). https://www.csoonline.com/article/3235970/what-is-quantum-cryptography-it-s-no-silver-bullet-but-could-improve-security.html

Kotsiantis, S. B., Zaharakis, I., & Pintelas, P. (2007). Supervised machine learning: A review of classification techniques. *Emerging Artificial Intelligence Applications in Computer Engineering, 160*, 3-24.

Kulchytskyy, B., Andriyash, E., Amin, M., & Melko, R. (2016). Quantum boltzmann machine. In *APS Meeting Abstracts.* Academic Press.

Kulkarni & Harihar. (2012). Research directions in quantum cryptography and quantum key distribution. *International Journal of Scientific and Research Publications, 2*, 6.

Kumar, V. (2014). *Text Encryption using Lattice-Based Cryptography. IOSR Journal of Computer Engineering* , 16.

Kuperberg, G. (2005). A subexponential-time quantum algorithm for the dihedral hidden subgroup problem. *SIAM Journal on Computing, 35*(1), 170–188. doi:10.1137/S0097539703436345

Kurzyk, D. (2012). Introduction to Quantum Entanglement. Institute of Mathematics, Silesian University of Technology.

L¨utkenhaus, N. (1999). *Security against individual attacks for realistic quantum key distribution.* Los Alamos Archives quant-ph/9910093.

L¨utkenhaus, N. (1999). Security of quantum cryptography with realistic sources. *Acta Physica Slovaca, 49*, 549–556.

L¨utkenhaus, N. (2000). Dim coherent states as signal states in the BB84 protocol: Is it secure? In P. Kumar, G. Mauro D'Ariano, & O. Hirota (Eds.), *Quantum Communication,Computing, and Measurement 2* (pp. 387–392). Kluwer Academic/Plenum Publishers.

Ladd, T. D., Jelezko, F., Laflamme, R., Nakamura, Y., Monroe, C., & O'Brien, J. L. (2010). Quantum computers. *Nature, 464*(7285), 45–53. doi:10.1038/nature08812 PMID:20203602

Lamata. (2020). Quantum machine learning and quantum biomimetics: A perspective. Machine Learning: Science and Technology 2020.

Langton, C. G. (1997). *Artificial Life: An overview*. MIT Press.

LaRose, R., Tikku, A., O'Neel-Judy, É., Cincio, L., & Coles, P. J. (2019). Variational quantum state diagonalization. *NPJ Quantum Information, 5*(1), 1-10.

Latorre, J. (2005). Image compression and entanglement. arXiv:quant-ph/0510031

Lee, M., & Cho, J.-D. (2014). Logmusic: context-based social music recommendation service on mobile device. In *Proceedings of the ACM International Joint Conference on Pervasive and Ubiquitous Computing (UbiComp '14)* (pp. 95–98). 10.1145/2638728.2638749

Lenstra, A. K., Lenstra Jr., H. W. (1993). The Development of the Number Field Sieve. *LNM, 1554*.

Lenstra, A. K., Lenstra, H. W., Manasse, M. S., & Pollard, J. M. (1990). The number field sieve. In *Proceedings of the 22nd Annual ACM Symposium on Theory of Computing* (pp. 564-572). ACM.

Le, P. Q., Dong, F., & Hirota, K. (2011). A flexible representation of quantum images for polynomial preparation, image compression, and processing operations. *Quantum Information Processing, 10*(1), 63–84. doi:10.100711128-010-0177-y

Le, P., & Iliyasu, A. (2011). *A flexible representation and invertible transformations for images on quantum computer, New advances in intelligent signal processing of studies in computational intelligence*. Springer.

Leprince-Ringuet, D. (2020). *ZDNet, What is the quantum internet? Everything you need to know about the weird future of quantum networks*. https://www.zdnet.com/article/what-is-the-quantum-internet-everything-you-need-to-know-about-the-weird-future-of-quantum-networks/

Li, J., Shi, Y., Zhang, Y. (2015). Searchable ciphertext-policy attribute-based encryption with revocation in cloud storage. *International Journal of Communication Systems International Journal of Communication System*.

Li, R., Alvarez-Rodriguez, U., Lamata, L., & Solano, E. (2017). Approximate Quantum Adders with Genetic Algorithms: An IBM Quantum Experience. Quantum Measurements and Quantum Metrology, 4(1), 1–7. doi:10.1515/qmetro-2017-0001

Liang, G., & Cao, J. (2013). CircleSense: a pervasive computing system for recognizing social activities. In *Proceedings of the 11th IEEE International Conference on Pervasive Computing and Communications (PerCom '13)* (pp. 201–206). IEEE.

LibreTexts. (2020). *Chemistry, Heisenberg's uncertainty principle*. https://chem.libretexts.org/Bookshelves/Physical_and_Theoretical_Chemistry_Textbook_Maps/Supplemental_Modules_(Physical_and_Theoretical_Chemistry)/Quantum_Mechanics/02._Fundamental_Concepts_of_Quantum_Mechanics/Heisenberg%27s_Uncertainty_Principle

Li, J. (2015). Quantum-inspired neural networks with application. *Ozean Journal of Applied Sciences, 5*(06), 233.

Li, J., Li, J., Xie, D., & Cai, Z. (2016). Secure auditing and deduplicating data in cloud. *IEEE Transactions on Computers, 65*(8), 2386–2396. doi:10.1109/TC.2015.2389960

Lin, Chen, Zhu, Yang, & Fengguo. (2018). Automated forensic analysis of mobile applications on Android devices. *Science Direct Digital Investigation Journal*.

Littman, M. L., & Szepesvári, C. (1996). A generalized reinforcement-learning model: Convergence and applications. In ICML (Vol. 96, pp. 310-318). Academic Press.

Liu, N., & Rebentrost, P. (2018). Quantum machine learning for quantum anomaly detection. Physical Review A, 97(4).

Liu, N., & Rebentrost, P. (2018). Quantum machine learning for quantum anomaly detection. *Physical Review Letters, 97*, 042315.

Li, Z., Liu, X., Xu, N., & Du, J. (2015). Experimental Realization of a Quantum Support Vector Machine. *Physical Review Letters*, *114*(14), 140504. doi:10.1103/PhysRevLett.114.140504 PubMed

Lloret, J., Canovas, A., Sendra, S., & Parra, L. (2015). A smart communication architecture for ambient assisted living. *IEEE Communications Magazine*, *53*(1), 26–33. doi:10.1109/MCOM.2015.7010512

Lloyd, S. & Shabrias, M. S. (2000). *Teleportation and Quantum Internet*. Massachusetts Institute of Technology.

Lloyd, S., Mohseni, M., & Rebentrost, P. (2013). Quantum algorithms for supervised and unsupervised machine learning. *Nature*.

Lloyd, S., Mohseni, M., & Rebentrost, P. (2014). Quantum principal component analysis. *Nature Physics*, *10*(9), 631–633. doi:10.1038/nphys3029

Lo, B. P., Ip, H., & Yang, G. Z. (2016). *Transforming health care: body sensor networks, wearables, and the internet of things*. Academic Press.

Lo, H. -K, & Chau, H. F. (1999). Unconditional Security of Quantum Key Distribution over Arbitrarily Long Distances. *Science*, *283*(5410), 2050-2056.

Long, P. M., & Servedio, R. (2010). Restricted Boltzmann machines are hard to approximately evaluate or simulate. In *Proc. of the 27th Int. Conf. on Machine Learning (ICML-10)*, (pp. 703–710). Brookline, MA: Microtome Publishing.

Loo, C. K., Peruš, M., & Bischof, H. (2004). Associative memory based image and object recognition by quantum holography. *Open Systems & Information Dynamics*, *11*(03), 277–289.

Lopez, E. M., Laing, A., Lawson, T., Alvarez, R., Zhou, X.-Q., & O'Brien, J. L. (2012). Experimental realisation of Shor's quantum factoring algorithm using qubit recycling. *Nature Photonics*, *6*(11), 773–776. doi:10.1038/nphoton.2012.259

Lorente, A. S., & Berres, S. (2017). A Secure Steganographic Algorithm Based on Frequency Domain for the Transmission of Hidden Information. *Security and Communication Networks*, *2017*, 1–14. Advance online publication. doi:10.1155/2017/5397082

Lütkenhaus, N. (n.d.). *Security against eavesdropping in quantum cryptography*. Physical.

Ma, C., Kulshrestha, S., Shi, W., Okada, Y., & Bose, R. (2018). E-learning material development framework supporting vr/ar based on linked data for iot security education. In *International Conference on Emerging Internetworking, Data & Web Technologies* (pp. 479–491). Springer. 10.1007/978-3-319-75928-9_43

Macdonald, F. (2019). *Science Alert, Scientists Just Unveiled The First-Ever Photo of Quantum Entanglement*. https://www.sciencealert.com/scientists-just-unveiled-the-first-ever-photo-of-quantum-entanglement

Mahalik, H., & Tamma, R. (2014). *Practical Mobile Forensics* (2nd ed.). https://hub.packtpub.com/mobile-forensics-and-its-challanges/

Malaney, R. (2010). Location-dependent communications using quantum entanglement. *Physical Review A.*, *81*(4). Advance online publication. doi:10.1103/PhysRevA.81.042319

Maltseva, D. (2018). *IoT Solutions for Healthcare Providers*. https://www.iotforall.com/topdigital-health-solutions/

Marand, C., & Townsend, P. D. (1995, August). Quantum key distribution over distances as long as 30 km. *Optics Letters*, *20*(15), 1695–1697. doi:10.1364/OL.20.001695 PMID:19862127

Margalikas, E., & Ramanauskaitė, S. (2019). Image steganography based on color palette transformation in color space. *J Image Video Proc.*, *82*(1), 82. Advance online publication. doi:10.118613640-019-0484-x

Marsland, S. (2015). *Machine learning: an algorithmic perspective*. CRC Press.

Martinis, J. (2019, October 23). *Google AI Blog*. Retrieved from ai.googleblog.com: https://ai.googleblog.com/2019/10/quantum-supremacy-using-programmable.html

Mashal, I., Alsaryrah, O., Chung, T.-Y., Yang, C.-Z., Kuo, W.-H., & Agrawal, D. P. (2015). Choices for interaction with things on Internet and underlying issues. *Ad Hoc Networks, 28*, 68–90. doi:10.1016/j.adhoc.2014.12.006

Mathew, A., Sa, F. A., Pooja, H. R., & Verma, A. (2015). Smart disease surveillance based on Internet of Things (IoT). *International Journal of Advanced Research in Computer and Communication Engineering, 4*(5), 180-183.

Ma, W. (2018). *Tresp*. Quantum Machine Learning Algorithm for Knowledge Graphs., doi:10.1145/1122445.1122456

Mayers. (1996). Quantum key distribution and string oblivious transfer in noisy channels. In *Advances in Cryptology: Proceedings of Crypto'96, Lecture Notes in Computer Science*, (Vol. 1109). Springer-Verlag.

Mayers, D. (2001). Unconditional security in quantum cryptography. *Journal of the Association for Computing Machinery, 48*(3), 351–406. doi:10.1145/382780.382781

McEliece, R. (1978). *A public-key cryptosystem based on algebraic number theory*. Technical report, DSN Progress Report 42-44, Jet Propulsion Laboratory.

McGrath, M. J., & Scanaill, C. N. (2013). *Body-worn, ambient, and consumer sensing for health applications. In Sensor Technologies*. Springer.

Mehrdad, S. (2009). Quantum Cryptography: A New Generation of Information Technology Security System. *Sixth International Conference on Information Technology: New Generations*, 1644-1647.

Micciancio, D. (2001). Improving Lattice Based Cryptosystems Using the Hermite Normal Form. In Cryptography and Lattices. CaLC 2001, Lecture Notes in Computer Science, vol 2146. Springer. doi:10.1007/3-540-44670-2_11

Miller, L. (1976). Riemann's hypothesis and tests for primality. *Journal of Computer and System Sciences, 13*(3), 300–313. doi:10.1016/S0022-0000(76)80043-8

Misbahuddin, M., & Sreeja, C. S. (2015). A Secure Image-Based Authentication Scheme Employing DNA Crypto and Steganography. *Proceedings of the Third International Symposium on Women in Computing and Informatics - WCI '15*. 10.1145/2791405.2791503

MIT Technology Review. (2013, May 6). *Government Lab Reveals It has Operated Quantum Internet for over Two Years*. Author.

Mohay, G. M., Anderson, A. A., Collie, B., McKemmish, R. D., & de Vel, O. (2003). *Computer and Intrusion Forensics*. Artech House.

Montanaro, A. (2016). Quantum algorithms: an overview. *NPJ Quantum Information, 2*, 15023.

Morales, G. (2015). Luna, Quantum Communication Protocols based on Entanglement Swapping. Computer Science Department, CINVESTAV - IPN, Mexico City, Mexico.

Mosca, M. (2018). Cybersecurity in an era with quantum computers: will we be ready? Institute for Quantum Computing and Department of Combinatorics and Optimization. University of Waterloo. doi:10.1109/MSP.2018.3761723

Mowla, N. I., Doh, I., & Chae, K. (2016). Securing information flow in content delivery networks with visual and quantum cryptography. *2016 International Conference on Information Networking (ICOIN)*, 463-468. 10.1109/ICOIN.2016.7427160

Murthy. (2019). *Novel Chaotic Quantum Based Homomorphic CPABE Authentication Protocol against Malicious Attack in Wireless Communication Networks*. Doi:10.6025/Jisr/2019/10/1/1-17

Narayanan, A., & Menneer, T. (2000). Quantum artificial neural network architectures and components. *Information Sciences*, *128*(3-4), 231–255. doi:10.1016/S0020-0255(00)00055-4

NASA. (2019). *Google and NASA Achieve Quantum Supremacy*. https://www.nasa.gov/feature/ames/quantum-supremacy/

Nayak, A., & Wu, F. (1999, May). The quantum query complexity of approximating the median and related statistics. In *Proceedings of the thirty-first annual ACM symposium on Theory of computing* (pp. 384-393). ACM.

Nelson, P. (2019). *Network World, Breakthroughs bring a quantum internet closer*. https://www.networkworld.com/article/3432509/breakthroughs-bring-a-quantum-internet-closer.html

Neven, H., Denchev, V. S., Drew-Brook, M., Zhang, J., Macready, W. G., & Rose, G. (2009). Binary classification using hardware implementation of quantum annealing Demonstrations at NIPS-09. In *24th Annual Conf. on Neural Information Processing Systems* (pp. 1-17). Academic Press.

Neven, J. R. (2020). Decoding Quantum Errors Using Subspace Expansions. *Nature Communications*, 636. PMID:32005804

Nguyen, P. Q. (1999). Cryptanalysis of the Goldreich-Goldwasser-Halevi Cryptosystem. *LNCS*, *1666*, 288–304.

Nield, D. (2019). *Science Alert, Physicists Just Achieved The First-Ever Quantum Teleportation Between Computer Chips*. https://www.sciencealert.com/scientists-manage-quantum-teleportation-between-computer-chips-for-the-first-time

Nielsen, M. A., & Chuang, I. (2002). *Quantum computation and quantum information*. Academic Press.

Nielsen, M. A., & Chuang, I. L. (2010). *Quantum Computation and Quantum Information*. Cambridge University Press. doi:10.1017/CBO9780511976667

Nolan, R. (2005). First Responders Guide to Computer Forensics. Academic Press.

O'Dowd. (2017). https://hitinfrastructure.com/news/how-ibm-universal-quantum-computing-impacts-hit-infrastructure

O'Gorman, B., Babbush, R., Perdomo-Ortiz, A., Aspuru-Guzik, A., & Smelyanskiy, V. (2015). Bayesian network structure learning using quantum annealing. *The European Physical Journal. Special Topics*, *224*(1), 163–188.

OSI Model: The 7 Layers Explained. (2014, April 12). *Skill Gurukul*.

Ostaszewski, M., Sadowski, P., & Gawron, P. (2015). *Quantum image classification using principal component analysis*. arXiv preprint arXiv:1504.00580.

Overill, R. E. (2012). *Digital quantum forensics: future challenges and prospects*. Department of Informatics, King's College London.

Overill, R.E., & Silomon, J.A.M. (2010). Digital Meta-Forensics: Quantifying the Investigation. *Proc. 4th International Conference on Cybercrime Forensics Education and Training (CFET 2010)*.

Paeng, S. H., Jung, B. E., & Ha, K. C. (2003). *A Lattice Based Public Key Cryptosystem Using Polynomial Representations. In Proc. Public Key Cryptography — PKC 2003* (Vol. 2567). Springer.

Panella, M., & Martinelli, G. (2008). Neurofuzzy networks with nonlinear quantum learning. *IEEE Transactions on Fuzzy Systems*, *17*(3), 698–710.

Pantelopoulos, A., & Bourbakis, N. G. (2010). A survey on wearable sensor-based systems for health monitoring and prognosis. *IEEE Transactions on Systems, Man and Cybernetics. Part C, Applications and Reviews, 40*(1), 1–12. doi:10.1109/TSMCC.2009.2032660

Park, K. C., & Shin, D.-H. (2017). Security assessment framework for iot service. *Telecommunication Systems, 64*(1), 193–209. doi:10.100711235-016-0168-0

Parvez, S., Dehghantanha, A., & Broujerdi, H. G. (2011). *Framework of digital forensics for the Samsung Star Series phone. ICECT'11.*

Patil, P. A., & Boda, R. (2016). Analysis of Cryptography: Classical verses Quantum Cryptography. *International Research Journal of Engineering and Technology, 3*(5), 1372–1376.

Patinformatics. (2018). *Quantum Computing Applications: A Patent Landscape Report.* Patinformatics, LLC. https://patinformatics.com/wp-content/uploads/2018/01/Quantum-Applications-Patent-Landscape-Report-Opt.pdf

Pednault Edwin, J. A. (2019, October 22). *Cornell University.* Retrieved from arxiv.org: https://arxiv.org/abs/1910.09534

Peikert, C. (2016). A decade of lattice cryptography. *Foundations and Trends in Theoretical Computer Science, 10*(4), 283–424. doi:10.1561/0400000074

Perera, C., Zaslavsky, A., Christen, P., & Georgakopoulos, D. (2013). Context aware computing for the internet of things: A survey. *IEEE Communications Surveys and Tutorials, 16*(1), 414–454. doi:10.1109/SURV.2013.042313.00197

Pfeiffer, P., Egusquiza, I. L., Di Ventra, M., Sanz, M., & Solano, E. (2016). Quantum Memristors. *Scientific Reports, 6*(1), 29507. doi:10.1038/srep29507 PubMed

Picard, R. W., & Picard, R. (1997). *Affective Computing* (Vol. 252). MIT Press.

Pirandola, S., & Braunstein, S. L. (2016, April). Physics: Unite to Build a Quantum Internet. *Nature Photonics.*

Plantard, T., Rose, M., & Susilo, W. (2009). Improvement of lattice-based cryptography using CRT. *Proc. QuantumComm'09*, 275-282.

Pramanik, S., Bandyopadhyay, S. K., & Ghosh, R. (2020). Signature Image Hiding in Color Image using Steganography and Cryptography based on Digital Signature Concepts. *2020 2nd International Conference on Innovative Mechanisms for Industry Applications (ICIMIA)*, 665-669. 10.1109/ICIMIA48430.2020.9074957

Pramanik, S., & Bandyopadhyay, S. (2013). Application of Steganography in Symmetric Key Cryptography with Genetic Algorithm. *International Journal of Computers and Technology, 10*(7), 1791–1799. doi:10.24297/ijct.v10i7.7027

Pramanik, S., & Bandyopadhyay, S. K. (2014). An Innovative Approach in Steganography. *Scholar Journal of Engineering and Technology, 2*(2B), 276–280.

Pramanik, S., & Raja, S. S. (2019). Analytical Study on Security Issues in Steganography. *Think India Journal, 22*(3), 106–114.

Pramanik, S., Singh, R. P., & Ghosh, R. (2019). A New Encrypted Method in Image Steganography. *Indonesian Journal of Electrical Engineering and Computer Science, 14*(3), 1412–1419. doi:10.11591/ijeecs.v14.i3.pp1412-1419

Pramanik, S., Singh, R. P., & Ghosh, R. (2020). *Application of bi-orthogonal wavelet transform and genetic algorithm in image steganography. Multimed Tools Appl.* doi:10.100711042-020-08676-1

Pramanik, S., Singh, R. P., Ghosh, R., & Bandyopadhyay, S. K. (2020). A Unique Way to Generate Password at Random Basis and Sending it Using a New Steganography Technique. *Indonesian Journal of Electrical Engineering and Informatics*, *8*(3). Advance online publication. doi:10.11591/ijeei.v8i3.831

Prasad, S., & Pal, A. K. (2017). An RGB colour image steganography scheme using overlapping block-based pixel-value differencing. *Royal Society Open Science*, *4*(4), 161066. doi:10.1098/rsos.161066 PMID:28484623

Quantaneo. (2019). *Delft University of Technology, World's first link layer protocol brings Quantum Internet closer to reality.* https://www.quantaneo.com/%E2%80%8BWorld-s-first-link-layer-protocol-brings-quantum-internet-closer-to-a-reality_a152.html

Quantum Key Distribution, Intercept and Resend. (2017). In *Wikipedia*.

Quantum Resistant Public Key Exchange: The Supersingular Isogenous Diffie-Hellman Protocol. (2016). CoinFabrik Blog.

Rao, S. (2019). *Evolution of IoT in Healthcare.* https://www.iotforall.com/evolution-iot-healthcare

Razzaque, M. A., Milojevic-Jevric, M., Palade, A., & Cla, S. (2016). Middleware for internet of things: A survey. *IEEE Internet of Things Journal*, *3*(1), 70–95. doi:10.1109/JIOT.2015.2498900

Rebentrost, P., Mohseni, M., & Lloyd, S. (2014). Quantum support vector machine for big data classification. *Physical Review Letters*, *113*(13), 130503. doi:10.1103/PhysRevLett.113.130503 PMID:25302877

Rebentrost, P., Mohseni, M., & Lloyd, S. (2014). Quantum Support Vector Machine for Big Data Classification. *Physical Review Letters*, *113*(13), 130503. doi:10.1103/PhysRevLett.113.130503 PubMed

Regev, O. (2003). New lattice based cryptographic constructions. *Proc. 35th ACM Symp. on Theory of Computing*.

Regev, O. (2004). Quantum computation and lattice problems. *SIAM Journal on Computing*, *33*(3), 738–760.

Regev, O. (2009). On lattices, learning with errors, random linear codes, and cryptography. *Journal of the Association for Computing Machinery*, *56*(1), 1–40.

Rehman, A., Saba, T., Mahmood, T., Mehmood, Z., Shah, M., & Anjum, A. (2019). Data hiding technique in steganography for information security using number theory. *Journal of Information Science*, *45*(6), 767–778. doi:10.1177/0165551518816303

Rghioui, A., & Oumnad, A. (2017). Internet of Things: Surveys for Measuring Human Activities from Everywhere. *International Journal of Electrical & Computer Engineering*, *7*(5).

Rghioui, A., & Oumnad, A. (2018). Challenges and Opportunities of Internet of Things in Healthcare. *International Journal of Electrical & Computer Engineering*, *8*.

Rghioui, A., Sendra, S., Lloret, J., & Oumnad, A. (2016). Internet of things for measuring human activities in ambient assisted living and e-health. *Network Protocols and Algorithms*, *8*(3), 15–28. doi:10.5296/npa.v8i3.10146

Ricks, B., & Ventura, D. (2004). Training a quantum neural network. In Advances in neural information processing systems (pp. 1019-1026). Academic Press.

Rigatos, G. G., & Tzafestas, S. G. (2006). Quantum learning for neural associative memories. *Fuzzy Sets and Systems*, *157*(13), 1797–1813.

Rivest, L., Shamir, A., & Adleman, L. (1978). A method of obtaining digital signatures and public-key cryptosystems. *Comm. Assoc. Comput. Math.*, *21*, 120–126.

Romero, J., Olson, J. P., & Aspuru-Guzik, A. (2017). Quantum auto-encoders for efficient compression of quantum data. Quantum Science and Technology, 2(4), 045001. doi:10.1088/2058-9565/aa8072

Romero, J., Olson, J., & Aspuru-Guzik, A. (2017). Quantum auto encoders for efficient compression of quantum data. Quantum Science and Technology, 2(4), 045001. doi:10.1088/2058-9565/aa8072

Rose, M. (2011). *Lattice-Based Cryptography: A Practical Implementation* (M.Sc. thesis). School of Computer Science and Software Engineering, University of Wollongong, New South Wales, Australia.

Ruan, Y., Xue, X., Liu, H., Tan, J., & Li, X. (2017). Quantum algorithm for k-nearest neighbors classification based on the metric of hamming distance. *International Journal of Theoretical Physics*, 56(11), 3496–3507.

Rubin, N. (2020). *Quantum Physics, "Hartree-Fock on a superconducting qubit quantum computer"*. https://arxiv.org/abs/2004.04174

Sachowski, J. (2018). *Digital Forensics and Investigations: People, Process, and Technologies*. CRC Press.

Sakthi Vignesh, R., Sudharssun, S., & Jegadish Kumar, K. J. (2009). Limitations of Quantum & The Versatility of Classical Cryptography: A Comparative Study. *Second International Conference on Environmental and Computer Science*, 333-337.

Sallis, Asbjorn, & MacDonell. (1996). Software Forensics: old methods for a new science. IEEE.

Salmilehto, J., Deppe, F., Di Ventra, M., Sanz, M., & Solano, E. (2017). Quantum Memristors with Superconducting Circuits. *Scientific Reports*, 7(1), 42044. doi:10.1038/srep42044 PubMed

Sank, D. (2019, February 7). *Google Research*. Retrieved from https://research.google.com: https://youtu.be/uPw9nkJAwDY

Sawand, A., Djahel, S., Zhang, Z., & Nait-Abdesselam, F. (2015). Toward energy-efficient and trustworthy eHealth monitoring system. *China Communications*, 12(1), 46–65. doi:10.1109/CC.2015.7084383

Scherping, N. (2016, Sept. 20). *Discover Magazine, Quantum Teleportation Enters the Real World*. https://www.discovermagazine.com/the-sciences/quantum-teleportation-enters-the-real-world

Schuld, M., Bocharov, A., Svore, K. M., & Wiebe, N. (2020). Circuit-centric quantum classifiers. *Physical Review. A,* 101(3), 032308.

Schuld, M., & Killoran, N. (2018). Quantum Machine Learning in Feature Hilbert Spaces. *Physical Review Letters*, 122(4), 040504. doi:10.1103/PhysRevLett.122.040504 PubMed

Schuld, M., & Petruccione, F. (2018). Quantum ensembles of quantum classifiers. *Scientific Reports*, 8(1), 1–12.

Schuld, M., Sinayskiy, I., & Petruccione, F. (2014). The quest for a quantum neural network. *Quantum Information Processing*, 13(11), 2567–2586.

Schuld, M., Sinayskiy, I., & Petruccione, F. (2015). An introduction to quantum machine learning. *Contemporary Physics*, 56(2), 172–185. doi:10.1080/00107514.2014.964942

Schuld, M., Sinayskiy, I., & Petruccione, F. (2016). Prediction by linear regression on a quantum computer. *Physical Review Letters*, 94(2), 022342.

Sen, D. (2014). The Uncertainty relations in quantum mechanics. *Current Science*, 107(2), 203–218.

Sergio Boixo, S. V. (2018). Characterizing quantum supremacy in near-term devices. *Nature Physics*, 595-600.

Sharbaf, M. S. (2011). Quantum Cryptography: An Emerging Technology in Network Security. Loyola Marymount University, California State University, Northridge.

Sharma & Khaliq. (2020). *A review on software forensics and software quality approach.* Department of Computer Science & IT, Khwaja Moinuddin Chishti Urdu, Arabi-Farsi University.

Sharma & Thind. (2019). A Quantum Key Distribution Technique Using Quantum Cryptography. *International Journal of Distributed Artificial Intelligence.*

Sharma, A., & Bhatt, A. P. (2019, September). Science Direct, Quantum Cryptography for Internet of Things Security. *Journal of Electronic Science and Technology, 17*(3). Retrieved November 28, 2020, from https://www.sciencedirect.com/science/article/pii/S1674862X19300345

Sharma, A., Ojha, V., & Goar, V. (2010, May). Security aspect of quantum key distribution. *International Journal of Computers and Applications, 2*(2), 58–62. doi:10.5120/625-885

Sharma, V., Lee, K., Kwon, S., Kim, J., Park, H., Yim, K., & Lee, S.-Y. (2017). *A consensus framework for reliability and mitigation of zero-day attacks in iot* (Vol. 2017). Security and Communication Networks.

SheaS. (2020). https://searchsecurity.techtarget.com/feature/Computer-Security-Fundamentals-Quantum-security-to-certifications

Sheng, Y.-B., & Zhou, L. (2017). distributed secure quantum machine learning. Science Bulletin, 62(14), 1025–1029. Advance online publication. doi:10.1016/j.scib.2017.06.007

Shor, P.W. (1994). Algorithms for quantum computation: discrete logarithms and factoring. *Proceedings 35th Annual Symposium on Foundations of Computer Science.* Doi:10.1109fcs.1994.365700

Shore, P. W., & Preskill, J. (2000). Simple Proof of Security of the BB84 Quantum Key Distribution Protocol. *Physical Review Letter, 85*(2), 441.

Shor, P. W. (1994). Algorithms for quantum computation: discrete logarithms and factoring. In *Proceedings of 35th Annual Symposium on Foundations of Computer Science* (pp. 124–134). Santa Fe, NM: IEEE.

Shor, P. W. (1994). Algorithms for quantum computation: discrete logarithms and factoring. *Proc. 35th Annual Symposium on Foundations of Computer Science,* 124-134. 10.1109/SFCS.1994.365700

Shor, P. W. (1997). Polynomial-time algorithms for prime factorization and discrete logarithms on a quantum computer. *SIAM Journal on Computing, 26*(5), 1484–1509.

Shouty, N. H., & Jackson, J. C. (1998). Learning DNF over the uniform distribution using a quantum example oracle. *SIAM Journal on Computing, 28,* 1136–1153. doi:10.1137/S0097539795293123

Silva, A., de Oliveira, W., & Ludermir, T. (2010). A weightless neural node based on a probabilistic quantum memory. 2010 Eleventh Brazilian Symposium on Neural Networks, 259–264. doi:10.1109/SBRN.2010.52

Singh, M. P., Radhey, K., Saraswat, V., & Kumar, S. (2017). Classification of patterns representing apples and oranges in three-qubit system. *Quantum Information Processing, 16*(1), 16. doi:10.1007/s11128-016-1472-z

Singh, M. P., & Rajput, B. S. (2016). Applications of Singh-Rajput MES in recall operations of quantum associative memory for a two-qubit system. *International Journal of Theoretical Physics, 55*(3), 1753–1770.

Singh, R. (2016). A proposal for mobile e-care health service system using IoT for Indian scenario. *Journal of Network Communications and Emerging Technologies, 6*(1).

Slattery, O. T. (2020). *Quantum Communications and Networks.* https://www.nist.gov/people/oliver-t-slattery

Smolensky, P. (1986). Information processing in dynamical systems: foundations of harmony theory. Technical Report no. CU-CS-321-86. University of Colorado Boulder, Department of Computer Science.

Sokouti, M., Zakerolhosseini, A., & Sokouti, B. (2016). Medical Image Encryption: An Application for Improved Padding Based GGH Encryption Algorithm. *The Open Medical Informatics Journal*, *10*(1), 11–22. doi:10.2174/1874431101610010011 PMID:27857824

Song, Wang, El-Latif, & Niu. (2014). Quantum image encryption based on restricted geometric and color transformations. *Quantum Inf Process*. doi:10.100711128-014-0768-0

Song, Z., & Sun, W. (2019). *Efficient model-free reinforcement learning in metric spaces.* arXiv preprint: 1905.00475.

Sousa, R. S., dos Santos, P. G. M., Verasa, T. M. L., de Oliveirac, W. R., & da Silva, A. J. (2020). Parametric probabilistic Quantum memory. *Neurocomputing*, *416*, 360–369. doi:10.1016/j.neucom.2020.01.116

Spiller, T. P. (1996, December). Quantum Information Processing: Cryptography, Computation, and Teleportation. *Proceedings of the IEEE*, *84*(12), 1719–1746. doi:10.1109/5.546399

Springer, P. O. (2019). *Quantifying how much quantum information can be eavesdropped.* https://phys.org/news/2019-01-quantifying-quantum-eavesdropped.html

Sreekanth, K. U., & Nitha, K. P. (2016). A study on health care in Internet of Things. *International Journal on Recent and Innovation Trends in Computing and Communication*, *4*(2), 44–47.

Srivastava, M., Moulick, S. R., & Panigrahi, P. K. (2013). *Quantum image representation through two-dimensional quantum states and normalized amplitude.* arXiv:1305.2251

Sufyan. (n.d.). *Defeating Man-in-the-Middle Attack in Quantum Key Distribution.* Academic Press.

Swain, G. (2019). Very High Capacity Image Steganography Technique Using Quotient Value Differencing and LSB Substitution. *Arabian Journal for Science and Engineering*, *44*(4), 2995–3004. doi:10.100713369-018-3372-2

Tang, E. (2019). Quantum-inspired classical algorithms for principal component analysis and supervised clustering, University of Washington. *Nature*.

Tan, R., Lei, T., Zhao, Q., Gong, L.-H., & Zhou, Z.-H. (2016). Quantum Color Image Encryption Algorithm Based on A Hyper-Chaotic System and Quantum Fourier Transform. *International Journal of Theoretical Physics*, *55*(12), 5368–5384. doi:10.100710773-016-3157-x

Thapliyal, K., & Pathak, A. (2018). Kak's three-stage protocol of secure quantum communication revisited. *Quantum Information Processing*, *17*(9). Advance online publication. doi:10.100711128-018-2001-z

Tibbetts. (2019). *Quantum Computing and Cryptography: Analysis, Risks, and Recommendations for Decisionmakers.* Center for Global Security Research, Lawrence Livermore National Laboratory.

Tittel, W., Sanders, B. C., & Lvovsky, A. I. (2009). Optical quantum memory. *Nature Photonics*, *3*(12).

Van Emde Boas, P. (1981). *Another NP-complete partition problem and the complexity of computing short vectors in a lattice.* Technical report 8104, University of Amsterdam.

Vas, G. (n.d.). *Economic Theory of Network.* Temple University.

Venegas-Andraca & Ball. (2009). *Processing images in entangled quantum systems, Quantum Inf Process.* Springer Science+Business Media, LLC.

Venegas-Andraca, S. E., & Ball, J. L. (2004). *Storing images in entangled quantum systems*. Report number: arXiv:quant-ph/0402085

Venegas-Andraca, S. E., & Ball, J. L. (2010). Processing images in entangled quantum systems. *Quantum Information Processing, 9*(1), 1–11. doi:10.100711128-009-0123-z

Ventura, D., & Martinez, T. (2000). Quantum associative memory. *Information Sciences, 124*(1-4), 273–296.

Vernacchia, S. (2019). *The darker side of quantum computing: risks and challenges*. Partner, Digital, Cyber Security, Resilience and Infrastructure. worldgovernmentsummit.org

Voas, J. (2016). *Networks of Things, NIST Special Publication (SP) 800-183*. National Institute of Standards and Technology.

Wallden, P., & Kashefi, E. (2019, April). *Cyber Security in the Quantum Era. Communications of the ACM, 62*(4), 120. doi:10.1145/3241037

Wan, K. H., Dahlsten, O., Kristjánsson, H., Gardner, R., & Kim, M. (2016). Quantum generalisation of feedforward neural networks. https://arxiv.org/abs/1612.01045

Wang, G. (2017). Quantum algorithm for linear regression. *Physical Review. A, 96*(1), 012335.

Wang, J., Geng, Y., Han, L., & Liu, J.-Q. (2019). Quantum Image Encryption Algorithm Based on Quantum Key Image. *International Journal of Theoretical Physics, 58*(1), 308–322. doi:10.100710773-018-3932-y

Wang, Y., Wang, R., Li, D., Adu-Gyamfi, D., Tian, K., & Zhu, Y. (2019). Improved Handwritten Digit Recognition using Quantum K-Nearest Neighbor Algorithm. *International Journal of Theoretical Physics, 58*(7), 2331–2340.

Wan, K. H., Dahlsten, O., Kristj'ansson, H., Gardner, R., & Kim, M. S. (2017). Quantum generalization of feed-forward neural networks npj. *Quantum Information, 3*, 36.

Washington Post. (2019). *The quantum revolution is coming, and Chinese scientists are at the forefront.* https://www.washingtonpost.com/business/2019/08/18/quantum-revolution-is-coming-chinese-scientists-are-forefront/

Watrous, J. (2001). Quantum algorithms for solvable groups. In *Proceedings of 33rd ACM STOC* (pp. 60-67). ACM.

Watrous, J. (2009). Zero-Knowledge against Quantum Attacks. *SIAM Journal on Computing, 39*(1), 25–58. doi:10.1137/060670997

Whurley, S. (2017). *7 things you need to know about Qubits.* https://superposition.com/2017/10/05/seven-things-need-know-about-qubits/

Wiebe, N., Kapoor, A., & Svore, K. M. (2014). Quantum deep learning. https://arxiv.org/abs/1412.3489

Wiebe, N., Kapoor, A., Granade, C., & Svore, K. M. (2015). *Quantum inspired training for Boltzmann machines*. arXiv preprint arXiv:1507.02642.

Wiebe, N., Kapoor, A., & Svore, K. M. (2015). Quantum algorithms for nearest-neighbor methods for supervised and unsupervised learning. *Quantum Information & Computation, 15*(3-4), 316–356.

Wittek, P. (2014). *Quantum machine learning: what quantum computing means to data mining*. Academic Press.

Wittek, P. (2014). *Quantum Machine Learning: What Quantum Computing Means to Data Mining*. Academic Press.

Wong, R., & Chang, W.-L. (2020). *Quantum algorithm for protein structure prediction in two-dimensional hydrophobic-hydrophilic model on square lattice.* Under review.

Wootters, W. K., & Zurek, W. H. (2016, Nov. 14). *The No Cloning Theorem*. Department of Physics, Williams College.

Xu, H., Chen, X., Li, P., Ding, J., & Eghan, C. (2019). A Novel RFID Data Management Model Based on Quantum Cryptography. In *Third International Congress on Information and Communication Technology. Advances in Intelligent Systems and Computing, vol 797*. Springer. 10.1007/978-981-13-1165-9_41

Xu, F., Curty, M., Qi, B., & Lo, H. (2015, March). Measurement-Device-Independent Quantum Cryptography. *IEEE Journal of Selected Topics in Quantum Electronics, 21*(3).

Yan, F. (2017). Quantum image processing: A review of advances in its security technologies. International Journal of Quantum Information, 15(3).

Yao, Z., Peng, W., Gao-yun, C., Dong-Dong, C., Rui, D., & Yan, Z. (2008). *Quantum clustering algorithm based on exponent measuring distance. In 2008 IEEE international symposium on knowledge acquisition and modeling workshop*. IEEE.

Yoshino, M., & Kunihiro, N. (2012). Improving GGH cryptosystem for large error vector. *International Symposium on Information Theory and its Applications ISITA*, 416-420.

Yu, L., Lu, Y., Tian, Y. M., & Zhu, X. L. (2012). Research on architecture and key technology of Internet of Things in hospital. *Transducer and Microsystem Technologies, 6*, 23.

Yuan, S., Mao, X., Xue, Y., Chen, L., Xiong, Q., & Compare, A. (2014). SQR: A simple quantum representation of infrared images. *Quantum Information Processing, 13*(6), 1353–1379. doi:10.100711128-014-0733-y

Zeidman, B. (2011). *The Software IP Detective's Handbook, Software forensics for embedded systems developers*. https://www.embedded.com/software-forensics-for-embedded-systems-developers/

Zhang, Y., Lu, K., Gao, Y., & Wang, M. (2013). NEQR: A novel enhanced quantum representation of digital images. *Quantum Information Processing, 12*(8), 2833–2860. doi:10.100711128-013-0567-z

Zhao, J.-C., Zhang, J.-F., Feng, Y., & Guo, J.-X. (2010). The study and application of the IOT technology in agriculture. *Proceedings of the 3rd IEEE International Conference on Computer Science and Information Technology (ICCSIT '10)*, 462–465.

Zhou, T., Shen, J., Li, X., Wang, C., & Shen, J. (2018). Quantum Cryptography for the Future Internet and the Security Analysis. Hindawi Security and Communication Networks. doi:10.1155/2018/8214619

Zhou, N. R., Hua, T. X., Gong, L. H., Pei, D. J., & Liao, Q. H. (2015). Quantum image encryption based on generalized Arnold transform and double random-phase encoding. *Quantum Information Processing, 14*(4), 1193–1213. doi:10.100711128-015-0926-z

Zhou, R. (2010). Quantum competitive neural network. *International Journal of Theoretical Physics, 49*(1), 110.

Zhou, R., Wang, H., Wu, Q., & Shi, Y. (2012). Quantum associative neural network with nonlinear search algorithm. *International Journal of Theoretical Physics, 51*(3), 705–723.

About the Contributors

Amandeep Bhatia is working as an Assistant Professor of Research at Chitkara University Research and Innovation Network, Chitkara University. He is also a visiting researcher in Prof Shenggen Zheng group at Center for quantum computing in Peng Cheng Laboratory, Shenzhen, China. Recently, he has received his PhD degree in the Department of Computer Science & Engineering Department from Thapar Institute of Engineering & Technology. His research focuses on quantum computation and information, quantum algorithms, post-quantum cryptography, quantum machine learning, formal languages, theory of computation, and computational complexity. He has five years of teaching and industrial experience. He has published more than 20 research articles in leading journals and conferences and 3 book chapters on different aspects of quantum computing.

Alekha Parimal Bhatt was born in Surat in 1997. She has completed her Bachelors in Technology (B.Tech) from Mody University of Science and Technology, Sikar. Currently she is working as a Software Engineer with Altran, Part of Capgemini. Her research interests include quantum computing and cryptography.

Satish Rupraoji Billewar (Ph.D.(Management), M.M.S.(Systems), M.E.(Computer Sci. &Engg), B.E.(Computer Sci. &Engg))is an Assistant Professor in the Department of Information Technology / Systems at Vivekanand Education Society's Institute of Management Studies & Research, Chembur(E), Mumbai. He has more than 15 years of teaching experience. His doctoral research was in identifying problems in the multidisciplinary field of E-Commerce Systems and providing solutions with the help of Total Quality Management. His contributions in the field of Software Project Management, E-Commerce, Total Quality Management and Software Testing Quality Assurance have been published in many Scopus Indexed Journals and International Conferences. He has written a book for the subject "Software Project Management", Dreamtech Technical Publication, Wiley India Pvt. Ltd., (Mumbai Univ. New Syllabus – BE-IT Sem-VII Regular & BE-Comp Sem-VI Elective), ISBN 978-93-5119-821-5, Mumbai University Approved Code: BEITC701, Link: https://www.wileyindia.com/software-project-management-includes-practicals.html.

Bhanu Chander is a research scholar at Pondicherry University, India, graduated from Acharya Nagarjuna University, A.P, in the year of 2013. A post-graduate degree from the Central University of Rajasthan, Rajasthan in the year 2016. Presently his main interesting areas include Wireless Sensor Networks, Machine Learning, Deep Learning, Neural networks, Cryptography, and Computer networks.

Aarti Dadheech received her M.E degree in Cryptography and Security, as well as B.Tech degree in Computer Science. She also served as Assistant Professor and is currently working towards the Ph.D. degree in Cloud Computing at Nirma University, India. Her main research fields are Quantum Cryptography, Deep Learning, and Video Processing.

Ankit Dholakiya has completed his B.E in Computer Engineering from Gujarat Technological University and M.Tech. in Cyber Security and Incidence Response from Gujarat Forensic Sciences University, Gandhinagar. He is interested in exploring about Cyber Security, Threat hunting, open source intelligence and cybercrime investigation. He has also undergone training in Digital Forensics at Directorate of Forensic Science Lab, Gandhinagar.

Bably Dolly pursed M.tech (Computer Science & Technology) from Integral University Lucknow in year 2016 . She is currently pursuing Ph.D. in Department of Computer Science, Babasaheb Bhimrao Ambedkar University, Lucknow. Her main research work focuses on Digital Image Processing, Computer Vision.

Vrunda Gadesha is working as Assistant Professor at K S School of Business Management. She is doing her research in the area of Quantum Computing and Cryptography.

Sunil Bahiru Ghane, M.E. (Computer Sci. & Engg), B.E. (Information Technology), is an Assistant Professor in the Department of Computer Engineering at Sardar Patel Institute of Technology, Andheri Mumbai. He has more than 11 years of teaching experience. He has published research papers in the field of Artificial Intelligence, Data Mining, Big Data Analysis in many Scopus Indexed Journals, and International Conferences.

Mangesh M. Ghonge is currently working as Assistant Professor at Sandip Institute of Technology and Research Centre, Nashik (MS), India. He received his PhD in Computer Science & Engineering from Sant Gadge Baba Amravati University, Amravati (MS), India on topic "Assignment based Selfish Node detection System in Mobile Ad hoc Networks" in 2019 and MTech degree in Computer Science & Engineering from Rashtrasant Tukadoji Maharaj Nagpur University, Nagpur (MS), India in 2012. He received his BE degree in Computer Science & Engineering from Sant Gadge Baba Amravati University, Amravati (MS), India in 2007. He has organized and chaired many national/international conferences and conducted various workshops. He received grant from Ministry of Electronics and Information Technology (MeitY) for organizing faculty development program. His more than 40 research papers published in various International journals including Scopus indexed journals. He has presented research paper in IEEE conferences at Singapore, Malaysia, also presented more than 10 papers in IEEE conferences. He Worked as Reviewer for Scopus Indexed IET Information Security journals. Also, reviewer in various international journals IJOAT, IJET, IJCA, and IJCSIT and for International Conferences held by different organization in India and well as abroad. He has invited as resource person in many workshop/seminars/FDP. His 02 patent are published by Indian Patent office. He has also contributed in Board of Studies, Computer Science & Engineering of Sandip University, Nashik as a Board Member. His research interest includes security in wireless networks, Ad-Hoc networks, and network protocols. Also includes implementation of open source software. He acquired knowledge in sciences/skills that covers areas of Computer Science, Networking, Databases and Programming, and more. He is member of CSI, IACSIT, IAENG, IETE and CSTA.

Ramkrishna Ghosh is an Assistant Professor in IT of Haldia Institute of Technology. He has 12 years of experience as an Assistant Professor, Lecturer, Software Faculty as well as Software Developer. He has published several engineering books online and international journals on Wireless Sensor Network and Cryptography. He completed M. Tech in IT from Jadavpur University after having qualified in GATE 2007 on paper IT with all India rank 180 and pursuing PhD in Computer Science. He has travelled all over India through his teaching only.

Mazhar Khaliq did M.C.A. from Aligarh Muslim University and got a Ph.D. (Computer Science) from Integral University, Lucknow. He has more than 20 years of teaching experience. Now he is an Assistant Professor & Subject In-charge Department of Computer Science, Khwaja Moinuddin Chishti Urdu, Arabi-Farsi University.

Mudassir Khan is currently working as an Assistant Professor in the Department of Computer Science at the College of Science & Arts Tanumah, King Khalid University Abha Saudi Arabia. He has completed his Ph.D. in Computer Science & Engineering from Noida International University Gautam Budh Nagar (NIU) India. He has completed his Graduation and Masters from India. He has more than 8 years of Teaching Experience at the King Khalid University of Saudi Arabia. He has published more than 20 papers in International Journals and conferences. He is the Member of various technical/ professional societies such as IEEE, UACEE, Internet Society, IAENG, and CSTA. His research interest includes Big data, IoT, deep learning, Computer Security, Cyber Security, and Cloud Computing, Cryptography.

Sujatha Krishnamoorthy is working as an Assistant professor in Department of Computer Science Kean Wenzhou University China and active member of CSI with 19 years of teaching experience. Her specialization is Digital image processing with Image fusion. She has published over 60 papers in International refereed journals like Springer and Elsevier. She has delivered several guest lectures, seminars and chaired a session for various Conferences. She is serving as a Reviewer and Editorial Board Member of many reputed Journals and acted as Session chair and Technical Program Committee member of National conferences and International Conferences. She has received a best researcher award during her research period.

Binod Kumar is Professor (MCA Dept.) at JSPM's Rajarshi Shahu College of Engineering, affiliated to Savitribai Phule Pune University, India. He is having more than 22 years of experience in various capacities in research, teaching and academic administration.He has obtained PhD (Computer Sc.) in 2010, M.Phil. (Computer Sc.) in 2006, MCA (NIT Jamshedpur) in 1998 and M.Sc.(BHU) & B.Sc.(BHU) in 1995 &1993 respectively.He worked as Associate Professor at School of Engineering and Computer Technology, Quest International University, MALAYSIA .He is recognized PhD guide in Computer Science under Savitribai Phule Pune University .He has been an evaluator for PhD dissertations of various Universities like Sardar Patel University (Gujarat), Bharathiar University (Coimbatore), M S.University Baroda (Gujarat).He has conducted PhD viva-voice as External Expert of 11 students at different universities. He has evaluated 42 PhD thesis and under his supervision 02 students have completed PhD and 05 students are pursuing PhD under Savitribai Phule Pune University, Pune, India.He is reviewer of Journals like Elsevier, SpringerPlus and TPC of various IEEE sponsored conferences. He is Editorial Board member of nearly 45 International Journals. He has been associated with Technical Program

Committee member (TPC) of nearly 60 International Conferences in India and abroad.He is Senior Member of IEEE Computer Society, Senior Member of Association for Computing Machinery (ACM, USA). He has filed one Patent. He has published three books, one chapter (IGI Global, USA) and nearly 45 papers in International & National Journals/Conferences. His areas of interest are Machine Learning.

Kamaljit I. Lakhtaria is working as Associate Professor in Department of Computer Science, Gujarat University. He is Coordinator for Department of Animation, ITIMS & Mobile Application, Gujarat University. More than 14 PhD Scholars are graduated under his guidance. 6 PhD Scholar working under him. He holds an edge in Information Retrieval, Next Generation Network, Web Services, Mobile Ad Hoc Networks, Network Security and Cryptography. He is author of 11 Reference Books in Computer Science. He Published 6 chapters in International Editorial Volumes. He presented many Research Papers in National and International Conferences. His Papers are published in the proceedings of IEEE, Springer, and Elsevier. He worked for E-Content Development in various Computer Science subjects. He has been invited by many universities as subject expert for Ph.D. Thesis evaluation as External Referee. He is Life-time member ISTE, IAENG and many Research Groups. He holds the post of Editor, Associate Editor in many International Research Journal. He is Program Committee member of many International Conferences. He is reviewer in IEEE WSN, Inderscience and Elsevier Journals.

Nilay Mistry holds a Bachelor's degree (BE) in Computers from Gujarat University, Ahmedabad - India And Master's degree (M.Tech.) in Computer Science & Engineering from Nirma University, Ahmedabad – India. He conducted Major Research projects on 'Smartphone multimedia forensics' at Directorate of Forensics Science, Gandhinagar and 'Gujarat Portal ID'; a project by Govt. of Gujarat at BISAG - Gandhinagar. He is NASSCOM NAC Certified expert. Presently working as Assistant Professor - Digital Forensic, at Gujarat Forensic Sciences University Gandhinagar. He is also a Teaching assistant and trainer for B.E. students at Institute of Technology, Nirma University, Ahmedabad and undertakes cyber forensics and cellphone forensics lectures for Bureau of Police Research & Development New Delhi and Intelligence Bureau – New Delhi, at Directorate of Forensic Science – Gujarat State, Gandhinagar. He also conducts computer forensics practical training for IPS/High Rank Officers and other Police Personnel of the country. Expertise: Cyber Forensics, Computer Security, Smart devices forensic analysis, Handled various cases related with Cyber Crime.

Parashu Ram Pal obtained Masters and Ph.D. in 1998 and 2010 respectively. He is working as a Professor in Department of Information Technology, ABES Engineering College, Ghaziabad, India. His area of interests are DBMS, Data Mining, Automata Theory, Computer Graphics and Computer Architecture. He has published more than 40 Research Papers in various International, National Journals & Conferences. He is devoted to Education, Research & Development for more than 22 years and always tries to create a proper environment for imparting quality education with the spirit of service to the humanity. He motivates to achieve excellence in education and research.

Digvijay Pandey is a Lecturer, Department of Technical Education, Research Scholar, IET Lucknow, India.

Pankaj Pathak obtained Masters and Ph.D. in 2005, 2014 respectively. He is working as an Assistant Professor in Symbiosis Institute of Digital and Telecom Management, a constituent of Symbiosis International (Deemed University), Pune. His area of interests are Data Mining, AI, and Smart Technologies. He has Published Several Research papers in the area of Data Mining, IOT security and Speech Recognition Technology.

Jay Prajapati is the employee of EY-Mumbai and working under domain of Cyber Security as Consultant since past 1 year and 11 months. Also, he had done 11 months Internship at EY-Mumbai in the domain of Cyber Security from June-2017 to May-2018. Jay Prajapati holds a Master's degree (M.Tech) in Cyber Security and Incident Response from Gujarat Forensic Sciences University, Gandhianagar-India. He did Bachelor's degree (B.E.) in Computer Engineering from Kadi Sarva Vishwavidyalaya University, Gandhinagar - India. He has good technical knowledge in Penetration Testing, Networking, Digital Forensics and Incident Response. Also, he has good consulting skills with client stakeholder management, team leadership and mentoring two person from the team. Apart from that, during Bachelor's he conducted major project on Application Development for iOS Platform. In addition to that he appeared for IELTS Examination which is conducted by British Council, Ahmedabad in Feb, 2016 and qualified it with 6.0 Bands. He also did a certification which is Diploma in Web Designing and Programming from AICSM Institute, Kota, Rajsthan - India.

Sabyasachi Pramanik obtained a Ph.D. in Computer Science and Engineering from the Sri Satya Sai University of Technology and Medical Sciences, Bhopal, India. Presently, he is an Assistant Professor, Department of Computer Science and Engineering, Haldia Institute of Technology, India. He is a Professional IEEE member. He has many publications in various reputed international conferences, journals, and online book chapter contributions (Indexed by SCIE, Scopus, ESCI, DBLP, etc). He is doing research in the field of Artificial Intelligence, Data Privacy, Cybersecurity, Network Security, and Machine Learning. He is also serving as the editorial board member of many international journals. He is a reviewer of journal articles from IEEE, Springer, Elsevier, Inderscience, IET, and IGI Global. He has reviewed many conference papers, has been a keynote speaker, session chair, and has been a technical program committee member in many international conferences. He has authored a book on Wireless Sensor Network. Currently, he is editing 6 books from IGI Global, CRC Press EAI/Springer, and Scrivener-Wiley Publications.

Sheetal Prasad is student of BTech Computer Science (IoT) SRM Institute of Science & Technology, Chennai. She qualified in First level of National Engineering Olympiad (NEO) 2.0 in 2019. She Completed online course of Taken Mind in association with Udemy on the topic Data Analysis and Visualisation- Complete Bootcampon. She completed online Certification from NPTEL in Problem Solving through Programming in C conducted IIT Kharagpur. She presented paper on IoT required from an Embedded Design Prospective and Impact in Healthcare: A Survey conducted by IEEE Student Chapter, SRM University . She published chapter in book "Quantum Cryptography and the Future of Cyber Security", Chapter name is " Cyber Security Techniques for Internet Of Things (IoT)", publisher is "IGI Global, USA."

Deepa Raj is working as an assistant professor in the Department of Computer Science Babasaheb Bhim Rao Ambedkar University. She did her Post Graduation from J.K Institute of applied physics and technology, Allahabad University and Ph.D. from Babasaheb Bhim Rao Ambedkar University Lucknow in the field of software engineering. Her field of interest is Software Engineering, Computer Graphics, and Image processing. She has attended lots of National and International conference and numbers of research papers published in her field.

Sandeep Kumar Sharma is currently working as a P.hD. research scholar at the Department of Computer Science & IT, Khwaja Moinuddin Chishti Language University. He had received his M.Tech. CS specialization in Network Management and Information Security, from SCSIT, Devi Ahilya Vishwavidyalaya, Indore M.P. He has ten years of teaching experience. He has qualified GATE, NET, and ICAR NET. His research area in software forensics and cyber security.

Renata Wong received her M.A. degree in sinology, as well as B.S. and M.S. degrees in computer science from Leipzig University, Germany, in 2008, 2011, and 2013, respectively. She is currently working towards the Ph.D. degree in quantum computing at Nanjing University, China. Her main research fields are quantum algorithms, protein structure prediction, foundations of physics, and linguistics.

Index

A

Access Control 10, 133-134, 184
amplitude amplification 82, 86, 98, 259, 272
application 12, 16, 28, 44, 47-49, 57, 61, 64, 77, 82, 102, 111, 123, 126-129, 133-134, 141-145, 147, 149, 158-159, 161-162, 165, 171, 173, 175-177, 182, 186, 188, 191, 195, 199, 226-227, 231, 264, 273
ASCII 202-203, 206-208, 212-213, 215
attack 8, 68, 73, 77, 103-104, 115-117, 119, 121-122, 130, 134-137, 140, 143, 147, 150, 152-154, 156, 172, 184, 221

B

BB84 2, 55, 61, 72, 74, 81, 140, 142, 154, 172

C

CBIR 186, 192
classical cryptography 1-2, 15, 19-20, 49, 60, 71, 74, 79, 102, 133, 136, 141, 145
Closest Vector Problem 108, 111
cryptography 1-8, 10-12, 14-15, 17, 19-20, 38, 47-52, 59-64, 71-75, 78-80, 82-84, 87-91, 98-99, 101-104, 108, 110-111, 122-124, 133, 135-136, 138-139, 141-150, 152-153, 155-157, 166-167, 170, 172-174, 177, 183, 185, 192, 194-195, 199-200, 202-203, 214, 219-221, 225-231, 259

D

decryption 1, 13-15, 51, 77, 103, 110-119, 121, 123, 137, 139, 148, 158, 219, 221, 225-226, 228
digital evidence 169, 173-174, 177-180, 182
digital forensics 169-170, 173, 175, 177, 179-180, 182-184
digital quantum forensics 169, 175, 177, 179, 182, 184
discrete logarithm problem 88, 103

E

encryption 1, 5, 8-10, 12-15, 18-19, 49, 51-52, 68, 71-72, 77, 86-87, 103-104, 111-112, 114-119, 121-123, 134, 137, 139, 148-150, 152-158, 165, 176, 183-184, 187, 193, 195, 200-201, 203, 214, 219-221, 225-227, 229

F

future 1, 11-12, 16-17, 20, 39, 51-52, 60, 63-64, 78-79, 90, 99, 102, 122, 143-145, 149-150, 156, 176, 180, 182-185, 187-188, 199-200, 227-230, 232, 241-242, 254, 257, 259

H

healthcare systems 124, 126, 129, 131-135, 141-144, 150, 161, 167
Heisenberg Uncertainty Principle 2-3, 47-48, 63, 68-69, 71, 79, 138-139, 170

I

image retrieval 192, 200
image searching 186, 193
Internet of Things 19, 80, 111, 124-125, 127, 145-147, 149-150, 158-159, 167-168
IoT 10, 68, 74-75, 78, 111, 122, 124-136, 141-151, 158-163, 165-168, 175
IoT infrastructure 125-126

K

kernel methods 257, 266, 268

L

LSB 202-207, 211-215, 219, 221, 225-228, 230-231

Recommended Reference Books

IGI Global's reference books are available in three unique pricing formats:
Print Only, E-Book Only, or Print + E-Book.

Shipping fees may apply.

www.igi-global.com

ISBN: 978-1-5225-9866-4
EISBN: 978-1-5225-9867-1
© 2020; 1,805 pp.
List Price: US$ 2,350

ISBN: 978-1-5225-8876-4
EISBN: 978-1-5225-8877-1
© 2019; 141 pp.
List Price: US$ 135

ISBN: 978-1-5225-7847-5
EISBN: 978-1-5225-7848-2
© 2019; 306 pp.
List Price: US$ 195

ISBN: 978-1-5225-6313-6
EISBN: 978-1-5225-6314-3
© 2019; 349 pp.
List Price: US$ 215

ISBN: 978-1-5225-1941-6
EISBN: 978-1-5225-1942-3
© 2017; 408 pp.
List Price: US$ 195

ISBN: 978-1-5225-0808-3
EISBN: 978-1-5225-0809-0
© 2017; 442 pp.
List Price: US$ 345

Do you want to stay current on the latest research trends, product announcements, news, and special offers?
Join IGI Global's mailing list to receive customized recommendations, exclusive discounts, and more.
Sign up at: **www.igi-global.com/newsletters.**

Publisher of Peer-Reviewed, Timely, and Innovative Academic Research

IGI Global
PUBLISHER of TIMELY KNOWLEDGE

www.igi-global.com   ✉ Sign up at www.igi-global.com/newsletters   f facebook.com/igiglobal   t twitter.com/igiglobal   in linkedin.com/igiglobal

Ensure Quality Research is Introduced to the Academic Community

Become an Evaluator for IGI Global Authored Book Projects

Premier Reference Source

Emerging GIS Applications for Emergency and Disaster Management

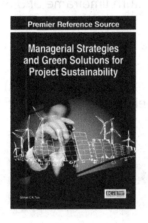

Premier Reference Source

Managerial Strategies and Green Solutions for Project Sustainability

Premier Reference Source

Comparative Approaches to Using R and Python for Statistical Data Analysis

Premier Reference Source

Solutions for High-Touch Communications in a High-Tech World

The overall success of an authored book project is dependent on quality and timely manuscript evaluations.

Applications and Inquiries may be sent to:
development@igi-global.com

Applicants must have a doctorate (or equivalent degree) as well as publishing, research, and reviewing experience. Authored Book Evaluators are appointed for one-year terms and are expected to complete at least three evaluations per term. Upon successful completion of this term, evaluators can be considered for an additional term.

If you have a colleague that may be interested in this opportunity, we encourage you to share this information with them.

IGI Global Author Services

Providing a high-quality, affordable, and expeditious service, IGI Global's Author Services enable authors to streamline their publishing process, increase chance of acceptance, and adhere to IGI Global's publication standards.

Benefits of Author Services:

- **Professional Service:** All our editors, designers, and translators are experts in their field with years of experience and professional certifications.

- **Quality Guarantee & Certificate:** Each order is returned with a quality guarantee and certificate of professional completion.

- **Timeliness:** All editorial orders have a guaranteed return timeframe of 3-5 business days and translation orders are guaranteed in 7-10 business days.

- **Affordable Pricing:** IGI Global Author Services are competitively priced compared to other industry service providers.

- **APC Reimbursement:** IGI Global authors publishing Open Access (OA) will be able to deduct the cost of editing and other IGI Global author services from their OA APC publishing fee.

Author Services Offered:

English Language Copy Editing
Professional, native English language copy editors improve your manuscript's grammar, spelling, punctuation, terminology, semantics, consistency, flow, formatting, and more.

Scientific & Scholarly Editing
A Ph.D. level review for qualities such as originality and significance, interest to researchers, level of methodology and analysis, coverage of literature, organization, quality of writing, and strengths and weaknesses.

Figure, Table, Chart & Equation Conversions
Work with IGI Global's graphic designers before submission to enhance and design all figures and charts to IGI Global's specific standards for clarity.

Translation
Providing 70 language options, including Simplified and Traditional Chinese, Spanish, Arabic, German, French, and more.

Hear What the Experts Are Saying About IGI Global's Author Services

"Publishing with IGI Global has been *an amazing experience* for me for sharing my research. The *strong academic production* support ensures quality and timely completion." – **Prof. Margaret Niess, Oregon State University, USA**

"The service was *very fast, very thorough, and very helpful* in ensuring our chapter meets the criteria and requirements of the book's editors. I was *quite impressed and happy* with your service." – **Prof. Tom Brinthaupt, Middle Tennessee State University, USA**

Learn More or Get Started Here:

For Questions, Contact IGI Global's Customer Service Team at cust@igi-global.com or 717-533-8845

IGI Global
PUBLISHER of TIMELY KNOWLEDGE
www.igi-global.com

www.igi-global.com

Celebrating Over 30 Years of Scholarly
Knowledge Creation & Dissemination

InfoSci®-Books

A Database of Nearly 6,000 Reference Books Containing Over
105,000+ Chapters Focusing on Emerging Research

GAIN ACCESS TO **THOUSANDS** OF
REFERENCE BOOKS AT **A FRACTION**
OF THEIR INDIVIDUAL LIST **PRICE**.

InfoSci®-Books Database

The **InfoSci®-Books** is a database of
nearly 6,000 IGI Global single and multi-volume
reference books, handbooks of research, and
encyclopedias, encompassing groundbreaking
research from prominent experts worldwide that
spans over 350+ topics in 11 core subject areas
including business, computer science, education,
science and engineering, social sciences, and more.

Open Access Fee Waiver (Read & Publish) Initiative

For any library that invests in IGI Global's InfoSci-Books and/or
InfoSci-Journals (175+ scholarly journals) databases, IGI Global
will match the library's investment with a fund of equal value to
go toward **subsidizing the OA article processing charges
(APCs) for their students, faculty, and staff** at that institution
when their work is submitted and accepted under OA into an
IGI Global journal.*

INFOSCI® PLATFORM FEATURES

- Unlimited Simultaneous Access
- No DRM
- No Set-Up or Maintenance Fees
- A Guarantee of No More Than a 5%
  Annual Increase for Subscriptions
- Full-Text HTML and PDF
  Viewing Options
- Downloadable MARC Records
- COUNTER 5 Compliant Reports
- Formatted Citations With Ability to
  Export to RefWorks and EasyBib
- No Embargo of Content (Research is
  Available Months in Advance of the
  Print Release)

*The fund will be offered on an annual basis and expire at the end of
the subscription period. The fund would renew as the subscription is
renewed for each year thereafter. The open access fees will be waived
after the student, faculty, or staff's paper has been vetted and accepted
into an IGI Global journal and the fund can only be used toward
publishing OA in an IGI Global journal. Libraries in developing countries
will have the match on their investment doubled.*

To Recommend or Request a Free Trial:
www.igi-global.com/infosci-books

eresources@igi-global.com • Toll Free: 1-866-342-6657 ext. 100 • Phone: 717-533-8845 x100

www.igi-global.com

www.igi-global.com

Publisher of Peer-Reviewed, Timely, and
Innovative Academic Research Since 1988

IGI Global's Transformative Open Access (OA) Model:
How to Turn Your University Library's Database Acquisitions Into a Source of OA Funding

Well in advance of Plan S, IGI Global unveiled their OA Fee Waiver (Read & Publish) Initiative. Under this initiative, librarians who invest in IGI Global's InfoSci-Books and/or InfoSci-Journals databases will be able to subsidize their patrons' OA article processing charges (APCs) when their work is submitted and accepted (after the peer review process) into an IGI Global journal.

How Does it Work?

Step 1: **Library Invests in the InfoSci-Databases:** A library perpetually purchases or subscribes to the InfoSci-Books, InfoSci-Journals, or discipline/subject databases.

Step 2: **IGI Global Matches the Library Investment with OA Subsidies Fund:** IGI Global provides a fund to go towards subsidizing the OA APCs for the library's patrons.

Step 3: **Patron of the Library is Accepted into IGI Global Journal (After Peer Review):** When a patron's paper is accepted into an IGI Global journal, they option to have their paper published under a traditional publishing model or as OA.

Step 4: **IGI Global Will Deduct APC Cost from OA Subsidies Fund:** If the author decides to publish under OA, the OA APC fee will be deducted from the OA subsidies fund.

Step 5: **Author's Work Becomes Freely Available:** The patron's work will be freely available under CC BY copyright license, enabling them to share it freely with the academic community.

Note: This fund will be offered on an annual basis and will renew as the subscription is renewed for each year thereafter. IGI Global will manage the fund and award the APC waivers unless the librarian has a preference as to how the funds should be managed.

Hear From the Experts on This Initiative:

"I'm very happy to have been able to make one of my recent research contributions *freely available* along with having access to the *valuable resources* found within IGI Global's InfoSci-Journals database."

– Prof. Stuart Palmer,
Deakin University, Australia

"Receiving the support from IGI Global's OA Fee Waiver Initiative *encourages me to continue my research work without any hesitation.*"

– Prof. Wenlong Liu, College of Economics and Management at Nanjing University of Aeronautics & Astronautics, China

For More Information, Scan the QR Code or Contact:
IGI Global's Digital Resources Team at eresources@igi-global.com.

Are You Ready to
Publish Your Research?

IGI Global
PUBLISHER of TIMELY KNOWLEDGE

IGI Global offers book authorship and editorship opportunities across 11 subject areas, including business, computer science, education, science and engineering, social sciences, and more!

Benefits of Publishing with IGI Global:

- Free one-on-one editorial and promotional support.

- Expedited publishing timelines that can take your book from start to finish in less than one (1) year.

- Choose from a variety of formats, including: Edited and Authored References, Handbooks of Research, Encyclopedias, and Research Insights.

- Utilize IGI Global's eEditorial Discovery® submission system in support of conducting the submission and double-blind peer review process.

- IGI Global maintains a strict adherence to ethical practices due in part to our full membership with the Committee on Publication Ethics (COPE).

- Indexing potential in prestigious indices such as Scopus®, Web of Science™, PsycINFO®, and ERIC – Education Resources Information Center.

- Ability to connect your ORCID iD to your IGI Global publications.

- Earn honorariums and royalties on your full book publications as well as complimentary copies and exclusive discounts.

Join Your Colleagues from Prestigious Institutions, Including:

Australian National University

MIT — Massachusetts Institute of Technology

JOHNS HOPKINS UNIVERSITY

TSINGHUA UNIVERSITY ~1911~

HARVARD UNIVERSITY

COLUMBIA UNIVERSITY IN THE CITY OF NEW YORK

Learn More at: www.igi-global.com/publish

or Contact IGI Global's Aquisitions Team at: acquisition@igi-global.com

Printed in the United States
By Bookmasters